Enhancing Employee Motivation Through Training and Development

Tricia Mazurowski
Adler University, USA

A volume in the Advances in
Human Resources Management
and Organizational Development
(AHRMOD) Book Series

Published in the United States of America by
IGI Global
Business Science Reference (an imprint of IGI Global)
701 E. Chocolate Avenue
Hershey PA, USA 17033
Tel: 717-533-8845
Fax: 717-533-8661
E-mail: cust@igi-global.com
Web site: http://www.igi-global.com

Copyright © 2024 by IGI Global. All rights reserved. No part of this publication may be reproduced, stored or distributed in any form or by any means, electronic or mechanical, including photocopying, without written permission from the publisher.
Product or company names used in this set are for identification purposes only. Inclusion of the names of the products or companies does not indicate a claim of ownership by IGI Global of the trademark or registered trademark.

Library of Congress Cataloging-in-Publication Data

Names: Mazurowski, Tricia, 1974- editor.
Title: Enhancing employee motivation through training and development / edited by Tricia Mazurowski.
Description: Hershey, PA : Business Science Reference, [2024] | Includes bibliographical references and index. | Summary: "This book provides relevant theoretical frameworks and the latest empirical research findings in the area of employee training and development"-- Provided by publisher.
Identifiers: LCCN 2024009384 (print) | LCCN 2024009385 (ebook) | ISBN 9798369316740 (hardcover) | ISBN 9798369316757 (ebook)
Subjects: LCSH: Employee motivation. | Employees--Training of. | Career development.
Classification: LCC HF5549.5.M63 E534 2024 (print) | LCC HF5549.5.M63 (ebook) | DDC 658.3/14--dc23/eng/20240229
LC record available at https://lccn.loc.gov/2024009384
LC ebook record available at https://lccn.loc.gov/2024009385

This book is published in the IGI Global book series Advances in Human Resources Management and Organizational Development (AHRMOD) (ISSN: 2327-3372; eISSN: 2327-3380)

British Cataloguing in Publication Data
A Cataloguing in Publication record for this book is available from the British Library.

All work contributed to this book is new, previously-unpublished material.
The views expressed in this book are those of the authors, but not necessarily of the publisher.

For electronic access to this publication, please contact: eresources@igi-global.com.

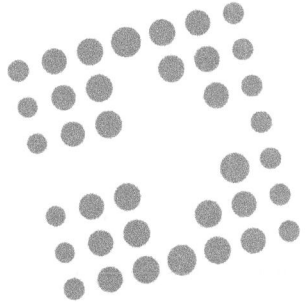

Advances in Human Resources Management and Organizational Development (AHRMOD) Book Series

Patricia Ordóñez de Pablos
Universidad de Oviedo, Spain

ISSN:2327-3372
EISSN:2327-3380

MISSION

A solid foundation is essential to the development and success of any organization and can be accomplished through the effective and careful management of an organization's human capital. Research in human resources management and organizational development is necessary in providing business leaders with the tools and methodologies which will assist in the development and maintenance of their organizational structure.

The **Advances in Human Resources Management and Organizational Development (AHRMOD) Book Series** aims to publish the latest research on all aspects of human resources as well as the latest methodologies, tools, and theories regarding organizational development and sustainability. The **AHRMOD Book Series** intends to provide business professionals, managers, researchers, and students with the necessary resources to effectively develop and implement organizational strategies.

COVERAGE

- Diversity in the Workplace
- Change Management
- Executive Education
- Employee Evaluation
- Succession Planning
- Process Improvement
- Organizational Development
- Upward Feedback
- Employment and Labor Laws
- Worker Behavior and Engagement

IGI Global is currently accepting manuscripts for publication within this series. To submit a proposal for a volume in this series, please contact our Acquisition Editors at Acquisitions@igi-global.com or visit: http://www.igi-global.com/publish/.

The Advances in Human Resources Management and Organizational Development (AHRMOD) Book Series (ISSN 2327-3372) is published by IGI Global, 701 E. Chocolate Avenue, Hershey, PA 17033-1240, USA, www.igi-global.com. This series is composed of titles available for purchase individually; each title is edited to be contextually exclusive from any other title within the series. For pricing and ordering information please visit http://www.igi-global.com/book-series/advances-human-resources-management-organizational/73670. Postmaster: Send all address changes to above address. Copyright © 2024 IGI Global. All rights, including translation in other languages reserved by the publisher. No part of this series may be reproduced or used in any form or by any means – graphics, electronic, or mechanical, including photocopying, recording, taping, or information and retrieval systems – without written permission from the publisher, except for non commercial, educational use, including classroom teaching purposes. The views expressed in this series are those of the authors, but not necessarily of IGI Global.

Titles in this Series

For a list of additional titles in this series, please visit:
http://www.igi-global.com/book-series/advances-human-resources-management-organizational/73670

Convergence of Human Resources Technologies and Industry 5.0
Pawan Kumar (Lovely Professional University, India) Sunil Kumar (Shoolini University, India) Rajesh Verma (Lovely Professional University, India) and Sumesh Dadwal (London South Bank University, UK)
Business Science Reference • © 2024 • 363pp • H/C (ISBN: 9798369313435) • US $290.00

Building Sustainable Human Resources Management Practices for Businesses
Cristina Raluca Gh. Popescu (University of Bucharest, Romania & The Bucharest University of Economic Studies, Romania) Javier Martínez-Falcó (University of Alicante, Spain & University of Stellenbosch, South Africa) Bartolomé Marco-Lajara (University of Alicante, Spain) Eduardo Sánchez-García (University of Alicante, Spain) and Luis A. Millán-Tudela (University of Alicante, Spain)
Business Science Reference • © 2024 • 364pp • H/C (ISBN: 9798369319949) • US $275.00

Demystifying the Dark Side of AI in Business
Sumesh Dadwal (Northumbria University, UK) Shikha Goyal (Lovely Professional University, India) Pawan Kumar (Lovely Professional University, India) and Rajesh Verma (Lovely Professional University, India)
Business Science Reference • © 2024 • 268pp • H/C (ISBN: 9798369307243) • US $275.00

Organizational Management Sustainability in VUCA Contexts
Rafael Perez-Uribe (Universidad de la Salle, Colombia) David Ocampo-Guzman (Santo Tomas University, Colombia & EAN University, Colombia) Carlos Salcedo-Perez (Politecnico Grancolombiano, Colombia) and Andrés Carvajal-Contreras (EAN University, Colombia)
Business Science Reference • © 2024 • 435pp • H/C (ISBN: 9798369307205) • US $275.00

Fostering Organizational Sustainability With Positive Psychology
Elif Baykal (Istanbul Medipol University, Turkey)
Business Science Reference • © 2024 • 338pp • H/C (ISBN: 9798369315248) • US $275.00

701 East Chocolate Avenue, Hershey, PA 17033, USA
Tel: 717-533-8845 x100 • Fax: 717-533-8661
E-Mail: cust@igi-global.com • www.igi-global.com

Table of Contents

Preface xiii

Chapter 1
The Aspects of Organizational Culture 1
    Nicholas Patrick, Adler University, Canada

Chapter 2
Shaping Organizational Culture Through Training and Development
Initiatives 32
    Ranjit Singha, Christ University, India
    Surjit Singha, Kristu Jayanti College (Autonomous), India
    V. Muthu Ruben, Christ University, India
    Melita Stephen Natal, Amity University, Greater Noida, India
    Alphonsa Diana Haokip, Christ King High School, India
    Elizabeth Mize, Rajiv Gandhi University, India

Chapter 3
Change Management in a Divergent World of Work 58
    Deepti Puranik, NMIMS University, India
    Madhumati Mulik, Independent Researcher, India

Chapter 4
Towards Understanding and Application of Learning and Development
Theories for Employee Motivation 79
    Peace Kumah, Knutsford University College, Ghana

Chapter 5
Training and Development to Enhance Motivation and Knowledge Transfer ... 117
    Neeta Baporikar, Namibia University of Science and Technology,
      Namibia & SP Pune University, India

Chapter 6
Into Action: Effective Knowledge Transfer in Employee Training 138
    Chelsea Craig, Adler University, USA

Chapter 7
Reinforcing Employee Motivation Through L&D: Proposed Organization Development Intervention Model 156
    Deepak Sharma, Narsee Monjee Institute of Management Studies, Bengaluru, India
    Mahima Guwalani, Narsee Monjee Institute of Management Studies, Bengaluru, India

Chapter 8
Examining the Relationship Between Learning Design and Organizational Citizenship Behavior 176
    Jennifer A. Bockelman, Adler University, USA

Chapter 9
Motivating Workplace Learners From a Place of Psychological Safety 207
    Rachel Frost, Adler University, USA

Chapter 10
Motivating Employees Through Continuous Professional Development and Training in the Retail Sector 233
    Gurmeet Singh, Glasgow Caledonian University, UK
    Vipin Nadda, University of Sunderland in London, UK
    Sunil Saini, Aksum University, Ethiopia
    Waseem Akram, University of West of Scotland, UK

Chapter 11
Role of Training and Development in Employee Motivation: Tourism and Hospitality Sector 248
    Amrik Singh, Lovely Professional University, India
    Amjad Imam Ansari, Lovely Professional University, India

Compilation of References 262

About the Contributors 301

Index 307

Detailed Table of Contents

Preface xiii

Chapter 1
The Aspects of Organizational Culture 1
    Nicholas Patrick, Adler University, Canada

This chapter explores the multidimensions or facets of organizational culture and how it creates a common culture between employees and their organization. It explores a formal and informal definition of organizational culture, why organizational culture matters, and the characteristics of organizational culture. Moreover, it explores a positive or negative organizational culture, the seven dimensions of organizational culture, Schein's cultural iceberg, Hofstede's model of organizational culture, and Charles Handy's model of organizational culture. These theories are investigated and summarized in the tables throughout the chapter to help understand how a summation of many parts can describe organizational culture. Additionally, it explores the four types of organizational culture, core values, subcultures, and countercultures, and their influence on shaping organizational culture. Lastly, Thomas Kilmann's conflict resolution model is explored as a summation of the theories above and explains how advancements in training and development lead to a positive organizational culture.

Chapter 2
Shaping Organizational Culture Through Training and Development
Initiatives 32
    Ranjit Singha, Christ University, India
    Surjit Singha, Kristu Jayanti College (Autonomous), India
    V. Muthu Ruben, Christ University, India
    Melita Stephen Natal, Amity University, Greater Noida, India
    Alphonsa Diana Haokip, Christ King High School, India
    Elizabeth Mize, Rajiv Gandhi University, India

This chapter explores the critical significance of development and training initiatives in molding and impacting an organization's culture. Organizational culture significantly influences employee satisfaction and motivation, making training programs crucial for fostering and harmonizing cultural values. In this analysis, the authors explore the theoretical underpinnings of organizational culture and evaluate its influence on the conduct and productivity of employees. Then, they investigate various development and training strategies that can influence, reinforce, or effectively transform corporate culture. Practical insights and real-world case studies demonstrate organizations' effective utilization of training initiatives to advance their intended cultural attributes. This chapter emphasizes the significance of ensuring that training initiatives align with the organization's overarching cultural objectives and the possible influence this may have on employee commitment and motivation.

Chapter 3
Change Management in a Divergent World of Work 58
Deepti Puranik, NMIMS University, India
Madhumati Mulik, Independent Researcher, India

Change management is an inevitable process of an organization that helps the organization's sustainable capacity in the ever-changing environment. The organizations have to develop various applied models of change management that would be apt for their strategic management. The chapter focuses on change management in this ever-changing work environment from an Indian perspective delving into certain cases where change management created an everlasting impact. It also looks at how certain models of change management have been applied to the organization's development. Change management is a difficult process which indulges into assessing need for change to the implementation of change and further assess the accomplishment of the change management for increase productivity.

Chapter 4
Towards Understanding and Application of Learning and Development
Theories for Employee Motivation 79
Peace Kumah, Knutsford University College, Ghana

This chapter examines how learning and development theories can be practically applied to enhance employee motivation. The chapter delves into various theories including adult learning, behavioral, cognitive, social learning, experiential learning, human resource development (HRD), and systems theory, and highlights their roles in shaping employee behavior and learning processes. The key constructs, strengths, limitations, and areas of applicability of these theories are discussed, emphasizing their potential to drive individual and organizational growth. By understanding and effectively applying these theories, organizations can design tailored training and development programs that cater to diverse learning needs, foster employee engagement, and promote a positive organizational culture. HR and learning and development professionals need to have a solid grasp of these theories to design training programs that address specific learning needs and promote positive outcomes. By leveraging theoretical frameworks, organizations can cultivate a culture of continuous learning and improve employee engagement and motivation.

Chapter 5
Training and Development to Enhance Motivation and Knowledge Transfer...117
Neeta Baporikar, Namibia University of Science and Technology,
Namibia & SP Pune University, India

Training and development have been a part of human resource development strategies for ages. However, many times these strategies have been merely to develop or improve the skills and competencies essential to do the job. This shortsighted approach has benefitted neither the individual employees nor organizations. More so in the current scenario of knowledge-based economies, where tenure is an issue and loyalty is towards professional growth and enhancement, it becomes essential to ensure that training and development focuses on enhancing motivation and ensuring knowledge transfer. Motivated employees are brand ambassadors for the organization and knowledge transfers help in retaining and ensuing career succession. In line with this thinking, adopting a qualitative approach, this chapter aims to discuss and deliberate on how training and development can enhance motivation and ensure effective knowledge transfer with a focus on public enterprises and suggest strategies to do training and development effectively to enhance motivation and effective knowledge transfer.

Chapter 6
Into Action: Effective Knowledge Transfer in Employee Training....................138
Chelsea Craig, Adler University, USA

This chapter discusses the importance of knowledge transfer and the mechanisms that go into successfully translating training material on the job. The essential nature of successful knowledge transfer within modern organizations and the common pitfalls experienced are explained. This chapter explores trainee personality-based, motivational, and social factors that influence which forms of training are effective for them. Adult learning principles that apply to knowledge transfer within training are also explored. Situational, personal, and organizational barriers to successful knowledge transfer are outlined. Finally, the chapter walks the reader through each element of the training design structure that can enhance the effectiveness of training translation. This allows readers to walk through the training design process with successful strategies for improving knowledge transfer at the heart of their design.

Chapter 7
Reinforcing Employee Motivation Through L&D: Proposed Organization
Development Intervention Model 156
    Deepak Sharma, Narsee Monjee Institute of Management Studies,
       Bengaluru, India
    Mahima Guwalani, Narsee Monjee Institute of Management Studies,
       Bengaluru, India

Planning of training and development activities needs to be done in such a way so that it triggers employee interest, on the one hand, and builds organizational capabilities leading to organisational effectiveness, on the other hand. In this post-pandemic-affected business world where traditional work and work relationships have changed with emerging gig workforce leading to creation of new kinds of work environment and employment relationships, there is a need to re-orient, reskill, and upskill the workforce in a different manner than used to happen. Accordingly, the deliverables for business, leadership, and HR have changed. Planned change for ensuring training interventions to work involves understanding assumptions of adult learning and use of technology in training process and system to facilitate right training interventions leading to organisational renewal. The chapter analyses a training and development system and its role in employee motivation as well as comprehensive OD intervention tool with the help of two broad themes.

Chapter 8
Examining the Relationship Between Learning Design and Organizational
Citizenship Behavior.. 176
    Jennifer A. Bockelman, Adler University, USA

This chapter will explore how training and development programs contribute to increased motivation to engage in prosocial organizational behaviors or organizational citizenship behaviors (OCBs). OCB refers to behaviors outside of an employee's core role that he or she performs for the benefit of an organization or other organizational members. While organizations have a considerable interest in increasing the motivation of employees to exhibit OCB, OCB may not be recognized by an organization's performance measurement system. Research has attempted to define predictors of OCB, such as personality traits, employee attitudes, and leadership behaviors. Potential motivations behind OCB will be explored, as well as adult learning theories that are most likely to promote OCB. In addition, this chapter will provide recommendations for the design of training and development with the goal of encouraging OCB and reducing counterproductive work behaviors (CWB).

Chapter 9
Motivating Workplace Learners From a Place of Psychological Safety............207
    Rachel Frost, Adler University, USA

This chapter delves into motivating workplace learners through the lens of psychological safety and adult learning theories. Grounded in self-determination theory, the exploration of felt support underscores the impact of intrinsic motivation on continuous learning and development. Multigenerational knowledge sharing is examined, revealing the interplay between psychological safety and generational cohort dynamics. The measurable impact of people-first training strategies and transformational leadership principles are emphasized for their positive effects on workplace thriving. A trauma-informed approach is integrated, advocating for inclusive and supportive organizational cultures. Lastly, insights from academic studies are woven throughout to contribute to a comprehensive understanding of effective strategies for fostering psychological safety, motivation, and holistic thriving in workforce development programs.

Chapter 10
Motivating Employees Through Continuous Professional Development and Training in the Retail Sector 233
    Gurmeet Singh, Glasgow Caledonian University, UK
    Vipin Nadda, University of Sunderland in London, UK
    Sunil Saini, Aksum University, Ethiopia
    Waseem Akram, University of West of Scotland, UK

Training and development could be a real motivating force for the company if they are provided in a well-organized manner. These activities could be considered as major strengths for HR management and can provide a firm base to the organizational objectives as it increases the individual's capacities. The major aim of this chapter is to get a better understanding of the benefits of training and continuous development in the retail sector. The major objective of this chapter is to contribute to making companies aware of the genuine benefits of training and continuous development. Further, the retail sector organizations can surely improve their training techniques and it will help them to adopt accurate teaching techniques. Different factors such as management, working conditions, reward system, teamwork, etc. can directly affect the performance of employees. It is significant for business to adopt various strategies through which they can continuously develop the performance of their employees.

Chapter 11
Role of Training and Development in Employee Motivation: Tourism and
Hospitality Sector 248

    Amrik Singh, Lovely Professional University, India
    Amjad Imam Ansari, Lovely Professional University, India

The contemporary hotel industry is facing many challenges that are closely connected to the changes that occur both in the field of tourist demand and tourist supply. The changes refer to the quality of services at first place, since the needs of tourists change rapidly towards higher quality and different products. Having in mind the character of the activities in the hospitality industry where direct contact between employees and guests is necessary for providing and realizing the services, the success of service realization and fulfilling guests' satisfaction depends the most on the employees. The present study aims to explore the issue of staff training in the hospitality sector as an important management activity for improved service quality. This study explores the importance of appropriate employee structure within the process of providing services. Staff training in the hospitality sector is very important for the continuous training of currently employed staff and for new employees as well.

Compilation of References 262

About the Contributors 301

Index 307

Preface

It is with great enthusiasm that we introduce this meticulously curated reference book, *Enhancing Employee Motivation Through Training and Development*, crafted by the esteemed Tricia Mazurowski of Adler University, United States. Within these pages, we embark on a transformative journey into the realm of organizational leadership and its profound impact on nurturing a culture of motivation and excellence within the workplace.

At its core, this publication is a testament to the symbiotic relationship between organizational success and the motivation of its workforce. Through a comprehensive review of the literature, we aim to illuminate the strategies and practices that enable organizational leaders to effectively support training and development initiatives, thereby enhancing employee motivation and performance.

Central to our endeavor is the dissemination of knowledge that is both informative and actionable. Each chapter is meticulously crafted to provide readers with relevant theoretical frameworks, empirical research findings, and practical insights aimed at enriching their understanding of employee training and development.

Our target audience comprises professionals and researchers working in the fields of Industrial/Organizational psychology, training and development, human resources, and organizational change management. Whether you are a seasoned practitioner seeking to refine your approach or a scholar eager to contribute to the discourse, this book offers a wealth of resources to inform and inspire.

As editors, we extend our heartfelt gratitude to Tricia Mazurowski for her dedication to this project and her invaluable contributions to the field. Additionally, we would like to thank our esteemed contributors whose expertise and insights have enriched the fabric of this publication.

In conclusion, we invite readers to embark on a journey of discovery and enlightenment as we explore the myriad facets of employee motivation and development. May this book serve as a catalyst for positive change, inspiring leaders and practitioners to cultivate environments where talent thrives and organizational success flourishes.

In this meticulously curated reference book, we embark on a transformative journey into the multifaceted landscape of organizational dynamics, exploring how various factors intersect to shape workplace culture, employee motivation, and organizational effectiveness. Here, we offer a brief overview of each chapter, providing readers with a glimpse into the rich tapestry of insights and perspectives that await within these pages.

Chapter 1: The Aspects of Organizational Culture

Authored by Nicholas Patrick of the Department of Psychology, Canada, this chapter delves into the intricate dimensions of organizational culture. From formal definitions to theoretical frameworks, readers will explore the various facets of organizational culture, including its positive or negative manifestations, dimensions, and influential models. By investigating core values, subcultures, and countercultures, this chapter illuminates how organizational culture shapes workplace dynamics and employee behavior.

Chapter 2: Shaping Organizational Culture Through Training and Development Initiatives

Authored by a team from various esteemed institutions in India, this chapter underscores the critical role of training and development initiatives in molding organizational culture. Through theoretical exploration and real-world case studies, readers will gain insights into how training programs can effectively reinforce cultural values and drive employee satisfaction and motivation. Emphasizing alignment with organizational objectives, this chapter offers practical strategies for leveraging training initiatives to shape and sustain a positive organizational culture.

Chapter 3: Change Management in a Divergent World of Work

Authored by scholars from NMIMS-Deemed to be University and beyond, this chapter examines the inevitability of change in organizational contexts and the imperative of effective change management. Drawing from Indian perspectives and case studies, the authors explore various models and approaches to change management, highlighting its role in enhancing organizational resilience and productivity in an ever-evolving landscape.

Chapter 4: Towards Understanding and Application of Learning and Development Theories for Employee Motivation

Authored by Peace Kumah of Knutsford University College, Ghana, this chapter delves into the intersection of learning and development theories with employee motivation. By adopting a qualitative approach, the chapter explores how training and development can transcend skill enhancement to foster motivation and facilitate knowledge transfer, particularly in public enterprises.

Chapter 5: Training and Development to Enhance Motivation and Knowledge Transfer

Penned by Neeta Baporikar of Namibia University of Science and Technology and SP Pune University, India, this chapter delves into the evolving landscape of training and development. It emphasizes the importance of aligning training initiatives with organizational goals while focusing on enhancing motivation and facilitating knowledge transfer. By examining strategies for effective training and development in public enterprises, the chapter offers valuable insights into cultivating a motivated workforce and fostering continuous learning.

Chapter 6: Into Action: Effective Knowledge Transfer in Employee Training

Authored by Chelsea Craig of Adler University, United States, this chapter sheds light on the crucial process of knowledge transfer within organizational training. By exploring factors influencing successful knowledge translation and outlining barriers to effective transfer, readers gain a comprehensive understanding of training design principles aimed at optimizing knowledge transfer. Practical strategies and design considerations empower readers to enhance training effectiveness and drive organizational success.

Chapter 7: Reinforcing Employee Motivation Through L&D: Proposed Organization Development Intervention Model

Authored by Deepak Sharma and Mahima Guwalani of Narsee Monjee Institute of Management Studies, Bengaluru Campus, India, this chapter offers a comprehensive analysis of training and development interventions. It highlights the importance of aligning training initiatives with organizational objectives and leveraging technology to facilitate organizational renewal. By proposing a comprehensive organizational development intervention model, the chapter equips readers with actionable strategies to foster employee motivation and enhance organizational effectiveness.

Chapter 8: Examining the Relationship Between Learning Design and Organizational Citizenship Behavior

Penned by Jennifer Bockelman of Adler University, United States, this chapter delves into the intersection of learning design and organizational citizenship behavior (OCB). It explores how training and development programs can influence employee motivation to engage in prosocial behaviors that benefit the organization. By identifying predictors of OCB and offering recommendations for training design, the chapter provides valuable insights into fostering a culture of organizational citizenship.

Chapter 9: Motivating Workplace Learners from a Place of Psychological Safety

Authored by Rachel Frost of Adler University, United States, this chapter explores the role of psychological safety in motivating workplace learners. Drawing from Self-Determination Theory and trauma-informed approaches, the chapter highlights the impact of supportive organizational cultures on intrinsic motivation and holistic thriving. Practical strategies and leadership principles empower readers to create psychologically safe learning environments conducive to employee motivation and development.

Chapter 10: Motivating Employees through Continuous Professional Development and Training in Retail Sector

Written by a team of scholars from various esteemed institutions, this chapter examines the benefits of continuous professional development and training in the retail sector. By exploring factors influencing employee performance and strategies for enhancing training effectiveness, the chapter offers valuable insights into fostering employee motivation and driving organizational success in the retail industry.

Chapter 11: Role of Training and Development in Employee Motivation: Tourism and Hospitality Sector

Authored by Amrik Singh and Amjad Ansari of Lovely Professional University, Punjab, India, this chapter delves into the importance of training and development in the hospitality industry. By exploring staff training as a critical component of service quality improvement, the chapter offers insights into fostering employee motivation and enhancing guest satisfaction in the tourism and hospitality sector.

As editors of this meticulously curated reference book, we are delighted to present a comprehensive exploration of the multifaceted realm of organizational dynamics. Through the lens of training and development, we have examined how various factors intersect to shape workplace culture, drive employee motivation, and enhance organizational effectiveness.

Each chapter offers a unique perspective, authored by esteemed scholars from around the globe, providing readers with a diverse range of insights and practical strategies. From delving into the intricate dimensions of organizational culture to exploring the critical role of change management in today's ever-evolving landscape, this book offers a wealth of knowledge for professionals and researchers alike.

Throughout these chapters, readers have gained valuable insights into aligning training initiatives with organizational objectives, fostering a positive organizational culture, and motivating employees to thrive in their roles. By synthesizing theoretical frameworks with real-world case studies, we aim to empower readers with actionable strategies to drive positive change within their organizations.

We extend our sincere gratitude to Tricia Mazurowski for her dedication to this project and to our esteemed contributors for their invaluable insights. It is our hope that this reference book will serve as a catalyst for positive change, inspiring leaders and practitioners to cultivate environments where talent thrives and organizational success flourishes.

In conclusion, we invite readers to delve into the rich tapestry of insights and perspectives offered within these pages. May this book inspire you to embark on a journey of discovery and enlightenment, as we collectively strive to enhance employee motivation through training and development in today's dynamic workplaces.

Tricia Mazurowski
Adler University, USA

Chapter 1
The Aspects of Organizational Culture

Nicholas Patrick
https://orcid.org/0009-0007-3804-9423
Adler University, Canada

ABSTRACT

This chapter explores the multidimensions or facets of organizational culture and how it creates a common culture between employees and their organization. It explores a formal and informal definition of organizational culture, why organizational culture matters, and the characteristics of organizational culture. Moreover, it explores a positive or negative organizational culture, the seven dimensions of organizational culture, Schein's cultural iceberg, Hofstede's model of organizational culture, and Charles Handy's model of organizational culture. These theories are investigated and summarized in the tables throughout the chapter to help understand how a summation of many parts can describe organizational culture. Additionally, it explores the four types of organizational culture, core values, subcultures, and countercultures, and their influence on shaping organizational culture. Lastly, Thomas Kilmann's conflict resolution model is explored as a summation of the theories above and explains how advancements in training and development lead to a positive organizational culture.

How can motivation be increased through understanding areas of organizational culture? The mission of this chapter is to educate the reader about how organizational culture impacts employee motivation and why it is important to develop a training plan or program. The concern will be that if the reader is unaware of organizational culture, it can impact their ability to develop a training program or increase employee motivation effectively. For example, if a leader is unaware of how their leadership

DOI: 10.4018/979-8-3693-1674-0.ch001

style impacts their subordinates, they cannot find ways to improve motivation. Thus, this chapter is crucial for the reader to develop a new understanding of how employee motivation happens.

A key to this chapter would be to create awareness because a lack of awareness would mean that organizations would not know how to use training and development to increase employee motivation. Moreover, if employees do not have adequate training in conflict resolution and leaders have training in self-reflection, it is difficult for these groups to improve problematic behaviors. For example, how can organizations improve their code of ethics to be more mindful or aware of behavior that negatively impacts the organizational culture? Thus, the objective is that the reader can understand and reflect on how they appear in their organization through these sections, as highlighted above. How does their behavior impact the culture they are a part of? Thus, the goal is to use theoretical frameworks and research in training and development. This chapter will also discuss adult learning of experiential learning and observation and how it relates to organizational culture.

KEY LEARNING OBJECTIVES

This chapter aims to define and understand how we can describe organizational culture through theory. If we can assign a way to define organizational culture and understand the various components or dimensions of organizational culture, organizations can use this knowledge to increase training and motivation. Enhancing employee motivation through training and development also encompasses identifying areas of organizational culture and what is needed to shift or change in an organization to create change. Training and development can occur individually due to changes in the organizational structure, etc. Thus, organizational culture informs readers that these various aspects can be altered, challenged, or identified as weaknesses or strengths. Once organizational members can identify weaknesses or strengths in the organizational culture, they understand what stands as a barrier to effective training and development. Similarly, what areas of an organization or an individual can be further developed or encouraged to keep employee motivation? However, it is important to understand how "organizational culture" is a subcategory of "culture."

DEFINING CULTURE AND ORGANIZATIONAL CULTURE

Throughout this chapter, we will explore the components of organizational culture and how subsystems, or multiple aspects of identity and environment, overlap to create an organizational vulture. Throughout history, culture has been thought of as something related to the region, an identity that embraces and encompasses aspects such as religion, language, food, etc. (Pappas & McKelvie, 2022). This broad understanding of culture is present today when considering how culture is seen as a commodity or a grouping of likenesses where groups share patterns in their behavior, socializations, interactions, etc. (Pappas & McKelvie, 2022). Hence, this unique set of commonalities shared amongst groups is unique to the members of groups who embrace and embody these aspects of identity. Moreover, culture can also be adapted or changed; we see this in various ways. For example, religions can be changed or adapted differently in different world regions. Christians in one part of the world might express their religious faith and belief systems differently than other groups. Hence, some larger systems or cultures exist, and smaller subsystems derive from larger cultures or systems.

Thus, this is exactly the way we should think of culture. Culture is a series of systems or subsystems that can be changed or adapted depending on the individuals who make up a culture (Pappas & McKelvie, 2022). Moreover, from the abovementioned concept, we can see that culture is unique to time and location. This means a culture can change over time due to external or internal influences (Pappas & McKelvie, 2022). The internal influences would be the people who share similar beliefs or values, and the external influences could be the environment, a change in thought process or thinking over time, etc. (Pappas & McKelvie, 2022). For example, when we accept things the way they are in the present moment, which is shared amongst groups, this becomes a common culture. When the way we see things changes amongst groups of people, the culture changes. We have seen how technology or limited beliefs have changed among groups and how this causes a cultural shift or change. For example, historically, the culture of gender norms amongst women and males has changed. Women were seen as the caretakers, and males were the providers. These ideologies or belief systems have shifted in the way we see culture. New knowledge or information disputes the idea that we should conform to gender roles. Hence, the change is a new understanding of how work is performed and the expected duties or roles that males or females were thought to perform over time. The shift is the idea that women are caretakers, and now women can be providers and caretakers, and males can also embody both roles. Hence, the idea of gender roles and conformability has changed with new knowledge.

Similarly, it is seen across organizations and roles within organizations that culture can also be changed or altered. For example, a Walmart operating in the United States might differ in culture from a Walmart in a country such as Thailand. The difference would be that the people working for Walmart within these locations change the culture. Walmart would have a set of core values, but the alternations or changes depend on location and time (Pappas & McKelvie, 2022). Thus, two Walmarts in Thailand could have a completely different culture depending on the group of employees, the systems and processes of how each organization conducts work, etc. Deductively, we can define organizational culture as the beliefs and values shared amongst employees (BDC, n.d.).

WHY ORGANIZATIONAL CULTURE MATTERS

Thus, from the explanation above, organizational culture is shared or normalized behavior amongst a group of two or more individuals (Nickerson, 2023). Organizational culture is shaped by the employees who work for their organization, their individual and collective values and beliefs, their relationships with each other, their work, themselves, and how they interact with their external environment (Nickerson, 2023). Culture always stays with us at work or in our personal lives (Nickerson, 2023). Hence, why is it important that we explore organizational culture? Organizational culture is important in enhancing employee motivation through training and development. Employees are more motivated when organizations and their members can better understand how to motivate, control, and shape culture. Training and development needs can be identified by understanding the current health of the organizational culture. The benefits of understanding organizational culture are better communication between stakeholders, which means better employee relationships (Nickerson, 2023). Organizational culture is vital to understanding how to unify employees through shared values (Nickerson, 2023). It also helps employees interact and connect by supporting them in achieving goals (Nickerson, 2023). Identifying barriers to growth, causes of burnout, resentment, and demotivation can also help improve employees' wellness or mental health (Nickerson, 2023). Thus, organizational culture helps us see what makes each organization different by its unique characteristics.

CHARACTERISTICS OF ORGANIZATIONAL CULTURE

We can think of organizational culture as the collective beliefs and values that interact to create a unique environment in an organization (Lumen Learning, n.d.). These core values or beliefs are shared amongst people, hence the idea of culture (Lumen Learning, n.d.; Pappas & McKelvie, 2022). The organizational part of the word refers to how these core values and beliefs are shared amongst people within an organization (Lumen Learning, 2022). Thus, we can think of how one feels or behaves and how this impacts culture. For example, when a new employee joins an organization and their core values or beliefs differ from their organization, they can shift the culture.

Conversely, when new employees join an organization and their core values and beliefs align with their organization, they merge into the existing organizational culture. Thus, the main difference between the term culture and organizational culture is that organizational culture is specific in that culture occurs within the context of how an organization's core values or beliefs can be shifted, changed, or formed (Lumen Learning, n.d.). Similarly, organizational culture encompasses how employees are guided by core values and beliefs that are part of an organization's philosophy. For example, when an organization has a core value of self-respect, this guideline or philosophy is shared amongst employees. Thus, the organization can set guiding principles or philosophies for its members or employees.

Furthermore, organizational culture affects the way employees interact with one another through guiding principles or core values (Lumen Learning, n.d.). For example, organizational culture can indicate how employees align with their organization's core values or beliefs or diverge from these core values and beliefs. Leaders are of primary importance in how culture is modeled in an organization through modeling core principles and values (Lumen Learning, n.d.). However, culture has different dimensions within an organizational context, from the employee how organizations conduct business practices, how power or hierarchy exists in the chain of command, etc. Thus, organizational culture exists in various dimensions or aspects that collectively form the definition of organizational culture. There are seven dimensions or aspects that make up organizational culture, and these are explored below.

A NEGATIVE OR POSITIVE ORGANIZATIONAL CULTURE

Now that we understand the differences and similarities between culture and organizational culture and their characteristics, it is important to identify positive and negative organizational culture. Moreover, how can we differentiate between the two types of workplace environments? We can differentiate these two by considering what a negative organizational culture entails, and this is an environment that leads to burnout, organizational stress, high turnover rates, etc. (Hetler, 2023). Thus, any unethical workplace environment that creates high-stress levels for employees, lacks diversity and inclusion, etc., can be seen as a negative organizational culture (Hetler, 2023). For example, an organization that lacks internal communication between employees can lead to a negative organizational culture. Suppose you are tasked to work on a team project, and all employees in that team do not communicate with one another. The result would be a lack of communication, collective thinking, or employees working towards the same goal. The outcome could be stress or burnout, where employees are unsure how to achieve the end goal of completing the team project.

Additionally, there are other examples of a negative organizational culture, including a lack of experiential learning, trust, role confusion, and career support (Hetler, 2023). For example, experiential learning allows employees to make mistakes and learn from them as part of their experiences to improve over time (Hetler, 2023). However, when employees fear making mistakes, a leader who does not allow them to make mistakes can create a negative workplace environment (Hetler, 2023). Thus, this example considers how leadership styles or how power is managed leads to a negative organizational culture. Likewise, a lack of trust can also lead to a negative organizational culture when trust is lacking between leaders and subordinates when employees are being closely micromanaged, and this constant level of supervision or surveillance can lead to a lack of trust, making the subordinate question their ability to perform work effectively (Hetler, 2023). Role confusion is another aspect that can be problematic when employees are unsure about their expected responsibilities. This can cause them to make mistakes and not trust their capability to perform work effectively (Hetler, 2023). Thus, the result could be a conflict between co-workers about what work they expect or their responsibilities (Hetler, 2023). Lastly, a lack of career support can also affect employees' ability to see a future with their organization (Hetler, 2023). Employees lacking career support may find it difficult to understand how their work allows them to grow professionally (Hetler, 2023). Hence, a positive organizational culture would be the opposite of these examples and would be more experiential learning, trust, role clarity, and career support (Hetler, 2023).

Throughout this chapter, various models of organizational culture are explored. These models or dimensions of organizational culture are explored to demonstrate how training and development can enhance organizational culture. For example, an organizational culture that focuses on a team orientation training strategy could use techniques such as cross-training to have employees learn each other's jobs, and this enhances the organizational culture because employees would be harder to replace (Lumen Learning, n.d.). Thus, the first model is the seven dimensions of organizational culture. According to one study, a weak organizational culture occurs when there is a lack of organizational goals that are communicated clearly by leadership (Pathiranage et al., 2020). Likewise, training and development should focus on leaders rather than their subordinates, as they are the ones who set the example for a positive organizational culture for their subordinates. A suggestion would be for training to include an aspect of conflict resolution where leaders understand the types of conflict and how to mitigate conflict to promote a positive organizational culture.

THE SEVEN DIMENSIONS OF ORGANIZATIONAL CULTURE

The layout of this chapter will start by identifying the seven areas of organizational culture: innovation, risk-taking, attention to detail, outcome orientation, people orientation, team orientation, aggressiveness, and stability (Lumen Learning, n.d.). The seven dimensions give us a list of values or core principles describing identifying an organization's culture. For example, when we look at a person's identity, we understand that there are different intersections of someone's identity. Intersectionality can present itself in the layers of an individual's identity (Lumen Learning, n.d.; Pappas & McKelvie, 2022). If someone says I am a person of color, male, and disabled, these are three layers of identity that collectively make up a person. Similarly, the seven dimensions identify different layers of an organization and how these layers collectively make up an organizational culture (Lumen Learning, n.d.). Culture informs us that identity or a shared identity makes up a culture (Pappas & McKelvie, 2022). We can identify aspects of organizational culture by considering the layers of identity that organizational culture has.

Thus, like a culture with rules and rituals, organizations have expectations of how employees should behave, perform work, etc. (Lumen Learning, n.d.; Pappas & McKelvie, 2022). Every organization has a set of practices based on the employees contributing to the organizational culture. Thus, organizational culture aims to identify the shared values amongst employees about what their expectations are from their organization and what they cannot do (Lumen Learning, n.d.; Pappas & McKelvie, 2022). Thus, organizational culture describes the shared identity of employees within an organization (Lumen Learning, n.d.). However, it is important to note that cultural dimensions can overlap to create multiple layers of identity (Lumen Learning, n.d.; Pappas & McKelvie, 2022). For example, an organization can be both team-oriented and innovative. Similarly, it is also possible for an organization to have a primary core value or layer of identity. For example, an organization has a primary core value of identity of being innovative. Thus, listed below is an explanation of each of the seven dimensions.

Innovation

How innovative or willing are you to take risks (Lumen Learning, n.d.)? This is a question that reflects the central idea behind innovation. Innovative cultures focus on experimenting with new ideas that help create advancement (Lumen Learning, n.d.). This level of curiosity encourages employees to take risks to advance an organization (Lumen Learning, n.d.). For example, an organization that offers an innovative way to package chips using paper bags instead of plastic is an example of an innovative culture (Lumen Learning, n.d.). Innovation can also be a training tool where employees are encouraged to self-teach themselves, and this benefits the organizational culture because employees are encouraged to make mistakes.

Attention to Detail

How important is attention to precision, analysis, and details (Lumen Learning, n.d.)? This is a question that reflects the central idea behind attention to detail. For example, when an organization sends out surveys to gather information about improving their practices, it allows them to serve their customers better. The goal of attention to detail is to pay attention to details to improve workplace practices, the customer experience, etc. (Lumen Learning, n.d.). Thus, attention to detail can be a competitive advantage for an organization as it prioritizes its customers (Lumen Learning, n.d.).

Outcome Orientation

How important are results (Lumen Learning, n.d.)? This is a question that reflects the central idea behind outcome orientation. The goal here is to consider what the organization has or will achieve and what actions are needed to achieve certain goals (Lumen Learning, n.d.). For example, an organization that aims to keep increasing sales every year focuses on outperforming itself yearly. In this organizational culture, all employees are accountable for the success or outcome the organization has achieved (Lumen Learning, n.d.).

People Orientation

How important is it that you make decisions to positively affect employees in your organization (Lumen Learning, n.d.)? This is a question that reflects the central idea behind people's orientation. Fairness, employee wellness, and individual rights are respected in this organizational culture, where how employees are treated is important (Lumen Learning, n.d.). Thus, organizations prioritize that employees are treated with respect and that ethics for employees are upheld (Lumen Learning, n.d.). For example, an organization with respectful workplace policies for employees or that offers health care benefits is people-oriented as they value their employees and prioritize their wellness.

Team Orientation

How important is it for activities to focus on teams and collaboration rather than individual work (Lumen Learning, n.d.)? This is a question that reflects the central idea behind team orientation. The importance of this organizational culture is that cooperation and harmony are amongst employees (Lumen Learning, n.d.). For example, an organization that uses cross-training to educate their employees in various job roles is centered around team orientation because the goal is how each employee can perform work to support one another (Lumen Learning, n.d.). The outcome would be better workplace relationships due to teamwork rather than individual work.

Aggressiveness

How important is it for you to be competitive with others (Lumen Learning, n.d.)? This is a question that reflects the central idea behind aggressiveness. Organizations with this culture value outperform competitors (Lumen Learning, n.d.). For example, an organization that has a mission to outperform its competitors in sales is an organization that has prominently an aggressive organizational culture. Training and development managers can use a reward system to reward employees for performance. This would enhance the organizational culture by creating standards and motivating employees to improve continuously.

Stability

How important is it for employees to understand their job role, expectations, etc. (Lumen Learning, n.d.)? This is a question that reflects the central idea behind stability. This type of organizational culture is focused on rules, and certain output levels are expected to be met (Lumen Learning, n.d.). For example, an organization that aims to have employees deliver 12 packages a day would expect consistent performance from their employees, not necessarily more or less than 12 parcels. Thus, the idea here is that there are consistent or the same levels of outputs produced by employees (Lumen Learning, n.d.). Consider Table 1 below, which summarizes the seven dimensions of organizational culture.

One study defined strong and weak organizational cultures and indicated that strong organizational cultures involve employees in decision-making and shared values across the organization (Pathiranage et al., 2020). Based on this study, an effective training and development plan should focus on all employees' mission, vision, and values and set a universal standard to ensure that all employees align with these aspects (Pathiranage et al., 2020). One suggestion could be to micromanage new employees in the development process to ensure they receive corrective action and align with the organization's vision, mission, and values (Pathiranage et al., 2020).

Table 1. The Seven Dimensions of Organizational Culture

Dimension of Organizational Culture	Explanation
Innovation	Employees take risks, leaders encourage creative decision-making, and employees adapt to change (Lumen, Learning, n.d.).
Attention to Detail	The organization values precision, an eye for detail, and record-keeping (Lumen Learning, n.d.).
Outcome Orientation	Focused on results (Lumen Learning, n.d.).
People Orientation	The organization is focused on the care of its employees (Lumen Learning, n.d.).
Team Orientation	Employees are encouraged to collaborate, cooperate, and support each other by working in groups (Lumen Learning, n.d.).
Aggressiveness	Competition is important, and what matters is performance and being a top competitor in the global marketplace (Lumen Learning, n.d.).
Stability	Employees understand what is expected from them, their leaders, and the chain of command (Lumen Learning, n.d.).

Note. This table summarizes the seven dimensions of organizational culture.

Schein's Cultural Iceberg Theory

Since organizational culture refers to an organization's values or beliefs, it is guided by principles and policies that form the collection of expected versus unexpected behaviors leaders expect from their subordinates (The World of Work Project, 2022). Thus, organizational culture determines how employees should behave and interact with one another (The World of Work Project, 2022). However, one professor named Edward Schein proposed that aspects of culture are not always visible (Juneja, n.d.). Schein proposed that organizations do not adopt a culture instantaneously; instead, culture is formed over time and can change and adapt to influences in the external environment (Juneja, n.d.; The World of Work Project, 2022). For example, are there invisible aspects of culture? Similarly, what aspects of culture are more visible to us? Moreover, how do an employee's experiences shape the culture they bring to an organization? Or how new employees change an existing organizational culture?

How can motivation be increased through understanding other aspects of organizational culture? Thus, Schein's cultural iceberg theory aims to identify visible versus invisible organizational culture (The World of Work Project, 2022). Understanding how these aspects arise in organizations and how leaders can use this to increase employee motivation is important. For example, when subordinates become more self-aware of disruptive or problematic behavior, it helps to increase motivation. Thus, Schein proposed that organizational culture can be described in three levels: artifacts, values, and assumed values (Juneja, n.d.).

Artifacts

This entails the visible part of organizational culture, such as observed behaviors and practices of employees (The World of Work Project, 2022). For example, consider a mandatory dress code in a work environment (Juneja, n.d.). This culture is considered a visible aspect of the expected dress code. Similarly, we could consider behavior a visible aspect of culture (Juneja, n.d.). Think of artifacts as tangible; we can see and identify them easily (Juneja, n.d.). Thus, artifacts exist on the iceberg's outer layer, the part that exists above sea level (Juneja, n.d.). The parts of the iceberg that we can see are not made invisible to us. Thus, artifacts can be observed, including things like office design, language, etc. (Juneja, n.d.). Changing artifacts in an organization would lead to too little to no changes overall, but it will not lead to significant changes in organizational culture (Juneja, n.d.). The reason is that the surface level of visible aspects has deeply rooted behaviors or beliefs that influence outward or external perceptions of someone. For example, if a manager is disrespectful, correcting the level of disrespect would be impossible without understanding the hidden or invisible layers of why they behave the way they do. Hence, are there hidden motivators for poor behavior or other reasons they might behave poorly?

Values

This includes less visible aspects that still exist and can be seen through behavior (The World of Work Project, 2022). Values include perceptions, attitudes, and beliefs (The World of Work Project, 2022). For example, an organization's mission statement or philosophy can indicate its values; although these aspects are less visible, they appear in employees' attitudes, belief systems, etc. (Juneja, n.d.). Thus, the philosophies, mission, goals, etc., are all in this category of the organizational culture (Juneja, n.d.). If we consider the values of an organization, we will have some insight into the organizational culture and what it entails. However, a change on this level would not create rapid or larger changes in the overall organizational culture because there are still invisible aspects that cannot be seen but are still driving certain behaviors.

Assumed Values

These aspects, such as external impacts, cannot be observed or visible (Juneja, n.d.). The assumed values are the inner layers of the iceberg and the parts submerged underwater (Juneja, n.d.). We cannot see this part of the iceberg because it is invisible, but it does exist and is comprised of feelings or beliefs that employees have but cannot perceive (Juneja, n.d.). Thus, these beliefs exist in an organization; however, most employees are unaware of these beliefs because they are unconscious beliefs (Juneja, n.d.). Assumed values, another term used to describe underlying beliefs, indicate how the organization operates (Juneja, n.d.). This section is the best indicator of organizational culture and is hard to influence or identify because it is not visible (Juneja, n.d.). However, this section indicates what beliefs could lead to workplace success. For example, if an organization has work-form-home policies, but employees have underlying beliefs that working from home is not a great policy, this will indicate the underlying beliefs that decrease motivation. Thus, Table 2 highlights and summarizes Schein's cultural iceberg.

Table 2. Schein's Cultural Iceberg Theory

Three Levels of Organizational Culture	Explanation of Terms
Artifacts	Visible elements of culture (The World of Work Project, 2022).
Values	Less visible are the organization's goals and values (The World of Work Project, 2022).
Assumed Values	Are invisible are unconscious beliefs (The World of Work Project, 2022).

Note. The above table summarizes Schein's cultural iceberg theory.

Thus, Schein's cultural iceberg demonstrates that understanding culture's visible and invisible aspects is important to improve employee motivation (The World of Work Project, 2022). In one study that considered health services in hospitals, the conclusion indicated that engaged employees were more proactive and collaborated with their peers more than other employees who were not engaged with their work (Srimulyani & Hermanto, 2022). This study showed that leaders are responsible for a positive organizational culture and employee engagement (Srimulyani & Hermanto, 2022). If leaders are responsible for driving a positive organizational culture, training, and development should focus on leadership development and visible and invisible aspects, such as leadership style, personal values, etc. (Srimulyani & Hermanto, 2022). Hence, Schein's cultural iceberg training and development should focus on leadership training since leaders are vital to employee engagement (Srimulyani & Hermanto, 2022). Furthermore, this study suggests that organizations should train leaders to be credible, understanding, and trustworthy and reinforce corrective and ethical behavior (Srimulyani & Hermanto, 2022).

Hofstede's Model of Organizational Culture

Geert Hofstede was a social psychologist whose ideas help us understand how culture influences individuals and how they interact with organizations (Nickerson, 2023). Hofstede's model of organizational culture makes us understand that culture is a shared experience where employees learn from each other and how to behave by observing behaviors from one another (Mind Tools Content Team, n.d.). Thus, their social environments influence the ones they are surrounded with, and our values or beliefs can change in the outer layers to merge into a group or to fit our environment, such as an organization (Mind Tools Content Team, n.d.). Hofstede established that there are six dimensions of cultural differences between organizations, and this indicates how we act within organizations, absorb certain rituals or traditions, or change organizational cultures (Mind Tools Content Team, n.d.). Hofstede's model of organizational culture is important in understanding cultural differences amongst different organizations, improving communication, and developing an organization's culture to be more positive through training and development practices (Nickerson, 2023).

Moreover, organizations want to find ways to train and develop their leaders to set a positive example for expected versus unexpected behaviors they want them to model to their subordinates (Nickerson, 2023). Thus, organizational culture indicates how we see employees interact with their external environment, which includes each other (Nickerson, 2023). Thus, Hofstede indicates below that there are five ways we can understand the organizational culture, which are the power distance index, masculinity versus femininity, individualism versus collectivism, uncertainty avoidance index, long-term versus short-term orientation, and indulgence versus restraint (Mind Tools Content Team, n.d.; Nickerson, 2023).

Power Distance Index

This section considers the degree of authority in an organization and how authority separates managers from their subordinates and gives each employee a rank within the organization (Nickerson, 2023). Hence, how does information flow between employees and leaders (Nickerson, 2023)? For example, organizations can distribute power evenly across all employees (Nickerson, 2023). This means that regardless of hierarchy, all employees experience equality in rights (Nickerson, 2023). Conversely, an organization can have unequal power distribution when superiors or leaders have special privileges, creating a power imbalance (Nickerson, 2023). Thus, the power distance index means the difference in how power is distributed or given to employees (Mind Tools Content Team, n.d.).

Masculinity Versus Femininity

This section indicates the degree to which an organization has feminine or masculine traits (Nickerson, 2023). Hence, how can we describe employee communication (Nickerson, 2023)? For example, to what degree does an organization have a culture where power and competitiveness (masculinity) versus collaboration and cooperation (femininity) qualities (Nickerson, 2023)? This also considers the differences that we might see where male and female stereotypical values are present in the organization's culture (Nickerson, 2023). Hence, an organization may consider male employees more aggressive than female employees, who might be seen as more compassionate and understanding (Nickerson, 2023). Although this section might vary depending on numerous factors of gender roles and stereotypes, it is important to consider how historical notions of power and authority have been associated with male figures, leading to inequality between the sexes (Mind Tools Content Team, n.d.; Nickerson, 2023)

Individualism Versus Collectivism

This section indicates whether employees prioritize their own goals or desires or consider the goals and desires of their team versus themselves (Nickerson, 2023). Hence, how do employees support themselves or each other (Nickerson, 2023)? Teamwork is a group of people who share something to work towards a common goal (Nickeson, 2023). Thus, do organizations rely on a teamwork culture where employees are encouraged to work together or individually? (Mind Tools Content Team, n.d.). How work is approached and tasks are completed varies between organizations. When organizations encourage teamwork, we might see more exchange of ideas, creativity, conflict, etc. (Mind Tools Content Team. n.d.). Organizations that encourage individual work might see decreased motivation, higher rates of burnout, organizational stress, etc. (Mind Tool Content Team, n.d.).

Uncertainty Avoidance Index

This section indicates a culture's ability to tolerate changes, especially those unseen in the future (Nickerson, 2023). Hence, how do organizations support risk-taking (Nickerson, 2023)? For example, how do employees respond to sudden organizational change, such as moving to a new department or performing work differently? Thus, the uncertainty avoidance index considers the degree to which an employee can tolerate and handle changes that are usually sudden (Nickerson, 2023).

Long-Term Versus Short-Term Orientation

This section indicates whether an organization cares more about the present or future (Nickerson, 2023). Hence, how do organizations support their employees for the next few years (Nickerson, 2023)? For example, when organizations support their employees in the long term, they help them see a future with their organization, perhaps a higher position or involvement with their employees in the future of their organization (Mind Tools Content Team, n.d.). Conversely, organizations that focus on short-term goals are focused on setting short-term objectives such as employee of the month or rewarding employees for performance measures in short periods; however, employees are only interested in meeting short-term objectives and do not see a future with their organization (Mind Tools Content Team, n.d.). Thus, the result would be that employees would leave their organization for better opportunities, such as better pay or a higher position (Mind Tools Content Team, n.d.).

Indulgence Versus Restraint

This section indicates employees' enjoyment or fulfillment (Nickerson, 2023). How do organizations celebrate their employees' successes (Nickerson, 2023)? For example, an indulgent organization focuses on satisfying its employees' needs and desires (Mind Tools Content Team, n.d.). This means an organization is concerned about employee health and safety, wellness, etc. (Mind Tools Content Team, n.d.). Conversely, a restrained organization is not concerned with individual needs or desires but rather aligns its employees with the needs and desires based on society's wants or societal norms (Mind Tools Content Team, n.d.). Thus, indulgent organizations focus on their employees' responsibility and duty to satisfy others (Mind Tools Content Team, n.d.). For example, employee safety is a restrained organizational culture, whereas focusing on productivity and meeting the demand for consideration is a restrained organizational culture (Mind Tools Content Team, n.d.).

Thus, consider Table 3 below, which summarizes Hofstede's model of organizational culture.

Charles Handy's Model of Organizational Culture

Several theories, researchers, psychologists, and philosophers have explored organizational culture and what entails organizational culture, such as how employees interact (Francis, n.d.). One of these theorists or philosophers was Charles Handy, who proposed that organizational culture could be described using a model describing how categories exist in organizational culture and outline the organizational structure

(Francis, n.d.; Fraraccio, 2023). Handy believes there are four organizational cultures within which organizations exist, including power, task, person, and role cultures (Francis, n.d.).

Table 3. Hofstede's Model of Organizational Culture

The Six Factors of Hofstede's Model	Explanation of Terms
Power Distance Index	Equality or Inequality (Nickerson, 2023).
Masculinity Versus Femininity	Power and competitiveness or collaboration and cooperation (Nickerson, 2023).
Individualism Versus Collectivism	Individualistic or collectivistic (Nickerson, 2023).
Uncertainty Avoidance Index	Risk tolerance versus risk intolerance (Nickerson, 2023).
Long-Term Versus Short-Term Orientation	Future, long-term, tradition, and short-term (Nickerson, 2023).
Indulgence Versus Restraint	Satisfaction or normative repression (Nickerson, 2023).

Note. The above table summarizes Hofstede's model of organizational culture.

Power Culture

Power is controlled and given to those in high leadership roles and remains in the hands of these people (Francis, n.d.; Fraraccio, 2023). Those in high leadership positions, as do subordinates, delegate and enjoy special privileges. Other employees cannot express their viewpoints in a way that allows them to share openly and freely with their superiors (Fraraccio, 2023). Power is concentrated and held by the few at the organization's top (Fraraccio, 2023). Thus, in a power culture, few rules exist; those at the top are the most important decision-makers, and subordinates must follow their superiors (Francis, n.d.; Fraraccio, 2023).

Task Culture

Teams are vital to meeting goals and solving problems, and groups of people who share a common goal come together to achieve work objectives (Fraraccio, 2023). The organizational culture is that power is shared or distributed amongst team members (Fraraccio, 2023). Teams are generally 4-5 members, each contributing equally to accomplishing goals (Francis, n.d.; Fraraccio, 2023).

Person Culture

The priority is self-interest versus the organization's best interests, and individuals are concerned about themselves (Fraraccio, 2023). The individual comes before the organization (Fraraccio, 2023). The organizational structure is that power is given solely to the individual (Fraraccio, 2023).

Role Culture

Employees have certain roles and responsibilities and are accountable for their work (Fraraccio, 2023). The organizational structure empowers those with work responsibilities (Fraraccio, 2023). Roles are assigned based on educational qualifications, specializations, etc. (Francis, n.d.; Fraraccio, 2023).

Thus, consider Table 4 below, which summarizes Charles Handy's model of organizational culture.

Table 4. Charles Handy's Model of Organizational Culture

Types of Organizational Cultures	Explanation of Terms
Power	Hierarchy, dominance over others, and few rules (Fraraccio, 2023).
Task	Cooperative teams and ambitious groups (Fraraccio, 2023).
Person	Individual talents and people are superior to their organization (Fraraccio, 2023).
Role	Personal power, lack of innovation, and role-specific authority figures are clearly defined (Fraraccio, 2023).

Note. The above table summarizes Charles Handy's model of organizational culture.

The Four Types of Organizational Cultures

There are also four types of organizational culture: clan culture, adhocracy culture, market culture, and hierarchy culture (Heinz, 2023). The first type of culture is clan culture, which considers how employees work together to achieve organizational goals or objectives or how employees work as a community (Heinz, 2023). Secondly, adhocracy culture considers how culture can change and is dynamic in that employees can vary in decision-making and personal expression (Heinz, 2023). Thirdly, market culture refers to how organizations conduct business practices, focusing on results, competition, and achievement (Heinz, 2023). Fourthly, hierarchical culture considers how power and information flow through the chain of command and creates an organizational structure where power or roles create power dynamics (Heins, 2023). Thus, a hierarchical culture emphasizes efficiency and processes (Heinz, 2023).

Clan Culture

Clan culture means employees are part of a family or community (Conmy, n.d.). Within clan culture, each employee can manage their work style according to their work style (Conmy, n.d.). The objective is to align an organization's values with its employees and similarly align employees with their organization's values (Conmy, n.d.). Organizations strive to have their employees identify with their organization and focus on employee wellbeing (Conmy, n.d.). The advantage of this type of organizational culture is that it can lead to the professional development of employees; however, the organization could lack structure (Heinz, 2023).

Adhocracy Culture

In adhocracy, managers have a vision for their subordinates and focus on innovation and creativity, including all employees of diverse backgrounds (Conmy, n.d.). In adhocracy, culture is related to innovation or creativity, where employees are challenged to experiment or think outside the box (Conmy, n.d.). The advantage of this organizational culture is that creativity or innovation can lead to new ideas and create a future for the organization (Heinz, 2023). The disadvantage of this organizational culture strategy is that employees and their organization do not have a concrete plan for the direction their organization will take in the future (Heinz, 2023). Thus, risk-taking can harm the organization when plans do not go according to plan, and it is unclear if employees will always accept new ideas (Heinz, 2023).

Market Culture

Market culture strives to focus on how the organization can always prioritize performance and customer service (Conmy, n.d.). Thus, the goal is to compete for the competition out the organization to become number one in their field (Conmy, n.d.). Market culture entails a culture that comes from a product or service, focusing on results in numbers, performance, etc. (Heinz, 2023). This type of organizational culture can be positive and negative in terms of the pressure that leaders have on their subordinates to perform their best and the pressure that subordinates have on themselves to deliver the best performance (Heinz, 2023). The advantage of market culture is that employees can be pushed to become and perform at their best, leading to professional and personal development (Heinz, 2023). However, the disadvantage of market culture is that it can also lead to employee burnout or a lack of employee motivation due to overworking (Heinz, 2023).

Hierarchical Culture

In a hierarchical culture, the focus is on how everyone accepts their role to fulfill a mission (Conmy, n.d.). Thus, this is a shared goal that team members commit to (Conmy, n.d.). Hierarchy culture is about the structure, and it mainly follows the top-down approach in the chain of commands where decisions are made from the highest point of leadership and then passed down to those with less power within the hierarchal structure, such as managers who pass this information to subordinates (Heinz, 2023). Hierarchical culture is about rules, processes, and procedures to keep an organization running smoothly (Heinz, 2023). The advantages of this type of organizational culture are that employees know what is expected of them and are prepared each day to perform work because there are no surprises in their job expectations (Heinz, 2023). The disadvantage of hierarchical culture is that it limits creativity or innovation because employees are held to rules or commands (Heinz, 2023). Similarly, employees might feel dissatisfied when their leader is unethical or pushes them to perform in a way that limits their creativity (Heinz, 2023).

Thus, consider Table 5 below, which summarizes the four types of organizational cultures.

Table 5. The Four Types of Organizational Cultures

Types of Cultures	Definition	Properties
Clan (Family, Merging into the Organizational Culture)	Working as a team (Heinz, 2023).	Working as a community of people (Heinz, 2023).
Adhocracy (Creative and Innovation)	Being flexible and taking risks (Heinz, 2023).	Entrepreneurial (Heinz, 2023).
Market (Results, Competitors)	Focus on profit and competitiveness (Heinz, 2023).	Focused on outcomes or results (Heinz, 2023).
Hierarchical (Control, Structure, and Rules)	Focusing on structure and stability (Heinz, 2023).	The focus is on control, efficiency, and avoiding risks (Heinz, 2023).

Note. The above table summarizes the four types of organizational cultures. The brackets in the "Types of Cultures" column are meant to summarize or give a synonym for what this term means.

Subcultures and Countercultures

What are subcultures and countercultures, and why are they relevant to organizational culture? Think of subculture as a culture within a larger culture, where beliefs, values, traditions, etc., can differ from the larger culture (Anuradha, 2021). For example, in the larger mainstream culture, a subculture could be bodybuilders prioritizing health and fitness (Anuradha, 2021; Keswani, 2020). The subculture is a part of the larger culture because bodybuilders belong to the group of people who are a part of mainstream culture; however, the subculture differs from the mainstream due to their differences in beliefs in health and fitness. However, the similarities are that both cultures share similar values, traditions, etc. (Keswani, 2020). Thus, we can think of a subculture as a group that, although it belongs to a larger group, also differs in its values, beliefs, and traditions from the larger culture (Keswani, 2020).

Another example would be a group of students; if this is the larger culture, then the subculture would be the students who are a part of the student council within the group of students. The student council group is the subculture group of students. Thus, subsystems or cultures exist within larger systems or cultures, and although the larger system or culture is greater, the subsystems do exist (Keswani, 2020). Accordingly, what is the significance of exploring subculture? Subcultures inform us that some subcultures or cultures are not always so visible if organizations have larger cultures or more observable cultures, such as the tip of the iceberg in Schein's theory (Keswani, 2020; Juneja, n.d.). Thus, to enhance employee motivation, we should understand the subcultures and cultures where shared values, beliefs, and traditions can hinder employee motivation (Juneja, n.d.).

Conversely, a counterculture is very different from a subculture because it is a group of individuals whose beliefs, values, and traditions differ from the mainstream or larger cultures (Keswani, 2020). Thus, when a group of people shares beliefs that are very different from what the mainstream or dominant culture accepts, we call this a counterculture (Keswani, 2020). For example, social justice groups throughout history that have advocated for women's rights or equality amongst races during that period would have been considered the counterculture because their beliefs differed from the dominant culture, mainstream culture, or norm (Anuradha, 2021). Thus, countercultures exist when a group shares different beliefs from the larger group (Anuradha, 2021). For example, when an organization has certain values or beliefs, such as a focus on customer service, meeting supply and demand, etc., and these beliefs or values differ from a group of employees, they would be the counterculture from the larger culture (Anuradha, 2021). Hence, countercultures are important to understand what might create employee demotivation, resistance, or a lack of training and development effectiveness.

Additionally, countercultures could indicate the importance of training and development and what an organization needs to do to ensure training and development increase employee motivation. Thus, the similarities between subculture and counterculture are that both are separate from another culture and can exist within another dominant culture (Anuradha, 2021). Hence, you can have numerous subcultures or countercultures within a dominant or mainstream culture (Anuradha, 2021). However, what is not always clear in organizations is how values, beliefs, and traditions form or appear in employees' primary and secondary values (Anuradha, 2021). For example, a subculture of students who belong to the student council, as seen above, could share similar or different primary or secondary values, such as prioritizing student wellbeing, ensuring funding is used appropriately, etc. (Anuradha, 2021). However, not all these values are clear or visible, so they exist within two categories, primary or secondary, explored below.

Core Values: Primary and Secondary

Thus, from the subcategories in this chapter, we have learned that organizational culture is much more dynamic and integrated into numerous factors, from how an individual thinks, feels, and behaves to organizational structures (Sutler-Cohen, 2019). It becomes clear that it is impossible to say that organizational culture is just one facet or aspect, as numerous factors are at play. These aspects of organizational culture that are sometimes visible or invisible are outlined in the core values of an individual or an organization (Sutler-Cohen, 2019). Core values in an organization are reflected in the mission statement, vision, and values (Sutler-Cohen, 2019). Hence, core values are just a person's or organization's beliefs that guide their behaviors (Sutler-Cohen, 2019). For example, when an organization has a mission to focus on customer service, this is essentially its core value. We would call customer service a primary core value since it is one of the organization's most visible and clear values (Sutler-Cohen, 2019). However, secondary values differ because they are not always easily visible or clear, but they still guide the organization (Sutler-Cohen, 2019). For example, perhaps the organization has an organizational culture of increasing profits generated for the organization. Although this core value might not be clear in the organization's code of conduct, mission, vision, and values, it is an important but not explicit or primary concern (Sutler-Cohen, 2019). However, the organization is still subconsciously guided by these values, thus making them secondary values (Sutler-Cohen, 2019).

Hence, primary and secondary core values influence belief systems, behavior, and decision-making (Sutler-Cohen, 2019). Thus, employees should know how core values influence biases or limit beliefs and learning capabilities. If employees have a core value that they are not equipped to perform other forms of work through cross-training, it limits their ability to adapt to a changing work environment (Sutler-Cohen, 2019). Similarly, by understanding core values, organizations can create training and development programs to change or redirect individual core values to align with their organization and vice versa. Employee motivation can also be improved if organizations can better understand work behavior, why employees are inclined to perform work in a certain way, what keeps them motivated and engaged at work, what makes them feel fulfilled, and what increases work satisfaction (Sutler-Cohen, 2019). Therefore, throughout this chapter, the theories and guidelines that explain the complexity of organizations strive to describe core values. They outline how organizational culture exists. Each theory can be described simply through a core set of primary and secondary values that an individual or organization has that make up core values that are essentially just the organizational culture. For example, consider the six factors of Hofstede's model; each factor outlines core values, whether primary or secondary, and this describes the organizational culture. One factor is the power distance index, which describes the level of dominance given to each level of authority in an organization through equality or Inequality (Nickerson, 2023).

Hence, the individual's core values describe the level of power an employee holds and the level of control or dominance over their subordinates (Nickerson, 2023). The organization's core values are the importance of hierarchy or organizational structure (Nickerson, 2023). Thus, organizational culture can be described as one where employees have authority based on ranking, as seen in the organizational structure. Moreover, an individual's core values outline or describe what type of culture we might see in organizational culture (Nickerson, 2023). Accordingly, we should use this as a tool or guide to understand the above theories, what is needed to improve a negative organizational culture, or what measures are needed in training and development plans to increase employee motivation.

Themes or Patterns in the Theories Above

Thus, an organizational culture appears to be formed through tradition, procedure, and work methods (Lumen Learning, n.d.; Pappas & McKelvie, 2022). Similarly, organizations have a set of core values, missions, and vision, which are guiding principles that reflect the type of culture or the seven dimensions of an organization (Lumen Learning, n.d.; Pappas & McKelvie, 2022). For example, a mission for Walmart to be a top competitor would indicate that an organization heavily reflects the layer of identity of competitiveness as indicated in its mission statement (Lumen Learning, n.d.). Similarly, an organization with a vision to focus on employee mental health heavily reflects people's orientation as their organizational culture (Lumen Learning, n.d.). However, culture can always be shaped depending on changes or advances in social justice, global perceptions, etc. The above theories have indicated that cultures can always change or adapt (Nickerson, 2023). We have seen how this can occur in organizations that rebrand themselves or change their vision or mission statement (Nickerson, 2023).

Thus, the theories throughout this chapter indicate how we can change or challenge an existing organizational culture (Nickerson, 2023). For example, in an organization with a power culture, as indicated in Charles Handy's model of organizational culture, dominance or authority is given to those in leadership (Francis, n.d.; Fraraccio, 2023). Accordingly, training and development to increase employee motivation should focus on leadership development since they are the ones who model expected behavior and influence employee engagement (Francis, n.d.; Fraraccio, 2023). Organizational culture has a role in motivation or demotivation; we can create training strategies outlining improving self-awareness, emotional intelligence, etc.

Thomas Kilmann Model: Conflict Resolution

This chapter explores organizational culture, and one aspect that we should consider is a negative organizational culture where conflict can occur. According to the Thomas Kilmann model, the various types of conflict are competing, avoiding, accommodating, collaborating, and compromising (Mishra, 2021). By identifying how to recognize conflict, we can improve organizational culture by offering strategies for conflict resolution. Hence, we can propose ways for subordinates to resolve disputes. Conflict resolution is vital for training and development strategies to give employees tools to become aware of types of conflict and motivate employees to make changes to improve relationships with their team members. When relationships digress from the organization's overall mission and vision, the result is a subculture of employees who either have a culture different from their organizations or a counterculture where employees completely diverge from the dominant culture (Mishra, 2021). Investigating conflict resolution increases employee motivation because organizations can better understand how to serve their employees and their needs to promote a healthy work environment (Mishra, 2021). Conflict resolution also improves training and development strategies because it allows organizations to understand what skills or knowledge their employees need to be successful in the work environment (Guzowski, 2022).

Competing

Competing involves a high level of assertiveness from one person but then a low level of cooperation between two or more individuals (Guzowski, 2022). We consider competing a conflict resolution strategy because the conflict revolves around one's assertiveness over another (Guzowski, 2022). This essentially means that one person is not cooperating with the other parties, and they hold the power position (Guzowski, 2022).

Avoiding

Avoiding is a conflict resolution strategy where you choose to pass on conflict, and argumentative or confrontation is better avoided (Guzowski, 2022). Thus, you do not express your opinions and shun the conflict (Guzowski, 2022). However, the downfall is that future conflicts could occur due to built-up resentment (Guzowski, 2022).

Accommodating

Accommodating happens when you want to resolve a conflict by giving up your opinions or position to satisfy the other party (Mishra, 2021). Thus, you express high levels of cooperativeness but minimal or low levels of assertiveness because you "give in" (Guzowski, 2022). You give up your stance to satisfy the other party (Guzowski, 2022).

Collaborating

Collaborating means that both parties are on the same side and want to cooperate and share power (Guzowski, 2022). Thus, a solution is reached to resolve conflict where both parties agree and receive benefits (Guzowski, 2022).

Compromising

Compromising is unique in that it is in the middle of being assertive and having cooperativeness (Guzowski, 2022). Both parties get a mutual benefit but must give up something they want to reach a conflict resolution (Guzowski, 2022). However, this can also present challenges as one party can receive more of a resolution closer to what they expected than the other party (Guzowski, 2022). Hence, one party may receive more benefits and give up less on something than another (Guzowski, 2022).

 The conflict resolution model helps us see that when assessing organizational needs for training and development to improve employee motivation, we should consider any existing or future problems (Mishra, 2021). Conflict resolution allows organizations to understand how to mitigate the effects of a negative organizational culture and address resolutions through training and development that focus on two main angles: assertiveness and cooperation, which exist in each aspect of the conflict resolution model (Mishra, 2021). Thus, the goal for organizations would be to focus on building lasting relationships among employees and helping employees understand their power in the hierarchy or organizational structure (Mishra, 2021).

For example, in one study, hospital nurses in Taiwan were given a questionnaire and a positive correlation was seen between leadership behavior and organizational culture (Tsai, 2011). Similarly, organizational culture positively correlates with job satisfaction (Tsai, 2011). This study concluded that organizational culture affected whether employees were satisfied with their work environment (Tsai, 2011). Effective leadership encourages a positive organizational culture where communication and collaboration are encouraged, enhancing job satisfaction (Tsai, 2011). Hence, training initiatives should focus on effective leadership, experiential learning processes, and conflict resolution. Less conflict means more employee motivation and job satisfaction.

Hence, consider Table 6 below, which summarizes Thomas Kilmann's conflict resolution model.

Table 6. Thomas Kilmann Model of Conflict Resolution

Types of Conflict	Explanation
Competing	Concern is for self and not for others (Guzowski, 2022).
Avoiding	You do not engage with the other party (Guzowski, 2022).
Accommodating	The concern is for others, and you accept the other person's perspective rather than your own (Guzowski, 2022).
Collaborating	You develop a solution that benefits both parties (Guzowski, 2022).
Compromising	You agree to some items and give up certain items for a mutually beneficial solution (Guzowski, 2022).

Note. The above table summarizes the types of conflict resolution strategies in Thomas Killman's conflict resolution model.

The Benefits of Training and Development

The benefits of training and development would be more employee growth, less turnover, and more productivity (Ottawa University, 2021). Training and development help retain employees because employees feel more comfortable performing their jobs with more knowledge and guidance, leading to lower turnover rates (Ottawa University, 2021). Employees with greater autonomy feel fewer mental health effects because they can make decisions (Ottawa University, 2021). Similarly, we would see increased engagement because employees would see growth opportunities within their organization and expand their skill sets by teaching and learning from other employees (Ottawa University, 2021).

How Effective Training and Development Create a Positive Organizational Culture

This chapter aims to encourage a learning culture where leaders are encouraged to give meaningful and constructive feedback and self-reflect on best practices to improve employee motivation. For example, being aware of how a new candidate can shift the organizational culture positively or negatively is important to create organizational changes. For example, another concept, such as modeling or experiential learning, allows you to make mistakes to learn, and reflecting on those mistakes is also important in enhancing employee motivation (Kumar, 2023; Patterson, 2023). Moreover, why should we consider an effective training plan, and how does this improve organizational culture? One reason would be that training plans and employee development through coaching, modeling, etc., create employee engagement and align employees and their organization to one common culture (Kumar, 2023). Rather than there being countercultures or subcultures or perhaps employees who have different core values than their organization's core values, training and development create a common organizational culture shared amongst all employees (Kumar, 2023; Lumen Learning, 2022; Mishra, 2021). Creating one common culture would result in a more engaged workforce, and employees would better understand how they serve their organization or align with their values (Kumar, 2023).

Hence, effective training and development lead to a positive organizational culture because employees start to understand the meaning of their work by aligning with the organization's values, mission, objectives, etc. (Kumar, 2023). Additional benefits would be a positive organizational culture that encourages knowledge sharing, and employees benefit from shared learning when they can help others align with the organization's values (Kumar, 2023). Effective training and development also allow for conflict resolution because it allows organizations to resolve conflicts by aligning employees with their values (Kumar, 2023). Another reason would be that when we explore the various types of organizational culture we might see in any organization, such as a hierarchical culture, it gives way for organizations to identify how to shift their current organizational culture or identify areas of weaknesses within their current organizational culture (Heinz, 2023; Kumar, 2023). Thus, training should align employees with the organization's vision and values, promoting knowledge sharing, collaboration, and conflict resolution strategies (Kumar, 2023; Patterson, 2023). Effective training and development create a positive organizational culture when employees are aware of what they can and cannot do, identify how an employee's work has significance or value to their organization, and how they can be more engaged with their work (Kumar, 2023; Patterson, 2023).

Lessons Learned

This chapter presents many theories describing organizational culture and its components. Although it may not always be clear that we can describe organizational culture, it is hard to identify just one common organizational culture. We saw this in the discussion on subcultures and countercultures, indicating that other emerging cultures can come from or oppose certain cultures (Anuradha, 2021). Additionally, this chapter has outlined and taught us six lessons: organizational culture is malleable, shaped by employees, is described through various theories, core values influence organizational culture, conflict resolution improves organizational culture, and training and development create a positive organizational culture. The following lessons learned are summarized below.

Organizational Culture Is Malleable

The significance of this lesson is that organizational culture can always change. It is not a fixed component that stays the same, but rather, it can be molded, adapted, and continuously changed because it is a dependent factor. This means organizational cultural changes depend on the environment, employees, societal norms, etc. Hence, measuring organizational effectiveness is difficult because it is a dependent factor. However, we can measure or identify visible and invisible aspects of organizational culture (Juneja, n.d.). Thus, organizations should focus on identifying aspects that make up organizational culture.

Employees Shape Organizational Culture

The significance of this lesson is that all employees collectively make up an organizational culture shaped by the employees who work for a particular organization (BDC, n.d.). This means that someone external from the organization would have less influence over the organizational culture than those who work and are engaged with that organization. Hence, when hiring and training practices are improved, the organization experiences fewer shifts or dramatic shifts in its organizational culture. If training and development practices do not improve to align employees with the existing organizational culture, you will have a subculture or counterculture (Anuradha, 2021).

Organizational Culture Described Through Various Theories

The significance of this lesson is that organizational culture is multidimensional and more complex than what is visible on the surface, as indicated in Schein's cultural iceberg (Juneja, n.d.). This chapter described what culture is and how culture can be described. Although there are numerous theories, the key takeaway is that we can describe the many facets of organizational culture. There may still be other areas of overlap or invisible that might not be so obvious (Juneja, n.d.). However, it is important to continuously explore areas of uncertainty where we think there may be a relationship between two or more variables influencing organizational culture to create a more positive one.

Core Values Influence Organizational Culture

The significance of this lesson is that if employees, especially new employees, core values do not align with their organizations, you could have a counterculture or a subculture, creating employee resistance, burnout, and demotivation (Sutler-Cohen, 2019). If an employee has different primary and secondary values, their organization may feel less inclined to work and support their organization's overall mission or objective (Sutler-Cohen, 2019).

Conflict Resolution is Needed to Improve Organizational Culture

The significance of this lesson is that with conflict resolution strategies, organizational culture improves because there is a strategy or resolution that employees are encouraged to use, leading to less disharmony and more cooperation and assertiveness (Guzowski, 2022). The Killman conflict resolution model offers insight into how conflict resolution can be resolved and the approaches employees should take to create harmony among each other (Guzowski, 2022). More harmony means a better and positive organizational culture.

Improving Training and Development Practices Creates a Positive Organizational Culture

The significance of this lesson is that training and development practices create KSAOs of knowledge, skills, abilities, and other competencies (Guzowski, 2022; Lumen Learning, n.d.). With improved employee skill sets, they are more confident in their work, can foresee a future with their organization, and are encouraged to use their skills to add value to the workplace. Hence, improving training and development creates more alignment between employees and their organization and a shared culture.

REFERENCES

Anuradha. (2021, September 2). *What is the difference between subculture and counterculture.* PEDIAA. https://pediaa.com/what-is-the-difference-between-subculture-and-counterculture/

BDC. (n.d.). *Organizational culture.* Entrepreneur's Toolkit. https://www.bdc.ca/en/articles-tools/entrepreneur-toolkit/templates-business-guides/glossary/organizational-culture

Conmy, S. (n.d.). *What are the four types of corporate culture?* The Corporate Governance Institute. https://www.thecorporategovernanceinstitute.com/insights/lexicon/what-are-the-four-types-of-corporate-culture/

Francis, A. (n.d.). *Charles Handy's Model of organizational culture.* MBA Knowledge Base. https://www.mbaknol.com/management-principles/charles-handys-model-of-organizational-culture/

Fraraccio, M. (2023, September 21). *Management theory of Charles Handy.* Business. https://www.business.com/articles/management-theory-of-charles-handy/

Guzowski, L. (2022, February 2). *Effective conflict resolution in the workplace with Thomas Kilmann model.* Human. https://www.human.pm/post/thomas-kilmann-model-conflict-resolution-workplace

Heinz, K. (2023, October 20). *The 4 types of organizational culture and their benefits.* Built In. https://builtin.com/company-culture/types-of-organizational-culture

Hetler, A. (2023, September 13). *11 signs of toxic workplace culture.* WhatIs. https://www.techtarget.com/whatis/feature/Signs-of-toxic-workplace-culture

Juneja, P. (n.d.). *Edgar Schein's model of organization culture.* Management Study Guide. https://www.managementstudyguide.com/edgar-schein-model.htm

Keswani, D. (2020, April 27). *Understanding organizational subcultures and countercultures.* Amity. https://www.ekoapp.com/blog/understanding-organizational-subcultures-and-countercultures

Kumar, P. (2023, October 26). *The importance of aligning the company culture with employee training*. eLearning Industry. https://elearningindustry.com/importance-of-aligning-company-culture-with-employeetraining#:~:text=It%20fosters%20a%20sense%20of, into%20their%20roles%20and%20responsibilities.&text=When%20 employees%20feel%20that%20the,out%20of%20their%20comfort%20zones.

Lumen Learning. (n.d.). *Key dimensions of organizational culture*. Principles of Management. https://courses.lumenlearning.com/wm-principlesofmanagement/chapter/reading-key-dimensions-of-organizational-culture/

Mind Tools Content Team. (n.d.). *Hofstede's cultural dimensions*. Mind Tools. https://www.mindtools.com/a1ecvyx/hofstedes-cultural-dimensions

Mishra, A. (2021, May 14). *Thomas Kilmann conflict model*. Management Weekly. https://managementweekly.org/thomas-kilmann-conflict-resolution-model/

Nickerson, C. (2023, October 24). *Hofstede's cultural dimensions theory & examples*. Simply Psychology. https://www.simplypsychology.org/hofstedes-cultural-dimensions-theory.html

Ottawa University. (2021, January 12). *5 benefits of training and development*. Why Is Training and Development Important? https://www.ottawa.edu/online-and-evening/blog/january-2021/5-benefits-of-training-and-development

Pappas, S., & McKelvie, C. (2022, October 17). *What is culture?* Live Science. https://www.livescience.com/21478-what-is-culture-definition-of-culture.html

Pathiranage, Y., Jayatilake, L., & Abeysekera, R. (2020). A literature review on organizational culture towards corporate performance. *International Journal of Management, Accounting and Economics, 7*(9), 522-544. https://www.ijmae.com/article_117964.html

Patterson, J. (2023, June 13). *Creating a culture of training and development in the workplace*. Forbes. https://www.forbes.com/sites/forbeshumanresourcescouncil/2023/06/13/creating-a-culture-of-training-and-development-in-the-workplace/?sh=447be1eb1038

Srimulyani, V. A., & Hermanto, Y. B. (2022). Organizational culture as a mediator of credible leadership influence on work engagement: Empirical studies in private hospitals in East Java, Indonesia. *Humanities & Social Sciences Communications, 9*(1), 1–11. doi:10.1057/s41599-022-01289-z PMID:35990765

Sutler-Cohen, S. (2019, March 6). *Core values: What they are, why they matter, and how to define yours.* Medium. https://medium.com/@scoutcoaching/core-values-what-they-are-why-they-matter-and-how-to-define-yours-93164383eada

The World of Work Project. (2022). *Edgar Schein's organizational culture triangle: A simple summary.* https://worldofwork.io/2019/10/edgar-scheins-culture-triangle/

Tsai, Y. (2011). Relationship between organizational culture, leadership behavior and job satisfaction. *BMC Health Services Research, 11*(1), 98. doi:10.1186/1472-6963-11-98 PMID:21569537

KEY TERMS AND DEFINITIONS

Adhocracy Culture: Managers have a vision for their subordinates and focus on innovation and creativity, including all employees of diverse backgrounds (Conmy, n.d.).

Clan Culture: Employees are part of a family or community (Conmy, n.d.).

Core Values: A person's or organization's beliefs that guide their behaviors (Sutler-Cohen, 2019).

Countercultures: When a group of people shares beliefs that differ from what the mainstream or dominant culture accepts. (Keswani, 2020).

Hierarchical Culture: Focuses on how everyone accepts their role to fulfill a mission (Conmy, n.d.).

Market Culture: Strives to focus on how the organization can always prioritize performance and customer service (Conmy, n.d.).

Organizational Culture: The beliefs and values shared amongst employees (BDC, n.d.).

Person Culture: The priority is self-interest versus the organization's best interests, and individuals are concerned about themselves (Fraraccio, 2023).

Power Culture: Power is controlled and given to those in high leadership roles and remains in the hands of these people (Francis, n.d.; Fraraccio, 2023).

Role Culture: Employees have certain roles and responsibilities and are accountable for their work (Fraraccio, 2023).

Subcultures: Are cultures within a larger culture, where beliefs, values, traditions, etc. can differ from the larger culture (Anuradha, 2021).

Task Culture: Teams are vital to meeting goals and solving problems, and groups of people who share a common goal come together to achieve work objectives (Fraraccio, 2023).

Chapter 2
Shaping Organizational Culture Through Training and Development Initiatives

Ranjit Singha
https://orcid.org/0000-0002-3541-8752
Christ University, India

Surjit Singha
https://orcid.org/0000-0002-5730-8677
Kristu Jayanti College (Autonomous), India

V. Muthu Ruben
https://orcid.org/0009-0006-7723-8596
Christ University, India

Melita Stephen Natal
https://orcid.org/0009-0004-1240-7817
Amity University, Greater Noida, India

Alphonsa Diana Haokip
https://orcid.org/0000-0003-2578-0114
Christ King High School, India

Elizabeth Mize
Rajiv Gandhi University, India

DOI: 10.4018/979-8-3693-1674-0.ch002

ABSTRACT

This chapter explores the critical significance of development and training initiatives in molding and impacting an organization's culture. Organizational culture significantly influences employee satisfaction and motivation, making training programs crucial for fostering and harmonizing cultural values. In this analysis, the authors explore the theoretical underpinnings of organizational culture and evaluate its influence on the conduct and productivity of employees. Then, they investigate various development and training strategies that can influence, reinforce, or effectively transform corporate culture. Practical insights and real-world case studies demonstrate organizations' effective utilization of training initiatives to advance their intended cultural attributes. This chapter emphasizes the significance of ensuring that training initiatives align with the organization's overarching cultural objectives and the possible influence this may have on employee commitment and motivation.

INTRODUCTION

It is impossible to exaggerate the significance of organizational culture concerning employee satisfaction and motivation. Corporate culture comprises fundamentally ingrained values, beliefs, customs, and behaviors that establish the identity of a given workplace. It significantly impacts individuals' perceptions of their roles, interactions with colleagues, and work methodologies. Organizational culture is a critical factor influencing employee motivation and satisfaction (Mariati & Mauludin, 2018; MacIntosh & Doherty, 2010). It promotes a deep sense of identification and affiliation, mainly when it corresponds with personal values, enhancing job contentment and encouraging active engagement in the professional community. In addition to establishing a motivational climate, positive and inclusive cultures promote innovation, collaboration, and the collective pursuit of organizational objectives. The alignment of leadership style and values with the corporate culture can stimulate and encourage personnel, thereby augmenting confidence and overall contentment (Reidhead, 2020; Mariati & Mauludin, 2018; Chang & Lee, 2007).

A robust organizational culture motivates members to perform their duties and align their goals with the company's, fostering employee engagement. Cultures that promote innovation and adaptability foster a dynamic workplace, increasing employee job satisfaction by ensuring they perceive their contributions as valuable. Establishing a supportive environment is influenced by cultural norms, which affect employee satisfaction through collaboration and conflict resolution (Reidhead, 2020; Reis et al., 2016; Bellou, 2010). Organizational culture profoundly impacts the work environment, which affects individual dispositions and fosters a sense of purpose and fulfilment. Organizations that strategically harmonize their culture with motivational principles have an enhanced ability to attract, retain, and motivate content and actively involve employees.

The correlation between an organization's training and development programs and its cultural values is crucial in influencing its employees' learning, development, and contributions within the workplace. The intrinsic cultural values of the organization significantly influence training programs rather than allowing them to operate independently. The reciprocal association is apparent in multiple aspects. Successful training initiatives intentionally complement and enhance the organization's cultural values. When these values align with prevalent norms, such as collaboration or innovation, they promote favorable employee engagement. Incorporating authentic illustrations and case studies that align with the organization's values reinforces this correlation by incorporating cultural context into educational resources (Polo et al., 2018; Widodo et al., 2017). Organizational leaders' active engagement in training programs and endorsement of leadership initiatives strengthen the connection between learning and cultural values. It unequivocally communicates the importance of integrating personal growth with the organizational culture.

Cultural values impact the learning environment by ensuring that training initiatives follow the cultural emphasis on customer satisfaction, open communication, and ongoing enhancement. Training initiatives foster an inclusive learning environment that values and respects workforce diversity, recognizing diverse perspectives and customary cultural values (Sugiyama et al., 2016; Zollers et al., 1999). Meticulously customizing feedback mechanisms to correspond with cultural values fosters an environment that values constructive criticism and ongoing progress in training programs. Practical training and development initiatives have a cumulative effect that shapes and strengthens an organization's culture. As personnel assimilate the skills and knowledge they have obtained, they integrate the cultural values into their day-to-day professional conduct, becoming essential contributors to the organization's overarching cultural tapestry. The interdependent and ever-changing connection between training initiatives and cultural principles amplifies staff involvement, cultivates a favorable professional atmosphere, and catalyzes the fulfilment of organizational objectives.

This chapter thoroughly examines the complex interplay among employee motivation, organizational culture, and the strategic execution of training and development endeavors. The stated goals function as a strategic guide, beginning with a concentrated effort to establish the importance of organizational culture within the broader framework of employee satisfaction and motivation. The following inquiry explores the intricate training-culture nexus, intending to reveal the potential benefits that can be strategically utilized to harmonize training initiatives with cultural values. The narrative is enhanced by including real-world case studies and practical insights, illustrating successful integrations, and contextualizing the impacts and outcomes observed in various organizational settings. The chapter deftly shifts its focus to the pivotal role of leadership and cultural alignment, emphasizing how the endorsement of leadership facilitates the harmonious integration of training initiatives with overarching cultural values. This chapter examines the impact of cultural values on the learning environment within organizations and suggests approaches to developing training programs sensitive to cultural subtleties. Promoting inclusion and diversity in training emphasizes cultivating an inclusive educational setting consistent with cultural values and demonstrating sensitivity towards various viewpoints. The investigation reaches its apex by scrutinizing feedback mechanisms and continuous improvement in training programs. It investigates how these mechanisms correspond with the cultural significance of fostering a culture of continuous learning and development. The chapter discusses the long-lasting effects of effectively planned training and development programs on organizational culture. It demonstrates how staff members gradually assimilate cultural values and skills, thereby contributing to the ongoing evolution and reinforcement of the corporate culture. The structured investigation culminates in a concise overview of significant discoveries, underscoring the interdependence of employee motivation, cultural values, and training and providing astute suggestions for further study and practical implementation. This chapter comprehensively analyzes how organizations can strategically utilize training and development initiatives to bolster employee motivation while following their distinct cultural values.

This chapter will examine the complex relationship between training and development initiatives and organizational culture. We aim to offer significant perspectives on how these initiatives influence and alter corporate cultures. Through an in-depth exploration of the fundamental mechanisms, obstacles, and prospective developments, our objective is to understand the operation dynamics comprehensively. Our investigation encompasses a wide-ranging analysis of the impact of training and development on an organization's culture. We collectively enhance our understanding of how these initiatives impact and shape organizational culture by navigating through various theoretical frameworks, such as Social Learning Theory, Organizational Socialization Theory, Cultural Assimilation Framework, Competing Values Framework, Schein's Model of Organizational Culture Change, and Kirkpatrick's Model of Training Evaluation. Real-world case studies provide concrete examples of how training initiatives achieve effective cultural transformation, offering actionable insights.

We provided organizations with pragmatic approaches to ensure that training programs harmonize with particular cultural characteristics. Recognizing the dynamic character of organizations, our experience underscores the increasing significance of fostering positive workplace cultures. The importance of training and development in deliberately molding and harmonizing cultures with strategic goals is duly recognized. In addition, we discuss the obstacles that arise from cultural transformation, emphasizing the ongoing requirement for research, practical advice, and flexibility to navigate the intricacies of the contemporary work environment. This chapter's primary objective is to contribute significantly to the current corpus of knowledge by presenting a comprehensive viewpoint on the interdependent connection between training, development, and organizational culture. By doing so, it seeks to cultivate work environments favorable to employee satisfaction and achievement.

UNDERSTANDING ORGANIZATIONAL CULTURE

The concept of organizational culture is complex and multifaceted, comprising the shared values, beliefs, customs, and behaviors that shape the fundamental nature of a work environment. It influences how individuals interact, perceive responsibilities, and approach professional endeavors. There are a range of definitions in academic and business circles that characterize it as the "personality" or "DNA" of an organization, effectively encapsulating the distinctive qualities that set apart a particular workplace. This collective comprehension influences behavior and decision-making and is often compared to a cohesive fabric, nurturing unity among organizational members (Assens-Serra et al., 2021). Essential components in forming corporate culture include norms, values, symbols, language, and leadership approaches (Wang & Huang, 2022). The elements above synergistically contribute to the ever-changing organizational culture, recognizing that it develops in reaction to internal and external factors. It is imperative for organizations that seek to harmonize their culture with evolving objectives to acknowledge this vitality. Gaining insight into organizational culture is the cornerstone for cultivating a productive workplace milieu, furnishing personnel with a framework to analyze their encounters, and nurturing a sense of unity, inclusion, and shared objectives. This comprehension becomes especially relevant when considering its significant influence on employee motivation, satisfaction, and the effectiveness of training and development endeavors.

Organizational culture, an intricate and multidimensional construct, comprises the customs, values, beliefs, and conduct that collectively establish the fundamental nature of a work environment. The collective perspective influences how individuals approach their work, perceive their roles, and interact with others. Diverse interpretations prevail in academic and business circles regarding the nature of organizational culture; some refer to it as the "DNA" or "personality" of a company (Viđak et al., 2021). These definitions emphasize its function in distinguishing one work environment from another, thereby establishing a distinct identity. Organizational culture, characterized as a cohesive fabric, fosters unity among its members by providing a shared understanding that guides decision-making and conduct. The development of this culture encompasses pivotal components, including values, norms, symbols, language, and leadership styles, all of which contribute to its ever-evolving character. It is imperative for organizations that seek to synchronize their culture with evolving objectives and respond to internal and external influences to acknowledge this vitality. A comprehensive comprehension of organizational culture is the bedrock for a flourishing workplace milieu, providing employees with a framework to analyze their experiences and cultivating a sense of unity, inclusion, and a common objective. This comprehension assumes added importance when considering its profound influence on employee motivation, satisfaction, and the efficacy of development and training endeavors (Robledo, 2023). Examining diverse definitions and viewpoints provides additional insight into the organizational culture's multifaceted character, enhancing our comprehension of its functioning within the complex structure of a company.

Various factors combine to shape the expected values, beliefs, and conduct that prevail in a professional setting, making the development of organizational culture a complex and multifaceted undertaking (Viđak et al., 2021). The founders' or leaders' vision frequently imbues fundamental values and convictions, establishing the structure of an organization's ethical system. Norms and customs, which are implicit regulations that dictate behavior and discourse, establish socially acceptable actions and engagements. Physical manifestations, including artefacts and symbols, establish a visual identity that reinforces and embodies cultural values. Language and communication patterns influence the reinforcement of cultural norms and the expression of ideas. As a fundamental component, leadership conduct establishes the ambience for an organization's culture; leaders advocate for values that foster a unified sense of identity. Socialization procedures, including training and induction, are vital for assimilating new members into a community of shared values and standards (Taormina, 2008). Collective experiences, rituals, and ceremonies all contribute to developing a feeling of cohesion and inclusion. Transiting an organization's history through stories and narratives influences collective memory and reinforces core values. Additionally, external influences, power structures, and organizational structures all contribute to the complex tapestry of culture. Understanding how these components interact provides valuable insights into establishing and maintaining corporate culture. (Larentis et al., 2018) Organizations that acknowledge the importance of these components can deliberately mold and oversee their culture, ensuring that it is in harmony with their fundamental objectives and principles to foster a harmonious and prosperous work environment.

Organizational culture significantly impacts numerous aspects of the work environment, influencing employees' conduct, perspectives, and productivity.

Understanding this effect is of the utmost importance for organizations striving to optimize their culture to attain the intended results. Organizational culture exerts a significant influence, intricately transforming employees' conduct, perspectives, and achievements, thus molding workplace dynamics (Viđak et al., 2021). The impact of culture is discernible in many employee behaviors, encompassing compliance with established standards and anticipations that govern interactions and cooperative efforts (Robledo, 2023). Cultural influences also shape decision-making patterns; prioritizing consensus promotes participatory processes, whereas hierarchical cultures favor top-down approaches. Cultural values profoundly affect the extent of risk-taking and innovation, either fostering or impeding the generation of creative contributions from personnel. Organizational culture substantially impacts employee attitudes concerning job satisfaction, commitment, and behavior. An environment characterized by positivity, support, and unity with personal values cultivates a sense of direction, enhancing employee engagement and dedication (Besley & Persson, 2022).

Cultural values impact employee motivation and accountability by setting performance standards that employees strive to surpass. Recognition and reward systems are profoundly influenced by culture, as they determine how the accomplishments of individuals or teams are validated (Stavrinoudis & Kakarougkas, 2019). The degree to which employees can adjust to change serves as evidence of the impact that organizational culture has, given that cultures that cherish transformation cultivate a labor force that is more robust and flexible. Personnel perceive change as an opportunity for growth and advancement in work settings, prioritizing innovation and ongoing enhancement (Abbas & Doğan, 2022). Cultural characteristics that deeply embed collaboration and communication foster a positive work environment, promoting open channels of communication and teamwork. It is critical to comprehend and purposefully oversee organizational culture, given its pivotal role in fostering a constructive and harmonious work environment, which ultimately facilitates the achievement of corporate objectives (Viđak et al., 2021).

A positive and robust organizational culture enhances individual and team performance by aligning employees with corporate objectives. A positive and robust organizational culture facilitates the alignment of employees with corporate objectives, which in turn enhances individual and team performance (Parent & Lovelace, 2018). An influential organizational culture fosters a favorable workplace atmosphere by cultivating employee engagement and satisfaction and promoting a sense of belonging and alignment with cultural values. Corporate cultures encourage innovation and creativity and motivate staff members to offer original concepts, resulting in improved product development and problem-solving outcomes (Dalain, 2023). An organization that fosters a positive culture is more likely to attract and retain exceptional personnel, enhancing its workforce with proficiency and drive. Cultures that embrace change foster adaptability, improving an organization's resilience and success as it navigates through dynamic business environments. Incorporating cultural values into customer interactions fosters favorable experiences, increases customer loyalty, and ultimately enhances organizational performance (Viđak et al., 2021). A culture that prioritizes efficiency, efficacy, and accountability has a positive impact on financial performance as it fosters operational excellence. A clearly defined culture influences the external perception of the organization, thereby bolstering its standing and attracting stakeholders who share its values. Civilizations prioritizing integrity and ethical conduct advance positive results by cultivating confidence and reducing the likelihood of legal and ethical disputes. Fostering a constructive and unified culture is critical to success in many organizational outcomes.

TRAINING AND DEVELOPMENT AS CULTURAL INFLUENCERS

Several theoretical frameworks within organizational dynamics illuminate the complex relationship between training and development initiatives and cultural change. These frameworks serve as indispensable resources for organizations wishing to implement training programs to propel and influence cultural transformation strategically. Bandura's Social Learning Theory posits that employees gain cultural values via structured instruction and unstructured encounters, with observation and imitation playing a pivotal role. Under the influence of Van Maanen and Schein, organizational socialization theory emphasizes the significance of training in assimilating personnel into the corporate culture. Employing practical training, the Cultural Assimilation Framework by D. E. Schneider emphasizes assimilating personnel into established cultural norms. Quinn and Rohrbaugh developed the Competing Values Framework, which classifies cultures and sees training as a mechanism to strengthen specific cultural orientations. Training facilitates the implementation of new values and behaviours for achieving deliberate cultural transformation, guided by Schein's Model of Organizational Culture Change. Although not explicitly centred on cultural shifts, Kirkpatrick's Model of Training Evaluation provides a valuable framework for evaluating the effects of training on cultural practices. As a result of their combined application, these frameworks offer organizations a sophisticated comprehension that enables them to strategically exploit training endeavors to cultivate and integrate preferred cultural values (Chao, 2012; Wanberg, 2012).

Numerous influential models offer significant insights regarding how training initiatives can mold and fortify the cultural values of an organization. D. E. Schneider developed the Cultural Assimilation Model, which emphasizes the importance of training employees to conform to prevailing cultural norms (Smokowski et al., 2017; Feinberg et al., 1979). This statement underscores the notion that practical training encompasses more than mere skill enhancement; instead, it places importance on communal experiences and fostering a feeling of inclusion. Change management models, including John Kotter's 8-Step Process (Albulescu & Bibu, 2020; Khankhoje, 2016), recognize the importance of training in informing and instructing personnel about novel values and conduct during organizational transitions. Schein's Model of Culture Change presents a systematic framework for purposeful cultural transformation, wherein training imbues intended cultural qualities. Quinn and Rohrbaugh's Competing Values Framework classifies organizational cultures and ensures that training initiatives align with particular cultural orientations (Yergler, 2012; Hogan & Coote, 2014). Albert Bandura's social learning theory emphasizes informal learning experiences within an organizational setting. It specifically examines the influence of training on cultural learning by employing peer interactions and role modelling (Rumjaun & Narod, 2020). These models provide a comprehensive comprehension of how deliberately crafted training programs impact the cultural transformation of an organization.

It is critical to ensure that training programs are in harmony with the organization's culture to promote employee engagement and further the overall goals of the culture. Commencing the alignment process requires a thorough cultural evaluation, employing interviews and surveys to extract knowledge of prevalent values and conventions. The involvement and endorsement of leadership in program development and the provision of a model for desired cultural behaviors establish leadership commitment as critical. Tailoring training materials guarantees they align with particular cultural characteristics by incorporating scenarios and illustrations that mirror the organization's values. Using narratives exemplifying desired behaviors and constructing a captivating cultural history strengthens cultural alignment through storytelling (Sony et al., 2020; Meek, 1988). Message consistency, incorporating organizational symbols, and interactive learning methods contribute to a unified cultural experience during training. Putting cultural principles into practice in the real world, having ways to keep rewarding people, and having a feedback loop that lets improvements be made repeatedly make constraints even stronger (Polo et al., 2018; Bunch, 2009). In essence, these approaches collaborate to produce training programs that impart expertise and competencies and strongly align with and fortify the organization's cultural identity, cultivating a motivated and interconnected workforce.

Organizations can effectively reinforce their cultural values by strategically integrating customized illustrations into the content and delivery of training. To illustrate, an approach that fosters a collaborative mindset and places significant emphasis on collaboration and cooperation is the development of training modules that incorporate case studies showcasing the successes of collective team efforts (Leonard & Lang, 2010; Sancho-Thomas et al., 2009). Similarly, fostering innovation and creativity entails incorporating educational materials emphasizing the significance of ground-breaking concepts in conjunction with interactive ideation sessions and seminars that enable staff members to contribute creatively. To instil customer-centric values, it is necessary to conduct role-playing and scenario-based exercises that simulate customer interactions; this ensures that employees comprehend the importance of placing customer satisfaction as a top priority (Cabral & Marques, 2022; Malik & Ahsan, 2019). Complementing modules on diversity and inclusion with inclusive training sessions cultivates an appreciation for the significance of inclusivity and the worth of varied viewpoints. Promoting discussions on ethical implications and using case studies and scenario-based training can effectively inculcate ethical decision-making. Incorporating change simulation exercises into one's change management approach facilitates adaptability development. Incorporating leadership development content and training sessions prioritizing mentoring, interactive discussions, and role modelling reinforces leadership values. Implementing recurring training sessions, workshops, or webinars fosters skill development and motivates staff members to adopt a learning-oriented mindset deeply ingrained in the organization's culture (Shapira-Lishchinsky, 2014; Booysen, 2013). These instances result in developing a training strategy that goes beyond the mere transmission of knowledge; it actively cultivates a workplace culture in which personnel exemplify and manifest the organization's values in their day-to-day conduct.

IMPORTANCE OF TRAINING AND DEVELOPMENT

Training and development initiatives are fundamental components in moulding the competencies of executives and managers to navigate the intricacies of the organization proficiently. These initiatives play a crucial role in refining leadership abilities that are essential for effectively navigating the intricacies of contemporary business settings (Xie, 2018). Effective communication is considered a fundamental ability in leadership because it promotes team members' clarity, collaboration, and alignment. Proficiency in decision-making is of equal importance, as it empowers executives to make well-informed and timely selections that propel the advancement of the organization. Proficiency in conflict resolution ensures the effective handling of disagreements, which maintains team unity and efficiency (Normore et al., 2019).

Strategic foresight, objective formulation, and goal congruence are fundamental elements of successful leadership, facilitating leaders in delineating an unambiguous trajectory for their teams in the face of dynamic market circumstances. Using training programs, executives acquire a deeper comprehension of the missions and values of the organization, which function as foundational tenets that direct behaviour and decision-making (Xie, 2018).

In the current business environment, transformation is perpetual; therefore, executives must possess proficient change management abilities to navigate through periods of transition smoothly. Training fosters an environment characterized by adaptability and resilience by providing leaders with the means to communicate change, rally support, and mitigate resistance effectively (Phillips & Klein, 2022).

Implementing training programs that prioritize cultural competence and diversity management plays a crucial role in cultivating inclusive workplace settings. Leaders who adopt an inclusive approach leverage the multitude of experiences and viewpoints in their teams, stimulating innovation and originality (Haun, 2022).

Coaching, mentoring, self-awareness, and emotional intelligence programs provide leaders with the necessary resources to facilitate the progress and advancement of their teams effectively. Leaders enable their teams to achieve their utmost capabilities and propel the organization's success by cultivating an environment that promotes ongoing wisdom and input.

Talent management and succession planning are essential components of leadership development. Organizations guarantee the continuity and sustainability of their operations by identifying and cultivating high-potential individuals who possess the necessary skills to spearhead growth and innovation.

It is critical to prioritize leaders' ongoing education and growth via training and development initiatives to cultivate successful leadership, influence a favourable organizational climate, and attain enduring prosperity in the rapidly evolving and competitive contemporary business environment.

TRAINING, DEVELOPMENT, AND WORKPLACE SAFETY

Training and development function as interdependent foundations that foster the advancement of employees and propel the triumph of the organization. Training design meets immediate employment requirements by disseminating task-related knowledge and skills. In contrast, development encompasses a more comprehensive outlook to improve overall capabilities, including problem-solving, critical thinking, and leadership aptitude (Garavan et al., 2020). By adopting this all-encompassing strategy, personnel are equipped to handle their present duties, tackle forthcoming obligations and progress professionally within the institution.

Training initiatives generally have an immediate and limited duration, intending to rectify particular deficiencies in skills or operational needs. These programs aim to enhance job performance and efficacy in the short term. Conversely, endeavours towards development adopt a longitudinal perspective, prioritizing ongoing progress and professional growth. By being more adaptable and customized to meet each participant's specific requirements and ambitions, development programs promote an environment of continuous learning and advancement within the entire organization (Bell et al., 2017).

Although they have different objectives and durations, both training and development contribute to the advancement of employees and impact the organization. They foster innovation, productivity, and efficiency by providing essential competencies and skills that enable personnel to thrive in their positions and contribute to achieving the organization's goals. Both procedures emphasize the significance of ongoing enhancement, necessitating consistent evaluation, input, and adaptation to align with changing organizational requirements and employee growth objectives (Garavan et al., 2020).

Training serves a pivotal function in augmenting the capabilities and aptitudes of personnel and fostering safety in the workplace by providing vital knowledge and skills that enable workers to recognize and alleviate hazards, comply with safety protocols, and securely operate equipment. Conversely, development initiatives cultivate an environment that promotes ongoing enhancements and improvements, thereby intrinsically aiding in improving ergonomics and workplace safety. Through encouraging innovative thinking and proactive resolution of safety issues, development programs can potentially foster a more secure and health-conscious workplace for every employee (Dodoo & Al-Samarraie, 2021).

When executed efficiently, training and development initiatives foster a culture of safety and ongoing enhancement within the organization. They provide workers with the essential competencies, understanding, and mentality required to give precedence to occupational safety and welfare, thereby positively contributing to the organization's overall achievement and longevity.

SHAPING ORGANIZATIONAL CULTURE

As the foundation of an organization's identity, organizational culture dictates its values, conduct, and decision-making. Employee relations and role performance are significantly impacted by an organization's demeanour, defined by shared beliefs, norms, and practices. The process of shaping organizational culture is purposeful and continuous, necessitating the involvement of leadership, strategic forethought, and the execution of diverse initiatives.

Training and development programs are of tremendous significance in influencing an organization's culture as they equip staff members with the essential knowledge, abilities, and mindsets required to exemplify and uphold preferred cultural principles. These initiatives function as frameworks for encouraging cultural congruence, cultivating staff involvement, and propelling the organization's overall effectiveness. By incorporating cultural values into training programs, organizations can foster a more cohesive and productive work environment by ensuring employees comprehend and exemplify the organization's ethos (Polo et al., 2018).

The ability of leaders to establish an atmosphere and exemplify desired conduct is critical to influencing an organization's culture. Leaders must exemplify the organization's values, effectively communicate those values, and actively foster a culture that embraces transparency, inclusiveness, and ongoing progress. Leaders employ their decisions and actions to impact employees' attitudes and behaviours, thereby molding the organization's collective identity and character (Day et al., 2014).

Organizational processes and systems are equally influential in shaping culture and leadership. Policies, procedures, and reward systems should be consistent with the organization's values to reinforce desired behaviours. Organizations can formalize cultural values and encourage pervasive integration by fostering an environment that incentivizes and reinforces behaviors that align with the desired culture (Tsai, 2011).

Collaboration and communication are indispensable for influencing the ethos of an organization. Communication channels that are open and transparent promote the exchange of information, ideas, and feedback, thereby cultivating an environment of trust and mutual regard among staff members. Collaboration that transcends departments and teams fosters a sense of cohesion and shared objectives, thereby fortifying the organization's culture and stimulating innovation and cooperation (Hebets, 2018).

Establishing an organizational culture necessitates implementing a comprehensive strategy that includes communication, leadership, training and development, and organizational processes. By harmonizing these components with the values and strategic goals of the organization, businesses can nurture a culture that motivates and enables personnel, stimulates achievement, and nurtures sustained prosperity (Day et al., 2021).

The theoretical frameworks provide distinct perspectives on how training and development programs influence an organization's culture and, by extension, employee engagement and motivation. Social Learning Theory highlights the significance of imitation and observation in the learning process. This theory suggests that employees acquire cultural values through informal interactions with supervisors and colleagues and formal training and development initiatives. Organizations can influence employee motivation and engagement by cultivating a sense of camaraderie and belonging through the establishment of mentorship programs and collaborative learning environments that facilitate the exchange of cultural values (Khalid et al., 2021).

The theory of organizational socialization centres on the progression by which members of an organization assimilate into its culture. By offering novices an understanding of the organization's standards, guidelines, and anticipations, training and development initiatives are crucial to this procedure. Organizations can enhance employee motivation and engagement by promoting assimilation into the organizational culture and harmonizing training initiatives with the organization's cultural context. This creates an environment that inspires and motivates workers to work diligently.

The Cultural Assimilation Framework emphasizes that training must follow the established organizational culture. Organizations can promote employee commitment and help uphold cultural norms by customizing training materials and delivery methods to align with their values, beliefs, and practices. By ensuring that training initiatives are in line with the interests and commitments of employees, this alignment fosters increased motivation and productivity, as well as greater engagement with the organizational culture.

Based on their emphasis on various dimensions, the Competing Values Framework divides organizational cultures into four quadrants. By developing training programs that emphasize particular cultural orientations within these four areas, businesses can mold their culture to correspond with their strategic goals. By fostering a culture that supports organizational objectives, training programs that reinforce desired cultural values and behaviors increase employee motivation and performance (Xie, 2018).

In promoting cultural change, Schein's Model of Organizational Culture Change emphasizes the significance of leadership, socialization, and reinforcement mechanisms. Training and development initiatives that equip personnel with the knowledge, abilities, and attitudes required to support new cultural norms are indispensable in this process. Organizations can bolster employee motivation and engagement by cultivating a culture of adaptability and inclusiveness by incorporating cultural change objectives into training programs and providing leadership support (Brown, 1992).

The Kirkpatrick Model of Training Evaluation offers a structured approach to evaluating the efficacy of training endeavors. Institutions can acquire valuable knowledge regarding employee motivation and cultural unity by systematically assessing training results. This capability allows organizations to enhance their strategies for cultural development, guaranteeing that training endeavors make a meaningful contribution to the organization's overall success (Heydari et al., 2019).

These theoretical frameworks support forming a corporate environment that nurtures a sense of unity, devotion, and shared purpose among staff members, propelling the organization's achievement via increased motivation, involvement, and productivity.

The critical relationship between organizational culture and training and development initiatives determines employee engagement, motivation, and output. By employing diverse theoretical frameworks, organizations can strategically mold their culture consistent with their values and strategic goals. By emphasizing communication, leadership, collaboration, and organizational processes, companies can foster a culture that motivates and enables its workforce, thereby facilitating long-term success and prosperity. In essence, a robust organizational culture inspires and unites members around a common objective, fostering collective success and organizational superiority.

CASE STUDIES AND PRACTICAL INSIGHTS

TNT Corporation effectively managed a cultural shift by implementing a comprehensive training and development initiative to cultivate collaboration and innovation among its heterogeneous teams. The organization implemented a comprehensive strategy encompassing periodic innovation seminars that fostered a culture of risk-taking and experimentation among employees through collaborative project development and brainstorming sessions. TNT Corporation dismantled organizational barriers by employing cross-functional training programs, which fostered a collective comprehension of each team member's various functions and viewpoints. The leadership team significantly influenced the transformation through their active engagement in training sessions, mentorship functions, and prioritization of the fundamental cultural values of innovation, transparency, and collaboration. The organization submitted significantly more patent applications due to these strategic initiatives. These results demonstrate that innovative ideas can be transformed into authentic products. Members' increased dedication to the organization's creative culture was evident in the significant improvements in employee engagement scores. The favorable cultural transformation significantly influenced the product development process, as groups cooperated harmoniously to expedite the introduction of ground-breaking solutions to the marketplace. This case study highlights the efficacy of training and development programs in facilitating substantial cultural transformation and cultivating a vibrant and inventive corporate climate at TNT Corporation.

Prominent service provider TCC Corporation initiated a cultural shift to place patient-centric care at the forefront; it understood the value of cultivating a collaborative and empathetic atmosphere. To accomplish this, the organization executed an all-encompassing training and development program emphasizing collaboration, communication, and empathy.

TCC Corporation implemented an essential tactic by integrating authentic client interaction simulations into the training process. By having actors portray patients from various backgrounds and with a range of needs during these simulations, personnel gained practical experience that improved their capacity for empathy and communication. The organization prioritized interdisciplinary training programs to unite healthcare professionals from diverse specialities; this strategy aimed to foster a more communicative and cooperative atmosphere while providing patient care.

In addition, TCC Corporation coordinated specialized workshops that focused on honing communication abilities, emphasizing the development of a compassionate bedside demeanour, active hearing, and clear communication. The seminars played a crucial role in providing healthcare professionals with the necessary competencies to interact with patients efficiently and promote enhanced communication among healthcare teams.

A culture shift toward customer-centric care resulted from this strategic training and development initiative at TCC Corporation; employees exhibited enhanced empathy, improved communication practices, and increased interdisciplinary collaboration. The TCC Corporation case study shows how purposeful training programs can change the culture of healthcare institutions, which enhances the quality of care for patients and the efficiency of the organizations.

TNT Corporation, a multinational technology company, effectively implemented a training and development program-driven cultural shift emphasizing collaboration and innovation. A significant surge in patent applications was among the concrete results produced by this transformation. As indicated by the substantial increase in patent applications, the emphasis on nurturing a culture of innovation and calculated risk-taking led to personnel effectively implementing their ground-breaking concepts.

The cultural transformation significantly influenced employee engagement, as surveys revealed a considerable rise in engagement ratings. Employees demonstrated a more significant commitment and affiliation with the organization's innovative culture, resulting in a more motivated and devoted labor force.

The positive cultural transformation directly and favorably impacted the product development cycle. The teams operating within TNT Corporation commenced their work in unison, capitalizing on their improved capacity for collaboration and forward-thinking to expedite the introduction of novel solutions to the market. Training and development initiatives can propel a focused cultural shift, generating tangible organizational advantages, including heightened employee engagement, enhanced innovation, and streamlined product development procedures.

A strategic and deliberate approach is necessary to ensure that training and development effectively align with an organization's culture. Commencing the procedure with a comprehensive cultural assessment establishes the foundation for comprehending the existing cultural environment, enabling institutions to identify precise domains that require enhancement. The subsequent phase involves selecting the desired cultural attributes, which serve as a definitive guide for advocating for the desired values and behaviors. Leadership participation is critical, as it guarantees dedication from the highest levels and showcases the organization's intention to foster cultural unity. Developing training materials to align with particular cultural characteristics, integrating narrative techniques, and employing interactive learning approaches all enhance the program's efficacy. Incorporating artefacts, symbols, and practical applications reinforces cultural values, linking theory and practice. In addition to leadership role modelling and mechanisms for continuous reinforcement, these elements fortify cultural transformation. By customizing training programs to suit various roles and integrating cross-functional training sessions, an organization can effectively cater to the diverse requirements of its members. When you use clear metrics to measure and analyze cultural change, you can learn important things leading to continuous improvement. Celebrating cultural successes is a form of positive reinforcement that creates an atmosphere of gratitude and recognition. By deliberately implementing these pragmatic recommendations, organizations may harmonize their culture, augment their overall efficacy, and triumph through development and training.

DISCUSSION

Training and development initiatives and organizational culture shape contemporary workplace dynamics. Training programs, functioning as influential tools, critically impact the dissemination and consolidation of cultural values among staff members, cultivating a collective sense of identity within the institution. The active participation of leadership in these endeavors conveys the strategic significance of cultural unity and establishes a model for the entire staff. Nevertheless, the process of effecting cultural change via training is full of obstacles; instead, it frequently encounters opposition to novelty and the complex endeavor of manoeuvring through firmly established conventions. An ongoing challenge is striking a balance between accommodating the diverse requirements of the workforce through the customization of training content and assessing cultural change qualitatively, necessitating the use of nuanced metrics (Knowles, 2021). Technological advancements indicate an increasing dependence on digital training platforms, particularly in remote work. Adaptive learning technologies are expected to improve the effectiveness of cultural training by tailoring content to meet the specific needs of each participant. Cultural training programs will be influenced by the increasing significance placed on diversity, equity, and inclusion, demonstrating a dedication to cultivating inclusive work environments. It is impossible to exaggerate the profound effect that a culturally aligned workforce has on employee motivation and satisfaction. This alignment fosters a sense of purpose and belonging among employees, enhancing their job satisfaction and fortifying their commitment to the organization's mission. A more committed, innovative, and engaged workforce results from motivated workers' reciprocal contributions (Philip et al., 2023). As organizations increasingly prioritize cultural alignment and adapt to changing trends, the interdependent connection between training and culture will significantly shape future workplaces.

When analyzing the correlation between training and development initiatives and organizational culture, it is essential to have a firm grasp of the theoretical underpinnings that support this dynamic relationship. Social learning theory provides significant contributions by elucidating how individuals assimilate cultural norms and values in an organizational setting via imitation and observation. This theory implies that training programs have the potential to effectively transmit cultural values by capitalizing on social interactions. The significance of socialization tactics in influencing the attitudes and actions of newcomers is underscored by organizational socialization theory. This theory emphasizes the necessity of incorporating these components into training programs to expedite the assimilation of new personnel into the intended cultural structure. The Cultural Assimilation Framework emphasizes the importance of harmonizing training initiatives with the prevailing organizational culture to promote effective assimilation. This guarantees that training materials strike a chord with staff members and serve to strengthen cultural conventions. The Competing Values Framework classifies organizational cultures into discrete quadrants, proposing that training programs may be purposefully crafted to foster particular cultural orientations that align with the organization's strategic goals. Schein's Model of Organizational Culture Change emphasizes the significance of reinforcement mechanisms and leadership in propelling cultural transformation. It further suggests that training programs provide employees with the essential competencies and mindsets to endorse emerging cultural conventions. Kirkpatrick's Model of Training Evaluation offers a systematic framework for evaluating the effects of training programs on diverse facets of organizational culture. This facilitates the process of cultural development for organizations and guarantees that such initiatives remain in line with their strategic objectives. Incorporating knowledge derived from these conceptual frameworks into training and development methodologies is critical to establishing and maintaining a dynamic and flexible organizational culture that propels the organization's achievements.

Theoretical frameworks have a wide range of impactful applications within the realm of training and development initiatives. They provide organizations with invaluable insights that aid in forming and reinforcing desired organizational cultures. By applying social learning theory, organizations can develop training programs that promote social interactions among staff members, thereby facilitating the transfer of cultural values and norms. The incorporation of cultural components into induction procedures is facilitated by Organizational Socialization Theory, which also accelerates the assimilation of newcomers into the organizational culture. By ensuring that training content follows the Cultural Assimilation Framework, organizations can bolster the efficacy of their training programs and reinforce cultural norms. The design of training initiatives that foster particular cultural orientations is guided by the Competing Values Framework, which stimulates performance and innovation following strategic priorities. By integrating cultural change objectives into training programs, Schein's Model of Organizational Culture Change promotes a culture of ongoing enhancement. By utilizing Kirkpatrick's Model of Training Evaluation, organizations can methodically evaluate the influence of training on cultural dimensions, thereby improving their cultural development strategies. By capitalizing on these frameworks, organizations can generally establish vibrant and robust cultures that foster innovation, employee commitment, and sustained prosperity.

FUTURE DIRECTION FOR RESEARCH

The prospective terrain of research about training, development, and organizational culture offers a stimulating array of potential directions for investigation. An examination of the incorporation of technology into cultural practices, an investigation into its enduring consequences, and an exploration of its global applicability highlight the ever-changing characteristics of modern work environments. To develop robust and welcoming organizational cultures, conducting a more comprehensive analysis of qualitative factors is crucial; accommodating remote work arrangements and integrating diversity, equity, and inclusion principles into training initiatives are vital. Comparative analyses across different industries provide valuable insights into employee perspectives' confluence and future leaders' development via cultural training. This approach enhances the overall comprehension of the subject matter. By exploring these research avenues, academics and professionals have the potential to make substantial contributions to the continuous improvement of practices that harmonize training and development with the culture of the organization in a dynamic professional environment.

CONCLUSION

This chapter concludes by emphasizing the significance of training and development in influencing an organization's culture, particularly emphasizing essential insights and wider ramifications for fostering a culturally aligned workforce. An extensive body of research has examined the complex interplay between training initiatives and corporate culture by employing a variety of theoretical frameworks and models. It has yielded valuable insights into the intricate relationship between the two. Scholarly frameworks, including Social Learning Theory, Organizational Socialization Theory, and the Competing Values Framework, offer detailed insights into how training can impact cultural transformation. Real-world examples, like TNT Corporation's transformation focused on innovation and TCC Corporation's customer-centric care initiative, demonstrate how effective training programs can facilitate cultural changes.

Organizations that aim to mold their culture deliberately can derive advantages from practical guidance on cultural alignment provided via training. This guidance consists of best practices and actionable steps. By integrating symbols, artefacts, and continuous reinforcement, as well as undertaking cultural assessments, these recommendations assist businesses in aligning their workforce with desired cultural values. The integration of interactive learning methods, leadership participation, and content customization are critical components of this procedure.

Employing personnel who are culturally aligned has considerably broader ramifications. An individual or group that embodies and resonates with the organization's values is more motivated and experiences greater job satisfaction. An influence that aligns with and personifies the organization's values fosters heightened motivation and job satisfaction. It, in turn, has a positive effect on employee engagement, culminating in increased dedication, cooperation, and flexibility. A positive corporate culture fosters innovation, increases consumer satisfaction, and contributes to the organization's overall success.

Cultivating a culturally aligned workforce promotes unity and inclusion, establishing a favorable professional atmosphere that effectively draws and retains exceptional personnel. Thus, incorporating training and development programs into the organizational culture is not simply a calculated decision but a highly influential factor with extensive consequences. In the face of the ever-evolving modern workplace, organizations must acknowledge the interdependent nature of training, development, and culture to ensure long-term prosperity and expansion.

REFERENCES

Albulescu, M., & Bibu, N. (2020). Change management strategy and ITIL implementation process in an IT company—Study case. In G. Prostean, J. Lavios Villahoz, L. Brancu, & G. Bakacsi (Eds.), *Innovation in Sustainable Management and Entrepreneurship. SIM 2019. Springer Proceedings in Business and Economics*. Springer. doi:10.1007/978-3-030-44711-3_46

Assens-Serra, J., Boada-Cuerva, M., Serrano-Fernández, M., & Agulló-Tomás, E. (2021). Gaining a better understanding of the types of organizational culture to manage suffering at work. *Frontiers in Psychology*, *12*, 782488. Advance online publication. doi:10.3389/fpsyg.2021.782488 PMID:34880819

Bell, B. S., Tannenbaum, S. I., Ford, J. K., Noe, R. A., & Kraiger, K. (2017). 100 years of training and development research: What we know and where we should go. *The Journal of Applied Psychology, 102*(3), 305–323. doi:10.1037/apl0000142 PMID:28125262

Bellou, V. (2010). Organizational culture as a predictor of job satisfaction: The role of gender and age. *Career Development International, 15*(1), 4–19. doi:10.1108/13620431011020862

Besley, T., & Persson, T. (2022). Organizational dynamics: Culture, design, and performance. *Journal of Law Economics and Organization*, ewac020. Advance online publication. doi:10.1093/jleo/ewac020

Booysen, L. (2013). The development of inclusive leadership practice and processes. In B. M. Ferdman & B. R. Deane (Eds.), *Diversity at Work: The Practice of Inclusion.*, doi:10.1002/9781118764282.ch10

Bunch, K. (2009). The influence of organizational culture on training effectiveness. In C. D. Hansen & Y. T. Lee (Eds.), *The Cultural Context of Human Resource Development*. Palgrave Macmillan. doi:10.1057/9780230236660_12

Cabral, A. M., & Marques, J. P. C. (2022). How innovation can influence customer satisfaction – A case study of the Saccharum Hotel in Madeira. *International Journal of Innovation Science, 15*(1), 80–93. doi:10.1108/IJIS-03-2021-0061

Chang, S., & Lee, M. (2007). A study on the relationship among leadership, organizational culture, the operation of learning organization and employees' job satisfaction. *The Learning Organization, 14*(2), 155–185. doi:10.1108/09696470710727014

Chao, G. T. (2012). Organizational socialization: Background, basics, and a blueprint for adjustment at work. In Oxford University Press eBooks (pp. 579–614). doi:10.1093/oxfordhb/9780199928309.013.0018

Dalain, A. F. (2023). Nurturing employee engagement at workplace and organizational innovation in time of crisis with moderating effect of servant leadership. *SAGE Open, 13*(2). doi:10.1177/21582440231175150

Day, D. V., Bastardoz, N., Bisbey, T. M., Reyes, D. L., & Salas, E. (2021). Unlocking Human Potential through Leadership Training & Development Initiatives. *Behavioral Science & Policy, 7*(1), 41–54. doi:10.1177/237946152100700105

Day, D. V., Griffin, M., & Louw, K. R. (2014). The climate and culture of leadership in organizations. In Oxford University Press eBooks. doi:10.1093/oxfordhb/9780199860715.013.0006

Dodoo, J. E., & Al-Samarraie, H. (2021). A systematic review of factors leading to occupational injuries and fatalities. *Journal of Public Health (Berlin)*, *31*(1), 99–113. doi:10.1007/s10389-020-01427-4

Feinberg, R., Bock, B., Bolton, R., Chambers, K. S., Claus, P. J., Deva, I., Gray, J. P., Güvenç, B., Hudson, C., Keesing, R. M., Lingenfelter, S., Mark, A. K., Montague, S. P., Ravenhill, P. L., Sewell, D., & Watson-Gegeo, K. A. (1979). Schneider's symbolic culture theory: An Appraisal [and Comments and Reply]. *Current Anthropology*, *20*(3), 541–560. https://www.jstor.org/stable/2742111. doi:10.1086/202324

Garavan, T. N., O'Brien, F., Duggan, J., Gubbins, C., Lai, Y., Carbery, R., Heneghan, S., Lannon, R., Sheehan, M., & Grant, K. (2020). The current state of research on training effectiveness. In Springer eBooks (pp. 99–152). doi:10.1007/978-3-030-48900-7_5

Haun, C. N. (2022). Diversity management and cultural competence in the healthcare field. In Springer eBooks (pp. 3378–3381). doi:10.1007/978-3-030-66252-3_3472

Hebets, E. A. (2018). A Scientist's Guide to Impactful Science Communication: A Priori Goals, Collaborative Assessment, and Engagement with Youth. *BioEssays*, *40*(8), 1800084. Advance online publication. doi:10.1002/bies.201800084 PMID:29882972

Heydari, M. R., Taghva, F., Amini, M., & Delavari, S. (2019). Using Kirkpatrick's model to measure the effect of a new teaching and learning methods workshop for health care staff. *BMC Research Notes*, *12*(1), 388. Advance online publication. doi:10.1186/s13104-019-4421-y PMID:31292006

Khalid, M. S., Zhan-Yong, Q., & Bibi, J. (2021). The impact of learning in a diversified environment: Social and cognitive development of international students for global mindset. *European Journal of Training and Development*, *46*(5/6), 373–389. doi:10.1108/EJTD-12-2020-0175

KhankhojeM. (2016). Change management in healthcare organizations. *Social Science Research Network*. doi:10.2139/ssrn.3232774

Knowles, S. (2021). Coaching for transformational, cultural change. In *Positive Psychology Coaching*. Springer. doi:10.1007/978-3-030-88995-1_20

Larentis, F., Antonello, C. S., & Slongo, L. A. (2018). Development of inter-organizational culture: the elements. In Springer eBooks (pp. 27–46). doi:10.1007/978-3-030-00392-0_3

Leonard, H. S., & Lang, F. (2010). Leadership development via action learning. *Advances in Developing Human Resources*, *12*(2), 225–240. doi:10.1177/1523422310367800

MacIntosh, E., & Doherty, A. (2010). The influence of organizational culture on job satisfaction and intention to leave. *Sport Management Review*, *13*(2), 106–117. doi:10.1016/j.smr.2009.04.006

Malik, M. I., & Ahsan, R. (2019). Towards innovation, co-creation and customers' satisfaction: A banking sector perspective. *Asia Pacific Journal of Innovation and Entrepreneurship*, *13*(3), 311–325. doi:10.1108/APJIE-01-2019-0001

Mariati, & Mauludin, H. (2018). The influence of organizational culture and work motivation on employee performance, job satisfaction as intervening variable (Study on Secretariat Staff of Pasuruan Regency). *IOSR Journal of Business and Management (IOSR-JBM)*, *20*(8). Available at SSRN: https://ssrn.com/abstract=3228300

Meek, V. L. (1988). Organizational culture: Origins and weaknesses. *Organization Studies*, *9*(4), 453–473. doi:10.1177/017084068800900401

Normore, A. H., Javidi, M., & Long, L. W. (2019). Handbook of Research on Strategic Communication, Leadership, and Conflict Management in Modern Organizations. In Advances in human resources management and organizational development book series. doi:10.4018/978-1-5225-8516-9

Parent, J. D., & Lovelace, K. J. (2018). Employee engagement, positive organizational culture and individual adaptability. *On the Horizon*, *26*(3), 206–214. doi:10.1108/OTH-01-2018-0003

Philip, J., Jiang, Y., & Akdere, M. (2023). Virtual reality technology for workplace training: The case for developing cultural intelligence. *International Journal of Cross Cultural Management*, *23*(3), 557–583. doi:10.1177/14705958231208297

Phillips, J., & Klein, J. D. (2022b). Change Management: From theory to practice. *TechTrends*, *67*(1), 189–197. doi:10.1007/s11528-022-00775-0 PMID:36105238

Polo, F., Cervai, S., & Kantola, J. (2018). Training culture. *Journal of Workplace Learning*, *30*(3), 162–173. doi:10.1108/JWL-01-2018-0024

Reidhead, C. (2020). Impact of organizational culture on employee satisfaction: A case of Hilton Hotel, United Kingdom. *Journal of Economics and Business*, *3*(1). Advance online publication. doi:10.31014/aior.1992.03.01.209

Reis, G. G., Trullén, J., & Story, J. (2016). Perceived organizational culture and engagement: The mediating role of authenticity. *Journal of Managerial Psychology*, *31*(6), 1091–1105. doi:10.1108/JMP-05-2015-0178

Robledo, M. A. (2023). Organizational culture. In Springer eBooks (pp. 1–3). doi:10.1007/978-3-319-01669-6_553-2

Rumjaun, A. B., & Narod, F. (2020). Social learning theory—Albert Bandura. In Springer Texts in Education (pp. 85–99). doi:10.1007/978-3-030-43620-9_7

Sancho-Thomas, P., Fuentes-Fernández, R., & Fernández-Manjón, B. (2009). Learning teamwork skills in university programming courses. *Computers & Education*, *53*(2), 517–531. doi:10.1016/j.compedu.2009.03.010

Shapira-Lishchinsky, O. (2014). Simulation-based constructivist approach for education leaders. *Educational Management Administration & Leadership*, *43*(6), 972–988. doi:10.1177/1741143214543203

Smokowski, P. R., Bacallao, M., & Evans, C. B. R. (2017). Acculturation. In R. Levesque (Ed.), *Encyclopedia of Adolescence*. Springer. doi:10.1007/978-3-319-32132-5_300-2

Sony, M., Antony, J., & Douglas, A. (2020). Essential ingredients for the implementation of Quality 4.0. *The TQM Journal*, *32*(4), 779–793. doi:10.1108/TQM-12-2019-0275

Stavrinoudis, T., & Kakarougkas, C. (2019). The synthesis of the variables formulates rewards system culture (ReSCulture). In Springer proceedings in business and economics (pp. 577–602). doi:10.1007/978-3-030-03910-3_39

Sugiyama, K., Cavanagh, K. V., Van Esch, C., Bilimoria, D., & Brown, C. (2016). Inclusive leadership development. *Journal of Management Education*, *40*(3), 253–292. doi:10.1177/1052562916632553

Taormina, R. J. (2008). Interrelating leadership behaviors, organizational socialization, and organizational culture. *Leadership and Organization Development Journal*, *29*(1), 85–102. doi:10.1108/01437730810845315

Tsai, Y. (2011). Relationship between Organizational Culture, Leadership Behavior and Job Satisfaction. *BMC Health Services Research*, *11*(1), 98. Advance online publication. doi:10.1186/1472-6963-11-98 PMID:21569537

Viđak, M., Barać, L., Tokalić, R., Buljan, I., & Marušić, A. (2021). Interventions for Organizational Climate and Culture in Academia: A scoping review. *Science and Engineering Ethics*, *27*(2), 24. Advance online publication. doi:10.1007/s11948-021-00298-6 PMID:33783667

Wanberg, C. R. (2012). The Oxford handbook of organizational socialization. In Oxford University Press eBooks. doi:10.1093/oxfordhb/9780199763672.001.0001

Wang, S., & Huang, L. (2022). A Study of the Relationship between Corporate Culture and Corporate Sustainable Performance: Evidence from Chinese SMEs. *Sustainability (Basel)*, *14*(13), 7527. doi:10.3390/su14137527

Widodo, H. P., Perfecto, M. R., Van Canh, L., & Buripakdi, A. (2018). Incorporating cultural and moral values into ELT materials in the context of Southeast Asia (SEA). In H. Widodo, M. Perfecto, L. Van Canh, & A. Buripakdi (Eds.), *Situating Moral and Cultural Values in ELT Materials. English Language Education* (Vol. 9). Springer. doi:10.1007/978-3-319-63677-1_1

Xie, L. (2018). Leadership and organizational learning culture: A systematic literature review. *European Journal of Training and Development*, *43*(1/2), 76–104. doi:10.1108/EJTD-06-2018-0056

Yergler, J. D. (2012). Organizational culture and leadership. *Leadership and Organization Development Journal*, *33*(4), 421–423. doi:10.1108/01437731211229331

Zollers, N. J., Ramanathan, A. K., & Yu, M. (1999). The relationship between school culture and inclusion: How an inclusive culture supports inclusive education. *International Journal of Qualitative Studies in Education : QSE*, *12*(2), 157–174. doi:10.1080/095183999236231

KEY TERMS AND DEFINITIONS

Cultural Alignment: The process of ensuring that organizational practices, behaviors, and values are consistent with its desired cultural identity and strategic objectives.

Cultural Transformation: The process of intentionally changing or evolving an organization's culture to better align with its strategic goals, values, and desired behaviors.

Cultural Values: Core principles and beliefs that guide behavior and decision-making within an organization, shaping its identity, practices, and interactions among members.

Employee Motivation: The internal drive and enthusiasm that influences an individual's behavior and effort towards achieving organizational goals and personal objectives.

Employee Satisfaction: The extent to which employees feel content, fulfilled, and engaged in their work, reflecting their perception of job-related factors such as work environment, compensation, and opportunities for growth.

Organizational Behavior: The study of how individuals and groups within an organization interact, behave, and make decisions, influencing its overall functioning, performance, and culture.

Organizational Culture: The shared values, beliefs, and norms that guide its members' conduct, interactions, and decision-making set the organization apart.

Training and Development: Training is the methodical procedure by which organizations equip their personnel with the requisite knowledge, skills, and abilities to execute their duties efficiently and foster their growth as members of the staff.

Training Strategies: Methods and approaches used to design, deliver, and evaluate training programs to enhance employee skills, knowledge, and performance.

Chapter 3
Change Management in a Divergent World of Work

Deepti Puranik
https://orcid.org/0000-0002-2628-8386
NMIMS University, India

Madhumati Mulik
Independent Researcher, India

ABSTRACT

Change management is an inevitable process of an organization that helps the organization's sustainable capacity in the ever-changing environment. The organizations have to develop various applied models of change management that would be apt for their strategic management. The chapter focuses on change management in this ever-changing work environment from an Indian perspective delving into certain cases where change management created an everlasting impact. It also looks at how certain models of change management have been applied to the organization's development. Change management is a difficult process which indulges into assessing need for change to the implementation of change and further assess the accomplishment of the change management for increase productivity.

INTRODUCTION

Humanistic Values, Training and Development, Employee Feedback system, systems thinking and action research are the five roots of an organizational development which were highlighted in the two early definitions of OD as: Beckhard (1969) defined it as "A planned effort, organisation-wide, managed from the top, to increase organisation effectiveness and health, through planned interventions in the organisation's processes using behavioural science knowledge." Bennis (1969) defined organization development as a "A response to change, a complex educational strategy intended to change the beliefs, attitudes, values and structure of organisations so that they can better adapt to new technologies, markets and challenges and the dizzying rate of change itself."

The continuous process that revitalizes an organization structure and at the same time overlooks the demand of stakeholders at internal as well as external level making it more apt for the global market and rebuilds an organization's direction and ability is change management. (Moran and Brightman, 2001: 111). Burnes (2004) looked at change being an inevitable part of the organization that occurs at operational as well as Strategic level. Consequently, the criticality for any organization to identify its future trajectory and effectively handle the necessary changes to reach that point cannot be overstated. Despite the acknowledged necessity of successful change management for survival and competitiveness in today's rapidly evolving landscape. A study conducted in the year 2004 by Balogun and Hope Hailey emphasized 70 percent failure in the programs of change management. This high rate of failure was due to the absence of a concrete framework that would have overlooked the change implemented in organization. The existing array of theories and methodologies available to academics and practitioners appears disparate, contradictory, and bewildering. Rune Todnem By (2005) proposed the need for additional research in response to the commonly observed low success rates of change programs, the limited empirical studies in change management within organizations, and a perceived absence of a robust framework for managing organizational change. Further investigating the change management intricacies were recommended by the research. The initial step suggested involves conducting exploratory studies aimed at enhancing the understanding of organizational change management, with the aim of identifying pivotal success factors crucial for effective change management. In addition, it was proposed that the change initiatives should be measured objectively so as to establish a consistent change management framework.

Kumkum Mukherjee (2015) emphasized the need for the change management due to globalization and its direct impact on organization. She highlighted the need for organizations to continuously redefining themselves so as to withstand the widespread element of change so as to sustain themselves in the realm of business culture. Either the organizations notice the environmental pressure which forces them to change or the organization themselves proactively seek this change. The most successful organizations also need to put continuous and conscious efforts as to maintain or regain their position in the market. The need to be constantly at the top position also motivates change. The development of an organization needs to be aligned with the environmental demands and thus change their functioning for the purpose of improved effectiveness. Mukherjee further emphasized the importance of contextual understanding for implementing change successfully and thus accentuated the significance of impact of prevailing forces that has a direct impact on organization productivity.

The methods, strategies and procedures that are used to plan and allocate resources along with actions for implementation of change constitutes Change management which is in contrast to organization development. Change management would also study the management of further changes instead of only imparting knowledge and expertise. Hence it is necessary to understand the organizational Development along with change management. Change is a constant aspect of an organizational life that is essential for thriving of the organization and this becomes intrinsic for success or an organization.

Success of an organization lies in the effective management of change which plays an pivotal role for the survival of an organization in today's evolving business scenario which has become extremely competitive in nature. There have been contradicting approaches for change management, also lack of empirical evidence which cannot be tested through the existing theories and knowledge. However, this chapter aims to offer a evaluation of several key theories and methodologies in organizational change management. This review would help in formulation of a comprehensive and novel approach for change management that could in a way fill the existing gap and also look at the theories from a new paradigm. The chapter also examines the concept of workplace change, its necessity, and the crucial role that effective change management plays in organizational development.

Organizational Change

The workplace will experience modifications in terms of shift schedules, work processes, attitudes, behaviors, and technology. The rapid pace of technological advancements and globalization has greatly accelerated the rate of change across multiple industries. In order to thrive in this dynamic work environment, it is imperative to take organizational change into account. Organizational change is driven by two distinct forces: internal and external forces.

The organization's internal environment is shaped by various factors, including its workforce, operational methods, ethical principles, and policies. Furthermore, these factors possess the potential to initiate transformative processes.

The human resources within an organization are considered to be a valuable asset due to their significant contributions to organizational development. The fluctuating nature of the workforce can either bolster or hinder an organization's productivity. The alterations in the workforce can be attributed to factors such as skills, interests, attitudes, and work behaviors. With a focus on the significance of workforce-related factors, Bragas et al. (2022) proposed strategies to aid organizations in formulating workforce policies and effectively managing workforce transitions. In the realm of service delivery, workforce supply plays a crucial role, as highlighted by Widdifield et al. (2021) underscoring the need to consider both supply and demand of the workforce. The decisions made by employees regarding joining and attrition have substantial effects on the organization, including alterations in job descriptions, job roles, and other work-related factors. The presence of a high attrition rate intensifies the demand for new recruitment and subsequent modifications. In this challenging period, the skilled management of acquired changes plays a crucial role in the organization's development, with employee support being of utmost importance.

Low employee resistance and adaptability is responsible for failure to change management (Evangelist-Roach, 2020). Rahi et al. (2021) established that the perceived competence, perceived autonomy, and perceived relatedness of employees significantly influence their readiness to change. Additionally, this study confirmed the crucial connection between employee readiness to change and the effective implementation of organizational changes. When organizational readiness is heightened, there is an increased probability of members initiating change, displaying resilience in the face of obstacles, and actively participating in cooperative or supportive actions to promote the change effort. The presence of psychological and behavioral preparedness is crucial in determining the readiness of an organization to undergo change and facilitates the successful implementation of change (Weiner, 2020).

The preparedness and willingness of employees to embrace change is demonstrated through their heightened level of engagement and commitment (Zulkarnain et al. 2024). The adherence to an organization's culture, policies, work ethics, and values plays a crucial role in shaping employee attitudes towards the organization. Hence, it is crucial to prioritize these factors when handling organizational changes. In addition to internal factors, external factors such as technological advancements, evolving market demands, and trends also serve as driving forces for change.

(Netflix was driven to modify the feature due to the predominant external forces of technological change and globalization. The introduction of new technology has caused a transformation in the expectations and behaviors of individuals. By effectively managing the change factors, Netflix achieved prosperity and success. The organization can be influenced to change its management by internal forces, including altering effectiveness, work climate, employee expectations, crisis, and managerial personnel. As an illustration, Netflix recognized that home movie-watching would alleviate both the financial burden of entertainment and the transportation predicament. As a result, Netflix acknowledged and accepted the organizational change. (Kobiruzzaman, 2022)

ORGANIZATIONAL DEVELOPMENT THROUGH CHANGE MANAGEMENT

The process of organizational change entails both internal and external transformations, which are essential for aligning with emerging market trends and improving organizational processes, ultimately contributing to organizational development.

Organization Development (OD) attracts and incorporate knowledge obtain through various fields that may include business, psychology, human resources, communication, and sociology. Richard Beckhard (1992) defined Organizational Development as: "an effort (1) planned, (2) organization-wide, (3) managed from the top, to (4) increase organization effectiveness and health through (5) planned interventions in the organization's 'processes', using behavioural-science knowledge". It is an initiative that looks at structured interventions for the wellbeing and augmented effectiveness as a part of comprehensive development plan by the management The approach directly applies principles of behavioral science for facilitating improvement in an organization.

Organizational Development differs significantly from change management and organization change though the objective of planned change may be integral part of both the systems. Organizational performance is enhanced by the processes, the activities conducted and the leadership strategies implemented in the organization development and change management. The main difference lies in cost, quality and schedule of the change as oppose to the human potential development, performance enhancement which serves as an competitive advancement in organizational development. Organizational Development emphasize the transfer of knowledge and skills, however change management does not look at transfer of knowledge or skills. Change Management may not include the elements of organizational development, however organizational development will encompass change management.

Donald Anderson (2016) mentioned Effective change management involves several key activities:

Motivating Change: This focuses on how to create readiness or acceptance of change for smooth transition. Organisational readiness to change represents organisations preparedness and willingness to change. The readiness to change process unfolds in two stages: the individual level and the organizational level. The concept of organisational readiness centers around the assessment of an organization's environment, including cultural, capacity readiness, and commitment as its integral components (Combe, 2014).

Creating a Vision: The vision of the organization needs to be aligned with the core ideology which should be properly articulated. Understanding the rationale for change and anticipating its desired outcome contribute to the development of a cohesive and mutually understood change vision. Establishing a clear and shared vision for change is the primary and critical step in the change process. Ensuring that the vision is embraced by all employees and the entire organization is of utmost importance in facilitating the successful implementation of change (Whelan-Berry, et al. 2010)

Developing Political Support: It is necessary to identify stakeholders, assess the power of change agents and influence their engagement in the process. The active participation of stakeholders is considered to be a significant factor in organizational change (Smith et al, 2014).

Managing the Transition: Management structures needs to be establish which can initiate various activities, enhance commitment. In the realm of change management, it is of utmost importance to ascertain the tool employed for implementing change, and one such tool is the empowerment of employees through training. Gathering feedback on the change process is crucial for understanding the challenges and obstacles involved. This feedback can provide valuable insights for effectively managing the transition (Errida et al. 2020)

Sustaining Momentum: Sustaining the momentum of change requires support from change agents, develop competencies through training and development and reinforce the behaviors that can ensure the consistency that is necessary through this entire process. As evidenced by the majority of change models analyzed in this research, there exists a widespread agreement that the achievement of successful change necessitates the establishment of a sustained process for preserving the gains and benefits of said change in the long run (Errida, et al. 2021)

CHANGE MANAGEMENT: A NEED BASED APPROACH

"Change Management Plan does not define what must be changed. It identifies the tactics to manage the risk factors of change management; creates the infrastructure of change management; integrates with the technical plan" (Graham, 2005).

The essential stages of Change Process given by Hayes in the year 2018 were as follows.

The initial step involves conducting a needs assessment and initiating the change process. It aids in the identification of the rationale and provides justification for the change. The process of change becomes more manageable when there is a clear identification of needs. Following that, it is necessary to diagnose the area of change and develop a plan for the future. The identification of a specific area will contribute to the prevention of unnecessary disorder in the work environment. In the third phase, strategic intervention is employed as a means to achieve change. Implementing strategies that take into account an organization's work conditions and culture will yield greater advantages than mere application of change. The fifth stage involves the planned execution and subsequent follow-up. The implementation of changes will provide us with insight into the challenges and barriers encountered during the change process. The sixth stage necessitates support for the initiatives of change in order to address the obstacles identified in the preceding stage. Issues pertaining to humans are also identified and addressed during this stage. Creating an environment that promotes learning and personal development is paramount during the seventh stage of the change process.

The effect of globalization and external factors on organization due to drafting of new government policies, market conditions, technological changes, political landscapes, the shift in societal attitudes, economic conditions. These external factors does impact an organization directly as well as influences the internal climate of an organization. The benefits of change management need to be realized and ensured for its achievement. Organizations must adapt quickly to the changing environment which would enhance acceptance of change management at the root levels. The products, strategies, processes are integral aspect of the organizational operation. The human side challenges that arise can derail the timeline, budgets and hence arises need for effective implementation of change management. The early adoption of change management is pivotal for increased efficiency of an organization and helps avoid unnecessary costs while garners support in team leaders. Motivation and engagement of employees is basic necessity which should be considered when implementing change in today's competitive landscape. The organization success depends on the right utilization of their employees' skills and abilities, failure to which may prove extremely costly and risky.

For example, in a banking sector, the implementation of Customer Relationship Management (CRM) became instrumental for the growth of banking business as the customer needs were considered. Based on CRM, customized solutions were offered which further aided a business. This further highlighted the customer centric approach taken by banks helping building success for private banks as compared to government banks. The change undertaken by the Indian banks had to be planned meticulously so as to avoid any pitfalls. It was also necessary that the change is implemented gradually giving time to customers and well as banks to adapt to this new change. The organization's strength and weakness should be considered when implementing change. When implementing change, one needs to adopt approaches that may be rigid or flexible considering all the factors that affect the organization. Hence a need-based evaluation would be imperative before the implementation of any change.

Change and Organizational Functioning

Sometimes a minor dispute in an organization may affect the operations from root levels to management. The changes in work climate, culture and environment may create a necessity for seeking alternative even in routine activities. The escalation due to mobilization and globalization brought in increase demand for workplace diversity, necessitating alterations in environment as well as skills development for adapting to the changing shifts. The progress of technology is incessant, necessitating a constant drive for enhancement, modification in technology usage, and acquisition of requisite skills. Work culture is not only affected by work conditions but also by environmental conditions. The recent COVID-19 pandemic has led to the development of a new work culture where working from home has become prevalent. The culture of working remotely has brought about significant changes in both work culture and attitudes towards work.

In order to address diverse alterations, it is imperative to establish a change management strategy. The process must be followed when implementing change. Following steps can help in it.

The Change Process

The necessity for change serves as a basis for initiating change processes. Distinct characteristics can be identified by analyzing situational factors and help regulate appropriate course of action. The identification and assessment process can lead to selecting promising action plan that can be suitable for everyone.

The next crucial step is to make a decision on the route to take from the current position to the intended endpoint. The effective management of change during this transitional period is an essential component of the change process. This is where the difficulties associated with introducing change become evident and necessitate proper management. These problems often involve low stability, misdirected energy, resistance to change, conflict, loss of momentum, and high levels of stress. Therefore, it is imperative to make every effort to anticipate reactions and potential obstacles when implementing change.

The installation phase can also be quite challenging. When considering change, individuals often assume that the process will follow a strictly logical and linear path. According to Pettigrew and Whipp (1991), the implementation of change can be described as an iterative, cumulative, and reformulation-in-use process.

Change Models

The most widely recognized change models are the ones developed by Lewin (1951) and Beckhard (1969). However, additional significant contributions to the comprehension of change mechanisms have been provided by Thurley (1979), Bandura (1986), and Beer et al (1990)

Lewin Model of Change

The fundamental methods for overseeing change, as described by Lewin (1951), are:

Unfreezing

Unfreezing is modifying the present stable work environment that supports existing behaviors and attitudes. The first stage of the change process entails preparing the organization to recognize the need for change, which necessitates dismantling the existing status quo and establishing a new operational approach. The pivotal element in this matter resides in crafting a persuasive message that effectively highlights the intrinsic drawbacks of the present strategy. The easiest way to frame this is by referencing declining sales figures, poor financial results, concerning customer satisfaction surveys, or similar indicators. These identify the need for change in a manner that is comprehensible to all.

In order to effectively prepare the organization, it is necessary to begin at its core by questioning the beliefs, values, attitudes, and behaviors that presently shape it.

The initial phase of the change process is often characterized by its difficulty and high levels of stress. Disrupting established norms and practices can cause disarray among individuals and systems. You have the potential to elicit strong reactions in individuals, which is precisely what should be pursued. By compelling the organization to reassess its core, you effectively create a (controlled) crisis, which in turn can foster a strong motivation to pursue a new equilibrium. Without this motivation, one will be unable to garner the requisite buy-in and participation essential for effecting any meaningful change.

Changing

The process involves the development of new responses in accordance with newly acquired information. Subsequent to the uncertainty introduced in the unfreeze stage, the change stage entails individuals actively addressing their uncertainty and seeking innovative methods. Individuals begin to develop beliefs and behaviors that align with the new course.

The process of transitioning from unfreeze to change does not occur abruptly: Individuals require time to fully adopt the new course and actively engage in the change. The Change Curve, a change model that is related, specifically addresses the issue of personal transitions within a changing environment, providing a more detailed understanding of this particular aspect. In order to effectively embrace and foster the success of change, individuals must gain an understanding of the benefits it will provide. Not all individuals will conform simply due to the necessity and potential benefits of the change for the company. It is advisable to avoid this common assumption and pitfall.

Refreezing

The change can be stabilized by incorporating the new responses into the personalities of those involved. Once the changes have materialized and individuals have embraced the new work methodologies, the organization can proceed with refreezing. The visible indications of the refreeze consist of job descriptions, a stable organization chart, and similar elements. The refreeze stage must also facilitate the internalization or institutionalization of changes for individuals and the organization. It is imperative to ensure that the changes are consistently implemented. The enhanced stability has instilled a sense of confidence and ease among employees, enabling them to adapt comfortably to the new ways of working. The justification for establishing a new sense of stability in our ever-changing world is frequently questioned. Despite the ever-present nature of change in numerous organizations, the refreezing stage remains crucial. In the absence of it, employees find themselves trapped in a transition dilemma, unsure about the appropriate procedures, resulting in incomplete productivity. Without the establishment of a new frozen state, effectively addressing the subsequent change initiative becomes extremely challenging. How can one effectively persuade others about the need for change if the latest modifications have not been given sufficient time to settle? In light of the unresolved modifications, any alteration will be perceived as change for the sake of change, leading to a lack of motivation to implement necessary changes. In order to facilitate the Refreezing process, it is important to acknowledge and commemorate the success of the change. This not only facilitates the attainment of closure for individuals, but also demonstrates gratitude for their tenacity amidst a demanding period, and nurtures faith in the prospective accomplishments of forthcoming modifications.

The Lewin's change model is a straightforward and comprehensible framework for. managing change.

The recognition of these three distinct stages of change allows for effective planning in implementing the required changes. The initial step involves establishing the motivation to change (unfreeze). Moving through the change process entails fostering effective communications and enabling individuals to embrace new work methods. The process concludes with the restoration of stability within the organization (refreeze), a crucial step in building the necessary confidence to proceed with the next unavoidable change.

Beckhard's Approach of Change Management

As per the findings of Beckhard (1969), a change management process include the following steps

The first step is a crucial step involves establishing objectives and effectively communicating the desired modified conditions within the organization that will be achieved through the implementation of the change. Second step is to assess the existing situation with respect to the organization objectives. The third step is to provide a comprehensive explanation of the anticipated adjustments in work behaviors that are essential for attaining the organizational objectives during a period of change. The fourth step is to develop strategic plans and action strategies to effectively manage change, considering an analysis of the factors that are anticipated to impact the implementation of the change.

Thurley's Approach to Change Management

To manage change, Thurley (1979) identified the five approaches.

Directive: Directive approach applicable in crises or when alternative methods have proven ineffective. Here, organizations use managerial rights without engaging in consultation, to manage change and handle critical situations.

Bargained: The shared power dynamics between employers and employees is in focus while applying bargained approach, emphasizing the necessity of negotiation, compromise, and agreement prior to implementing any changes.

Hearts and mind: A comprehensive effort to transform the values, beliefs, and attitudes, of the entire workforce. The approach labeled as 'normative', defined by management's preconceived idea of what is considered appropriate or 'normal', places emphasis on commitment and a shared vision rather than involvement or participation.

Analytical: This is the preferred approach, favored by both external and internal consultants, due to its rational and logical nature. The existence of power politics, emotions and external pressures poses a formidable obstacle to maintaining the rational approach, despite its initial feasibility.

Action-based: The actions of managers reflect their thoughts. The line between managerial action and managerial thought becomes indistinguishable in practice. The process of identifying potential solutions, frequently through experimentation.

This leads to an enhanced comprehension of the challenge and resolution, or at the very least, a structure for revealing solutions.

Bandura Approach to Change Management

Bandura (1986) described the manner in which individuals undergo change. He recommended that individuals make deliberate choices regarding their behaviors. People derive the information for their decision-making from their surroundings, and their choices are influenced by their values, self-perceptions, and anticipated outcomes of their actions.

According to Bandura, The stronger the correlation between a specific behavior and a specific outcome, the higher the likelihood of our participation in that behavior. The more desirable the outcome, the higher the probability of engaging in behavior that we perceive as leading to it. The more confident we are in our ability to adopt a new behavior, the more inclined we are to give it a try.

In order to modify people's behavior, it is necessary to first modify the working environment in which they operate.

Beer et al (1990) approach to Change Management

According to this theory, alterations in attitudes result in alterations in behavior. As per this model, change can be likened to a conversion experience (Beer, et al.,1990). Indeed, the behavior of individuals is significantly influenced by the roles they assume within the organization. To induce behavioral changes effectively, it is necessary to place individuals in a changed work environment that entails new duties. It convincingly compels individuals to adopt new attitudes and behaviors. Based on this Beer et al., (1990) introduced Steps of change management.

The first step is to promote the responsibility to change by collectively analyzing problems. The second step is to foster a collective vision for organizing and managing to attain objectives. The third step is to encourage agreement towards the new vision, exhibit proficiency in its implementation, and foster unity to propel its advancement.

The fourth step is to facilitate the dissemination of revitalization across all departments without exerting top-down pressure: refrain from enforcing the matter, allowing each department to discover its own path towards the new organizational structure. In fifth step there is revitalization through the establishment of systems, structures, and formal policies. Adjust and monitor strategies when encountering issues in the revitalization process is the sixth step.

It is evident that each change management process adheres to four steps: initiating change, planning change, implementing the change, and measuring and confirming the change.

Initiating Change

Prior to implementing any changes, it is imperative to identify the underlying need for change or any specific modification requirements. After identifying need it is necessary to make employee understand the importance of change and how change will help them for development. Attitude towards change or vision to see the change plays very important role in change inculcation. All these things will make the workplace ready for the change.

Planning Change

It is imperative to plan for change after establishing readiness in the workplace. The distinctiveness of every organization necessitates the use of varied change implementation models. The introduction of the change can be decided based on the type of organization, which can be categorized as formal and informal. In the process of change planning, it is imperative to conduct a study of the targeted population or the intended beneficiaries of said change. The importance of considering employees' position within the organization, the nature of their work, and the potential impact of any changes cannot be overstated in the planning process. Change agents are instrumental in facilitating the implementation of plans therefore identification of change agents is required (Miller, 2002).

Implementing the Change

The most challenging task in change management is the inculcation of it (Cawsey, et al., 2012).

While implementing the change way of communicating that change is very important. Effective communication motivates employees to be part of the change activity. Planned changes don't always produce the intended results. Therefore, when implementing changes, it is crucial to exercise caution and consider the various factors that have both direct and indirect impacts.

Implementing and Measuring the Change

The objective of the change is to enhance development across various dimensions, such as productivity, workplace environment, and work attitude. Measuring change will aid in comprehending the extent to which the implemented plan has been incorporated and the magnitude of the change. Following the implementation, it is necessary to assess the effectiveness of the program. It is necessary to conduct an evaluation to identify the deficiencies in the process of change management.

The process of change management becomes continuous in workplaces because of shifts in environment, technology, and workplace conditions. Gaining knowledge in change management will empower individuals to effectively tackle the challenges associated with it, while considering various perspectives can assist in change management planning. As discussed in change management process attitude towards change, work environment are some factors that plays very important role in change management. In order to achieve effective change management, it is imperative to give attention to different dimensions.

Case Study

CCD found itself in a massive debt of Rs 7,000 crore, an amount so significant that it posed a serious threat to the company's survival and marked the culmination of its remarkable journey. Malvika Hegde officially took on the position of CEO at Coffee Day Enterprises Limited (CDEL) in December 2020, with a strong determination to rejuvenate the esteemed brand.

The employed strategy, characterized by wisdom and courage, ensured its effectiveness beyond mere survival. Despite the external pressure stemming from the Covid-19 pandemic and an unprecedented financial crisis, Malavika displayed courage in making strategic decisions to consolidate and restructure the business operations.

An astute business strategy she employed was to abstain from raising prices on the brand's iconic products, a decision that defied convention considering the substantial debt. However, her attention was directed towards downsizing and streamlining the operations, ultimately leading to the closure of unprofitable outlets.

Additionally, Malavika Hegde forged a strategic alliance with Blackstone and Shriram Credit Company to effectively reduce costs and increase revenue. As a result of her unwavering dedication, the company's debt had diminished by 2021 and further decreased to a manageable Rs 465 crore by 2023.

However, what truly sets Malavika's leadership apart is her commendable, empathetic approach when dealing with her employees. Considering the brand's financial challenges, she assumed the responsibility of assuring the nearly 25,000 CCD employees that she would unwaveringly advocate for the brand's survival, effectively cultivating trust and confidence during a highly demanding period.

The study presented explores the strategies employed by organizations to ensure survival and evaluates their impact on business expansion. And the role of a leader as a catalyst for change.

Some Dimensions of Change Management at Workplace as Follows

1. Individual (cognitive) factors
2. Work environment/ Culture
3. Communication
4. empowerment and Participation

Individual Factors in Change Management

The impact of change on individuals within an organization is more profound than its effect on the organization as a whole (Bridges, 1986; Jick, 1990) therefore, it is required to focus on behavioral factors. The introduction of change often results in fatigue and discomfort, which in turn leads to resistance towards it. Employees' lack of motivation to accept change hinders their involvement in the new process. The need for every employee to be involved in the change is crucial, as their inability to relate to it may hinder their participation in the change process.

Work Environment

According to Bandura (1986), in his theory of change, employees' decision-making process relies on the information they receive from their surroundings. Therefore, the work environment plays a crucial role in determining decisions regarding change. In order to observe a change in employees' behavior at the workplace, it is necessary to modify the work environment as it serves as a catalyst for such changes. Altering the environment can assist employees in shifting their mindset towards forthcoming workplace changes. A change in the work environment consistently serves as a reminder to employees about the necessity of adapting their work behaviors. Leadership, work structure, work values and ethics, and the vision and mission of an organization are all important factors that contribute to the establishment of a conducive work environment.

Communication

The factor that greatly influences the success of change management is communication. The manner in which change is communicated to employees holds great significance, as it sets the course for the entire change management process. Positively communicated change is easy to manage. Effective communication plays a crucial role in maintaining transparency in the change management process. The utilization of effective communication assists in conveying the relatability of the change to employees. Instead of solely focusing on communicating the benefits of the organization, it is important to communicate the individual benefits of change to employees.

Empowerment and Participation

The empowerment of employees and the increase in employee participation heavily rely on effective communication. Effective communication by leaders can raise awareness among their teams about the empowerment brought by change. The involvement of both leaders and employees in decision-making processes pertaining to change not only enhances participation but also empowers employees for the new change (Rothermel & LaMarsh, 2011). Without establishing a connection with change, employees may find it challenging to become involved. Consequently, it is necessary to inform them about their own empowerment. The sensation of empowerment contributes to the enhancement of engagement in the process of change. The involvement of employees in decision-making processes fosters a sense of autonomy and enhances participation.

Case Study

From early 2014, when Satya Nadella assumed the position of CEO, Microsoft Corporation (Microsoft), a multinational computer technology company, has implemented change management strategies.

Since its establishment, Microsoft has garnered recognition for its employee-friendly HR practices and innovation. However, during the late 1990s, as the company underwent substantial expansion, specific elements of its corporate culture shifted towards a rigid atmosphere defined by bureaucracy, detrimental competition, and a lack of innovative mindset. Upon assuming leadership of the company, Nadella found Microsoft lagging behind competitors like Apple. within the market for mobile phones. Furthermore, according to industry experts, the company missed opportunities to leverage significant technological trends of the 2000s, such as social networking, mobile phones, and search engines. Meanwhile, their primary revenue source remained stagnant. A licensing fee was generated by Microsoft for the sale of Windows on laptops and desktops.

Faced with the task of executing a strategy that would completely transform the company's focus from software to devices and services, Nadella proposed a cultural shift at Microsoft. Alongside the recently appointed Chief People Officer, Kathleen Hogan, he played a leading role in integrating empathy and a growth mindset into Microsoft. This achievement was accomplished through the implementation of HR practices that were mutually supportive. Analysts opined that a cultural transformation of such magnitude had not previously been witnessed in a corporation as large as Microsoft, nor had they observed a company that had encountered such significant challenges rebound so successfully.

Above mentioned case study shows how culture affect change management process. Acquire a thorough comprehension of the issues and challenges inherent in change management, along with those encountered in the management of a cultural transformation. Gain an understanding of the leadership and management approach employed by Satya Nadella. Conduct an evaluation of the potential challenges Microsoft may encounter in the future and examine possible strategies it can implement to overcome them.

Challenges in Change Management

The ever-changing landscape of the professional domain presents a substantial challenge to attaining stability. The existence of extensively diverse workplaces requires a more inclusive approach to managing change, thereby presenting a challenge to the competence of leaders. The task of fostering employee readiness for change is fraught with challenges, primarily during the unfreezing stage, which is complicated by individual variances. The shifting of economic conditions can be attributed to organizational failures, terrorist attacks, natural disasters, and various other factors. The constantly evolving consumer behavior and market demand pose challenges that must be addressed in change management. The shift in social structure and practice mandates the inclusion of such considerations in work activities. Sithambaram et al. (2021) state that the alteration of work processes and modes has given rise to novel difficulties, namely executive support, incongruity between agile methods and business objectives, limited understanding of agile principles, insufficient collaboration, and inadequate skillset among project stakeholders.

These challenges develops occupational stress, study conducted by Kern et al. (2021), revealed that challenge stressors create both positive impact in the context of organisational change. According to the data, challenge stressors were found to have positive effects on emotional exhaustion. Nevertheless, it was determined that the control group experienced solely beneficial outcomes in terms of professional efficacy. The moderator analyses conducted on the change group demonstrated that the presence of time pressure and concentration demands had a beneficial impact on the professional efficacy of individuals exhibiting high levels of ambiguity tolerance and low levels of procrastination, whereas it had adverse effects on individuals with low ambiguity tolerance and high procrastination tendencies. The research findings suggest that organizational change also impacts the well-being of employees in the workplace. Therefore, it is essential to develop strategies for the process of change management.

Strategic Change Management

An Organizational Change Management Strategy entails the systematic development, planning, and execution of measures to effectively introduce change throughout the organization. It involves the mitigation of risks and maximizing change management efforts to achieve desired outcomes. Leader is accountable for setting the direction of change management initiatives. The success of organizational change is determined by various factors, however, with proper preparation and a well-defined roadmap, this journey can become significantly easier.

The implementation of strategic change management serves to minimize employee resistance, enhance comprehension of the change necessity, and boost participation. Change management strategies aid in determining priorities and mitigating risks. When strategically managing change, it is necessary to follow a set of steps as outlined below.

Define Organization vision and goal of organizational change: In order for an organization to derive maximum benefits from changes, it is imperative that the organization's vision and goal for change management are in sync.

Participant Identification: In order to effectively manage change, it is essential to conduct a thorough study of the target population. Identifying the specific population within the organization that will be impacted is essential for successful implementation of the change. This will prove advantageous when determining the course of action.

Plan communication channel: The effectiveness of change management hinges on the communication strategy employed to inform employees or participants of the change. Informing participants about the rationale for the change and the benefits it will bring to organizational development will enhance employee engagement in the change process. Establishing clear communication prior to initiating the change process is instrumental in cultivating readiness for change.

Providing resources and support required to manage change: The success of organizational change is entirely contingent upon the level of support it garners from all organizational levels. The establishment of a supportive environment is an essential factor in organizational change. The presence of essential resources, both in terms of materials and processes, is of utmost importance in efficiently managing the change process.

Inculcation and Evaluation of change: It is imperative to implement alterations in standard work conditions and evaluate the efficacy of the modified work processes or conditions. The implementation of this change is imperative as it aids in recognizing the challenges and barriers associated with the esteemed change. This allows for the evaluation of the change process and implementation of necessary modifications.

Change is not a singular event, but rather a continuous process. The effective implementation of a change management strategy can empower an organization to successfully navigate uncertainties and emerge stronger and more resilient. The implementation of strategic change management enables organizations to take into account not just technological and trend-related factors, but also behavioral and psychological factors. which has a significant impact on the overall process of change management. In light of the ongoing evolution of the professional landscape, it is imperative for leaders to enhance their proficiency in comprehending and executing change management protocols, which poses a significant challenge for upcoming leaders.

REFERENCES

Anderson, D. (2016). *Organization Development: The Process of Leading Organizational Change* (6th ed.). Sage Publications, Inc.

Beckhard, R., & Wendy, P. (1992). *Changing the essence: The art of creating and leading fundamental change in organizations* (Vol. 10). Jossey-Bass.

Bragas, C. M., Bragas, L. F., & Soliman, C. (2022). The Changing Workforce And Its Implications To Productivity: A Literature Review. Sachetas An International, Peer Reviewed. *Open Access & Multidisciplinary Journal., 1*(2), 55–69.

Bridges, W. (1986). Managing organizational transitions. *Organizational Dynamics, 15*(1), 24–33. doi:10.1016/0090-2616(86)90023-9

By, R. T. (2005). Organisational change management: A critical review. *Journal of Change Management, 5*(4), 369–380. doi:10.1080/14697010500359250

Cawsey, Deszca, & Ingols. (2012). Organisational Change: An Action-Oriented Toolkit (2nd ed.). Academic Press.

Chenglieh, P. (1985). In Search of the Chinese style of management. *Malaysian Management Review, 20*(3).

Combe, M. (2014). *Change readiness: Focusing change management where it counts*. Project Management Institute.

Cummings, T. G., & Worley, C. G. (2009). *Organization Development & Change* (9th ed.).

Errida, A., & Lotfi, B. (2020). Measuring change readiness for implementing a project management methodology: An action research study. *Academy of Strategic Management Journal, 19*(1), 1–17.

Errida, A., & Lotfi, B. (2021). The determinants of organizational change management success: Literature review and case study. *International Journal of Engineering Business Management, 13*. Advance online publication. doi:10.1177/18479790211016273

Evangelist-Roach, M. (2020). *Workforce Agility Strategies for Improving the Success Rate of Change Initiatives* (Doctoral dissertation, Walden University).

Garrow, V. (2009). *OD: past, present and future*. Institute for Employment Studies.

Graham, J. (2005). Organizational change management and projects. Paper presented at PMI® Global Congress 2005—North America, Toronto, Ontario, Canada. Newtown Square, PA: Project Management Institute.

Hayes, J. (2018). *The theory and practise of change management*. Red Globe Press.

Jick, T. D. (1990). Note: the recipients of change. In *Harvard Business School 9-491-039*. Harvard Business School Press.

Kern, M., & Zapf, D. (2021). Ready for change? A longitudinal examination of challenge stressors in the context of organizational change. *Journal of Occupational Health Psychology, 26*(3), 204–223. doi:10.1037/ocp0000214 PMID:33705194

Kobiruzzaman, M. M. (2022). Netflix Organizational Change & Structure Case Study 2022. Newsmoor- Best Online Learning Platform. https://newsmoor.com/netflixorganizational-change-organizational-managementchange-examples

Kreutzer, R. T., & Land, K. (2014). The Necessity of Change Management: Why our traditional communication and organizational structures are becoming obsolete. In Springer eBooks (pp. 209–248). doi:10.1007/978-3-642-54401-9_9

Miller, D. (2002). Successful Change Leaders: What makes them? What do they do that is different? *Journal of Change Management, 2*(4), 359–368. doi:10.1080/714042515

Mirzoyan, S., & Tovmasyan, G. (2022). The role and necessity of change management in organizations. Investing CRM as an effective system to manage customer relations. *Business Ethics and Leadership, 6*(1), 6–13. doi:10.21272/bel.6(1).6-13.2022

Mukherjee, K. (2015). *Organizational Development and Change*. Pearson.

Rahi, S., Alghizzawi, M., Ahmad, S., Munawar Khan, M., & Ngah, A. H. (2022). Does employee readiness to change impact organization change implementation? Empirical evidence from emerging economy. *International Journal of Ethics and Systems, 38*(2), 235–253. doi:10.1108/IJOES-06-2021-0137

Rothermel, R., & LaMarsh J. (2011). Managing change through employee empowerment. *Global Business and Organizational Excellence: A Review of Research and Best Practices, 31*(2), 17-23.

Sithambaram, J., Nasir, M. H. N. B. M., & Ahmad, R. (2021). Issues and challenges impacting the successful management of agile-hybrid projects: A grounded theory approach. *International Journal of Project Management, 39*(5), 474–495. doi:10.1016/j.ijproman.2021.03.002

Smith, R., King, D., Sidhu, R., & Skelsey, D. (Eds.). (2014). *The effective change manager's handbook: Essential guidance to the change management body of knowledge.* Kogan Page Publishers.

Weiner, B. J. (2020). A theory of organizational readiness for change. In *Handbook on implementation science* (pp. 215–232). Edward Elgar Publishing. doi:10.4337/9781788975995.00015

Whelan-Berry, K. S., & Somerville, K. A. (2010). Linking change drivers and the organizational change process: A review and synthesis. *Journal of Change Management, 10*(2), 175–193. doi:10.1080/14697011003795651

Widdifield, J., Bernatsky, S., Pope, J. E., Kuriya, B., Barber, C. E., Eder, L., & Thorne, C. (2021). Evaluation of rheumatology workforce supply changes in Ontario, Canada, from 2000 to 2030. *Healthcare Policy, 16*(3), 119–135. doi:10.12927/hcpol.2021.26428 PMID:33720829

Zulkarnain, Z., Hadiyani, S., Ginting, E. D., & Fahmi. (2024). Commitment, employee engagement and readiness to change among oil palm plantation officers. *SA Journal of Human Resource Management, 22*, 2471. doi:10.4102/sajhrm.v22i0.2471

Chapter 4

Towards Understanding and Application of Learning and Development Theories for Employee Motivation

Peace Kumah
Knutsford University College, Ghana

ABSTRACT

This chapter examines how learning and development theories can be practically applied to enhance employee motivation. The chapter delves into various theories including adult learning, behavioral, cognitive, social learning, experiential learning, human resource development (HRD), and systems theory, and highlights their roles in shaping employee behavior and learning processes. The key constructs, strengths, limitations, and areas of applicability of these theories are discussed, emphasizing their potential to drive individual and organizational growth. By understanding and effectively applying these theories, organizations can design tailored training and development programs that cater to diverse learning needs, foster employee engagement, and promote a positive organizational culture. HR and learning and development professionals need to have a solid grasp of these theories to design training programs that address specific learning needs and promote positive outcomes. By leveraging theoretical frameworks, organizations can cultivate a culture of continuous learning and improve employee engagement and motivation.

DOI: 10.4018/979-8-3693-1674-0.ch004

INTRODUCTION

Learning and development are two crucial concepts in human resource management that aim to enhance the knowledge, skills, and abilities of employees in an organization. Learning pertains to acquiring new knowledge, skills, or behaviors using various methods such as training programs, workshops, seminars, on-the-job experiences, and formal education (Belte, 2021). The focus of learning is often to acquire specific competencies or skills that directly relate to an individual's current role or job responsibilities. Learning can be formal (structured training programs) or informal (peer-to-peer learning, self-directed learning). The main goal of learning is to improve individual performance, enhance job-related skills, and increase knowledge in a specific area.

Development, on the other hand, is a broader concept that includes not only acquiring new skills but also focuses on long-term growth, career advancement, and personal development (Bednarek, 2023). Development activities prepare employees for future roles, responsibilities, and challenges within the organization. These initiatives may include mentoring programs, leadership development programs, job rotations, coaching, and opportunities for career advancement. The primary objective of development is to foster continuous growth, career progression, and overall professional development of employees (Cho, 2023). Thus, learning is more focused on acquiring specific skills and knowledge relevant to current job roles, while development is geared toward preparing individuals for future roles, career advancement, and overall growth within the organization. Learning and development are critical components of a comprehensive human resource strategy to enhance employee capabilities and drive organizational success.

Theories of learning and development are essential for understanding how individuals learn and grow, designing effective training programs, personalizing learning experiences, improving knowledge transfer, enhancing employee development, measuring learning outcomes, and promoting a culture of continuous learning within organizations. By leveraging theoretical frameworks, learning and development professionals can create impactful learning interventions that drive individual and organizational success. However, it is critical to have a better understanding and applicability of learning and development theories to achieve these objectives. A theory is a well-substantiated explanation or framework based on a set of principles, concepts, or laws that help to explain and predict phenomena (Bereiter, 1990). In the context of research and academia, theories are developed to provide a systematic understanding of a particular subject or area of study. Theories are often used to guide research, make predictions, and understand complex relationships between variables (Weinstein & Mayer, 1986). In the field of management and human resources, learning and development theories play a crucial role in shaping our understanding of organizational behavior, decision-making processes, and performance outcomes (Perriton, 2022).

Learning and development theories vary based on their focus, scope, timeframe, application, and emphasis. Learning theories primarily concentrate on how individuals gain knowledge, skills, and behaviors through cognitive, behavioral, and social processes. These theories explore the mechanisms of learning, memory, attention, and motivation that affect individual learning outcomes (Shuell, 1986). On the other hand, development theories focus on human growth, maturation, and change over time, including physical, cognitive, emotional, and social development across different life stages (Garavan et el., 2007). Learning theories are more specific and narrower in scope, focusing on the mechanisms and processes involved in acquiring new knowledge, skills, or behaviors. These theories often emphasize the role of reinforcement, conditioning, observation, and cognition in learning. Development theories have a broader scope, considering the overall growth and progression of individuals from infancy to adulthood. These theories consider biological, psychological, and environmental factors in shaping individuals' development across different domains (Perriton, 2022). Learning theories focus on relatively short-term changes in behavior or knowledge acquisition that occur through specific learning experiences or interventions. These theories are concerned with how individuals learn new information or skills in the present moment (McConnell, 1942). Development theories take a long-term perspective, examining the continuous and sequential changes that occur over an individual's lifespan. These theories consider the cumulative effects of experiences, interactions, and maturation processes on individuals' growth and development over time (Yawson, 2012).

Learning theories are often applied in educational settings, training programs, and behavior modification interventions to facilitate learning, skill acquisition, and behavior change. These theories inform instructional design, teaching strategies, and learning interventions aimed at enhancing individual learning outcomes. Development theories are applied in various fields, including psychology, education, healthcare, and social work, to understand human growth and development across different life stages (Weinstein & Mayer, 1986). These theories inform interventions, assessments, and policies that support individuals' holistic development and well-being. Learning theories emphasize the acquisition of specific knowledge, skills, or behaviors through cognitive, behavioral, or social processes. These theories focus on how individuals learn, remember, and apply information in different contexts (Kolb & Kolb, 2005). Development theories emphasize the broader aspects of human growth and change, including physical, cognitive, emotional, and social development. These theories explore the factors that influence individuals' overall development and maturation over time.

However, when learning and development theories are misunderstood or misapplied in organizational settings, they can have several negative implications for both employees and the organization. Misunderstanding and misapplying learning and development theories can have detrimental effects on employees, organizational performance, and the overall learning culture within an organization (Hammer, 2021). By understanding the differences between learning and development theories, researchers, educators, and practitioners can apply relevant theoretical frameworks to address specific learning or developmental needs and promote positive outcomes in individuals' cognitive, emotional, and social growth. Human resource (HR) and learning and development (L&D) professionals need to have a solid understanding of learning theories and apply them effectively to design and deliver impactful learning and development initiatives that drive individual and organizational success. This chapter presents seven important theories of learning and development, discusses their focuses and key constructs, strengths and limitations, and areas of applicability.

BACKGROUND

Behavioral and cognitive theories of training offer distinct perspectives on how individuals learn and develop skills (Baluch & Ridder, 2020). Table 1 summarizes the key differences between the two theories. Some training programs may integrate both behavioral and cognitive theories to provide a comprehensive learning experience that addresses both behavioral and mental processes. Learning and development theories provide frameworks for understanding how individuals learn, develop skills, and acquire knowledge in organizational settings. Figure 1 shows the key learning and development theories discussed in this chapter including:

- Adult Learning Theory
- Behavioral Theories
- Cognitive Theories
- Systems Theory
- Experiential Learning Theory
- Human Resource Development (HRD) Theory
- Social Learning Theory

Training theories can be classified into several categories. Behavioral theories are centered around observable behaviors and employ reinforcement techniques to shape desired behavior. One famous theory in this category is Operant Conditioning by Skinner (1988), which emphasizes the use of positive and negative reinforcement to encourage desired behaviors. On the other hand, cognitive theories of training focus on the role of mental processes in learning and skill development. Cognitive Load Theory, proposed by Sweller al et. (2011), focuses on how cognitive load affects learning and retention of information. Social Learning Theory, developed by Bandura (1977a, 1977b), suggests that individuals learn through observing, imitating, and modeling others' behaviors. This theory highlights the significance of social interactions and role modeling in the learning process. Adult Learning Theory, known as Andragogy, is a theory of adult learning that emphasizes self-directed learning (Knowles, 1984), the practical application of knowledge, and the relevance of learning to adult learners' experiences and goals (Allen et al., 2022).

Experiential Learning Theory, developed by Kolb (1984), suggests that learning is a cyclical process that involves concrete experience, reflective observation, abstract conceptualization, and active experimentation. This theory emphasizes the importance of hands-on learning experiences. Human Resource Development (HRD) Theory focuses on the development of human capital within organizations through training, career development, and performance management initiatives (Lester, 2022). These theories aim to enhance individual and organizational effectiveness through continuous learning and development. Systems Theory views training and development as part of a larger organizational system (Von Bertalanffy, 1968). Individual learning and development contribute to overall organizational performance (Adams, 2014). This perspective emphasizes the interconnectedness of training initiatives with organizational goals and culture.

Table 1. Differences between behavioral and cognitive theories

Measures	Behavioral Theories	Cognitive Theories
Key Concepts	Focus on observable behaviors and posit that behaviors can be learned through reinforcement and punishment.	Emphasize the role of mental processes in learning, such as memory, attention, and problem-solving.
Focus	Focus on observable behaviors and external stimuli.	Emphasize internal mental processes and understanding
Learning Approach	Emphasize learning through reinforcement and conditioning	Focus on understanding, problem-solving, and information processing
Application	Used in skill-based training programs. Training programs based on behavioral theories often use techniques like positive reinforcement, feedback, and rewards to encourage desired behaviors.	Applied in programs that require critical thinking, problem-solving, and decision-making skills. Training programs based on cognitive theories focus on enhancing cognitive processes to improve learning and skill development.

Figure 1. Learning and Development Theories

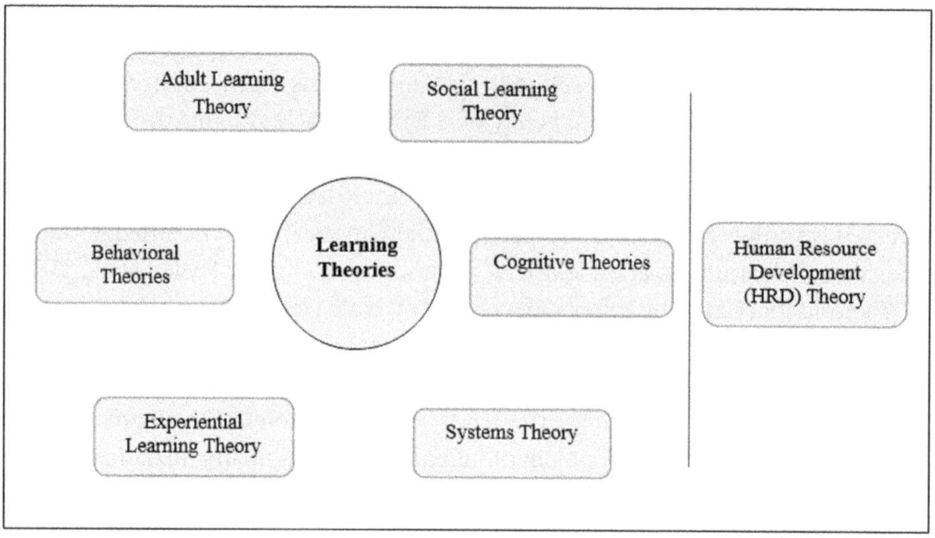

[Figure: A diagram showing "Learning Theories" at the center, connected to: Adult Learning Theory, Social Learning Theory, Behavioral Theories, Cognitive Theories, Experiential Learning Theory, and Systems Theory. Separately shown: Human Resource Development (HRD) Theory.]

LEARNING AND DEVELOPMENT THEORIES

Adult Learning Theory

Adult Learning Theory, also known as Andragogy, is a framework that recognizes the distinct characteristics and learning needs of adult learners. It was developed by Knowles (1984) and emphasizes that adult learners are self-directed individuals who take responsibility for their learning. They are motivated to learn when they perceive the relevance of the content to their goals and experiences. Therefore, adult learning programs should empower learners to set goals, identify learning needs, and engage in self-directed learning activities (Jackson, 2009). Adult learners bring a wealth of life experiences and prior knowledge to the learning process. Learning is most effective when it is based on real-life experiences, problem-solving activities, and reflection on past experiences. By incorporating experiential learning opportunities such as case studies, simulations, and group discussions, educators can enhance adult learners' understanding and retention of new concepts.

Adult learners are more motivated to learn when they see the immediate applicability of the content to their personal or professional lives. Therefore, it is important to make learning relevant, practical, and applicable to real-world situations (Perry, et al., 2023). By connecting new information to learners' existing knowledge and experiences, educators can enhance engagement and motivation among adult learners. While adult learners value independence and self-direction, Adult Learning

Theory also recognizes the benefits of collaborative learning environments. Adults can benefit from sharing perspectives, engaging in discussions, and collaborating with peers to deepen their understanding of complex topics (Jackson, 2009). By incorporating group activities, peer feedback, and collaborative projects, educators can foster a sense of community and mutual learning among adult learners.

Figure 2. Adult Learning Theory

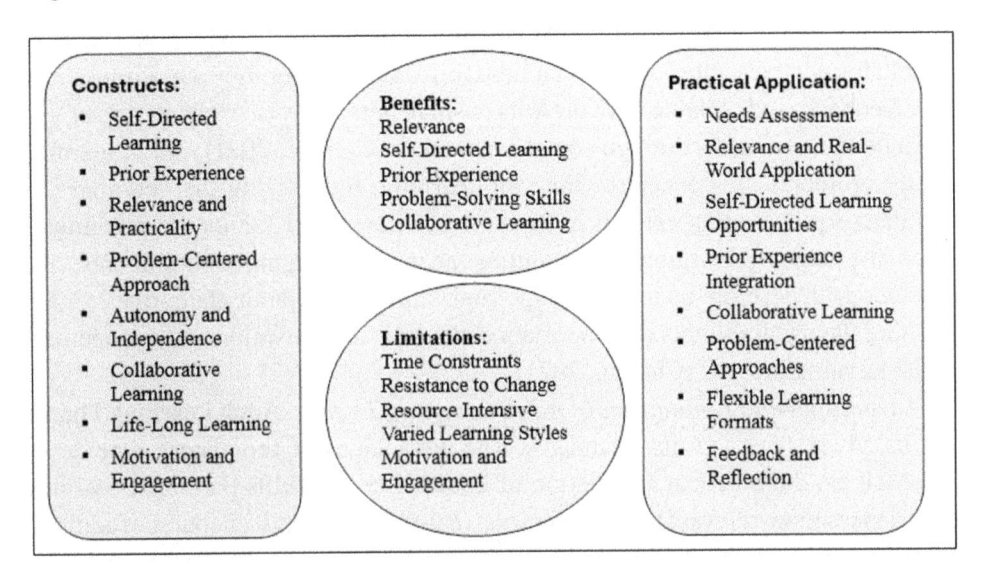

Constructs:
- Self-Directed Learning
- Prior Experience
- Relevance and Practicality
- Problem-Centered Approach
- Autonomy and Independence
- Collaborative Learning
- Life-Long Learning
- Motivation and Engagement

Benefits:
Relevance
Self-Directed Learning
Prior Experience
Problem-Solving Skills
Collaborative Learning

Limitations:
Time Constraints
Resistance to Change
Resource Intensive
Varied Learning Styles
Motivation and Engagement

Practical Application:
- Needs Assessment
- Relevance and Real-World Application
- Self-Directed Learning Opportunities
- Prior Experience Integration
- Collaborative Learning
- Problem-Centered Approaches
- Flexible Learning Formats
- Feedback and Reflection

Constructs of Adult Learning Theory. Adult Learning Theory comprises several key constructs that are essential for effective learning (Refer to Figure 2). These constructs include self-directed learning, prior experience, relevance and practicality, problem-centered approach, autonomy and independence, collaborative learning, life-long learning, motivation, and engagement. Self-directed learning is a crucial component of Adult Learning Theory, highlighting the importance of individuals taking responsibility for their own learning process, setting goals, and actively engaging in acquiring knowledge and skills based on their interests and needs (Garner & Shank, 2023).

Adults bring a wealth of prior experiences, knowledge, and skills to the learning process. Adult learning theory recognizes the value of leveraging these experiences as a foundation for new learning, building on existing competencies, and connecting new information to prior knowledge. Adult learners are motivated by the relevance and practicality of the learning content. Adult learning theory emphasizes the importance of connecting new information to real-world applications, addressing immediate challenges, and demonstrating the practical value of learning outcomes. Adult learning theory often adopts a problem-centered approach, where learners engage in solving real-world problems, case studies, or challenges (Allen et al., 2022). This approach promotes critical thinking, problem-solving skills, and the application of theoretical concepts to practical situations. Adult learners value autonomy and independence in their learning process. Adult learning theory emphasizes providing opportunities for self-directed exploration, decision-making, and reflection, allowing learners to take ownership of their learning journey.

While autonomy is important, adult learning theory also recognizes the benefits of collaborative learning. Adults can benefit from engaging in group discussions, peer feedback, and collaborative projects to share perspectives, exchange ideas, and enhance their learning through social interaction (Chuang, 2021). Adult learning theory promotes the concept of life-long learning, recognizing that learning is a continuous process that extends beyond formal education. Adults are encouraged to pursue ongoing learning opportunities, adapt to changing environments, and continuously develop their knowledge and skills throughout their lives. Adult learning theory highlights the importance of intrinsic motivation and engagement in the learning process (Chuang, 2021).

Advantages and Limitations of Adult Learning Theory. Adult Learning Theory has its advantages and disadvantages. The advantages of this theory include its emphasis on the practical application of knowledge and skills that make learning experiences more relevant to adult learners' real-world needs. It encourages adults to take ownership of their learning process, set goals, and pursue self-directed learning opportunities, which fosters autonomy and independence in learning. Additionally, leveraging adults' prior experiences, knowledge, and skills as a foundation for new learning can enhance understanding, retention, and application of new information (Becerra, & Mshigeni, 2022). The theory also promotes critical thinking, problem-solving skills, and collaborative learning, allowing adults to engage in group discussions, peer feedback, and collaborative projects to enhance learning through social interaction.

On the other hand, there are several disadvantages to Adult Learning Theory. Adult learners often have busy schedules and competing priorities, making it challenging to dedicate sufficient time and effort to learning activities, especially if they are self-directed or require extensive engagement. Some adult learners may also be resistant to new learning approaches or unfamiliar teaching methods, particularly if they have established preferences or habits based on prior educational experiences (Arghode et al., 2017). Moreover, implementing adult learning theory effectively may require resources such as time, expertise, technology, and support services, which can be challenging for organizations or educators with limited resources. Adult learners have diverse learning styles, preferences, and backgrounds, making it challenging to design learning experiences that cater to the individual needs and preferences of all learners (Leslie, 2021). Finally, while adult learning theory emphasizes intrinsic motivation and engagement, some adult learners may struggle to stay motivated or engaged in the learning process, particularly if they do not see the immediate relevance or value of the learning content.

Practical Application of Adult Learning Theory. To effectively apply adult learning theory, it is necessary to conduct a detailed needs assessment. This will help you to understand the specific learning goals, preferences, and challenges of adult learners. To gather information about the learners' prior experiences, knowledge gaps, and preferred learning styles, use various tools such as surveys, interviews, and feedback mechanisms.

Design learning experiences that emphasize the practical relevance of the content to adult learners' professional roles, goals, and challenges (Mukhalalati, 2019). To demonstrate the application of theoretical concepts in practical situations, use case studies, simulations, and real-world examples. It also provides adult learners with opportunities for self-directed learning, such as project-based assignments, independent research projects, or self-paced modules (Mukhalalati, 2019). Encourage learners to set goals, explore topics of interest, and take ownership of their learning journey. Use adult learners' prior experiences, knowledge, and skills as a foundation for new learning. Encourage learners to reflect on their experiences, share insights with peers, and connect new information to their existing knowledge base. Foster collaborative learning experiences that allow adult learners to engage in group discussions, peer feedback, and collaborative projects. Encourage teamwork, knowledge sharing, and peer support to enhance learning outcomes through social interaction.

Incorporate problem-solving activities, case studies, and real-world challenges into the learning curriculum. A supportive learning environment encourages adult learners to apply critical thinking skills, analyze complex problems, and develop practical solutions (Allen et al., 2022). Offer flexible learning formats to accommodate the diverse needs and preferences of adult learners. These could include online courses, blended learning options, evening classes, or weekend workshops. Provide multiple pathways for learning to cater to different learning styles and schedules. Encourage regular feedback and reflection opportunities for adult learners to assess their progress, receive constructive feedback from instructors or peers, and reflect on their learning experiences.

Significance of Adults Learning Theory. Adult Learning Theory provides a framework for creating effective learning experiences for adult learners. By incorporating principles like self-directed learning, collaboration, and motivation, educators can tailor their instructional strategies to cater to the unique needs of adult learners (Lindgreen, 2022). To optimize learning outcomes, it's essential to recognize the advantages and disadvantages of adult learning theory and customize learning environments and support mechanisms accordingly. By applying these principles, educators can create effective learning experiences that encourage continuous growth.

Behavioral Theories

Behavioral theories of training focus on how behaviors can be learned, reinforced, and modified through training interventions in organizational settings (Skinner, 1988). These theories emphasize observable behaviors and the use of reinforcement techniques to shape employee behavior (Sahu, 2020). Behavioral theories in organizational management encompass various constructs that focus on understanding how individuals' actions, interactions, and responses are influenced by external stimuli, reinforcement, and environmental factors (Westaby, 2005). Figure 3 shows some key constructs, strengths and limitations, and areas of application of behavioral theories.

Constructs/Theories. Operant conditioning is a fundamental concept in behavioral theories that explains how behavior is shaped by its consequences (Skinner, 1988). It involves the use of reinforcement, which can be either positive or negative, and punishment to increase or decrease the likelihood of specific behaviors occurring in the workplace. Reinforcement refers to the process of strengthening desired behaviors by providing positive consequences, like rewards, or by removing negative consequences, such as punishments (Skinner, 1988). Behavioral theories explore how reinforcement strategies can motivate employees, improve performance, and shape organizational culture. Punishment, on the other hand, involves applying negative consequences to decrease or eliminate undesirable behaviors in the workplace. Behavioral theories examine the use of punishment as a deterrent for inappropriate actions and its impact on employee behavior and compliance with organizational norms (Kwon, 2019).

Observational learning, also known as social learning or modeling, focuses on how individuals acquire new behaviors by observing and imitating others. Behavioral theories explore how observational learning processes influence employee behavior, skill acquisition, and knowledge transfer in organizational settings (Scherrens et al., 2018). Behavior modification techniques involve systematically applying principles of reinforcement, punishment, and shaping to modify and manage employee behavior effectively. Behavioral theories provide frameworks for implementing behavior modification programs to address performance issues, enhance skills, and promote desired behaviors. Contingency management principles in behavioral theories emphasize the relationship between specific behaviors and their consequences. Managers use contingency management strategies to establish clear expectations, provide feedback, and reinforce desired behaviors based on predetermined contingencies in the workplace.

Behavioral contracts are agreements between managers and employees that clearly outline the expectations, goals, and consequences regarding specific behaviors. These contracts are based on behavioral theories, which emphasize the use of such agreements to establish performance standards, monitor progress, and recognize positive behaviors through rewards (Kwon & Silva, 2023). Behavioral modeling is another important aspect of these theories. It involves demonstrating desired behaviors, skills, or attitudes for employees to observe and emulate. By doing so, managers can shape organizational culture, increase leadership effectiveness, and promote learning and development among employees. Behavioral economics integrates principles of psychology and economics to understand how individuals make decisions and choices based on cognitive biases, heuristics, and social influences. Behavioral theories in organizational management apply behavioral economics concepts to analyze employee decision-making, motivation, and performance (Kwon & Silva, 2023). Finally, behavioral contingencies refer to the relationship between specific behaviors and their consequences, which determine the likelihood of behavior recurrence. Behavioral theories explore how managers can use behavioral contingencies to reinforce desired behaviors, address performance issues, and create a positive work environment based on consistent reinforcement principles.

Figure 3. Behavioral Theories

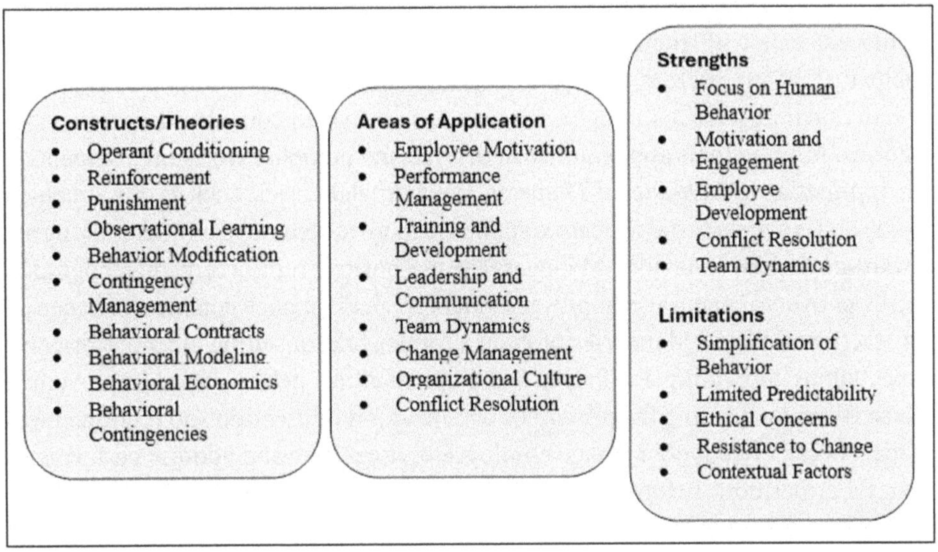

Constructs/Theories	Areas of Application	Strengths
• Operant Conditioning • Reinforcement • Punishment • Observational Learning • Behavior Modification • Contingency Management • Behavioral Contracts • Behavioral Modeling • Behavioral Economics • Behavioral Contingencies	• Employee Motivation • Performance Management • Training and Development • Leadership and Communication • Team Dynamics • Change Management • Organizational Culture • Conflict Resolution	• Focus on Human Behavior • Motivation and Engagement • Employee Development • Conflict Resolution • Team Dynamics **Limitations** • Simplification of Behavior • Limited Predictability • Ethical Concerns • Resistance to Change • Contextual Factors

Strengths and Limitations. Focusing on human behavior is an essential aspect of behavioral theories that helps managers and leaders create a positive and productive work environment. By studying these theories, organizations can implement strategies to motivate employees, increase engagement, and enhance job satisfaction, thereby leading to improved performance and retention (Kwon & Silva, 2019). These theories also provide a framework for developing employees' skills, capabilities, and attitudes through training, coaching, and feedback, contributing to individual and organizational growth (Qi, 2023). Moreover, understanding behavioral theories can help managers manage conflicts and interpersonal issues effectively within the organization by addressing the underlying causes of behavior. Lastly, behavioral theories offer insights into group dynamics, communication patterns, and collaboration within teams, enabling leaders to build cohesive and high-performing teams.

Behavioral theories have limitations in explaining human behavior as they oversimplify it by focusing only on observable actions and neglecting the complexity of individual motivations, emotions, and cognitive processes (Klonoff, 2019). Additionally, human behavior is inherently unpredictable and influenced by various internal and external factors, making it challenging to predict and control behavior solely based on behavioral theories. Furthermore, some behavioral management techniques, such as behavior modification and reinforcement strategies, raise ethical concerns related to manipulation, coercion, and invasion of privacy. This can lead to potential conflicts and resistance to change, as employees may resist behavioral interventions or modifications that are perceived as intrusive, controlling, or inconsistent with their values and beliefs (Arnott & Gao, 2022). Moreover, contextual factors such as the broader organizational context, cultural differences, or individual differences in behavior may not always be considered by behavioral theories, limiting their applicability in diverse and complex work environments.

Application of Behavioral Theories. Behavioral theories, such as reinforcement theory and expectancy theory, can be applied to motivate employees by identifying and rewarding desired behaviors. Managers can use positive reinforcement, recognition, and incentives to encourage employees to achieve performance goals and enhance job satisfaction. Behavioral theories provide a framework for setting clear performance expectations, providing feedback, and implementing performance improvement plans. By understanding the principles of behavior modification and reinforcement, managers can effectively manage employee performance and address performance issues. Furthermore, behavioral theories inform training and development programs by emphasizing the importance of learning through reinforcement, practice, and feedback (Burke-Smalley & Mendenhall, 2020). Training initiatives can be designed to reinforce desired behaviors, improve skills, and enhance job performance based on behavioral principles. Additionally, behavioral theories help leaders understand how their actions and communication styles influence employee behavior. By applying principles of effective communication, feedback, and role modeling, leaders can create a positive work environment, build trust, and inspire commitment among employees. Lastly, behavioral theories guide managers in understanding group dynamics, conflict resolution, and collaboration within teams. By promoting positive behaviors, fostering open communication, and addressing interpersonal issues, managers can build cohesive and high-performing teams.

Behavioral theories are also important in change management initiatives as they help address employee resistance, promote acceptance of change, and facilitate transition processes. Managers can use communication, participation, and reinforcement strategies to encourage behavioral change and support organizational change efforts. These theories also help in developing a positive organizational culture by promoting desired behaviors, values, and norms (Ratiu et al., 2016). By aligning organizational practices with behavioral expectations, managers can shape a culture that supports employee engagement, innovation, and performance. Behavioral theories also provide insights into managing conflicts and resolving interpersonal issues within the organization. By understanding the underlying causes of conflict, applying conflict resolution techniques, and promoting constructive behaviors, managers can address conflicts effectively and maintain a harmonious work environment.

Significance of Behavioral Theories. Behavioral theories can help managers develop strategies and policies to shape employee behavior and improve organizational outcomes (Arnott & Gao, 2022). Applying these theories can create a supportive and motivating work environment that enhances productivity and fosters positive relationships among employees. However, it's important to consider limitations and take a balanced approach that integrates multiple perspectives (Ratiu et al., 2016). Integrating behavioral principles into management practices is essential for enhancing employee motivation, improving performance, and achieving organizational success.

Cognitive Theories

Cognitive theories of training focus on the mental processes involved in learning, and understanding how individuals acquire knowledge, develop skills, and solve problems. These theories emphasize the role of cognitive processes such as attention, memory, and problem-solving in learning and skill development (Sweller al et., 2011). In organizational training programs, cognitive theories can inform instructional design strategies that promote active learning, problem-solving, and critical thinking. By incorporating techniques such as scaffolding, modeling, and practice with feedback, organizations can enhance employees' cognitive skills and performance (Shuell, 1986).

Constructs of Cognitive Theories. Cognitive theories in organizational management encompass various constructs that focus on understanding how individuals perceive, process information, make decisions, and behave in the workplace (see Figure 4). Some key constructs of cognitive theories include (Cervone, 2023):

- **Perception**: This refers to how individuals interpret and make sense of sensory information from their environment. Cognitive theories explore how perception influences employees' understanding of situations, tasks, and interactions in the workplace.
- **Attention**: Attention involves the cognitive process of selectively focusing on specific stimuli while filtering out irrelevant information. Cognitive theories examine how attentional processes impact employees' ability to concentrate, prioritize tasks, and maintain focus in work settings.
- **Memory**: Memory encompasses the storage, retention, and retrieval of information over time. Cognitive theories investigate how memory processes, such as encoding, storage, and retrieval, influence learning, decision-making, and problem-solving in organizational contexts.
- **Problem-solving**: This involves the cognitive processes used to identify, analyze, and resolve challenges or obstacles. Cognitive theories explore how individuals approach problem-solving tasks, apply strategies, and generate solutions based on cognitive processes such as reasoning and decision-making.
- **Decision-Making**: This refers to the process of selecting a course of action from multiple alternatives. Cognitive theories examine how individuals make decisions, evaluate risks, weigh options, and consider consequences based on cognitive biases, heuristics, and judgment processes.
- **Cognitive Biases**: These are systematic patterns of deviation from rationality in judgment and decision-making. Cognitive theories identify and explain common biases, such as confirmation bias, anchoring bias, and availability heuristics, that can influence employees' perceptions and choices in organizational settings.
- **Cognitive Flexibility**: This refers to the ability to adapt cognitive strategies, shift perspectives, and adjust mental frameworks in response to changing circumstances. Cognitive theories explore how cognitive flexibility enhances problem-solving, creativity, and adaptability in dynamic work environments.
- **Metacognition**: This involves awareness and control of one's own cognitive processes, including monitoring, planning, and evaluating thinking strategies. Cognitive theories examine how metacognitive skills enable individuals to regulate their cognitive activities, reflect on their performance, and improve learning outcomes.

- **Information Processing**: Information processing models in cognitive theories describe how individuals acquire, encode, store, retrieve, and use information. These models outline the stages of cognitive processing, such as attention, perception, memory, and decision-making, to understand how employees process and respond to information in the workplace.
- **Cognitive Load**: Cognitive load theory focuses on the mental effort and capacity required to process information effectively. Cognitive theories explore how cognitive load influences learning, task performance, and decision-making, and how managers can optimize cognitive load to enhance employee productivity and well-being.

Figure 4. Cognitive Theory

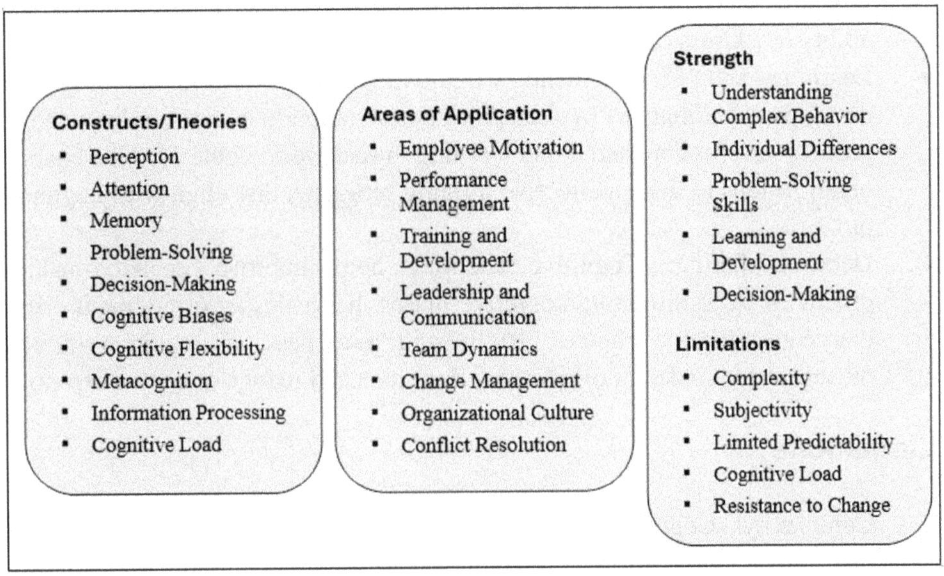

Constructs/Theories	Areas of Application	Strength
• Perception	• Employee Motivation	• Understanding Complex Behavior
• Attention	• Performance Management	• Individual Differences
• Memory	• Training and Development	• Problem-Solving Skills
• Problem-Solving	• Leadership and Communication	• Learning and Development
• Decision-Making	• Team Dynamics	• Decision-Making
• Cognitive Biases	• Change Management	**Limitations**
• Cognitive Flexibility	• Organizational Culture	• Complexity
• Metacognition	• Conflict Resolution	• Subjectivity
• Information Processing		• Limited Predictability
• Cognitive Load		• Cognitive Load
		• Resistance to Change

Strengths and Limitations. Cognitive theories in organizational management focus on understanding how individuals perceive, process information, and make decisions in the workplace. These theories offer valuable insights into human cognition and behavior. Here are some advantages and disadvantages of cognitive theories (Ritchie, 2021):

Strengths

- Understanding Complex Behavior: Cognitive theories provide a deeper understanding of complex human behaviors, such as problem-solving, decision-making, and creativity. By examining cognitive processes, managers can gain insights into how employees think and act in various work situations.
- Individual Differences: Cognitive theories recognize and account for individual differences in perception, learning styles, and problem-solving approaches. This allows managers to tailor training, communication, and decision-making processes to accommodate diverse cognitive preferences among employees.
- Problem-solving skills: Cognitive theories emphasize the development of problem-solving skills and critical thinking abilities. By promoting cognitive flexibility and analytical thinking, organizations can enhance employees' ability to address challenges and adapt to changing circumstances.
- Learning and Development: Cognitive theories inform learning and development initiatives by focusing on how individuals acquire knowledge, process information, and apply learning in real-world contexts. This enables organizations to design effective training programs that align with cognitive processes.
- Decision-Making: Cognitive theories help improve decision-making processes by highlighting cognitive biases, heuristics, and judgment errors that can influence choices. By raising awareness of cognitive pitfalls, managers can make more informed decisions and reduce cognitive errors.

Limitations

- Complexity: Cognitive theories can be complex and abstract, making them challenging to apply in practical organizational settings. Managers may struggle to translate theoretical concepts into actionable strategies for managing employee behavior.
- Subjectivity: Cognitive processes are subjective and influenced by individual perceptions, beliefs, and experiences. This subjectivity can introduce variability and uncertainty into how cognitive theories are interpreted and applied in organizational contexts.
- Limited Predictability: Human cognition is dynamic and influenced by multiple factors, making it difficult to predict and control cognitive processes with precision. This unpredictability can hinder the effectiveness of cognitive theories in anticipating and managing employee behavior.

- Cognitive Load: Cognitive theories may overlook the cognitive load and mental strain experienced by employees in demanding work environments. Overloading employees with cognitive tasks or information processing requirements can lead to cognitive fatigue and reduced performance.
- Resistance to Change: Employees may resist cognitive interventions or changes that challenge their existing cognitive frameworks or habits. Implementing cognitive strategies that require significant cognitive restructuring or adaptation may face resistance and pushback from employees.

Application of Cognitive Theories. Application of cognitive theories in organizational management involves using insights from cognitive psychology to understand and influence employee behavior, decision-making, and performance in the workplace. Some practical applications of cognitive theories include (Ford et al., 2020):

- Design training programs that align with cognitive processes to enhance learning outcomes.
- Provide decision-making support tools that account for cognitive biases and help employees make rational decisions.
- Offer constructive feedback and performance evaluations that consider employees' cognitive strengths and limitations.
- Optimize cognitive load, attentional focus, and information processing to enhance productivity.
- Implement change management strategies that address employees' cognitive responses to change.
- Foster creativity and innovation by promoting cognitive flexibility and problem-solving skills.
- Support employee mental health and performance through stress management and well-being programs.
- Provide leadership development programs and coaching to improve leadership effectiveness and team performance.

Significance of Cognitive Theory. Cognitive theories can help managers understand the cognitive processes that influence employee behavior, decision-making, and performance in organizations. By applying these theories, organizations can design interventions, training programs, and strategies that align with employees' cognitive capabilities and enhance overall organizational effectiveness. However, managers need to balance the advantages and disadvantages of cognitive theories when applying them in practical organizational settings. Integrating cognitive insights into various aspects of organizational management can lead to improved decision-making, problem-solving, and overall effectiveness in achieving strategic goals and objectives.

Systems Theory

Systems Theory is a comprehensive framework that views organizations as complex systems composed of interconnected and interdependent parts that work together to achieve common goals (Von Bertalanffy, 1968). This theory emphasizes the interactions and relationships between various components within an organization and how they influence the overall functioning and performance of the system (Checkland, 1999).

Constructs of Systems Theory. Systems theory in organizational management encompasses various constructs that focus on viewing organizations as complex, interconnected systems with dynamic interactions and interdependencies (see Figure 5). Holism is a key concept of systems theory that highlights the importance of viewing organizations as integrated entities, where the collective behavior of the system is more than the sum of its individual parts (Adams, 2014). A holistic approach considers the interconnectedness and interdependence of various components within the organization. Interdependence emphasizes the relationships and dependencies among different parts of the organization, showing how changes in one area can impact the entire system. Systems theory acknowledges the interconnected nature of organizational functions, departments, and processes that influence each other's performance and outcomes (Fischer-Lescano, 2011). Feedback loops are mechanisms within systems that enable information to be circulated and processed, leading to adjustments and adaptations in response to internal and external stimuli. Positive feedback loops amplify changes, while negative feedback loops help maintain stability and balance within the organization. Emergence refers to the phenomenon where new patterns, behaviors, or properties arise from the interactions of system components, leading to novel outcomes that cannot be predicted solely by analyzing individual elements. Systems theory acknowledges the emergent properties that result from the dynamic interactions within organizations (Gittner, 2023).

Boundaries define the scope and limits of the system, distinguishing it from its external environment and other systems. Understanding boundaries helps identify inputs, outputs, and interactions that influence the system's functioning and performance. Equifinality suggests that multiple paths or processes can lead to the same outcome within a system. Systems theory recognizes that organizations can achieve similar goals through different strategies, structures, or approaches, allowing for flexibility and adaptation in achieving desired results (McMahon & Patton, 2022).

Systems theory also acknowledges the existence of nested systems within organizations, where subsystems interact and operate within larger systems. Understanding the hierarchy of systems helps analyze the relationships, dependencies, and interactions at different levels of the organization (Fischer-Lescano, 2011). Open systems theory posits that organizations are influenced by and interact with their external environment, exchanging resources, information, and feedback. Open systems adapt to external changes, incorporate feedback, and maintain a dynamic equilibrium to survive and thrive in a complex environment. Nonlinear dynamics in systems theory recognize that organizational behavior and outcomes are often nonlinear, meaning small changes can lead to disproportionate effects or nonlinear relationships between variables. Understanding nonlinear dynamics helps predict and manage complex organizational phenomena (McMahon & Patton, 2022). Systems theory emphasizes the adaptive capacity and resilience of organizations to respond to internal and external challenges, disruptions, and changes. Adaptive systems can adjust their structures, processes, and strategies to maintain stability, learn from experiences, and evolve.

Merits and Demerits of Systems Theory. Systems theory provides a comprehensive and interdisciplinary view of organizations, emphasizing the interconnectedness and interdependencies of various components. This holistic perspective enables managers to understand the organization as a whole system, rather than just focusing on isolated parts. By drawing from multiple disciplines like biology, engineering, and sociology, systems theory offers tools and concepts to manage complexity within organizations. It analyzes relationships, feedback loops, and emergent properties to enable managers to navigate complex systems, anticipate the impact of changes, and consider diverse factors influencing organizational performance (Gittner, 2023). Systems theory recognizes organizations as open systems that interact with their environment, promoting adaptability and resilience. Organizations can respond to external changes, learn from feedback, and adjust their strategies to maintain competitiveness. By fostering systems thinking skills among managers, systems theory encourages them to consider the long-term consequences of decisions, identify patterns of behavior, and leverage feedback mechanisms to improve organizational performance.

Systems theory is a complex and abstract concept that can be difficult to apply in practical organizational settings. Managers may require specialized training and expertise to fully understand the intricate concepts and terminology. Due to the dynamic and nonlinear nature of systems, predicting outcomes with certainty can be challenging, leading to uncertainty and unpredictability when implementing changes or interventions based on systems theory principles (Andersen, 2020). Applying systems theory in organizational management may require significant resources, including time, expertise, and technology, and investing in training, data analysis tools and organizational restructuring might be necessary. However, introducing systems theory concepts and practices in traditional organizational structures may face resistance from employees accustomed to hierarchical or siloed approaches, making overcoming resistance to systemic thinking and fostering a culture of collaboration challenging (McMahon & Patton, 2022). Moreover, systems theory's focus on relationships, feedback loops, and emergent properties may lead to an overemphasis on structural aspects of organizations, potentially overlooking individual behaviors, motivations, and emotions that also influence organizational dynamics.

Constructs

Figure 5. Systems Theory

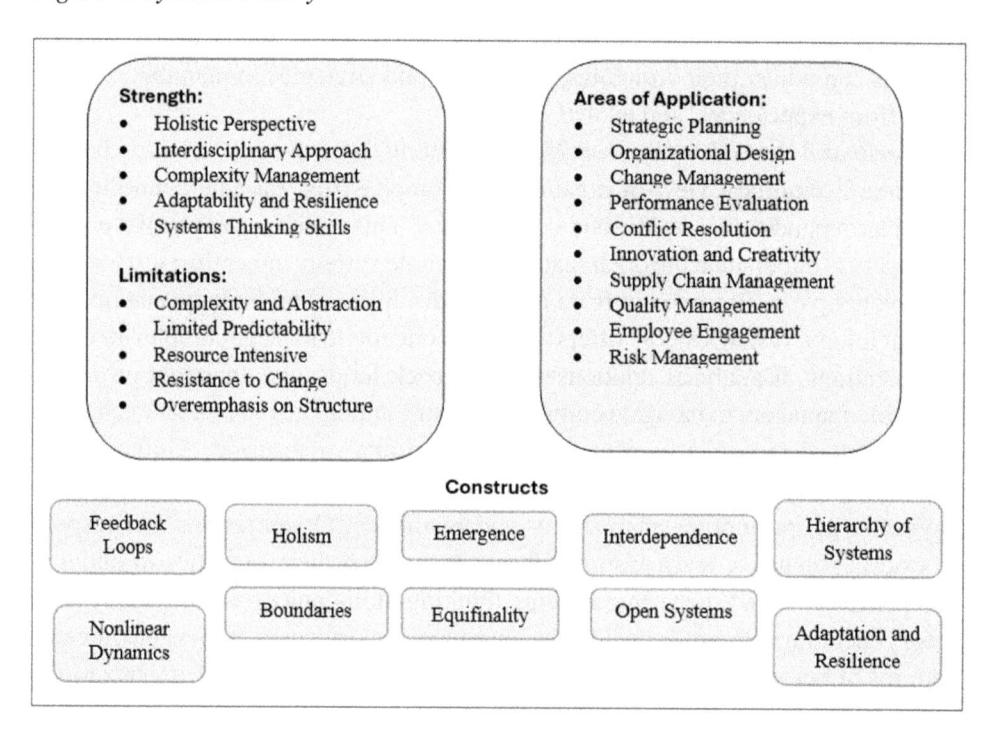

Strength:
- Holistic Perspective
- Interdisciplinary Approach
- Complexity Management
- Adaptability and Resilience
- Systems Thinking Skills

Limitations:
- Complexity and Abstraction
- Limited Predictability
- Resource Intensive
- Resistance to Change
- Overemphasis on Structure

Areas of Application:
- Strategic Planning
- Organizational Design
- Change Management
- Performance Evaluation
- Conflict Resolution
- Innovation and Creativity
- Supply Chain Management
- Quality Management
- Employee Engagement
- Risk Management

Constructs

- Feedback Loops
- Holism
- Emergence
- Interdependence
- Hierarchy of Systems
- Nonlinear Dynamics
- Boundaries
- Equifinality
- Open Systems
- Adaptation and Resilience

Application of Systems Theory. Systems theory offers a valuable approach to various aspects of organizational management, such as strategic planning, organizational design, change management, performance evaluation, conflict resolution, innovation and creativity, supply chain management, quality management, employee engagement, and risk management (Klier, 2022). In strategic planning, managers can use systems theory to view organizations as complex systems with interconnected parts. By analyzing feedback loops, relationships between departments, and emergent properties, managers can develop strategic initiatives that align with the organization's goals and adapt to changing environments. In organizational design, systems theory can help managers focus on the interdependencies and interactions among different functions, teams, and processes. By creating flexible structures that promote collaboration, communication, and adaptability, managers can enhance overall performance.

When implementing organizational changes, systems theory can help managers anticipate the ripple effects across the organization. By understanding how changes in one area can impact other parts of the system, managers can proactively address resistance, manage transitions, and ensure successful change implementation. In performance evaluation, systems theory emphasizes the interconnectedness of individual and organizational performance (Andersen, 2020). Managers can use feedback mechanisms to assess performance, identify areas for improvement, and align individual goals with organizational objectives to enhance overall effectiveness. Systems theory can also be applied in conflict resolution by recognizing the underlying interdependencies and dynamics that contribute to conflicts within the organization. Managers can address conflicts by considering the systemic causes, promoting open communication, and fostering collaborative solutions that benefit the entire system.

Systems theory encourages innovation and creativity by recognizing the emergent properties of dynamic interactions. It helps optimize supply chain networks and guide quality management practices (Klier, 2022). By using systems thinking, managers can foster experimentation, learning, and adaptation to improve coordination, efficiency, and responsiveness across the supply chain while enhancing overall quality performance within the organization. Systems theory recognizes the interconnectedness between employee satisfaction, motivation, and organizational performance. Managers can use this to create a positive work environment, promote communication, and align employee goals with organizational objectives to enhance productivity. In risk management, systems theory can be applied to identify potential risks, develop contingency plans, and ensure organizational sustainability.

Significance of System Theory. Systems Theory is a valuable approach for organizational leaders to gain a holistic view of organizational dynamics, promote collaboration and communication, and foster a culture of continuous learning and improvement. By analyzing complex interactions within the organizational system, organizations can enhance their ability to adapt, innovate, and thrive in dynamic and uncertain environments. Applying Systems Theory principles can help managers and leaders navigate complexity, improve decision-making processes, and enhance overall performance and effectiveness.

Experiential Learning Theory

Experiential Learning Theory, proposed by Kolb (1984), is a prominent model that emphasizes the importance of experience in the learning process. According to Kolb (1984), learning is a continuous process that involves the transformation of experiences into knowledge. The theory suggests that individuals learn best when they actively engage in experiences, reflect on those experiences, conceptualize the information, and apply it to new situations (Kolb & Kolb, 2005).

Constructs of Experiential Learning Theory. Experiential Learning Theory consists of four key constructs that explain the process of learning. These include concrete experience, reflective observation, abstract conceptualization, and active experimentation (Kolb & Kolb, 2005). Concrete experience is the first stage of the learning cycle, where individuals engage in hands-on experiences and encounter new situations or challenges (Morris, 2020). Reflective observation follows, where individuals reflect on their experiences, analyze what happened, and consider the outcomes (Satyam & Aithal, 2022). Abstract conceptualization is the stage where individuals make sense of their experiences by developing abstract concepts, theories, or models to understand the underlying principles and patterns. In this stage, individuals create generalizations, theories, or frameworks based on reflective observations and concrete experiences (Kolb & Kolb, 2005).

The final stage of the learning cycle is active experimentation, where individuals apply their new knowledge and insights in practical situations, test hypotheses, and explore alternative solutions (Kolb & Kolb, 2005). This stage allows individuals to learn by doing, adapt their approaches, and refine their understanding through practical application. Experiential Learning Theory also identifies four different learning styles – diverging, assimilating, converging, and accommodating. Diverging learners prefer to observe and reflect on experiences, assimilating learners excel in abstract conceptualization and theoretical understanding, and converging learners are inclined towards active experimentation and practical application while accommodating learners thrive in hands-on experiences and active experimentation (Seaman, et al., 2017).

Merits and Demerits of Experiential Learning Theory. Experiential learning theory promotes active engagement and participation in the learning process, leading to increased motivation, interest, and retention of knowledge (Okoye & Edokpolor, 2021). By emphasizing hands-on experiences and practical application, learners can connect theoretical concepts to real-world situations, enhancing their understanding and ability to apply knowledge in practical scenarios. This allows individuals to learn at their own pace, explore their interests, and tailor their learning experiences based on their preferences and learning styles, promoting personalized and self-directed learning. Through reflective observation and abstract conceptualization, experiential learning theory fosters critical thinking skills, problem-solving abilities, and the capacity to analyze and evaluate information from multiple perspectives (Jackson, 2022). Furthermore, experiential learning facilitates the development of practical skills, such as communication, teamwork, decision-making, and leadership, by providing opportunities for hands-on practice and active experimentation.

Implementing experiential learning activities, like simulations, field trips, and hands-on projects, can be resource-intensive in terms of time, effort, and costs (Holst & Kuk, 2018). This can make it challenging for organizations with limited resources to adopt this approach. The interpretation of experiences and reflective observations in experiential learning can be subjective, leading to varying perspectives and outcomes among learners. This subjectivity may impact the consistency and objectivity of the learning process. Evaluating experiential learning outcomes and assessing the effectiveness of hands-on experiences can be complex (Hedin, 2010). Traditional assessment methods may not fully capture the depth and breadth of learning that occurs through experiential activities. Engaging in experiential learning activities may require additional time for planning, implementation, and reflection. This can be challenging for learners with busy schedules or organizations with tight deadlines and operational demands (Kolb, 2015). While experiential learning enhances practical skills and real-world application of knowledge, there may be limitations in transferring theoretical concepts and abstract learning to different contexts or domains. This can potentially restrict the generalizability of learning outcomes.

Practical Application of Experiential Learning Theory. There are numerous ways organizations can apply experiential learning theory to enhance learners' skills, knowledge transfer, and personal growth. Some of these practical applications include (Chen et al., 2022):

- **Internship Programs**: Organizations can offer internship programs to provide students or professionals with hands-on experience in a real work environment. Through internships, individuals can apply theoretical knowledge, engage in active experimentation, and reflect on their experiences to enhance their skills and understanding of the industry.
- **Simulation Exercises:** Using simulation exercises, such as business simulations, virtual reality scenarios, or role-playing activities, allows learners to experience realistic situations in a controlled environment. This practical application of experiential learning theory helps individuals develop problem-solving skills, decision-making abilities, and teamwork dynamics.
- **Field Trips and Site Visits:** Organizing field trips or site visits to relevant locations, such as factories, museums, or research centers, provides learners with firsthand experiences and exposure to different contexts. By engaging

in concrete experiences and reflective observation during these visits, individuals can deepen their understanding and connect theory to practice.
- **Project-Based Learning:** Implementing project-based learning approaches where learners work on real-world projects, challenges, or case studies encourages active experimentation, collaboration, and critical thinking. By working on projects, individuals can apply theoretical concepts, test hypotheses, and develop practical solutions.
- **Experiential Workshops and Training Sessions**: Conducting experiential workshops, training sessions, or team-building activities that involve hands-on exercises, group discussions, and problem-solving tasks can enhance learning outcomes. These interactive sessions promote engagement, skill development, and knowledge transfer through experiential learning methods.
- **Outdoor Education Programs:** Outdoor education programs, such as leadership camps, wilderness expeditions, or adventure-based activities, offer opportunities for experiential learning in natural settings. Participants engage in physical challenges, teamwork exercises, and reflection activities that promote personal growth, resilience, and interpersonal skills.
- **Service-Learning Initiatives:** Integrating service-learning initiatives into educational programs allows learners to apply academic knowledge to community service projects or social causes. By engaging in service activities, individuals gain practical experience, develop empathy, and contribute to societal impact while reflecting on their learning experiences.

Significance of Experiential Learning Theory. Experiential Learning Theory is a framework for creating effective learning experiences that promote deep understanding, skill development, and application of knowledge in real-world settings. Educators, trainers, and organizations can create opportunities for learners to actively participate in the learning process, fostering a culture of continuous improvement. To optimize learning outcomes, it's important to recognize both the advantages and disadvantages of this theory and leverage its practical applications in educational and organizational settings.

Social Learning Theory

Social Learning Theory (Bandura, 1977a) highlights the role of social interactions, observational learning, and modeling in learning and behavior change. The theory emphasizes that individuals can learn new behaviors by observing others and the consequences of their actions. Reinforcement plays a crucial role in the learning process, and individuals are more likely to imitate behaviors that are rewarded or reinforced (Bandura, 1977a). Social context and self-efficacy are also important factors in learning and behavior change. The theory can inform the design of training programs that incorporate modeling, observational learning, and social reinforcement, however, it may oversimplify the complexity of human behavior and individual differences may influence the effectiveness of social learning interventions.

Constructs of Social Learning Theory. The Social Learning Theory consists of several key components that explain how individuals learn from their social environment. These components include observational learning, modeling, reinforcement, cognitive processes, self-efficacy, reciprocal determinism, vicarious reinforcement, and social context (Bandura, 1977a).

Observational learning involves acquiring new behaviors, skills, or knowledge by observing and imitating others. This construct highlights the importance of modeling and vicarious learning in shaping behavior. Modeling refers to the process of observing and emulating the behaviors, attitudes, or actions of role models or significant others. Individuals are more likely to imitate behaviors that are demonstrated by models they perceive as credible, competent, or similar to themselves. Reinforcement plays a crucial role in the acquisition and maintenance of learned behaviors. Positive reinforcement increases the likelihood of behavior repetition, while negative reinforcement decreases the likelihood of behavior recurrence. Cognitive processes, such as attention, retention, reproduction, and motivation, mediate observational learning and behavior change. Individuals actively process and interpret information from their social environment to guide their learning and behavior.

Self-efficacy refers to individuals' beliefs in their ability to successfully perform a specific task or behavior. Social Learning Theory highlights the importance of self-efficacy in influencing motivation, persistence, and performance outcomes, as individuals are more likely to engage in behaviors they believe they can successfully execute (Reed et al., 2023). Reciprocal determinism suggests that behavior is influenced by the interaction between personal factors, environmental factors, and behavior itself. This dynamic interplay underscores the bidirectional relationship between individuals and their social environment. Vicarious reinforcement occurs when individuals observe the consequences of others' behaviors and adjust their own behavior based on the observed outcomes. Positive or negative consequences experienced by models can influence observers' likelihood of imitating similar behaviors. Social interactions, peer influences, cultural norms, and societal expectations play a critical role in modeling, reinforcement, and the transmission of behaviors within social groups (Wojciechowski, 2021). The social context is therefore a crucial factor in shaping learning and behavior.

Advantages and disadvantages of Social Learning Theory. Social Learning Theory has both advantages and disadvantages. The theory recognizes the importance of social context, cultural norms, and peer relationships in shaping individuals' development and behavior (Li, 2022). It highlights the role of observational learning in acquiring new behaviors, skills, and knowledge by observing and imitating others. It also emphasizes the significance of modeling behavior by credible and competent role models. Additionally, the principles of Social Learning Theory can be applied to various settings, making it a versatile framework for understanding and promoting behavior change. The theory also emphasizes cognitive processes, such as attention, retention, reproduction, and motivation, in mediating observational learning and behavior change, highlighting the active role of individuals in processing and interpreting social information.

However, some critics argue that Social Learning Theory may oversimplify the complexity of human behavior by focusing primarily on observable behaviors and external influences, potentially overlooking the role of internal factors, individual differences, and personal experiences in shaping behavior. Some researchers suggest that the theory may have limited predictive power in explaining all aspects of behavior, as it may not fully account for the dynamic interplay of cognitive, emotional, and situational factors that influence behavior in real-world contexts (Al-Yaaribi & Kavussanu, 2018). Ethical concerns are also raised about the modeling of behaviors, particularly when individuals observe and imitate harmful behaviors exhibited by role models, leading to potential reinforcement of undesirable behaviors in society. Critics also argue that Social Learning Theory may underestimate the role of individual agency, autonomy, and personal responsibility in behavior change, as it primarily focuses on external influences and social determinants of behavior (Kabiri et al., 2020). Lastly, the theory may not always adequately address the emotional aspects of learning and behavior change, such as motivation, self-regulation, and emotional barriers to learning, which can significantly impact individuals' engagement and persistence in learning and behavior change efforts.

Practical Application of Social Learning Theory. Social Learning Theory is a useful tool for enhancing teaching and training methods in educational, workplace, and therapeutic settings (Li, 2022). By incorporating modeling, peer learning, and observational learning strategies, educators, employers, and therapists can promote positive behavior change and skill acquisition among individuals. In educational settings, positive role models, collaborative learning opportunities, and feedback can reinforce desired behaviors and skills acquisition among students. In the workplace, mentoring, on-the-job training, and job shadowing can facilitate knowledge transfer and skill development among employees (Bond et al., 2020). In therapeutic settings, social modeling, role-playing exercises, and peer support groups can promote positive behavior change and social skills development in individuals.

Social Learning Theory can also inform health promotion and wellness initiatives by leveraging social support, peer influence, and role modeling to encourage healthy behaviors (Kabiri et al., 2020). In parenting and family interventions, parents can use positive reinforcement, modeling desired behaviors, and clear expectations to promote prosocial behaviors and skills acquisition in children (Pusch, 2022). Furthermore, Social Learning Theory can guide community-based programs aimed at addressing social issues, such as bullying prevention, substance abuse prevention, and violence reduction (Wojciechowski, 2021). By changing social norms, promoting positive role models, and fostering social support networks, community organizers can create a culture of respect, empathy, and cooperation within the community.

Lastly, Social Learning Theory can also guide leadership development programs in professional settings by emphasizing the importance of role modeling, feedback, and social learning in shaping effective leadership behaviors (Shadmanfaat et al., 2020). Organizations can provide opportunities for mentorship, peer coaching, and collaborative projects to enhance leadership skills and promote a culture of continuous learning and development among employees.

Significance of Social Learning Theory. The Social Learning Theory highlights the importance of social interactions, observational learning, and modeling in learning and behavior change. By understanding the role of social factors in learning, organizations can design effective training programs that promote positive behavior change, skill acquisition, and learning outcomes. Practitioners can leverage social influences, observational learning processes, and social reinforcement mechanisms to facilitate behavior change and positive social interactions. However, it is important to critically evaluate the theory's limitations and applicability in promoting positive social learning outcomes in diverse contexts.

HRD Theory

Human Resource Development (HRD) Theory is a comprehensive framework that focuses on improving the skills, knowledge, and capabilities of individuals within an organization to enhance performance and achieve organizational objectives (Bednarek, 2023). HRD includes a variety of practices, processes, and interventions aimed at developing human capital, fostering a culture of learning, and supporting the growth and development of employees at all levels of the organization (Lester, 2022). Key components of HRD Theory include training and development, career development, performance management, organizational development, and talent management (see Figure 6). All these components work together to help organizations develop their human resources and achieve their goals.

Constructs of Human Resource Development (HRD) Theory. Human Resource Development (HRD) theory is based on several essential constructs that are critical for enhancing employees' knowledge, skills, and abilities to improve their performance and achieve organizational goals (Cho, 2023). These constructs include Training and Development, Career Development, Performance Management, Organizational Development, Leadership Development, Employee Engagement, Knowledge

Management, Workforce Planning, Diversity and Inclusion, and Employee Well-being. Training and Development focuses on continuous learning and professional growth to support individual and organizational development (Perriton, 2022). Career Development aims to align individual career goals with organizational objectives and promote career advancement opportunities. Performance Management sets performance expectations, provides feedback, and evaluates employee performance to enhance individual and organizational effectiveness. Organizational Development improves organizational effectiveness and facilitates change through HRD interventions, such as team building, change management, and organizational culture development.

Figure 6. Human Resource Development (HRD) Theory

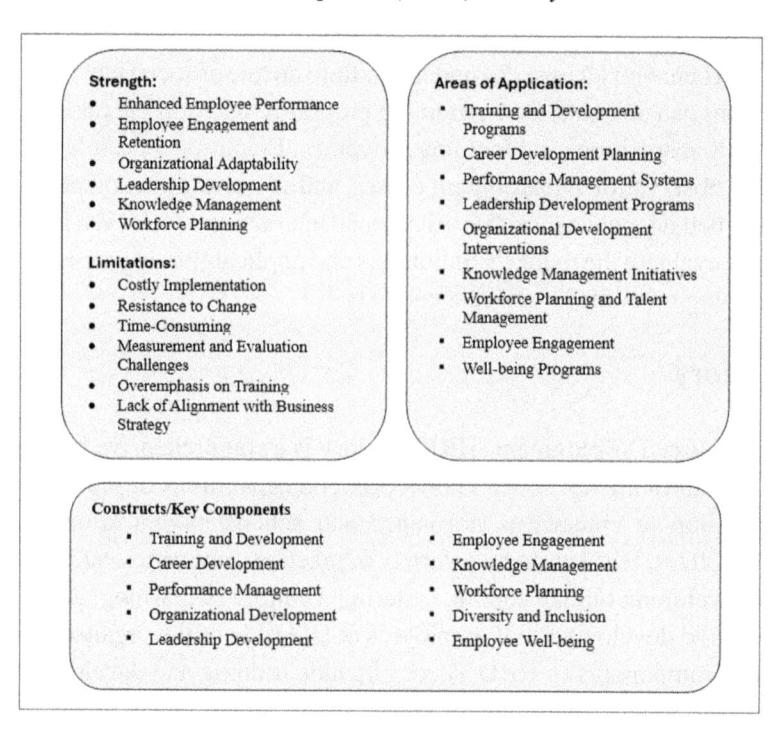

Strength:
- Enhanced Employee Performance
- Employee Engagement and Retention
- Organizational Adaptability
- Leadership Development
- Knowledge Management
- Workforce Planning

Limitations:
- Costly Implementation
- Resistance to Change
- Time-Consuming
- Measurement and Evaluation Challenges
- Overemphasis on Training
- Lack of Alignment with Business Strategy

Areas of Application:
- Training and Development Programs
- Career Development Planning
- Performance Management Systems
- Leadership Development Programs
- Organizational Development Interventions
- Knowledge Management Initiatives
- Workforce Planning and Talent Management
- Employee Engagement
- Well-being Programs

Constructs/Key Components
- Training and Development
- Career Development
- Performance Management
- Organizational Development
- Leadership Development
- Employee Engagement
- Knowledge Management
- Workforce Planning
- Diversity and Inclusion
- Employee Well-being

Leadership Development emphasizes the identification, development, and succession planning of organizational leaders to drive organizational success. Employee Engagement focuses on creating a positive work environment, fostering employee motivation, and enhancing employee commitment to the organization through employee involvement, empowerment, and recognition (Li, 2023). Knowledge Management is essential for capturing, sharing, and leveraging organizational knowledge and expertise through knowledge transfer, learning initiatives, and knowledge-sharing platforms. Workforce Planning aligns human resource needs with organizational goals and strategies through forecasting future workforce requirements, identifying talent gaps, and implementing recruitment and retention strategies. Diversity and Inclusion create a diverse and inclusive workplace that values and respects individual differences through diversity training, inclusive policies, and diversity initiatives.

Employee Well-being promotes the physical, mental, and emotional health of employees through achieving work-life balance, wellness programs, and employee assistance initiatives (Hammer, 2021). By incorporating these constructs of HRD theory into organizational practices and strategies, organizations can effectively develop their human capital, enhance employee performance and engagement, and achieve sustainable growth and success.

Advantages and Disadvantages of Human Resource Development (HRD) Theory

Advantages

- **Enhanced Employee Performance**: HRD theory focuses on developing employees' knowledge, skills, and abilities through training and development initiatives, leading to improved performance and productivity within the organization.
- **Employee Engagement and Retention**: By investing in career development, leadership development, and employee well-being programs, HRD theory can increase employee engagement, satisfaction, and retention, reducing turnover rates and enhancing organizational stability (Hammer, 2021).
- **Organizational Adaptability**: HRD theory emphasizes organizational development and change management practices, enabling organizations to adapt to evolving market trends, technological advancements, and competitive landscapes effectively.
- **Leadership Development**: HRD theory prioritizes leadership development initiatives, fostering a pipeline of skilled and competent leaders who can drive organizational growth, innovation, and strategic success.
- **Knowledge Management**: HRD theory promotes knowledge sharing, learning initiatives, and continuous improvement practices, facilitating the creation, dissemination, and application of organizational knowledge and expertise.

- **Workforce Planning**: HRD theory helps organizations align their human resource needs with strategic goals, enabling effective workforce planning, talent management, and succession planning to build a skilled and diverse workforce.

Disadvantages

- **Costly Implementation**: Implementing HRD initiatives such as training programs, leadership development, and career planning can be costly for organizations, especially for small businesses with limited resources.
- **Resistance to Change**: Employees may resist HRD interventions that require them to change their behaviors, attitudes, or work practices, leading to challenges in implementing organizational development and change management initiatives.
- **Time-Consuming**: Developing and implementing HRD programs, such as performance management systems, career development plans, and knowledge-sharing platforms, can be time-consuming and may require significant organizational commitment and resources.
- **Measurement and Evaluation Challenges**: Assessing the effectiveness and impact of HRD initiatives on employee performance, engagement, and organizational outcomes can be challenging, as measuring intangible outcomes like learning and development can be subjective and complex.
- **Overemphasis on Training**: HRD theory may sometimes focus too heavily on training and development as the primary solution to organizational challenges, overlooking other factors such as leadership, culture, and organizational structure that also influence performance and effectiveness.
- **Lack of Alignment with Business Strategy**: HRD initiatives may not always align with the organization's overall business strategy, leading to disconnects between HRD goals and organizational objectives, which can hinder the effectiveness and relevance of HRD practices.

Practical application of HRD Theory. Human Resource Development (HRD) Theory involves implementing various strategies and initiatives to develop employees' knowledge, skills, and abilities, enhance organizational performance, and foster a culture of continuous learning and improvement. Here are some practical applications of HRD Theory in organizations (Nimon, 2015):

- **Training and Development Programs**: Organizations can implement training and development programs to enhance employees' job-related skills, competencies, and knowledge. These programs can include on-the-

job training, workshops, seminars, e-learning modules, and mentoring opportunities to support employee growth and development.
- **Career Development Planning**: Facilitating career development planning for employees to identify their career goals, aspirations, and development needs. Organizations can offer career pathing, job rotation, and succession planning initiatives to help employees advance in their careers and align their goals with organizational objectives.
- **Performance Management Systems**: Establishing performance management systems to set clear performance expectations, provide regular feedback, and evaluate employee performance. Performance appraisals, goal setting, and performance feedback mechanisms can help employees understand their strengths and areas for improvement.
- **Leadership Development Programs**: Implementing leadership development programs to identify and develop future leaders within the organization. Leadership training, coaching, and mentoring initiatives can help build a pipeline of skilled leaders who can drive organizational success and innovation.
- **Organizational Development Interventions**: Introducing organizational development interventions to improve organizational effectiveness, foster teamwork, and manage change. Team-building activities, change management initiatives, and organizational culture development programs can enhance collaboration and adaptability within the organization.
- **Knowledge Management Initiatives**: Promoting knowledge sharing, learning initiatives, and best practices within the organization to capture, disseminate, and apply organizational knowledge and expertise. Knowledge-sharing platforms, communities of practice, and learning forums can facilitate continuous learning and innovation.
- **Workforce Planning and Talent Management**: Conducting workforce planning to align human resource needs with organizational goals and strategies. Talent management initiatives, recruitment strategies, and succession planning efforts can help organizations build a skilled and diverse workforce to meet current and future business needs.
- **Employee Engagement and Well-being Programs**: Implementing employee engagement and well-being programs to create a positive work environment, foster employee motivation, and support employee health and wellness. Recognition programs, wellness initiatives, and work-life balance policies can enhance employee satisfaction and retention.

Significance of HRD Theory. HRD Theory can help organizations develop their human capital, improve employee performance and engagement, and achieve sustainable growth. By investing in employee development, organizations can improve engagement, productivity, and job satisfaction, leading to improved performance and competitiveness.

CONCLUSION AND RECOMMENDATIONS

This paper explores how learning and development theories can be used to motivate employees in organizational settings. It discusses various theories, such as Behavioral, Cognitive, Social Learning, Adult Learning, Experiential Learning, HRD, and Systems Theory. The document highlights the key differences between Behavioral and Cognitive Theories and explores the limitations of Behavioral Theories in explaining human behavior. Additionally, the application of Systems Theory in organizational management is discussed. The paper emphasizes the importance of a balanced approach that considers the unique characteristics of the organization and employees when applying learning and development theories to enhance organizational performance and employee well-being.

Learning and development theories are essential in shaping organizational behavior, enhancing employee motivation, and driving performance outcomes. Integrating theories such as Behavioral, Cognitive, Social Learning, Adult Learning, Experiential Learning, HRD, and Systems Theory into management practices can create impactful learning interventions that support individual growth and organizational success. HR and L&D professionals should understand these theories and apply them effectively to design training programs that address specific learning needs and promote positive outcomes. By leveraging theoretical frameworks and considering the unique characteristics of their workforce, organizations can cultivate a culture of continuous learning and achieve sustainable success.

REFERENCES

Adams, K. M., Hester, P. T., Bradley, J. M., Meyers, T. J., & Keating, C. B. (2014). Systems theory as the foundation for understanding systems. *Systems Engineering, 17*(1), 112–123. doi:10.1002/sys.21255

Al-Yaaribi, A., & Kavussanu, M. (2018). Consequences of prosocial and antisocial behaviors in adolescent male soccer players: The moderating role of motivational climate. *Psychology of Sport and Exercise, 37*, 91–99. doi:10.1016/j.psychsport.2018.04.005

Allen, S. J., Rosch, D. M., & Riggio, R. E. (2022). Advancing leadership education and development: Integrating adult learning theory. *Journal of Management Education*, *46*(2), 252–283. doi:10.1177/10525629211008645

Andersen, N. A. (2020). The constitutive effects of evaluation systems: Lessons from the policymaking process of Danish active labour market policies. *Evaluation*, *26*(3), 257–274. doi:10.1177/1356389019876661

Arnott, D., & Gao, S. (2022). Behavioral economics in information systems research: Critical analysis and research strategies. *Journal of Information Technology*, *37*(1), 80–117. doi:10.1177/02683962211016000

Baluch, A. M., & Ridder, H.-G. (2020). Mapping the research landscape of strategic human resource management in nonprofit organizations: A systematic review. *Nonprofit and Voluntary Sector Quarterly*, *50*(3), 591–614.

Bandura, A. (1977a). *Social learning theory*. Prentice-Hall.

Bandura, A. (1977b). Self-efficacy: Toward a unifying theory of behavioral change. *Psychological Review*, *84*(2), 191–215. doi:10.1037/0033-295X.84.2.191 PMID:847061

Becerra, M., & Mshigeni, S. (2022). A quasi-experimental evaluation of a flipped class in a public health course. *Journal of Applied Learning and Teaching*, *5*(1), 178–182.

Bednarek, R. (2023). Using interpretive methods to unleash the potential of human resource development. *Human Resource Development Review*, *22*(1), 169–186.

Belte, A. (2021). New avenues for HRM roles: A systematic literature review on HRM in hybrid organizations. *German Journal of Human Resource Management*, *36*(2), 157–176.

Bereiter, C. (1990). Aspects of an Educational Learning Theory. *Review of Educational Research*, *60*(4), 603–624. doi:10.3102/00346543060004603

Bond, M. A., & Blevins, S. J. (2020, March). Using faculty professional development to foster organizational change: A social learning framework. *TechTrends*, *64*(2), 229–237. doi:10.1007/s11528-019-00459-2

Burke-Smalley, L. A., & Mendenhall, M. E. (2020). Facilitating Transfer of Learning in Professional Development Programs: A Cognitive-Behavioral Tool. *Management Teaching Review*, *7*(2), 155–163. doi:10.1177/2379298120953532

Cervone, D. (2023). Theory and Application in Personality Science: The Case of Social-Cognitive Theory. *Psychology and Developing Societies*, *35*(2), 231–250. doi:10.1177/09713336231178366

Checkland, P. (1999). Systems thinking. In W. Currie & B. Galliers (Eds.), *Rethinking Management Information Systems: An Interdisciplinary Perspective* (pp. 45–56). Oxford University Press. doi:10.1093/oso/9780198775331.003.0004

Chen, L., Jiang, W.-J., & Zhao, R.-P. (2022). Application effect of Kolb's experiential learning theory in clinical nursing teaching of traditional Chinese medicine. *Digital Health*, *4*, 1–5. doi:10.1177/20552076221138313 PMID:36406155

Cho, Y. (2023). Special issue on qualitative methods for theory building in HRD: Why now? *Human Resource Development Review*, *22*(1), 3–6. doi:10.1177/15344843221146358

Chuang, S. (2021). The applications of constructivist learning theory and social learning theory on adult continuous development. *Performance Improvement*, *60*(3), 6–14. doi:10.1002/pfi.21963

Fischer-Lescano, A. (2011). Critical Systems Theory: A Challenge for Law and Society. *Philosophy and Social Criticism*, *38*(1), 3–23. doi:10.1177/0191453711421600

Ford, T. G., Lavigne, A. L., Fiegener, A. M., & Si, S. (2020). Understanding district support for leader development and success in the accountability era: A review of the literature using social-cognitive theories of motivation. *Review of Educational Research*, *90*(2), 264–307. doi:10.3102/0034654319899723

Garavan, T. N., O'Donnell, D., McGuire, D., & Watson, S. (2007). Exploring Perspectives on Human Resource Development: An Introduction. *Advances in Developing Human Resources*, *9*(1), 3–10. doi:10.1177/1523422306294342

Garner, J. K., & Shank, M. D. (2023). Using adult learning theory to explore student perceptions of the flipped class method. *Journal of Marketing Education*, 1–16. doi:10.1177/02734753231196501

Gittner, A. B., Dennis, S. A., & Forbis, J. S. Jr. (2023). Diversion: A systems theory perspective. *Journal of Contemporary Criminal Justice*, *39*(4), 485–489. doi:10.1177/10439862231189415

Hammer, E. (2021). HRD interventions that offer a solution to work-life conflict. *Advances in Developing Human Resources*, *23*(2), 142–152. doi:10.1177/1523422321991192

Hedin, N. S. (2010). Experiential Learning: Theory and Challenges. *Christian Education Journal, 7*(1), 109–117. doi:10.1177/073989131000700108

Holst, J. D., & Kuk, L. (2018). A dissection of experiential learning theory: Alternative approaches to reflection. *Adult Learning, 29*(4), 151–157.

Jackson, L. D. (2009). *Revisiting Adult Learning Theory through the Lens of an Adult Learner. Journal Name, Volume(Issue)*. Page Range.

Jackson, M. K. (2022). Working remotely: How organizational leaders and HRD practitioners used the experiential learning theory. *New Horizons in Adult Education and Human Resource Development, 46*, 1–5.

Kabiri, S., Akbari, H., & Hosseini, S. A. (2020). Performance-enhancing drug use among professional athletes: A longitudinal test of social learning. *Crime and Delinquency, 68*(5), 869–893.

Kabiri, S., Smith, H., & Akers, R. L. (2020). A Social Learning Model of Antisocial Coaching Behavior. *International Journal of Offender Therapy and Comparative Criminology, 64*(8), 874–889. doi:10.1177/0306624X19899608 PMID:31928277

Klier, J. D., Bamberger, M., & Raimondo, E. (2022). Grounding Evaluation Capacity Development in Systems Theory. *Evaluation, 28*(2), 231–250. doi:10.1177/13563890221088871

Klonoff, D. C. (2019). Behavioral Theory: The Missing Ingredient for Digital Health Tools to Change Behavior and Increase Adherence. *Journal of Diabetes Science and Technology, 13*(2), 276–281. doi:10.1177/1932296818820303 PMID:30678472

Kolb, A., & Kolb, D. (2005). Learning styles and learning spaces: Enhancing experiential learning in higher education. *Academy of Management Journal, 4*(2), 193–212.

Kolb, D. (1984). *Experiential learning: Experience as the source of learning and development*. Prentice Hall.

Kolb, D. A. (2015). *Experiential learning: experience as the source of learning and development* (2nd ed.). Pearson Education.

Kwon, H. R., & Silva, E. A. (2019). Mapping the landscape of behavioral theories: Systematic literature review. *Journal of Planning Literature, 35*(2), 161–179. doi:10.1177/0885412219881135

Kwon, H. R., & Silva, E. A. (2023). Matching Behavioral Theories and Rules with Research Methods in Spatial Planning-Related Fields. *Journal of Planning Literature, 38*(2), 245–259. doi:10.1177/08854122231157708

Leslie, H. J. (2021). Facilitation fundamentals: Redesigning an online course using adult learning principles and trifecta of student engagement framework. *Journal of Research in Innovative Teaching & Learning, 14*(2), 271–287. doi:10.1108/JRIT-09-2019-0068

Lester, J. N. (2022). Introduction to special issue: Qualitative research methodologies and methods for theory building in human resource development. *Human Resource Development Review, 22*(1), 1–8.

Li, B. (2023). Thinking diffractively with data in human resource development. *Human Resource Development Review, 22*(1), 15–35. doi:10.1177/15344843221135670

Li, C. K. W. (2022). The applicability of social structure and social learning theory to explain intimate partner violence. *Journal of Interpersonal Violence, 37*(23-24), 1–26. doi:10.1177/08862605211072166 PMID:35200042

Lindgreen, A., Di Benedetto, C. A., Brodie, R. J., & Zenker, S. (2022). Teaching: How to ensure quality teaching, and how to recognize teaching qualifications. *Industrial Marketing Management, 100*, A1–A5. doi:10.1016/j.indmarman.2021.11.008

McConnell, T. R. (1942). Introduction. In N. B. Henry (Ed.), Theories of learning (41st Yearbook, National Society for the Study of Education, Part 2 (pp. 3-13). Chicago: University of Chicago Press.

McMahon, M., & Patton, W. (2022). The Systems Theory Framework of career development: News of difference and a journey towards acceptance. *Australian Journal of Career Development, 31*(3), 195–200. doi:10.1177/10384162221120464

Morris, T. H. (2020). Experiential learning: A systematic review and revision of Kolb's model. *Interactive Learning Environments, 28*(8), 1064–1077. doi:10.1080/10494820.2019.1570279

Mukhalalati, B. A., & Taylor, A. (2019). Adult learning theories in context: A quick guide for healthcare professional educators. *Journal of Medical Education and Curricular Development, 6*, 6. doi:10.1177/2382120519840332 PMID:31008257

Nimon, K. (2015). Secondary Data Analyses from Published Descriptive Statistics: Implications for Human Resource Development Theory, Research, and Practice. *Advances in Developing Human Resources, 17*(1), 26–39. doi:10.1177/1523422314559805

Okoye, K. R., & Edokpolor, J. E. (2021). Effect of industrial work experience in developing technical and vocational education undergraduates' employability skills. *Asian Journal of Assessment in Teaching and Learning, 11*(1), 1–12. doi:10.37134/ajatel.vol11.1.1.2021

Perriton, L. (2022). Guest editorial: Historical perspectives. *Human Resource Development Review, 21*(2), 152–159. doi:10.1177/15344843221088145

Perry, S. A. B., Barefield, T., & Cox, A. B. (2023). Review of the book Generative Knowing: Principles, Methods, and Dispositions of an Emerging Adult Learning Theory, by A. Nicolaides. *New Horizons in Adult Education and Human Resource Development, 35*(3), 176–177. doi:10.1177/19394225231200262

Pusch, N. (2022). A meta-analytic review of social learning theory and teen dating violence perpetration. *Journal of Research in Crime and Delinquency, 61*(2), 171–223. doi:10.1177/00224278221130004

Qi, Y., Wang, B., & Liu, J. (2023). Behavioural economics theories in information-seeking behaviour research: A systematic review. *Journal of Librarianship and Information Science*, 1–13. doi:10.1177/09610006231219246

Ratiu, L., David, O. A., & Baban, A. (2016). Developing managerial skills through coaching: Efficacy of a cognitive-behavioral coaching program. *Journal of Rational-Emotive & Cognitive-Behavior Therapy, 34*(4), 244–266. doi:10.1007/s10942-016-0256-9

Reed, M. S., Collins, D., & Cronin, A. (2023). Assessing the efficacy of online learning in disparate business subjects: Lessons from distributed practice theory. *Journal of Management Education, 47*(5), 512–541. doi:10.1177/10525629231178916

Ritchie, L. (2021). *Yes I can: Learn to use the power of self-efficacy*. Effic Research Ltd.

Sahu, A. K., Padhy, R. K., & Dhir, A. (2020). Envisioning the future of behavioral decision-making: A systematic literature review of behavioral reasoning theory. *Australasian Marketing Journal, 28*(4), 145–159. doi:10.1016/j.ausmj.2020.05.001

Satyam, B., & Aithal, P. S. (2022). Reimagining an Experiential Learning Exercise in Times of Crisis: Lessons Learned and a Proposed Framework. *Journal of Marketing Education, 44*(2), 191–202. doi:10.1177/02734753221084128

Scherrens, A.-L., Pype, P., Van den Eynden, B., Mertens, F., Stichele, R. V., & Deveugele, M. (2018). The use of behavioural theories in end-of-life care research: A systematic review. *Palliative Medicine*, *32*(1), 1065–1079. doi:10.1177/0269216318758212 PMID:29569998

Shadmanfaat, S. M., Howell, C. J., Muniz, C. N., Cochran, J. K., Kabiri, S., & Fontaine, E. M. (2020). Cyberbullying perpetration: An empirical test of social learning theory in Iran. *Deviant Behavior*, *41*(3), 278–293. doi:10.1080/01639625.2019.1565513

Shuell, T. J. (1986). Cognitive conceptions of learning. *Review of Educational Research*, *56*(4), 411–436. doi:10.3102/00346543056004411

Skinner, B. F. (1988). *About Behaviorism*. Random House.

Sweller, J., Ayres, P., & Kalyuga, S. (2011). *Cognitive load theory*. Springer. doi:10.1007/978-1-4419-8126-4

Von Bertalanffy, L. (1968). *General System Theory: Foundations, Development*. George Braziller.

Weinstein, C. E., & Mayer, R. E. (1986). The teaching of learning strategies. In M. C. Wittrock (Ed.), *Handbook of research on teaching* (3rd ed., pp. 315–327). Macmillan.

Westaby, J. D. (2005). Behavioral reasoning theory: Identifying new linkages underlying intentions and behavior. *Organizational Behavior and Human Decision Processes*, *98*(2), 97–120. doi:10.1016/j.obhdp.2005.07.003

Wojciechowski, T. W. (2021). The relevance of the dual systems model for social learning theory: Testing for moderation effects. *Criminal Justice and Behavior*, *48*(12), 1791–1807. doi:10.1177/00938548211017927

Yawson, R. M. (2012). Systems theory and thinking as a foundational theory in human resource development: A myth or reality? *Human Resource Development Review*, *12*(1), 53–85. doi:10.1177/1534484312461634

Chapter 5

Training and Development to Enhance Motivation and Knowledge Transfer

Neeta Baporikar
https://orcid.org/0000-0003-0676-9913
Namibia University of Science and Technology, Namibia & SP Pune University, India

ABSTRACT

Training and development have been a part of human resource development strategies for ages. However, many times these strategies have been merely to develop or improve the skills and competencies essential to do the job. This shortsighted approach has benefitted neither the individual employees nor organizations. More so in the current scenario of knowledge-based economies, where tenure is an issue and loyalty is towards professional growth and enhancement, it becomes essential to ensure that training and development focuses on enhancing motivation and ensuring knowledge transfer. Motivated employees are brand ambassadors for the organization and knowledge transfers help in retaining and ensuing career succession. In line with this thinking, adopting a qualitative approach, this chapter aims to discuss and deliberate on how training and development can enhance motivation and ensure effective knowledge transfer with a focus on public enterprises and suggest strategies to do training and development effectively to enhance motivation and effective knowledge transfer.

DOI: 10.4018/979-8-3693-1674-0.ch005

Copyright © 2024, IGI Global. Copying or distributing in print or electronic forms without written permission of IGI Global is prohibited.

INTRODUCTION

Training and development has been a part of human resource development strategies since ages. However, many times these strategies have been merely to develop or improve the skills and competencies required by the organization. This shortsighted approach has neither benefitted the individuals' employees nor did organizations; much less enabled them to achieve the organizational goals and objectives. More so in the current scenario of knowledge-based economies, where tenure is an issue and loyalty is towards professional growth and enhancement, it becomes essential to ensure that training and development focuses on enhancing motivation and ensuring knowledge transfer. Motivated employees are brand ambassadors for the organization and knowledge transfers help in retaining and ensuing career succession. In line with this thinking, adopting a qualitative approach, this chapter aims to discuss and deliberate on how training and development can enhance motivation and ensure effective knowledge transfer with a focus on public enterprises and suggest strategies to do training and development effectively to enhance motivation and effective knowledge transfer.

BACKGROUND

Human resources forms a critical component of modern businesses. Salah (2016) asserts that success or failure of an organisation can be attributed to the quality of human resources in the organisation. To become a successful organisation, employees need to be trained. According to Karim, Musfiq, and Wasib (2019), training is essential as it improves employees' capacities, outlook, knowledge, and skills, which then leads to an improvement in their level of performance. According to Saleem, Shahid, and Naseem (2011), training is a process that enhances an employee's knowledge, exposure, and talents as well as their current skill set. According to McDowall and Saunders (2010), the importance of training has increased recently because more competent and moderately successful firms invest heavily in staff training Employers heavily rely on the expertise and abilities of their staff to remain competitive and successful in the rapidly evolving technological world. As a result, significant and ongoing investment in training is necessary (Oluwaseun, 2018).

According to Blen (2021), the most significant effect of training on staff and the organisation is an improvement in output quality and quantity, enabling staff to operate more productively and effectively. As personnel with adequate training are less likely to make expensive mistakes, the effects extend to the growth in income. However, Blaine (2009) advises that training needs should be determined first in order to establish a well-structured training programme. Training and development strategies need to be designed based on gap analysis produced by using the information acquired to help identify the mismatch between employee capabilities and what the organisation requires of them (Hussen, 2021). According to Goldstein and Ford (2002), the process of developing a training programme is intended to address an employee's training needs. According to Redmond and Johnson (2016), employees are more dedicated and willing to participate in training programmes if they are aware of the need for training.

LITERATURE REVIEW

Holden and Biddle (2017) make the case that investing in education has a clearly high rate of return and the potential to help achieve significant societal objectives. According to the concept of human capital, measures that support education could hasten both economic growth and the eradication of poverty. In addition, the developing empirical evidence connecting education to those aims could be convincingly explained using the Human Capital Theory. According to the Human Capital Theory, training and development can help people perform and produce better (Becker, 1964). The argument backs up the inclination to invest in training and development because it improves employee performance and fosters an organisation's expansion (Salah, 2016). There is now sufficient proof to show that an increase in training and development has a favourable impact on workers' performance.

Ruso and Fouts (1997) postulate that in the resource-based theory view, resources are classified into three categories. The tangible resources refer to financial services while physical resources such as plant and equipment are intangible and personnel-based. Intangible resources refer to human resource and reputation. Personnel based resources include culture, expertise of employees and commitment. On their own, these resources are not very productive. Since training is seen as an intangible resource that an organisation can use to gain a competitive edge, a variety of criteria must be taken into account when making decisions on training and development.

TRAINING NEEDS ANALYSIS

For any training programme to be a success, training needs to be first identified. According to Cascio (1992), there are three levels of analysis to figure out the firm requirements. The three levels are organisational, operational and individual. Operational analysis focuses on where training is needed and helps the firm to avoid wastage in resource on doing training programmes that need not to be done and optimising the use of resources to programmes that need to be done which can make employees perform better for the overall benefit of the organisation. The second level of analysis is the operational analysis. This type of analysis focuses on the work to be performed after an employee has received training. The third and final level of analysis is the individual analysis. This takes into account both the employee's actual performance and the performance that the company expects from the employee (Cascio, 1992).

Training Methods

Dessler (2008) postulates that training must have five steps for it to be effective. Analysing the needs of the employees is the first step. This looks at the area of skills which employees lack and come up with a programme that addresses the lack of knowledge and skills. It is very important that this step includes input from both the employee and organisation to come up with an effective training programme. The second step is the instruction design where the trainer prepares the training programme based on the needs analysis of step one. This includes programme content such as workbooks, power point slides, exercises, activities and so forth. Step 3 is validation. This step essentially does a pilot test on a small audience to see if the programme can work. Step 4 is where the actual training starts. This step is called the implementation step. Step 5 is the evaluation step. After the implementation programme, it is anticipated that the trainees would have acquired the necessary information to successfully complete their tests. In this step, management does the assessment to see if the training programme was a success or not. It is important at this stage for management to provide feedback to the trainer and trainees.Types of employee training

According to Salah (2016), the training methods used by an organisation determine whether the majority of training programmes are successful or not. According to Temesgen (2019), training can be assumed to have a beneficial effect on employee performance if performance is higher after training than it was before. Temesgen (2019), states that there are a variety of training programmes available, all of which are intended to provide employees with the information and abilities they need to perform their jobs effectively and successfully. The two most common types of training are off-the-job training and on-the-job training (Naftal, 2018). The effectiveness of employees is frequently impacted by the various training approaches. A brief description of each training programme under consideration is provided below:

- **On the job training** refers to a programme that is primarily carried out at the workplace This type of training includes apprenticeship, job rotation, coaching etc.. Since this type of training is internal, many consider it as the

most cost effective because employees are trained at the workplace (Naftal, 2018).
- **Off the job training** refers to a programme that is primarily done off site which includes case studies, role plays, lectures, seminars, group discussions, and multimedia learning. According to Blen (2021), training is a deliberate attempt to help people develop the information, abilities, and attitudes needed to complete a certain activity. In so doing, employees are assisted in learning and applying new knowledge and abilities in a safe working environment. This kind of training emphasises learning more so that employee performance improves. Since it requires the individual to leave the workplace, this sort of training is expensive for an organisation.
- **Induction** – This according to Dragomiroiua, Hurloiua and Mihai (2014) reduces the negative effects of the drastic change of environment and lifestyle and accelerates adaptation to conditions that employees meet at the new job. Three types of induction processes include pre-induction where a new employee is provided information before commencing with work, induction which refers to the first day and the transition in the new work and post induction which deals with feedback or follow up after induction has been provided.

According to Sultana (2013), a key element of training is the trainer's capacity to help employees apply the knowledge they have learned in the classroom to their daily work. Poor training material and trainer delivery methods are likely to prevent participants from achieving the desired learning outcomes.

Benefits of Employee Training

There are a numerous benefits of training employees. In a 2014 study, Onyango and Wanyoike examined how training impacts worker performance and the following benefits were a result of their study: Training improves the morale of employees, trained employees are happier and less stressed when conducting their work. Training increases the morale of employees, with a boost in morale, employees are less likely to be absent from work which decreases the chance of having employees quit their jobs. Due to the competency they develop after training, employees are more likely to secure work on a permanent basis as their skills help them secure the job. Competency helps employees become more employable and this increase their chances of promotion within the organisation.

A well-trained employee requires minimal supervision since he or she has the ability to do the work independently. This reduces wastage of time and effort for the employee and the supervisor. Training also enhances productivity of employees, which ultimately leads to higher profits for the organisation. Itika (2011) states that the benefits of training to both an individual and the organisation include the improvement of existing skills and knowledge, higher morale end motivation, improved customer service, increased opportunities of getting promoted which finally results in an increase in performance of the employee and the organisation. In conclusion, training makes an employee a valuable asset to the organisation and helps the employee earn more income.

Mullins (2007) talks on the benefits of training to employees and the organisation and asserts that some of the benefits of training include an increase in confidence and commitment of employees, increase in effectiveness and efficiency and increase in productivity and performance. Employees are more likely to be promoted and earn more after training. Employees are less likely to be absent from work and thus the turnover of employees decreases. In summary, a trained employee is valuable for any organisation. With training, an employee's morale is uplifted. With an elevated morale, an employee is likely to be more efficient and effective. An employee with an elevated morale is happier and most likely to be satisfied at the workplace. The level of risks such as wastage of resource or unnecessary accidents in the work place are minimised. An organisation with a skilled workforce has its image enhanced and the increase in revenue is inevitable.

Employee Development

While development is more focused on the growth of people inside an organisation, training focuses on providing the necessary information and skills needed for the employees to perform their duties more efficiently and effectively (Meraghni., Bekkouche., & Demdoum. (2021)). Pallavi (2013) states that development is more about general knowledge and attitudes, which is more useful and helpful for employees in higher positions such as supervisors and managers. Salah (2016) emphasises further that employees must evolve in order to become aware of and be prepared for the requirements of predicted future responsibilities and positions. In other words, there is a conscious effort made to provide workers with the tools they need to help the organisation achieve its objectives. The efforts towards employee development largely depend on personal drive and ambition of employees. To effect this development of employees, development programmes are essential in this process. Ekpo (1989) opines that development programmes are structured in such a way to help employees enhance their personality, knowledge, attitude, behaviour and to develop their professional and leadership skills which are all ingredients in improving their abilities to perform their duties within an organisation. When the training requirements are clearly identified in advance as a result of the input from the employee and employer, the efficacy of a training programme can be realised.

Employees can participate in a variety of development programmes to advance their careers (Salah, 2016).

Oshionebo (2003) extends that there are other development programmes such as mentoring, career planning, proficiency courses, professional certification just to name but a few, which are all geared towards improving the current and future performance of employees within an organisation. Oshionebo further stresses that no matter what development method is used, what is of utmost importance is that the development programme should be designed in such a way that it meets specific objectives which contribute to the employee and organisational effectiveness.

Since development is based on personal drive and ambition it becomes challenging because it requires an individual to have the will power to advance further in life. Human beings naturally are in a state of inertia unless compelled by an external force. This makes it very complicated for human beings to optimally take advantage of opportunities that come with career development. It also becomes a challenge when employee development programmes are not aligned to organisational goals and objectives. Oshionebo (2003) opines that employee development programmes are ineffective when there is lack of feedback from superiors. According to Antonacoupoulou (2000), employee development focuses on progress and accepting difficult and more responsible roles in an organisation's future. Employee development is dependent on each employee's willingness to participate in the development programme. According to Antonacoupoulou (2000), organisational culture, senior management's attitude toward staff development, and the lack of advancement chances all affect the growth of an employee.

TRAINING AND DEVELOPMENT PROCESS

Desimone, Werner, and Harris (2002) as the phase or stage within the training and development programme that is followed to guarantee that organisational goals are reached define the training and development process. The training and development process has four stages, as defined by Hussen (2019), and they are as follows:

- Identification of training needs
- Training design
- Delivery of the training
- Monitoring and evaluation

According to Cooke (2000), performance is defined as the accomplishment of particular goals as assessed against specified targets. Therefore, an organisation's ability to attain its mandate heavily relies on the performance of its employees.

According to Kidane (2021) employee performance should be evaluated in relation to the performance standards established by an organisation. When employees fulfil the performance requirements set by their organisation, they are deemed good performers; when they do not, they are deemed poor performers. Performance of employees is usually measured by output. Kidane (2021) claims that organisational performance standards are used to evaluate employee performance. Profitability, efficiency, and the effectiveness of executing a certain activity are examples of performance metrics. The capacity of a business to generate profits continuously throughout time is known as profitability (Kidane, 2021), efficiency is the ability of employees to optimise the use of resources to achieve the desired outcome and effectiveness is the ability to meet the set targets (Stoner, 1996). Abdelhakim and Madgy (2019) define performance as the accomplishment or merely functional efficiency of employees. The author further stresses that every organisation's primary goal is to raise performance levels. Only consistently effective employee performance can allow for this to happen. Employee effectiveness thus contributes to an organisation's overall expansion. For a company to effectively manage its human resources and evaluate its employees in a way that fosters personal growth, enhances organisational performance, and informs business planning, performance evaluation (Ahmed, Sultana, Paul and Azeem, 2013).

Further, besides training there are many other factors that affect employee performance (Shahim, 2018). Some of the most important factors include leadership, coaching, empowerment, participation, motivation, working environment and organisational culture. According to Northouse's definition from 2007, leadership is the act of motivating and inspiring a group of individuals to accomplish common goals and objectives. According to Champathes (2006), coaching is a process aimed at enhancing employees' current performance. This involves a two-way communication where the need enhancement is recognised and the way to improve is established. Empowerment according to Duvall (1999) is a process of equipping individuals and an organisation to achieve collective goals and objectives. Participation is about involvement or inclusion. Chen and Tjosvold (2006) stated that employee performance increases when they feel involved as this gives them the sense of responsibility and authority. Organisational culture is about the collective beliefs and attitudes of the people working in an organisation. Schein (1990) argues that the determining factor of organisational culture is the mindset of the people. Motivation influences people to behave in a certain way. Jobber (1994) asserts that a poorly motivated workforce can be very costly to an organisation. Maintaining high motivation of employees has many benefits for an organisation because employees who are highly motivated are more likely to perform better. Motivated workers make less mistakes and this minimises operating expenses. In addition, absenteeism becomes outdated, turnover is reduced, and less time is wasted (Shahim, 2018). According to Collis and Hussey (2009), numerous elements influence how well individuals perform in an organisation. This covers elements like an employee's aptitude, the training they receive, their drive and commitment, their welfare, management rules, their access to fringe benefits, their pay and benefits packages, their promotion prospects and their communication skills. A high performing employee has the ability to offer exceptional customer service, practise standard operational procedures and is more accurate, effective and efficient. This leads to organisational competence and growth.

Challenges of Training and Development

Some of the challenges commonly faced by training and development department in organizations include:

- Budget: Budgets are limited or minimal and no funds are available for training and development of employees given the tough economic situation most organisations are going through. Budget cuts on training are now more frequent due to the COVID-19 pandemic. It was also reported that there was no sufficient budget for outsourced training. The lack of budget makes it very difficult to provide consistent training to the employees.
- Training programmes offered are too expensive making it impossible to partake in such training programmes.
- Insufficient time for employee development. Employees are not allocated sufficient time to attend to career development programmes to enhance their performance.
- Lack of qualified trainers. Owing to the lack of qualified trainers, senior employees are then expected to train junior employees which then take a lot of time from seniors to perform other duties. As a result of this shortage, it is very difficult for the company to train new staff or graduates. To make matters worse, trainers also are not well compensated. This brings up a lot of challenges in that the companies are unable to attract qualified trainers from outside and the training they receive from unqualified trainers is not up to standard.
- Training providers cannot come up with tailor- made training programmes to match the organisation goals. This is because unqualified trainers do not understand the training process. Needs assessment and outcomes identification are done haphazardly making the training process unsuccessful.
- Poor understanding and knowledge of the benefits of the training. No needs assessment has been done by management to determine the areas that the employee needs to work on in order to improve their performance. Without proper needs assessment and the outcome identification process, employees

are more likely to remain in the dark about the company expectations on them.
- Management is not fully supporting the training needs. The main challenge is that management is not keen on employee development and usually does merely lip-service. Group training is usually rushed and does not cater for individual needs and differences.
- Training programmes need to be implemented to allow employees to get additional skills apart from those on the job training. Other training methods in use can be off the job training, refresher training, health and safety training just to name but a few. There are ineffective training modules leading to employees being inadequately engaged with learning platforms and content.
- Training and development are not prioritised as it is seen as an unnecessary expense to the organisation. Education and training are not considered useful.
- There is lack of career succession planning. If there is lack of a clear career succession plan in place, employees are most likely to remain in the dark. This can make employees easily move to other organisations where career succession plans are clear and in line with the organisational goals and objectives.
- Poor or lack of effective feedback. This is an important activity in the employee development process that involves a trainer to guide an employee to achieve both personal and organisational goals. Feedback affords the employee a chance to access strengths and weaknesses. After an employee has gone through the development process the next step will be an evaluation that gets done to assess whether the employee understood what was expected of him / her.

EMPLOYEE MOTIVATION

Motivation in general reflects the level of energy, commitment and creativity that a company's workers bring to their jobs. Motivation is an emotional feature that encourages an employee to act towards a desired goal. Employee motivation means to motivate employees by giving rewards to them to attain the organizational goals (Baporikar, 2021). The individual motivation of employees plays an important role in getting high-level satisfaction (Petcharak, 2004). Motivation is a process in which people are influenced to move on for performing something especially to fulfill their needs and get satisfaction (Butkus and Green, 1999). Baron (1893) defined motivation in his own right. He says, "Motivation is a collection, or arrangements of procedures involved in push and pull forces that makes the actions stronger towards success". Kinicki and Kreitner (2001) assume that motivation corresponds to such emotional processes that cause the inspiration and determination of voluntary actions that help to attain the goals. Rutherford (1990) found in his research that motivation is the effective agent in an organization because motivated employees are always innovative in their jobs. It is task for the organization to appreciate and understand the procedures necessary to have an effect on encouragement of their workers.

The majority of theorists in the area of motivation argue that there is an unquestionable link between motivation and job satisfaction and motivation with employee loyalty to the organization (Basset-Jones and Lloyd, 2005; Chen et al., 2004; Lok and Crawford, 2004; Pool and Pool, 2007). Sirotaet al. (2005), in a major study of motivation and job satisfaction, involving 135,000 respondents from different countries and groupings, found that organizations employing motivation strategies, that include three major things, i.e. justice, companionship and achievement. Barber and Bretz (2000) mentioned that reward management systems have major impact on organizations ability to catch, retain and motivate high potential employees and as a result getting the high levels of performance.

Extrinsic Rewards

Extrinsic rewards are tangible and are exterior to work and efficiency of the employees. Salary/pay, incentives and bonuses are the types of extrinsic rewards. Pay has direct link with efficiency of the employee (Bishop, 1987). There must be a successful extrinsic reward system to get better performance and high efficiency of the employees (Carraher, 2006). Extrinsic rewards as tangible rewards obtained due to doing the job, such as pay and promotion (Porter and Lawler, 1968). Mottaz (1985) says that extrinsic rewards are also defined as social and organizational rewards. Organizational rewards are like pay, bonuses and fringe benefits, which can be seen (Katz & Van Maanen, 1977; Malhotra et al., 2007; Mottaz, 1985). Whilst Kuvaas (2006) said that employee's loyalty depends upon pay and bonuses given to them. Social rewards help employees to create interest for achieving company's objective (Burke, 2002). Reio and Callahon (2004) conclude that extrinsic rewards motivate the employee and obtain high efficiency from them. Professor Elton Mayo, who said that motivating employees is the main work of an organization conducted many researches. Frey (1997) argues that pay plays an important role in motivating the employees. He also argues that if employees get bonuses and incentives, they will be satisfied and motivated and work hard to obtain the organizational goal.

Intrinsic Rewards

Intrinsic rewards are intangible in nature. We cannot touch them with our hands but only feel them such as appreciation, caring attitudes from employer and job rotation. Intrinsic rewards are the rewards within the job itself such as satisfaction from completing a task, appreciation from employer (Ajila, 2004). Loyalty of employees depends upon rewards and recognition (Andrew, 2004). Porter and Lawler (1968) said that the satisfaction,which an employee gains by doing his work, is intrinsic reward. Mottaz (1985) said that intrinsic rewards are of different kinds. Task rewards are example of it and they refer duties and responsibility of an employee. Intrinsic non-monetary rewards are the appreciation, which an employee gets, by his or her efforts by completing his job (Porter & Lawler, 1968). Malhotra *et al.* (2007) explained that intrinsic non-monetary rewards influence the loyalty of an employee more effectively than extrinsic rewards. Adeyemo and Aremu (1999), said that employer who is more helpful to his employees is also a big reason of employee loyalty.

Burke (2002) said that if controllers are loyal to their employees and behave nicely with them than employees will be more loyal to their employers and their jobs. Reio and Callahon (2004) argued that intrinsic rewards are used to motivate employees for higher efficiency. Dee prose (1994) said that intrinsic rewards are very effective for getting motivation and efficiency of employees. Therefore, they will work better for organization. The overall success of an organization depends on how an organization motivates its employees and how they differentiate their performance. Lawler (2003) said that success of the organizations depends on how they motivate their employees. Many researches indicate that motivating employees is the main work of an organization.

TRAINING EFFECTIVENESS

On Organization commitment and employee motivation, the training producers used by companies both have direct and indirect effect (Meyer and Allen, 1991) "An intrusion system is developed to increase the job performance on individual basis" (Chiaburu and Tekleab, 2005, p. 29). According to Swart et al. (2005) the motivation of the individual, the individual"s needs and training system are the source of individual improvement. The mainstream of theorists in the area of motivation argue that, there is an undeniable link between motivation with employee commitment to the organization and motivation.(Basset-Jones and Lloyd, 2005; Chen et al., 2004;The fear occur during job performance due to lack of skills unfavorable causes, lack of communication skill, annoyance and other factors to control situations and increase work productivity training is much important (Chen et al., 2004). Row den and Connie (2005), through training the organization employee know well how to satisfy their customer. Tsai et al. (2007), when employees are trained and satisfy their jobs and loyal to their organization will show a positive effect on organizational goals.

According to Harrison (2000), training is main component and his key factor learning also help the organization to achieve their objective and goals would create a positive effect. In general, it can be argued that the outcome or results the organization is expected usually are low. According to few studies, employee's thoughts moreover change through training. Lang (1992) argued the training system developed by the organization help to increase the productivity of employees and achieve goals. Another survey, conducted by Gaertner and Nollen (1989) in manufacturing firms, concealed employee loyalty linked with the concealed HRM methods. These methods were inner encouragement, and training opportunity.

Training has positive impact on employee motivation. It has significant relation and impact on employee motivation. Employee will more motivate in presence of training. In training organizations, have to teach them about their job and organization culture. It will create confidence in employees and they will do their work with full interest. It will create a positive influence as hypothesis result shows. Expectancy is the apparent chance that effort goes to good presentation; variables affecting the individual's expectancy discernment include self-efficacy, goal difficulty, and perceived control. We get the targeted performance through expectancy on the basis of experience and knowledge. Expectancy usually is supported by tentative verification (Tien, 2000; Vansteenkiste et al., 2005) and it is normally used theories of motivation in the workplace/organization (Campbell and Pritchard, 1976; Henemne and Schwab, 1972; Mitchell and Biglan, 1971) employee motivation play important role in job performance.

KNOWLEDGE TRANSFER

To enable employees to work together efficiently knowledge transfer is essential (Baporikar, 2017). To increase the organization's efficiency managers should encourage their employees. Employee motivation cannot be controlled on profit. Employees transfer their knowledge related to their individual learning when they are intrinsically motivated (Huysman and de Wit, 2004).Employee motivation has two important roles in knowledge transfer. First, it is reward of process itself and second it is the source of enhancing individual participation of knowledge (Lucas and Ogilvie, 2006).

Role of Motivation in the Knowledge Transfer

Two relatively clear trends characterize human resource management in today's organizations. Individuals are encouraged to maximize their potential, develop their abilities to perfection and show personal competitive spirit and abilities and realize their career plan by rising in the organizational structure. The second trend emphasizes the need to acquire constantly new knowledge, abilities and skills of all employees. Intellectual capital becomes irreplaceable with the role and content in the competitive positions of organizations. Considering these two trends, one of the questions is how do you encourage individuals who have acquired the necessary knowledge to transfer them to other members of the organization? Alternatively, why would someone pass on their knowledge as a personal source of career advancement and career advancement to others?

It is not possible to give completely satisfactory answers to these questions since it is an extremely complex matter. It is argued that knowledge transfers will be effective when we become self-aware of our emotions, strengths and weaknesses, only then can we begin to think about how to manage that knowledge to apply them to help us achieve our goals and pass them on to others (Zeidner et al., 2004). People, who focus mainly on themselves and lack empathetic preferences and values, do not have enough self-awareness. Some authors point to the need to emphasize the perceived usefulness of acquiring and transferring knowledge, which depends on the extent to which participants in the acquisition and transfer will be able to exercise self-actualization (Burke & Hutchins, 2007). In the acquisition and transfer of knowledge, the importance of learning style indicates that in the management activities of human resources management should intensively work on adopting organizational models and learning styles. This will reduce the possible risks in acquiring knowledge, implementing it more effectively in work and transferring knowledge to others (Tharenou, 2010). Research findings confirm that the effectiveness of training content acquisition and transfer of acquired knowledge is highly correlated with certain employee dimensions that come from characteristics of their personality such as conscientiousness, extroversion, self-control, empathetic orientation (Burke & Hutchins, 2007). The emphasis on self-evaluation should be on the formative use of one's learning or achievement based on a nomothetic or group comparison. This implies that the trainees are compared with several potential achievements themselves (Klein & Buckingham, 2002).

Motives and Motivation for the Transfer of Knowledge

Motives and motivation for knowledge transfer in organizations can include different internal and external incentives. External (extrinsic) can take the form of salary, incentives, promotion, bonuses, etc. Internal (intrinsic) is intangible such as praise, empathetic inclination, loyalty to the organization etc. Managers are interested in generating both external and internal motives to get the best out transmitted acquired knowledge among employees. Intrinsic motives are becoming increasingly the focus of interest today in management for several reasons. One is that external motives very often prove to be insufficiently effective in transferring knowledge. Besides, knowledge transfer has long been the focus of pedagogy (as a scientific area primarily concerned with knowledge transfer) on efficiency in the sphere of intangible motives. Whether or not someone transfers their knowledge to another usually depends on a series of motives that are not materially based but have some deeper psychological meanings. There are at least eight intrinsic motives that can be accepted as incentives for individuals to transfer their acquired knowledge to other members of the organization:

1. The expected reward for knowledge transfer
2. Position (rank, role) in the organization
3. Personal responsibility
4. Job satisfaction
5. Empathic values and preferences
6. Effects of training (learning)
7. Personal experience in knowledge transfer
8. Loyalty to the organization

The expected reward for the transfer of knowledge is here understood through intangible forms such as acknowledgements of a successful transfer, praise, gratitude and appreciation expressed by the employer (Ajila & Abiola, 2004). It is quite certain that individuals who have these expectations will be more inclined to transfer their knowledge to others and vice versa. Managers need to be able to create these expectations, because they do not arise spontaneously and spontaneously, but are a reflection of the knowledge and skills of managing expectations. Low expectations of rewards will not successfully create knowledge transfers, as well as unrealistic and high ones that cannot be realized.

An employee who could transfer his / her knowledge to others starts from his / her position (place, rank, and role) in the organization. It tries to position its inputs and outputs in the process. What does he potentially gain and lose? Most often, it depends on whether the individual who is potentially transferring their knowledge is in a subordinate or superior role to the one to whom that knowledge is to be transferred (Baporikar, 2017; 2016a; 2016b and 2015). The more an employee is personally and directly responsible for the job, the more difficult it is to transfer their knowledge to others. He then estimates what they will gain and what they will lose if they pass on their knowledge to others. Responsibility for the job creates a side not only for the person who needs to transfer their knowledge but also for the person who needs to take them. This fear of job transfer occurs to the person who needs to take that knowledge due to possible skills shortages and adverse opportunities and causes for poor job performance, lack of communication skills and disabilities, and other factors. This is considered to be very important in controlling the situation of how the training was performed and what strategies will be used to transfer knowledge to preserve and maintain responsibility for the work done (Chen et al., 2004; Rowden & Conine, 2005). A more satisfied associate will more transfer their knowledge to others and vice versa. Therefore, management must always strive to enable trainees to apply the acquired knowledge in their workplaces to increase their satisfaction. Employees who cannot apply the acquired knowledge in their work are generally always dissatisfied. Not only will they not pass on this knowledge to others, but it will also deter them from engaging in training and thus create negative attitudes towards knowledge acquisition in organizations.

Empathic values and abilities of employees are directly related to the acquisition and transfer of knowledge. Donacefard and associates position emotional intelligence as one of the most productive forms of learning in organizations (Danacefard et al., 2012). These authors also include mental models in the dimensions of learning, placing the learning culture as a key feature of the corporate culture. In their opinion, emotional intelligence reflects on learning and transfer of knowledge through self-awareness, self-regulation, sympathy, social skills and self-stimulation of employees. In a larger study, it was demonstrated that managers who spread positive emotions and create an emotional landscape in the organization toward learning led to the acceptance of learning among all employees and the transfer of knowledge (Pinkley, 1990).

If the trainee did not acquire the expected knowledge himself, then how will he transfer it to others? The effects of training have a significant impact on the transfer of acquired knowledge. Employees transfer their knowledge related to their learning and acquisition only when intrinsically motivated (Chiaburu & Tekleab, 2005; Huysman, & Wit, 2004). Several studies so far confirm and imply that training is the most important factor in gaining knowledge. However, very few authors have demonstrated that the quality and effects of training also affect the success of knowledge transfer (Odigie & Li-Hua, 2008). More authors point to the need to emphasize the perception of the usefulness of training and its research, which depends on the extent to which the trainees will be able to monitor the contents of the training (Burke & Hutchins, 2007). Poor perceptions of training create low effects of the training and thus prevent the transfer of acquired knowledge (Baporikar, 2020).

Its members are not only loyal to the organization through time spent in the organization and by identifying their life goals and interests with those of the organization. They also demonstrate this loyalty through their willingness and ability to transfer their acquired knowledge to other members of that organization. In this way, the individual and the employee creates and reinforces his or her views that he or she is an active participant in the source of increasing organizational knowledge as primary capital (Baporikar, 2015). Individual participation in the creation of organizational knowledge through the transfer of personally acquired knowledge is one of the essential motives of this transfer (Lucas & Ogilvie, 2006). A higher level of devotion indicates a greater tendency to transfer knowledge to others.

FUTURE AREAS FOR RESEARCH

Knowledge transfer plays a significant role, but it is observed, for example, that introverted training participants are not inclined to transfer the acquired knowledge to their co-workers and team members, as they have no experience in doing so (Tharenou, 2010). There is no longitudinal research on the experience of training participants in knowledge transfer, which is crucial to ensure that the training and developments initiatives of an organization lead to multiplier effect and promote knowledge repositories. Another area for research is to design and develop methods and framework for the unquestionable predictive value of training self-evaluation in the acquisition, application and transfer of acquired knowledge. These research and results obtained from such studies can be very useful for decision-makers in engaging trainees for future training (Obach, 2003).

CONCLUSION

Developed workers are more likely to be promoted, take on far more difficult duties, and be able to earn more money. A well-groomed employee is better equipped to handle stress, anxiety, aggravation, and disputes. The growth and competency the organisation achieves are the benefits of training and development to the organisation. Workers who have received training are more likely to increase an organisation's profitability. Training and development of employees can increase a company's appeal and encourage others to associate with it. A business that values employee development typically has devoted workers who will advance through the ranks because of well-defined succession plans. Making a business competitive requires training and development. Therefore, training and development should be a crucial component of every organisation that wants to succeed and remain competitive. However, a training requirement analysis must be done for the training to be effective. For this to be implemented effectively, the involvement of the management is quite crucial for ensuring that the knowledge transfer and organizational learning occurs. In a similar vein, organisations must design staff development programmes that are in line with their strategic goals and objectives if they want to promote career development.

Funding

This research received no specific grant from any funding agency in the public, commercial, or not-for-profit sectors.

REFERENCES

Adeyemo, D. A., & Aremu, A. O. (1999). Career commitment among secondary school teachers in Oyo state, Nigeria: The Role of biographical mediators. *Nigerian Journal of Applied Psychology*, *5*(2), 184–194.

Ajila, C., & Abiola, A. (2004). Influence of Rewards on Workers Performance in an Organization. *Journal of Social Sciences*, *8*(1), 7–12. doi:10.1080/09718923.2004.11892397

Baporikar, N. (2015). Understanding professional development for educators. [IJSEM]. *International Journal of Sustainable Economies Management*, *4*(4), 18–30. doi:10.4018/IJSEM.2015100102

Baporikar, N. (Ed.). (2016a). *Management education for global leadership*. IGI Global.

Baporikar, N. (2016b). Lifelong learning in knowledge society. In *Impact of Economic Crisis on Education and the Next-Generation Workforce* (pp. 263–284). IGI Global. doi:10.4018/978-1-4666-9455-2.ch012

Baporikar, N. (2017). Knowledge transfer issues in teaching: Learning management. In *Innovation and Shifting Perspectives in Management Education* (pp. 58–78). IGI Global. doi:10.4018/978-1-5225-1019-2.ch003

Baporikar, N. (2020). Learning link in organizational tacit knowledge creation and dissemination. *International Journal of Sociotechnology and Knowledge Development*, *12*(4), 70–88. doi:10.4018/IJSKD.2020100105

Baporikar, N. (2021). Effect of Reward on Motivation and Job Satisfaction. *International Journal of Applied Management Sciences and Engineering*, *8*(1), 12–51. doi:10.4018/IJAMSE.2021010102

Baron, R. A. (1983). *Behavior in organizations*. Allyn & Bacon, Inc.

Basset-Jones, N., & Lloyd, G. F. (2005). Does Herzberg"s motivation theory have staying power? *Journal of Management Development*, *24*(10), 929–943. doi:10.1108/02621710510627064

Bishop, J. (1987). The recognition & Reward of Employee Performance. *Journal of Labor Economics*, *5*(4), S36–S56. doi:10.1086/298164

Burke, W. W. (2002). *Organizational Change: Theory and Practice*. Sage.

Campbell, J. P., & Pritchard, R. D. (1976). Motivation theory in industrial and organizational psychology. In M. D. Dunnette & L. M. Hough (Eds.), *Handbook of Industrial and Organizational Psychology* (pp. 63–130). Wiley.

Carraher, R., Gibson, A., & Buckley, R. (2006). Compensation in the Baltic and the USA. *Baltic Journal of Management*, *1*(1), 7–23. doi:10.1108/17465260610640840

Chen, T. Y., Chang, P. L., & Yen, C. W. (2004). A study of career needs, career development programs, job satisfaction and the turnover intensity of R & D personnel. *Career Development International*, *9*(4), 424–437. doi:10.1108/13620430410544364

Chen, Y., & Lou, H. (2002). Toward an understanding of the behavioral intention to use a groupware application. *Journal of Organizational and End User Computing*, *14*(4), 1–16. doi:10.4018/joeuc.2002100101

Chiaburu, D. S., & Tekleab, A. G. (2005). Individual and contextual influences on multiple dimensions of training effectiveness. *Journal of European Industrial Training*, *29*(8), 604–626. doi:10.1108/03090590510627085

Deeprose, D. (1994). *How to recognize and reward employees*. AMACOM.

Eby, L. T., Freeman, D. M., Rush, M. C., & Lance, C. E. (1999). Motivational bases of affective organizational commitment: A partial test of an integrative theoretical model. *Journal of Occupational and Organizational Psychology*, *72*(4), 463–483. doi:10.1348/096317999166798

Frey, B. (1997). On the Relationship between Intrinsic and Extrinsic Work Motivation. *International Journal of Industrial Organization*, *15*(4), 427–439. doi:10.1016/S0167-7187(96)01028-4

Gartner, K. N., & Nollen, S. D. (1989). Career experiences, perceptions of employment practices and psychological commitment to the organization. *Human Relations*, *42*(11), 975–991. doi:10.1177/001872678904201102

Harrison, R. (2000). *Employee Development*. Beekman Publishing.

Herzberg, F. (2003). *One more time: how do you motivate employees? Harvard Business Review on Motivating People*. Harvard Business School Press.

Huysman, M., & de Wit, D. (2004). Practices of managing knowledge sharing: Towards a second wave of knowledge management. *Knowledge and Process Management*, *2*(1), 81–92. doi:10.1002/kpm.192

Katz, R., & Van Maanan, J. (1977). The loci of work satisfaction: Job interaction and policy. *Human Relations*, *30*(5), 469–486. doi:10.1177/001872677703000505

Landy, F. J., & Becker, W. S. (1990). Motivation theory reconsidered. In B. M. Staw & L. L. Cummings (Eds.), *Work in Organizations* (pp. 1–38). Jai Press.

Lang, D. L. (1992). Organizational culture and commitment. *Human Resource Development Quarterly*, *2*(3), 191–196. doi:10.1002/hrdq.3920030211

Lawler, E. E. (2003). *Treat people right*. Jossey-Bass Inc. McGraw-Hill Irwin.

Locke, E. A. (1976). The nature and causes of job satisfaction. In M. D. Dunnette (Ed.), *Handbook of industrial and organizational psychology* (pp. 1297–1349). Rand McNally.

Lucas, L. M., & Ogilvie, D. (2006). Things are not always what they seem. How reputations, culture and incentives influence knowledge transfer. *The Learning Organization*, *13*(1), 7–24. doi:10.1108/09696470610639103

Luthans, F. (1998). Organizational Behavior. Boston: Irwin McGraw-Hill. Luthans, Fred, Harriette S. McCaul, Nancy G. Dodd (1985). Organizational Commitment: A Comparison of American, Japanese, and Korean Employees. *Academy of Management Journal*, *28*(1), 213–219. doi:10.2307/256069

Odigie, H. A., & Li-Hua, R. (2008). Unlocking the channel of tacit knowledge transfer. *The Learning Organization*, *32*(4), 124–141.

Tharenou, P. (2010). Training and development in organizations. In A. Wilkinson, N. Bacon, T. Redman, & S. Snell (Eds.), *The Sage handbook of human resource management* (pp. 155–172). Sage. doi:10.4135/9780857021496.n10

KEY TERMS AND DEFINITIONS

Business: Pertains broadly to commercial, financial, and industrial activities.

Challenges: Something that by its nature or character serves as a call to make special effort, a demand to explain, justify, or difficulty in a undertaking that is stimulating to one engaged in it.

Core Competences: Knowledge based technical and human abilities and skills.

Globalization: Worldwide integration and development, the process enabling financial and investment markets to operate internationally, largely because of deregulation and improved communications.

Government: The organization, machinery, or agency through which a political unit exercises authority and performs functions and which is usually classified according to the distribution of power within it. It is a political system by which are administered and regulated.

Knowledge Exchange: The act, process, or an instance of exchanging acquaintance with facts, truths, or principles, as from study or investigation for and including general erudition creating, involving, using, or disseminating special knowledge or information.

Management: Any act by an individual member on the behalf of a group, with the intent to get the group to meet better its goals. It includes acts, activities, or process of looking after and making decisions about something.

Motivation: The act or an instance of motivating, arousing desire to do, creating interest or drive by incentive or inducement. It is a psychological aspect that arouses, sustains and regulates human behavior.

Policy: Refers to guidelines as issued by the governance.

Stakeholder: A person with an interest or concern in something, especially in an organization or institution. Stakeholder is a member of a type of organization or system in which as a member or participant seen as having an interest in its success.

Strategies: Method chosen and plans made to bring about a desired future, achievement of a goals or solutions to a problem. Strategies are a result of choices made and a set of managerial decisions and actions that determine the long-term performance of a business enterprises.

Chapter 6
Into Action:
Effective Knowledge Transfer in Employee Training

Chelsea Craig
Adler University, USA

ABSTRACT

This chapter discusses the importance of knowledge transfer and the mechanisms that go into successfully translating training material on the job. The essential nature of successful knowledge transfer within modern organizations and the common pitfalls experienced are explained. This chapter explores trainee personality-based, motivational, and social factors that influence which forms of training are effective for them. Adult learning principles that apply to knowledge transfer within training are also explored. Situational, personal, and organizational barriers to successful knowledge transfer are outlined. Finally, the chapter walks the reader through each element of the training design structure that can enhance the effectiveness of training translation. This allows readers to walk through the training design process with successful strategies for improving knowledge transfer at the heart of their design.

INTO ACTION: EFFECTIVE KNOWLEDGE TRANSFER IN EMPLOYEE TRAINING

Training and development are an integral part of organizational functioning. Regardless of the industry, new employees must acquire the skills and knowledge they need to be successful in their roles, and current members of the organization need access to the tools they need to evolve within their career. Knowledge and information are vital intangible assets that must be continuously distributed to members. To remain competitive, organizations are constantly acquiring new information for better practices and ideas. Disseminating the organization's constantly evolving knowledge to the right people at the right time is only one step of this process – employees must be willing and able to put newly acquired information and skills to use in their role for the organization to benefit (Mambo & Smuts, 2022). When knowledge transfer in training occurs successfully, employees can practice new skills in their role that improve their performance. Ideally, the sharing of knowledge occurs organically amongst employees, and learning and growth become part of the organizational culture. The organization remains competitive in the industry and its members are prepared to take on new challenges.

When knowledge transfer through the training process is ineffective, organizations suffer the consequences. According the 2023 *Training* industry report, businesses in the United States spent $101.8 billion dollars on training and development (Frefield, 2023). However, recent studies have documented that 70% of employees do not feel that they have the skills they need to successfully perform their job, only 12% transferred the knowledge they obtained through training on the job, and only 25% felt that their organization's training programs were beneficial to overall performance (Glaveski, 2021). Ineffective training transfer is a costly crisis that increases turnover, leads to poor business decisions, and creates barriers to innovation.

To solve the prevalent problem of breakdowns in knowledge and training transfer, an organization must focus in on the factors within its control that can increase the translation of training to skill development. These factors occur both at the individual and organizational level, and include trainee personalities and learning style, organizational culture, and training program design. To design a training program that sets trainees up for success, it is important to consider the influence of each of these factors (Matthews, 2023). This chapter will explore the knowledge transfer process, employee traits and circumstances that influence motivation for knowledge transfer, how organizations store and disseminate information and how organizational culture effects the rate of knowledge transfer. Finally, we will also explore the process of designing a training program that encourages knowledge transfer and avoids common barriers.

Knowledge Transfer: Concepts and Core Components

Most organizations will need to efficiently distribute the knowledge acquired collectively about core organizational operations, goals and changes so employees will be adequately prepared for them. The need for efficient knowledge transfer occurs often when new employees are hired, or current employees change duties or positions. New projects and interests the organization chooses to take on will often require additional training and education. Within many industries, best practices are also changing and evolving in a way that mandates ongoing training and development for all employees.

Knowledge transfer must occur both during training and within the organization on a regular basis. Both situations require the creation, sharing and translation of information and skills into action. Knowledge creation, while vital to innovation in any field, is useless if the organization cannot apply it. An effective knowledge transfer process benefits both the growth of the individual and the organization as a whole (Mambo & Smuts, 2022).

The transfer of knowledge occurs primarily through different types of interaction between members and departments of the organization. These interactions may occur through written or digital communication, on the job or within a training session. Knowledge transfer involves learning, unlearning, and relearning to effectively adapt new information to a new or changing work environment. In turn, those who can apply learned information successfully may transfer their knowledge on to others (Rosellini & Hawamdeh, 2020).

The Importance of an Effective Knowledge Transfer Process

One of the key benefits of effectively transferring knowledge across the organizational team is that it fosters a knowledge-sharing culture. A knowledge-sharing culture is one where new hire are easily able to understand and apply primary concepts of their role, communication and feedback are frequent, and support is accessible. This leads to greater innovation and more rapid development of internal talent. Current employees are also more likely to be retained within the organization if they feel they can easily access the tools they need to excel.

Supporting individual growth through skill development and continuous learning is integral part of organizational evolution. If employees cannot successfully attain and implement new skills, the organization cannot function capably, and its members cannot grow their own skillsets. Nearly every organization or business has some form of training process to impart new skills and structures to its team members; however, only some find that their training efforts are consistently translated to the work environment. This lack of application of what is learned in a training program on the job is a common problem in many industries and harms everyone from the company itself to its management and employees (Grossman &Salas, 2011). Often, it is clear to leadership that enhanced training is needed, and vast resources are often dedicated to workshops, short courses and orientation programs that somehow fail to yield results in the workplace. The design of an effective training program, therefore, must focus on designing training that aligns individual and organizational goals to cultivate an effective learning experience that continues throughout one's career.

Into Action

The fortunate news is that the business world has begun to recognize that refining the knowledge transfer process is vital to organizational competitiveness. By placing the proper tools in the hands of all employees and ensuring that everyone has the confidence to use them, the entire organization can continue to seamlessly evolve within its rapidly changing sector. In today's fast-paced, interconnected culture, it is vital that organizations and their members can quickly adapt to new opportunities. Successful knowledge transfer enables employees to be cross-trained and advance to new roles, as well as allowing the organization to grow its workforce and take advantage of new talent.

The Knowledge Management Process

Knowledge management refers to the way an organization collects, stores, and disseminates its collective knowledge. Knowledge management systems (KMS) refer to the ways knowledge is shared between members of an organization (Isrialidis, 2021). An effective knowledge management process is crucial to ensuring that each member of the organization has the information they need to perform their duties effectively, as well as being able to communicate with other members and coordinate efforts. Effective knowledge management also means supporting the growth and development of talent to strengthen the organization, transferring newly acquired information and skills readily (Kaur, 2022).

The knowledge management process begins with an organization choosing how to effectively store its collective knowledge. Implicit knowledge is stored by members of the organization, through the procedures and practices that best serve them in their roles. The second part of the knowledge management process involves disseminating tacit information to members of the organization. An organization that encourages a culture of learning and readily sharing information with new and current members. Members feel supported in efforts to learn and expand their skills and have access to the tools they need to perform at their best. The fluid transfer of knowledge between members allows organizations to put their total informational resources to use (Kaur, 2022).

Research into the enhancers and barriers of the knowledge management process regarding effective healthcare practices indicates that organizational structure and culture play a key role in encouraging the transfer of acquired knowledge into practice. Factors that improve the distribution and implementation of organizational knowledge include trust, human relationships among management and staff, and motivation. However, a strict hierarchical structure that over-regulates the dissemination of knowledge amongst members can act as a barrier toward the quality of services (Radevic et al, 2023).

Organizations that are resistant to change, have rigid policies and a high degree of bureaucracy can be said to have a poor knowledge management system. A common flaw that leads to dysregulation in knowledge management is an organization that is overly siloed or process-driven; one that adopts elaborate processes through which information can be obtained that makes it difficult for members to access the information they need (Radevic et al, 2023). An open channel of communication regarding new information, beneficial skills and operational tools is vital for any organization to function effectively.

Different Types of Knowledge: Implicit, Explicit, and Tacit

Training and knowledge transfer often inherently occur in different forms, both during formal training processes and on the job. Knowledge can be disseminated in several different ways, often depending on the type of information. One common form of knowledge transfer involves explicit knowledge. Explicit knowledge refers to information that is able to be obtained through data, analyzed and presented, often in written or digital form. Such information is intended to be comprehended, recalled and applied as needed on the job. Examples of explicit knowledge transfer may include being given an employee handbook or having access to descriptions of company-wide policies and procedures. Knowledge that is obtained through education or other structured training is also considered explicit knowledge.

Explicit knowledge is typically selected and disseminated through training programs based on the needs of the organization. The information selected is often reusable and can be applied to solve problems in a number of similar situations. This type of information is often conveyed in training through lectures, print, electronic formats or demonstrations. Employees are more likely to apply explicit knowledge on the job when they feel it applies to their role and enhances their efficiency on the job, so it is often helpful to involve trainees in the process of selecting the explicit information to be covered in training (Rosellini & Hawamdeh, 2020).

Implicit knowledge refers to how operations, tasks or concepts are best applied. This may involve a discussion between coworkers about how to best perform a task. For example, a more seasoned employee may have created a system to effectively manage daily tasks and communicate that to a new hire. Additionally, many best practices and industry standards are types of implicit knowledge that can be carried between roles or organizations. Implicit knowledge can often be unconscious and can be developed through experience or experimentation (Gallemard, 2023).

Implicit knowledge can be more difficult to identify and define. The key to understanding which unspoken elements ingredients to the organization's success are comes through encouraging insight and self-reflection. This can occur through self-evaluation, performance reviews, or even conversations between colleagues

(Gallemard, 2023). Identifying and transmitting implicit knowledge begins with pinpointing the hidden strengths that one brings to their role and cultivating those strengths in others.

Tacit knowledge is knowledge that is obtained through experience. It can be difficult to describe or translate to others and is often acquired through hands-on training. Examples of tacit information can include the best way to make a certain recipe, or the type of muscle movements required to operate a machine. Tacit knowledge can often be the missing element that makes a skill feel natural and evokes a sense of flow on the job (Rosellini & Hawamdeh, 2020(.

One might ask how it is possible to "train" skills that are not easily defined or neatly organized. Most often, implicit knowledge is disseminated through direct interactions through mentorships, peers, supervisors, and other colleagues. These interactions tend to be individualized and based on personal, first-hand experience. To encourage the sharing of implicit knowledge within an organization, it can be helpful for leaders to encourage trust and openness through frequent visual and verbal contact with employees (Gallemard, 2023). Apprenticeships and shadowing experiences also allow students to pick up vital tacit skills while obtaining their credentials.

An Inside Job: Individual Factors That Affect Knowledge Transfer

Successful knowledge transfer requires the conscious consideration of all interacting factors that influence the knowledge transfer process. These include intrinsic factors of the trainee, such as motivation and learning style. Knowledge transfer is also heavily influenced by external factors that exist in the training and work environment, as well as management styles and the organizational culture. Finally, the design of the training program itself can either help or hinder the knowledge transfer process. Common barriers to effective knowledge transfer include a lack of time and flexibility to conduct a training course, an unsupportive work environment that is not conducive to skill transfer, and a sense that new skills or information will not be effective or helpful in the work environment (Grossman & Salas, 2011). We will explore these barriers further in the chapter.

The personal makeup and situational disposition of the trainee are primary elements that influence the effectiveness of knowledge and skill transfer. Whether a trainee is willing and able to incorporate their training material on the job is influenced by their personality, their type and degree of motivation and their capacity to learn the information in the format it is presented. When considering the personality of the trainee, we can understand their primary source of motivation and emphasize that during training. We can also understand how to harness both intrinsic and extrinsic sources of motivation to encourage employees to obtain and utilize training (Rowold, 2007). Finally, an effective training program utilizes what we know about adult learning to impart knowledge and supports trainees as they practice new skills.

Personality Traits and Their Interaction With Knowledge Transfer

Each trainee that attends a training program has an implied desire to learn new skills and information. However, whether this motivation will be maintained and translated into practice on the job depends partially on the personal makeup of the trainee. People with different personality traits sustain this motivation through the learning process under different conditions. For example, one person may feel more supported in practicing their training with frequent supervisory check-ins, while another may feel a greater sense of autonomy with less direct supervision.

Within the study of personality, one of the popular models to examine is the Five Factor Model. This model is frequently utilized in human resource management research to consider the interactions between organizations and personalities. Recent studies considering the relationships between Five Factor Model traits and motivation to transfer new skills in the workplace have determined significant correlations between these traits and rates of knowledge transfer (Rowold, 2007).

One of these traits is conscientiousness. Conscientiousness refers to one's desire to do the right thing, live cohesively with others and observe a social and moral code. People with a high degree of conscientiousness are more likely to be motivated to apply new skills when they see those skills as valuable to the goals of the organization or to helping them become more effective in their role. Trainees with a high degree of conscientiousness are also more likely to set high goals for themselves and monitor their own progress (Rowold, 2007).

Trainees who have a higher degree of extraversion also have a high degree of intrinsic motivation regarding their desire to improve their performance through the acquisition of new skills. Extraverted trainees respond well to interactive training experiences and often prefer direct feedback and peer and management support as they progress in their role. They also tend to have more confidence in their ability to practice new skills and feel optimistic about their own ability to succeed (Ng & Ahmed, 2018).

Agreeableness has been debated in prior research with regard to its impact on motivation to transfer knowledge and skills to the work environment. While some studies suggest that it has little correlation with the effectiveness of knowledge transfer, some recent studies have indicated that it does act as a supportive factor (Ng & Ahmed, 2018). Trainees who have a higher degree of agreeableness often value being helpful and competent in their role and may be more motivated by a desire to offer more support to others through enhanced skill acquisition (Ng & Ahmed, 2018).

There has been some evidence to suggest that neuroticism can hinder the knowledge transfer process. Indeed, it seems clear that trainees with a higher degree of neuroticism are less likely to feel confident in practicing new skills in their work environment and are more likely to require a high degree of support. Conversely, trainees with a greater degree of emotional stability are less likely to fear a loss in value if they experience a learning curve and are more confident in their ability to become successful through practice. Finally, highly neurotic trainees are often less likely to seek support from peers or supervisors due to their fear of losing value (Rowold, 2007).

Finally, openness refers to the depth of one's thought process, degree of creativity and desire to obtain new experiences and knowledge. A trainee with a high degree of openness is likely to be intrinsically motivated by their desire to diversify their own knowledge and skillset (Rowold, 2007). These employees are additionally suited to impart knowledge to their peers and conduct training in turn. Finally, due to their intellectual curiosity, such trainees have a higher absorptive capacity that enhances knowledge transfer to the workplace.

Motivation to Learn

Beyond the influence of relatively stable personality traits, certain dispositional and environmental factors additionally contribute to the knowledge transfer success rate. One primary influence is the trainee's motivation to learn and apply new skills and information. This degree of motivation is often influenced by how the employees view themselves and their ability to learn and apply new skills. It is also informed by the perception of benefits to mastering new skills. Finally, one's attitude toward learning and career development in general affects how likely a trainee is to practice and retain new information (Rhodes et al, 2008).

Self-efficacy refers to one's perception of one's own competence regarding a particular skillset. A trainee's degree of confidence in their ability to learn, understand and successfully apply new training can be influenced by traits such as age, social environment, and current career outlook (Burke & Hutchins, 2007)). When a trainee feels that they are less cognitively agile than they once were, feels unsupported by their colleagues, or do not foresee a long career involving the use of their current skillset, they will be less motivated to absorb material presented in mandatory training, as well as less likely to embrace voluntary training. Another personal factor that has shown consistent correlation with motivation for employee development is one's prior experience with training; whether it felt positive and necessary or stressful and tedious in the past often informs the attitude of the trainee toward future experiences (Burke & Hutchins 2007).

Another, less-considered variable effecting employee motivation to develop through training is the social environment within which the trainee is embedded in. Do they belong to a culture that identifies heavily with professionalism and achievement, or do they feel that their energy is best invested elsewhere? Have they come from an environment that values or condescends learning and career growth? Finally, it is also important to consider whether the trainee's social environment supports ongoing access to learning opportunities and affords the time and energy to focus on learning (Rhodes et al, 2008). It is much more difficult to focus on understanding and implementing new training if one has inconsistent transportation to attend or is too overburdened to focus on understanding new material.

Trainees' perception of the information or skillset being presented is also an influential factor in whether the material will be utilized in their work environment or not. Information that is presented with clear benefits to the trainee at work, such as by increasing efficiency or using new resources, they will be subsequently more motivated to put it into practice. Additionally, employees who identify with their organization's values and have long-term career goals will be more likely to embrace new training and apply more effort to refine their skills (Burke & Hutchins, 2007)).

Adult Learning Principles: Fortifying the Learning Process

How a trainee learns- and under what conditions- is another dynamic and powerful variable in the knowledge transfer process. A key tenant of adult learning is that, essentially, there is no one overarching way for adults to learn effectively. One's learning style is incredibly personal, and for adults, it is additionally impacted by prior experiences on the job, in the educational system and in their personal lives (Dwyer, 2004). While some adults may respond well to a short lecture or demonstration, others may need to practice new skills hands-on to understand them. More extroverted trainees may benefit more from group-based activities during training, while an online course might be a better fit for more reserved trainees. There is no one "right way" to conduct instruction; a blending of methods or multiple options of modality can help trainees learn in a way that works for them.

It is key to understand one's audience and incorporate their personal needs and experiences into the objectives of the training program. While a universal set of objectives is key to ensuring the needs of the organization are met, giving trainees some autonomy in the choice and presentation of material communicates respect and mutual understanding. Giving trainees a voice in what is important for them to learn to achieve mutual goals is more likely to motivate them to learn new information. Additionally, when adult learners can customize their experience based on their learning style and circumstances, it gives more employees access to effective learning. Different learners with different strengths will have a more equal chance to participate in evolving with the organization (Dwyer, 2004).

While learning stye may vary significantly for adults, some central elements have been identified as generally helpful for large groups. Aside from building autonomy into the training process, individual attention and feedback are often helpful when people are learning at different rates. Personal attention may be needed when one trainee is struggling with a certain concept that others have mastered, so they are not left behind. Another useful strategy is to involve learning through teaching by using peer-led training sessions or discussion groups. This interactive style of training allows more advanced trainees to practice their own skills by training the next set, reinforcing what they have recently learned.

While personalizing the training experience is ideal, one must also consider whether certain methods are appropriate for the material being discussed (Dwyer, 2004). This is where instructors and course designers must strike a balance between catering to different learning styles and meeting the training needs of the organization. For instance, it is difficult to teach a complex surgical procedure through an online course, or to learn to operate a new vehicle through a lecture. It can be helpful to blend essential elements of the training with segments that are more suited to being personalized. This might look like a mixture of modalities, such as an online course combined with an in-person skills training seminar.

Another powerful tool that frequently enhances adult learning experience is called interval training. Interval training is a way to structure a training program into short segments that are immediately put into practice. This practice segment is followed by a follow-up session involving mutual discussion between supervisors and trainees. Interval training was introduced as a way to combat the "forgetting curve"- a pattern common among adult learners to immediately begin to gradually forget a large amount of new information they have recently learned all at once (Dwyer, 2004).

Organizational Factors: Moving the Learning Process From "I" to "We"

There are many organizational factors that impact the knowledge transfer process as well. An organizational culture and its approach to employee learning can impact the trainee experience. Trainees are more likely to retain and apply knowledge when they are in an environment that encourages them to think critically about new concepts and practice skills until they are fully mastered.

An organizational culture that incentivizes employees to embark on additional training and acknowledges progress is one that trainees feel more comfortable and motivated in. It is important for an organization to recognize and reward individual efforts to broaden their skillset and transfer those skills to others. Additionally, encouraging group knowledge-sharing and peer training creates an environment where trainees feel empowered to take their skills to the next level.

The relationship between the organization and its trainees is also important when designing an effective training program. Knowledge transfer occurs most effectively when trainees have a comfortable and accessible environment to learn in, when their individual needs are considered and when new information is easily available to them (Rhodes et al, 2008).

Building a Culture of Trust

A culture of trust refers to the relationship between organizational supervisors, management and employees. This type of organizational culture encourages knowledge sharing between employees and distributes new knowledge rapidly in accessible forms (Sajaghi & Najafi, 2013). This can include presentations, training courses, internal magazines and formal meetings.

This type of culture is one where employees feel readily able to access information and skills, share information amongst each other and feel supported by upper management in their development process. This type of organizational culture practices transparency and goes out of its way to invest time, effort and resources into employee growth (Sanjaghi & Najafi, 2013). A culture of trust is one that values and demonstrates respect for the growth potential of its employees.

It has become clear through recent research that the degree of social support trainees receive is a large determinant of whether they are confident and motivated to apply new skills. While a lack of supervisory availability can spell disaster in the knowledge transfer process, support from peers and management often predicts better utilization of training.

Lost in Translation: Improving Contextual Similarity Between the Training Environment and Work Environment

Another organizational factor that typically creates barriers to successful knowledge transfer is the lack of contextual similarity between the training experience that a new skill is practiced in and the work environment itself. When employees practice a new skillset under one set of conditions that differ significantly from those they work in, it is much more difficult to translate those skills while suddenly introducing new, previously unencountered variables. Another common pitfall in the knowledge transfer process is that the information trainees acquire does not fit their particular role (Lim, 2000)

It is frustrating for trainees when an organization implements new procedures or requirements that do not fit the role or cause additional difficulty on the job (Lim 2000). This is why it is vital for training program designers to work with trainees and organizational leaders to determine which skills are actually needed and desired to enhance performance. This can be accomplished through brainstorming sessions that include new hires, current employees and organizational leaders.

Encouraging Growth and Change

Just as the workplace needs to be conducive to the new skills trainees are learning, the organizational culture itself needs to be open to its own growth process. A culture that praises adaptation is often much more receptive to new practices. Some organizational cultures struggle to adapt to new processes when change is viewed as difficult or complex. Employees accustomed to business-as-usual in a stagnant environment are often less open to adopting new procedures and absorbing additional information.

Organizational leaders can alleviate resistance to change by demonstrating the immediate benefits of utilizing new information (Martinelli et al, 2023). For instance, training in a new medical procedure may involve a demonstration or practice with new instruments. When trainees can see the benefits of a new skill for themselves, they often become more invested in pursuing it.

It can also be beneficial for trainers to offer trainees the opportunity to experiment with new procedures before adopting them on a regular basis. This can also help trainees see the benefits of the new procedure firsthand without the pressure of implementing it permanently. The experimentation process also allows trainees to gain mastery of a new skill before it becomes a regular part of their duties.

A culture that encourages internal growth through the dissemination of new information, training and skills that develop in the field also encourages motivation to learn on an individual level. Organizations can encourage this desire to grow through cultivating ample opportunities to share knowledge. This can include organizing social gatherings, including a reward system to encourage training and knowledge sharing, and a thorough orientation for new hires to the knowledge management systems in use (Israilidis et al, 2021).

Designing a Truly Effective Training Program

The design and implementation of a training program is a huge investment for any organization. As such, it is important to ensure that it is utilized by trainees to meet the organization's goals and enhance their own professional growth. To design a training course that yields a high adoptability rate, several factors must be first taken into consideration. Who are the trainees, and what personal or environmental barriers exist for them? What is motivating them to obtain additional training? What skills do they need, and how can they be taught efficiently?

The organization itself must also examine its values. Historically, has innovation and change been encouraged or avoided? If the culture has been slower to adopt new ideas in the past, it may need to take additional care in reassuring team members of the benefits of a new direction. Finally, the organization needs to consider the degree to which it is fostering trust and transparency amongst its members.

Finally, the work environment must be considered in terms of how conducive it is to the practice of new skills or procedures. Individual roles should also be examined closely to ensure that new information applies to those receiving it. It is also important to ensure that trainees will have access to peers and supervisors as they begin practicing new skills and receive regular feedback as they progress.

The Needs of the Many: Choosing Focal Points

Once the climate is amenable to knowledge transfer, one can begin designing a training course by identifying what information needs to be disseminated to particular trainees. When selecting focal points for training, including current employees and new hires who will be participating in the course for can be incredibly beneficial. This enhances trainee motivation by harnessing their professional interests and validating their on-the-job needs. Informed by organizational goals, these discussions can serve as a filter to capture the elements trainees need and value (Awais Bhatti & Kaur, 2010).

It is important to begin to consider the goals of the training program for both the organization and its trainees before the process begins. Precious time that could be spent engaging with new skills can be eaten up by goal-setting discussions if the program is already underway (Uzialko, 2023).

Finally, one must also consider the expectations trainees have for the training program. Pre-training discussions should include a clear outline of the results trainees will have when they utilize new skills on the job, and how they will assist them in their specific role. Highlighting specific personal benefits for trainees to learn a new skillset, such as career growth, lets trainees feel individually invested in it (Hajjar et al, 2018).

Personalization: Consider the Human Factors

Additional training is useless if trainees cannot access it or cannot learn information in the way it is presented to them. This is why it is important to consider the personal barriers trainees may face and work to resolve them. When considering the characteristics of a training group, it is important to determine accessibility needs. Are there trainees who have a disability, or face transportation barriers? Are they unable to attend a multi-day seminar due to family obligations? Working with trainees to find a modality that works for them demonstrates support for the individual in their career growth process. It also allows the organization to benefit from the talents of employees with a variety of backgrounds (Rhodes et al, 2007).

Setting the Stage With Expectations

Once a set of goals for the training program has been established and individual needs have been taken into account, training program designers can begin to consolidate training goals and expectations for trainees (Wilson & Kelly, 2022). These expectations may include certain attendance requirements, progress evaluations or proficiency testing. Additionally, formal communication of the goals of the training program helps to prime trainees, letting them mentally prepare for the learning experience ahead (Martinelli et al, 2023).

Trainees may also benefit from an itinerary of periodic benchmark evaluations, team meetings or required examinations that will be incorporated into the training process (Martinelli et al, 2023). When trainees are aware of how the course will be paced, when opportunities to check in will occur and when they are expected to acquire certain competencies, they will be better able to plan ahead for extra skill practice or study they may need.

Preparing for Trainee Success

As previously mentioned, training instructors must be prepared to recognize and work with the diverse variety of communication needs, learning styles and circumstances trainees enter the environment with. It is crucial to form a plan for any adjustments to the course trainees may need to attend or learn effectively. One way to achieve this is by utilizing a variety of learning modalities (Martinelli et al, 2023). These may include both online and in-person audio and visual instruction as well as group discussion, peer-led practice and on-the-job training sessions. A socially responsible organization will also recognize and attempt to assist with any transportation or language barriers that may exist for certain trainees, assuring equal access to opportunities for talented employees, regardless of personal background or circumstance.

Creating opportunities for on-the-job training is of particular importance. Many trainees find that this method is both a more convenient and motivating way to practice applying new skills. Not only are trainees already present in the training environment, but it also allows them to experience the applicability and benefits of applying their training firsthand.

Ensure Appropriate and Applicable Goals Are in Focus

One of the most common reasons knowledge and skills disseminated through training programs are not readily applied on the job is that there is little opportunity to do so. Far too often, training programs are designed strictly by human resource professionals who do not have direct experience in the work environment and are not as familiar with the protocols and objectives the department may require. As such, it is highly recommended that managers, current employees and site supervisors have direct input into the focal points of the training course (Glaveski, 2021).

Those who are directly immersed in the work environment are in the best position to determine its needs, as well as how to best implement new procedures. They are also familiar with the most appropriate times for shadowing and hands-on demonstrations.

Providing Support During and Post Training

One of the greatest opportunities to nurture the effectiveness of the knowledge transfer process is by providing ongoing support to trainees as they experiment with and begin applying new skills. Support from supervisors and peers throughout the process allows trainees to feel like supported team members. By providing support, trainees often feel more comfortable in the knowledge that there is always somewhere to turn to ask questions or communicate when they need help applying new concepts on the job,

Support can be provided through ongoing check-ins with trainees throughout the training process. These discussions can help trainers evaluate trainee progress in mastering new skills and track their growth, as well as offer an opportunity for trainees to discuss any difficulties they are having. Supervisors can be more aware of trainees who might require additional review or practice to succeed and provide extra attention early in the process. This ensures that no one is left behind to the degree where extensive catch-up is required.

Review: Knowledge Transfer Is a Team Effort

When designing a training program, it is vital that the skills and knowledge being disseminated is successfully applied in the work environment. To ensure that training courses are making an impact in the workplace, it is crucial to make both the needs of trainees and the goals of the organization equally important considerations.

Tools for encouraging a successful knowledge transfer process include understanding different trainee personalities and finding the most effective sources of motivation for them. Knowing why a person has chosen to undertake additional training and what their goals are is key to cultivating and maintaining motivation throughout the training process. Understanding a trainee's individual personality makeup also helps to inform program designers of potential modes of instruction best suited for them.

Encouraging knowledge transfer also requires one to understand that adults have a wide variety of learning styles and finding ways to cater to each. This may involve utilizing different modalities of presentation and practice, so each trainee has the opportunity to learn new information in a way that works for them. Additionally, training program designers need to reckon with the reality of certain barriers trainees may face and build flexibility into their course to ensure equitable access.

Setting appropriate goals for the training program involves considering the realities of the work environment and ensuring that the skills being taught will translate into on-the-job benefits. Trainees should emerge into a work environment where they can readily apply new skills and see their benefits firsthand. Ensuring that applicable and realistic goals are set can be achieved through discussion with current employees and managers as well as with trainees. This can allow for a merging of organizational goals and individual career goals. Finally, trainees should be actively supported through direct and frequent interaction with and feedback from training supervisors to ensure that they remain on course and receive additional support as needed.

Successful knowledge transfer includes a combination of enhancing motivation for acquiring new skills and creating ample opportunity for their practice. Both of these elements, when baked into the design of the training program itself, can dramatically improve the benefits of a training program for the organization as well as encouraging the growth of its members. For an organization to thrive, its team must constantly grow its own skillset. Remaining competitive becomes synonymous with successful ongoing training of new and current members- keeping them at the forefront and evolving as a team.

REFERENCES

Awais Bhatti, M., & Kaur, S. (2010). The role of individual and training design factors on training transfer. *Journal of European Industrial Training, 34*(7), 656–672. doi:10.1108/03090591011070770

Burke, L. A., & Hutchins, H. M. (2007). Training Transfer: An Integrative Literature Review. *Human Resource Development Review*, *6*(3), 263–296. Advance online publication. doi:10.1177/1534484307303035

Dwyer, R. J. (2004). Employee development using adult education principles. *Industrial and Commercial Training*, *36*(2), 79–85. doi:10.1108/00197850410524851

Freifeld, L. (2023, November 15). *2023 Training Industry Report*. Training. https://trainingmag.com/2023-training-industry-report/#:~:text=final%20purchase%20decision-TRAINING%20EXPENDITURES,the%20payroll%20of%20small%20companies

Gallemard, J. (2023, August 25). Implicit Knowledge - What is It & How to Transfer in The Workplace. *Smart Tribune*. https://blog.smart-tribune.com/en/implicit-knowledge

Glaveski, S. (2021, January 20). *Where Companies Go Wrong with Learning and Development*. Harvard Business Review. https://hbr.org/2019/10/where-companies-go-wrong-with-learning-and-development

Grossman, R., & Salas, E. (2011). The transfer of training: What really matters. *International Journal of Training and Development*, *15*(2), 103–120. doi:10.1111/j.1468-2419.2011.00373.x

Hajjar, E. L. (2018). Exploring the Factors That Affect Employee Training Effectiveness: A Case Study in Bahrain. *SAGE Open*, *8*(2). doi:10.1177/2158244018783033

Israilidis, J., Siachou, E., & Kelly, S. (2021) Why organizations fail to share knowledge: an empirical investigation and opportunities for improvement. *Information Technology & People, 34*(5), 1513-1539.

Kaur, G. (2022, February 9). *What is knowledge management? definition, process, examples, strategy, best practices, and Trends*. Spiceworks. https://www.spiceworks.com/collaboration/content-collaboration/articles/what-is-knowledge-management/

Lim, D. H. (2000). Training design factors influencing transfer of training to the workplace within an international context. *Journal of Vocational Education and Training*, *52*(2), 243–258. doi:10.1080/13636820000200118

Mambo, S., & Smuts, H. (2022). The impact of organisational culture on knowledge management: The case of an international multilateral organisation. *EPiC Series in Computing*, 184–171. doi:10.29007/bkxv

Martinelli, M., Silverman, J., & Helou, J. E. (2023, September 1). *Design tactics for training transfer*. ATD. https://www.td.org/magazines/td-magazine/design-tactics-for-training-transfer

Matthews, P. (2023, September 22). *The Case for Learning Transfer*. People Alchemy. https://peoplealchemy.com/blog/the-case-for-learning-transfer/

Ng, K. H., & Ahmad, R. (2018). Personality traits, social support, and training transfer: The mediating mechanism of motivation to improve work through learning. *Personnel Review, 47*(1), 39–59. doi:10.1108/PR-08-2016-0210

Radević, I., Dimovski, V., Lojpur, A., & Colnar, S. (2023). Quality of healthcare services in focus: The role of knowledge transfer, hierarchical organizational structure and trust. *Knowledge Management Research and Practice, 21*(3), 525–536. doi:10.1080/14778238.2021.1932623

Rhodes, J., Lok, P., Yu-Yuan Hung, R., & Fang, S. C. (2008). An integrative model of organizational learning and social capital on effective knowledge transfer and perceived organizational performance. *Journal of Workplace Learning, 20*(4), 245–258. doi:10.1108/13665620810871105

Rosellini, A., & Hawamdeh, S. (2020). Tacit knowledge transfer in training and the inherent limitations of using only quantitative measures. *Proceedings of the Association for Information Science and Technology, 57*(1). 10.1002/pra2.272

Rowold, J. (2007). The impact of personality on training-related aspects of motivation: Test of a longitudinal model. *Human Resource Development Quarterly, 18*(1), 9–31. doi:10.1002/hrdq.1190

Sanjaghi, M., Akhavan, P., & Najafi, S. (2013). Fostering knowledge sharing behavior: The role of organizational culture and trust. *International Journal of the Academy of Organizational Behavior Management, 2*(5), 9-33.

Uzialko, A. (2023, October 23). *How to develop a New Hire Training Plan*. Business News Daily. https://www.businessnewsdaily.com/15839-new-hire-training.html

Wilson, T., & Kelly, S. (2022, November 30). *Barriers to effective training and development*. https://strategichrinc.com/barriers-to-effective-training/

Chapter 7
Reinforcing Employee Motivation Through L&D:
Proposed Organization Development Intervention Model

Deepak Sharma
Narsee Monjee Institute of Management Studies, Bengaluru, India

Mahima Guwalani
https://orcid.org/0009-0009-4145-5486
Narsee Monjee Institute of Management Studies, Bengaluru, India

ABSTRACT

Planning of training and development activities needs to be done in such a way so that it triggers employee interest, on the one hand, and builds organizational capabilities leading to organisational effectiveness, on the other hand. In this post-pandemic-affected business world where traditional work and work relationships have changed with emerging gig workforce leading to creation of new kinds of work environment and employment relationships, there is a need to re-orient, reskill, and upskill the workforce in a different manner than used to happen. Accordingly, the deliverables for business, leadership, and HR have changed. Planned change for ensuring training interventions to work involves understanding assumptions of adult learning and use of technology in training process and system to facilitate right training interventions leading to organisational renewal. The chapter analyses a training and development system and its role in employee motivation as well as comprehensive OD intervention tool with the help of two broad themes.

DOI: 10.4018/979-8-3693-1674-0.ch007

INTRODUCTION

Training refers to "the systematic accretion of skills, command, concepts or mindset leads to improve performance" (Lazazzara and Bombelli 2011).

When training & development activities are planned in such a way that leads to enhancing of organizational capabilities leading to organisational effectiveness, it may be considered as an OD intervention. Defined in simple terms, an OD intervention is a planned, participative change effort. OD intervention involve effective and collaborative management of organizational culture. Employees in an organization would only be motivated towards training and development activities when there exists right training culture where participants feel that training activities lead to real change in behaviour of employees and application of training on the job involves not only support for training programmes but diagnosis into factors that would create interest in assumptions of learning & training. The intrinsic motivation of participants also needs to be taken into account. It may also involve looking deeper into practices that would facilitate learning as far as training interventions for adult learners are concerned.

If knowledge workers were to be motivated to keep their learning ability intact on the job, their intrinsic motivation needed to be triggered by making them realise that they were making improvement & going on growth path and task of applying learning on the job was meaningful (Pollock, Jefferson and Wick, 2015).

Baldwin et al. (1991) asserted that employees with higher amount of pre-training motivation on the basis of their interest and willingness to attend training had greater learning outcomes in comparison to employees who had lower pre-training motivation.

Adult learners' interest in training may not automatically be triggered but it involves exploration of conditions under which training & development may be perceived to be interesting, and of value-addition to learner. Similarly as covid had created need for online training, a question arose how organisational renewal may be brought in by looking into factors such as enhanced motivation for participants as far as training is concerned and also introspection as to what leads to better learning outcomes. There are many obstacles to implementing effective training interventions. One of the main obstacles is that designing programmes which appear interesting, relevant and also actually effective might be extremely difficult within a large & ever-changing corporate environment (Schmude, 2023). With new technological development and altered economic circumstances comes a continuous need to adjust training methods. This requires training to be an adaptable process, with programmes continuously being evaluated in order to keep them relevant. Moreover, employees' individual learning styles and preferences must be taken into account to increase their engagement with the training material as well as retention of such resources. Interactive elements such as hands-on exercises and simulations be included in training. Through this more dynamic, flexible approach to training organizations can also prepare their employees with skills capable of handling complexities related to algorithmic decision making.

Training programmes in the corporate world have long been accustomed to knowledge acquisition. However, people are increasingly agreeing that only providing theoretical knowledge in training is not enough. The new paradigm puts its primary emphasis on enabling practical skills which directly enable an organisation to make decisions and solve problems. This represents not only a change in content, but also one of method. Learning has become much more interactive and application oriented(Mandi et al., 2023).

The themes discussed here would be further examined in review of the literature.

Review of the Literature

Pink (2008) worked on motivation and explored that for most individuals the intrinsic desire to attain self-satisfaction as well as self-efficacy was much more motivating in comparison to what constitutes extrinsic reward like money and position.

There was evidence that if an individual's efforts were ignored it was a big source of de-motivation (Ariely, 2011).

Another source of destruction of intrinsic motivation was lack of acknowledgement. If individuals need to apply their learnings their efforts need to get acknowledged. The critical area for professionals is that if employees are to be encouraged to make efforts to apply their learning then certainly it needs to be ensured that their effort are acknowledged and achievements recognized. It has been seen that historically departments entrusted with training have not been doing enough to tap the intrinsic motivation of participants by ensuring that participants receive recognition as they put in efforts towards application of what they have learnt in training while they go back on the job. In other words, acknowledgement of achievement may be considered as integral part of employee learning experience(Pollock, Jefferson and Wick, 2015).

For large number of people, expertise on a skill or concept works as a reward in itself. Starting life as infants, human beings manifest a high sense of intrinsic motivation to learn (Pasupathi, 2013). The drive to learn is fairly persistent and adults continue to learn throughout their life and also that there is no upper age limit to learn. Adults have a tendency to look at learning tasks with a pragmatic viewpoint. "Adults need to know why they need to learn something before undertaking to learn it" (Knowles, Holton, & Swanson, 2011).

Expectancy Model of motivation was developed as a way to explain what motivated employees (Vroom, 1994). Vroom came out with a proposal that effort is proportional to motivation and that motivation in organisations was the result of three factors:

- Expectancy—the expectation that the new approach will improve performance
- Instrumentality—the expectation that improved performance will be rewarded
- Valence—the relative value of the reward for the individual

Three factors largely determine whether employees in organization are motivated to transfer and apply their learning:

- The extent to which employees believe that application of new skills would lead to improvement in their performance;
- The extent to which they believe that improvement in performance would be recognized and rewarded; and
- The extent to which they value the potential rewards and recognition that may come their way through such efforts

Two additional factors also contribute to employee motivation. The first is the employee's personal confidence in his ability of adaptability and improvement.

Dweck (2007) referred to concept of growth mindset—employees who very strongly believe in their ability to grow and change—are more motivated and more likely to go forward with application of new learning, than those who feel they are victims of their environment etc. The extent to which the learners were prepared to participate in the training to begin with may also have impact on motivation. Training and development department have to ensure that vigilant, and continuous performance support is available after traditional course is complete. Such support may improve participant's success possibilities, may enhance participant motivation, lead to extension of learnings, provide possibilities of acceleration of learning transfer, and finally may lead to enhanced performance. Participant's confidence in his or her ability to transfer learning on the job may also influence motivation to transfer the learnings from training.

Many research studies point out that manager & peer support may be vital for training, along with employee motivation to participate in training programmes. Critical success factors may be right & positive attitude among peers, managers, and employees about participation in training activities; managers' and peers' openness as well as willingness to provide information to participants about how they may utilise the knowledge, skills, or behaviours learned in training programmes to perform their jobs more meaningfully & effectively; and opportunities for trainees to use content learnt during training in their jobs(Rouiller and I. Goldstein, 1993; Noe and J. Colquitt, 2002).

If it is workable, employees maybe offered a choice of kind of training programmes they want to attend. Employees need to digest how actual training assignments are made, to maximize their motivation to learn. Research studies point out that providing trainees a choice towards kind of programs they may attend and then living upto those choices maximize employee motivation to learn. Offering employees choices but later not necessarily fulfilling them or living upto them can undermine employee motivation to learn(Quinones, 1995; Baldwin, R. J. Magjuka and B. T. Loher, 1991).

Noe (2023) asserts that managers need to work towards following areas for ensuring that trainee motivation increases at workplace:

1. Providing job related information & resources, and other work aids vital for employees to use new skills or behaviour even before they participate in training programs.
2. Spreading positive word of mouth about the company's training programs to employees.
3. Employees need to be told that they are doing a good job as they use training resources in their job
4. Work group members need to be encouraged to collaborate with each other in trying to use new skills by soliciting feedback, sharing of training experiences & situations in which training was useful
5. Employees to be provided space and opportunities for practice and application of new skills or behaviour within their work

Individual traits, input, output, consequences, and feedback have a high impact on the motivation to learn. Motivation to learn may be considered as participant's desire to learn the content of training programmes(Bauer, K. Orvis, K. Ely, and E. Surface, 2016; Noe, 1986; Noe and J. Colquitt, 2002).

Many researches point out that motivation to learn is linked to knowledge gained, behaviour changes, or skill acquisition as a result of training(Baldwin, R. T. Magjuka, and B. T. Loher, 1991; Tannenbaum, Mathieu, Salas and Cannon-Bowers, 1991; Colquitt, LePine and Noe, 2000).

Other than focusing on the factors of person traits, input, output, consequences, and feedback in determining whether training is the best remedy for a performance problem, managers need to take into account such factors when selecting employees for attending a training program. These factors are linked to the employees' motivation to learn.

Kulkarni et al. (2023) in a survey of 812 randomly selected respondents from the organization in Belagavi, found factors such as learning goals, social interaction, time management and personalization had a vital role to play in motivation of respondents and building training intention in the online environment, and the successful realization of the training goals.

McKinsey and Company, in a survey found that 375 million employees may be required to change their profession, or influenced by digitalization, may need to acquire new skills by 2030. In addition, 87% of the workforce would be facing skill gaps and also lack motivation to upskill (Manyika et al., 2017). Employees need to equip themselves with the necessary skills for effective performance in the online work environment (Rahman et al., 2022; Yang, 2023). Workplaces are using online or remote training for employee training(Rahman et al., 2022). For conceptualizing and designing online content, organizations need to do analysis of their workplace culture, content of courses, delivery mode, tools used for digitalization, and certain other factors to ensure that employees are motivated as they receive the training (Antony et al., 2023; Chatterjee & Kar, 2020; Malik et al., 2023).

Employee's willingness to participate in learning process is influenced by employee motivation to learn (Khan & Khan, 2022). Existing research (Alshaikh, 2020; Bhatti et al., 2022; Chawla, 2020; Pham et al., 2022) indicates that training process undertaken by organization is going to impact employees' motivation to engage with the training. Impact of online training programmes on employee motivation is still debated (Bijaniaram et al., 2023; Singh et al., 2021).

Online training programs may suffer from employee engagement issues (Clardy, 2018; Cortellazzo et al., 2019; Meister & Willyerd, 2010; Turban et al., 2017).

Based on review of the literature two themes broadly emerge when we look towards role of L&D in contributing towards employee motivation and organisational renewal: (i)incorporating Adult Learning Principles in L&D for Organisational Renewal, and (ii) Training interventions (traditional and online) as OD tool.

Theme 1: Incorporating Adult Learning Principles in L&D for Organisational Renewal: Research indicates that usage of Adult learning principles such as focus on need to know for the learner affects motivation to learn, learning outcomes and post-training motivation to use learning. Lindeman (1926a, 1926b) also worked upon and chalked out certain critical assumptions which stood true for adult learners across variety of situations. Such assumptions got support of later research as well. He asserted that adults were motivated to learn with different kinds of learning needs and interests and they looked upon kind of learning that would satisfy such need. He further stressed upon that adults' inclination to learn was more 'life-centered' and as such they looked more on applicability of life situations. Experience provided them most enriching opportunities to learn therefore best method to make them learn was 'experiential learning and analysis of experience. Adults were more inclined to self-directed learning so the teacher was required to engage them in mutual enquiry process in place of providing knowledge transmission and evaluation of conformity thereafter. As age increase individual differences increase and therefore, adult learning needs to be more customised for individual differences in style, place, time and pace of learning.

Attempts to arrive at theoretical concepts about what we may already know form our experiences and researches on characteristics of adult learners were in progress since five decades. Earlier, the efforts were made in the direction and found that adults were learning best in flexible, informal, non-threatening set up (Knowles, 1950).

Such principles may provide a guiding light to L&D professionals who may use these to design training in such a way that modules include applicability of models/principles through relating to learner's own life situations and analysis of experiences. Also, once trainer knows the trainee/learner/participant's profile he may accordingly customise certain cases/exercises based on such experiences.

Caffarella and Daffron (2013), discussed principles of learning that were relevant for adult learners:

- Adults were practical and placed high value on relevance.
- Adults were goal-oriented.
- Adults learn from experience.
- Adult learners need to be shown respect.
- Adults were autonomous and self-directed.

Research in organizational training suggests there are three aspects to the need to know: the need to know how the learning will be conducted, what will be learned, and why it will be valuable. Hicks and Klimoski (1987) in a study of group of managers attending training on performance appraisals found that group that received a more clear and real preview of areas to be covered and the expected outcomes, as well as being provided a choice about whether or not to attend the training, were more likely to feel the workshop was appropriate for them. Baldwin et al. (1991) tested the proposition that whether trainee involvement in their planning of learning intervention would enhance the learning process and found that the importance of choice about learning has impact on learning process. Factors such as role of prior experiences of the learner, level of readiness to learn and orientation to learning need to be effectively utilised to shape learning for better organisational outcomes and for building long term organisation's capabilities.

Clark et al. (1993) explored another dimension of a learner's need to know when they studied 15 training groups across 12 different organizations which represented a wide range of organizational types and training topics. They found that career utility and job were significant predictors of training motivation. When employees were provided opportunity to give input into the decision-making in training affecting them, they were more likely to perceive job and career utility.

Argyris (1982) and Schon (1987) have written extensively about the difficulties and importance of overcoming the natural tendency to resist new learning that challenges existing mental schema from prior experience. Argyris(1982) labelled learning as single-loop or double-loop learning. Single-loop learning is may be considered as learning that adjusts/fits into the prior experiences and existing values of the individual, and enables the learner to respond accordingly. Double-loop learning means learning that would not fit the individual's prior experiences or schema. Schon (1987) proposed "knowing-in-action (automated responses relying on individual's existing schema that equip him to perform effectively in day to day actions)" and "reflection-inaction (process where individual reflects while performing to explore when existing schema no longer work and according changes schema)." Effective learners are good in double loop learning and reflection in action.

Such kinds of learning may serve as indicators for L&D professionals to carve out effective modules based on what may relate well to profile of participants. Any learning resources/ material that is totally unrelated to learner's traits/competencies or experiences may be difficult to learn as it would not fit in the learner's prior experiences and its usefulness and applicability later.

Adult experiences have a critical impact on the learning process of people. Practitioners of adult learning need to realise the role of such experiences as a trigger for and resource for learning. Experience may catalyze learning new knowledge if new knowledge is packaged in a way that it may fit in or relate to knowledge already existing. However, already existing knowledge/mental models may become obstacles to new learning if new learning does not fit the individual's prior experiences.

As such, the unlearning process within learner assumes critical significance as much as learning mechanism/process when new learning is dissimilar to existing knowledge/mental model. Kurt Lewin (1951) the founding father of OD proposed such stage of change to be called as the "unfreezing" stage (the other two being "change" and "refreezing"). Although Lewin's model is more used in the perspective of organisations, it may apply for individual learning perspective as well. Individuals would try to change only when they unfreeze existing mindset.

Kolb (1984) stressed that learning may be considered a continuous process such that all learning can be perceived as relearning. This may hold good for adults who enjoy a rich repository of events/episodes/experience. Again, L&D practitioners may take a note of such assumption son learning and then may design such modules to serve as a motivational value for participants in L&D such that there is maximum transfer of learning and then there is effective transfer for organisational outcomes.

Theme 2: Training interventions (traditional and online) as OD tool— Today's rapidly changing business world means that effective organisational development (OD) strategies are of prime importance. One of the foundational enablers of these strategies may be considered as training interventions, both physical and virtual in nature. Whether such interventions are effective or not depends on the extent to which they help in achievement of organisational goals, and particularly on improving problem-solving capabilities of organizations. This theme traces the development of training models from learning-centred methods to strategic results-based approaches, use of technology, the challenges and benefits of online training and ROI factor.

To be effective, training must produce targeted competencies that result in organisational success. Such approach favours a more tailor-made training regimen (Zhou et al., 2022). Training interventions are designed to develop skills that can make a direct contribution to an organisation's strategic goals in areas like leadership, communication, decision-processing and creativity. Targeted training makes sure staff are learning rather than just getting knowledge, and that they know how to apply what they learn.

The success of any training initiative is largely dependent on the level of managerial support it receives. The involvement of course instructors guarantees that the training objectives coincide with managers' goals and the organization's strategic vision. Upgrade of training programmes through the use of technology is another dimension adding to organisational effectiveness (Gouvenelle et al., 2023). From virtual reality to AI-based learning platforms, these technologies offer interactive and personalized solutions to learning. They also entail challenges such as providing fair access to learning resources, managing costs and training employees to use these new instruments properly.

In terms of job satisfaction, performance, and engagement positive impact was found as far as effect of online training programmes on employee motivation was concerned (Chowkase et al., 2022; Dang et al., 2022; Ranjit, 2022).

Researches point in direction that online training programs equip an employee with new skills & knowledge, consequentially providing improved confidence and motivation to perform the job (Chowkase et al., 2022; Jaiswal & Arun, 2022; Neeley & Leonardi, 2022).

Studies also point that if poorly designed and implemented there may be negative impact of online training programmes on employee motivation(Chawla, et al., 2022; Mushtaque et al., 2022; Singh et al., 2022; Vikas & Mathur, 2022). Quality of online training programs plays a vital role as far as motivation of employees is concerned toward online training programmes (Balakrishnan et al., 2022; Chawla et al., 2022; Gokak et al., 2022; Mushtaque et al., 2022; Vikas & Mathur, 2022).

Factors found to have an impact on motivating employees in the context of online training programs, are individual and contextual factors, learner autonomy, goals, social interaction, elements triggering intrinsic and extrinsic motivation of employees (Deci & Ryan, 2000; Gegenfurtner et al., 2017; Keller, 2010; Song et al., 2016).

Specific and challenging goals that are set in online training programmes, with timely feedback, may enhance motivation of employees by creating a sense of direction, purpose, and feeling of accomplishment (Kluger & DeNisi, 1996; Locke & Latham, 2019).

Autonomy of learners may involve providing learners with autonomy and control over their learning process. Online training programs that facilitate employees in making decisions(or choices) about their learning activities, pace, and content can increase employee motivation by creating a sense of ownership and control over their own learning (Deci & Ryan, 1985; Reeve, 2018).

Social interaction and collaboration among learners (such as discussion forums, virtual group activities, and peer feedback) in online training programs may improve employee motivation by providing social support, opportunities for shared learning, and a sense of community (Bandura, 2019; Deci & Ryan, 1985; Dennen, 2005; Vallerand, 1997).

Individual factors (involving personal goals, prior knowledge of employees, learning styles, skills and attitudes) may influence the relationship between online training programmes and employee motivation, as participants/learners may vary in their preferences, aspirations, desires, needs, and motivations for learning (Eisenbeiss, 2012; Kim & Keller, 2010; Pintrich & De Groot, 1990).

Contextual factors at workplace such as organizational culture, job relevance of the training, leadership support may have an impact on employee motivation in the online training programmes (Noe et al., 2013; Salas et al., 2012). Training programs conducted online need to be designed to provide learners with flexibility and autonomy, but studies found that learner motivation is more in case of face-to-face contact with the learners (Milao et al., 2022; Mitchell et al., 2021). Traditional training programmes involving face to face interaction and online training programs require different pedagogical approaches for their effectiveness. In online training programs, instructors need to have additional expertise for adapting their training/teaching methods to effectively engage learners in an online work environment (Kraiger et al., 2022; Lapitan et al., 2021; Singh et al., 2022). Studies have also indicated that as far as online training programmes are concerned technology access and expertise as well as internet connectivity may create hindrances in effectiveness of online training programmes (Kraiger et al., 2022; Lapitan et al., 2021; Singh et al., 2022).

It is a difficult but necessary step to look at the effectiveness of training interventions in terms of ROI. Rightly designed metrics can be used to evaluate the concrete outcomes in terms of organisational performance, which result from training(Singh et al., 2023). This means going beyond the usual measures of learning and measuring how training can increase productivity, improve product quality, reduce staff turnover, leading to higher profits. ROI can be measured accurately, which encourages businesses and paves the way for investment in training programmes and future trainings. If we apply quantitative assessment to the return on investment, organizations may develop a closer view towards which interventions work best and thus may work towards allocation of resources appropriately. Furthermore, by measuring ROI one would be enabled to make continuous improvement and fine-tuning of training strategies in order to optimize the impact on organizational outcomes.

To sum up, organisational development & renewal to be successful, training interventions are needed that are of the face-to-face and online types. The power to enhance key organisational skills of the employees, especially decision making and problem solving is highly integral to their success.

Proposed Model

The STRIVE (Strategic Training Integration for Vital Engagement) Model is designed to provide a comprehensive framework for organizations to enhance employee engagement and performance through strategic training initiatives.

Incorporating Adult Learning Principles: This aspect of the model emphasizes tailoring training and development/learning and development efforts to individual needs by utilizing the principles of adult learning. By focusing on the experience-based, person-centered approach, organizations can stimulate motivation among employees while also meeting organizational objectives effectively. This involves recognizing the diverse learning needs and interests of adult learners, emphasizing practical relevance, and promoting self-directed learning.

Training Interventions as OD Tools: The model highlights the importance of viewing training programmes as integral tools for organizational development (OD). It emphasizes the need for specific design considerations in training programmes, ensuring they go beyond mere knowledge acquisition. This includes addressing obstacles such as securing managerial support and integrating technology effectively. Additionally, the model emphasizes the significance of meaningful collaboration among participants in online training programs, which can enhance employee motivation by fostering shared learning and a sense of community. Individual and contextual factors, such as learning styles, workplace culture, and leadership support, are also recognized as influencing factors in employee motivation in training programmes.

Overall, the STRIVE Model provides organizations with a structured approach to strategically integrate training initiatives that not only enhance employee skills and knowledge but also foster a culture of engagement, motivation, and continuous learning. Under the STRIVE Model, training professionals/L&D experts are supposed to partner with Organization Development (OD) experts as well as with Human Resources (HR) professionals in order to ensure renewal of organisational capabilities and to boost employee motivation.

Figure 1. STRIVE Model

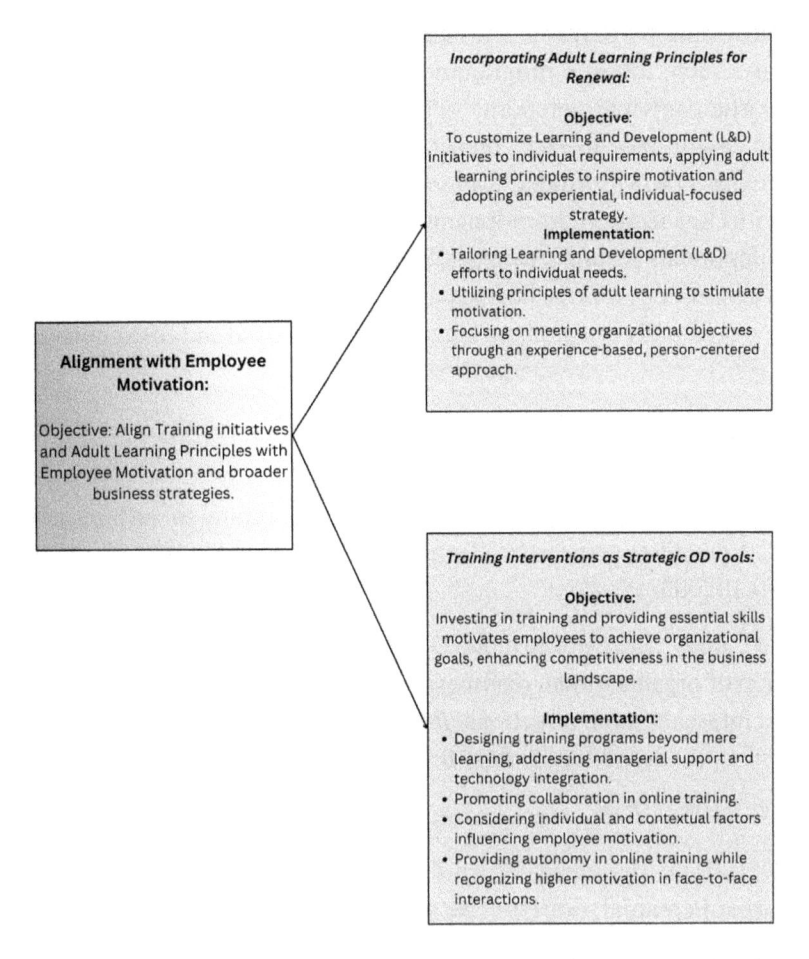

Alignment with Employee Motivation:

Objective: Align Training initiatives and Adult Learning Principles with Employee Motivation and broader business strategies.

Incorporating Adult Learning Principles for Renewal:

Objective:
To customize Learning and Development (L&D) initiatives to individual requirements, applying adult learning principles to inspire motivation and adopting an experiential, individual-focused strategy.

Implementation:
- Tailoring Learning and Development (L&D) efforts to individual needs.
- Utilizing principles of adult learning to stimulate motivation.
- Focusing on meeting organizational objectives through an experience-based, person-centered approach.

Training Interventions as Strategic OD Tools:

Objective:
Investing in training and providing essential skills motivates employees to achieve organizational goals, enhancing competitiveness in the business landscape.

Implementation:
- Designing training programs beyond mere learning, addressing managerial support and technology integration.
- Promoting collaboration in online training.
- Considering individual and contextual factors influencing employee motivation.
- Providing autonomy in online training while recognizing higher motivation in face-to-face interactions.

STRIVE (Strategic Training Integration for Vital Engagement) Model

CONCLUSION

Usage of Adult learning principles focusing more on the need to know for the learner affects learner motivation, learning outcomes and post-training motivation to use learning. Employee's traits, input, output, consequences, and feedback have considerable influence on the motivation to learn. Factors found to have profound effect on motivating employees in the context of training programmes—especially online, are individual and contextual factors, goals, autonomy offered, degree of social interaction, factors causing intrinsic and extrinsic motivation of employees to be triggered. Specific and challenging goals that are set in online training programmes, with timely feedback, may enhance motivation of employees by creating a sense of direction, purpose, and feeling of accomplishment. Autonomy of participants may involve providing participants with a certain degree of control over their learning process. As such, training programmes conducted online need to be designed to provide participants with autonomy, but researches also found that learner motivation is more in case of face-to-face contact.

Under the STRIVE Model, training professionals/L&D experts need to work closely with Organization Development (OD) specialists as well as Human Resources (HR) professionals in order to create a smooth linkage between the training and development strategy and the business environment at large. At the end, this strategic integration eventually brings about organizational renewal and continuous excellence.

REFERENCES

Alshaikh, M. (2020). Developing cybersecurity culture to influence employee behavior: A practice perspective. *Computers & Security*, *98*, 102003. doi:10.1016/j.cose.2020.102003

Antony, J., Sony, M., McDermott, O., Jayaraman, R., & Flynn, D. (2023). An exploration of organizational readiness factors for Quality 4.0: An intercontinental study and future research directions. *International Journal of Quality & Reliability Management*, *40*(2), 582–606. doi:10.1108/IJQRM-10-2021-0357

Argyris, C. (1982). *Reasoning, Learning and Action*. Jossey-Bass.

Ariely, D. (2011). *The upside of irrationality: The unexpected benefits of defying logic*. Harper Perennial. doi:10.1109/AERO.2011.5747214

Balakrishnan, S. R., Soundararajan, V., & Parayitam, S. (2022). Recognition and rewards as moderators in the relationships between antecedents and performance of women teachers: Evidence from India. *International Journal of Educational Management*, *36*(6), 1002–1026. doi:10.1108/IJEM-12-2021-0473

Baldwin, T. T., Magjuka, R. J., & Loher, B. (1991). The perils of participation: Effects of the choice of training on trainee motivation and learning. *Personnel Psychology*, *44*(1), 51–65. doi:10.1111/j.1744-6570.1991.tb00690.x

Bandura, A. (2019). Applying theory for human betterment. *Perspectives on Psychological Science*, *14*(1), 12–15. doi:10.1177/1745691618815165 PMID:30799756

Bauer, K., Orvis, K., Ely, K., & Surface, E. (2016). Re-examination of Motivation in Learning Contexts:Meta-analytically Investigating the Role Type of Motivation Plays in the Prediction of Key TrainingOutcomes. *Journal of Business and Psychology*, *31*(1), 33–50. doi:10.1007/s10869-015-9401-1

Bhatti, M. K., Soomro, B. A., & Shah, N. (2022). Predictive power of training design on employee performance: An empirical approach in Pakistan's health sector. *International Journal of Productivity and Performance Management*, *71*(8), 3792–3808. doi:10.1108/IJPPM-09-2020-0489

Bijaniaram, R., Tehrani, M., Noori, R., & Pak, J. (2023). What does it take for organizations to adopt massive open online courses (MOOCs)? A fuzzy DANP analysis. *Journal of the Knowledge Economy*, 1–36. doi:10.1007/s13132-023-01178-z

Caffarella, R. S., & Daffron, S. (2013). *Planning programs for adult learners: A practical guide* (3rd ed.). Jossey-Bass.

Chatterjee, S., & Kar, A. K. (2020). Why do small and medium enterprises use social media marketing and what is the impact: Empirical insights from India. *International Journal of Information Management*, *53*, 102103. doi:10.1016/j.ijinfomgt.2020.102103

Chawla, P. (2020). Impact of employer branding on employee engagement in business process outsourcing (BPO) sector in India: Mediating effect of person–organization fit. *Industrial and Commercial Training*, *52*(1), 35–34. doi:10.1108/ICT-06-2019-0063

Chawla, S., Sareen, P., & Gupta, S. (2022). Wellness programs an employee engagement technique pre and during pandemic: A systematic literature review. *ECS Transactions*, *107*(1), 3505–3521. doi:10.1149/10701.3505ecst

Chowkase, A. A., Datar, K., Deshpande, A., Khasnis, S., Keskar, A., & Godbole, S. (2022). Online learning, classroom quality, and student motivation: Perspectives from students, teachers, parents, and program staff. *Gifted Education International*, *38*(1), 74–94. doi:10.1177/02614294211060401

Clardy, A. (2018). 70-20-10 and the dominance of informal learning: A fact in search of evidence. *Human Resource Development Review*, *17*(2), 153–178. doi:10.1177/1534484318759399

Clark, C. S., Dobbins, G. H., & Ladd, R. T. (1993). Exploratory Field Study of Training Motivation. *Group & Organization Management*, *18*(3), 292–307. doi:10.1177/1059601193183003

Colquitt, J., LePine, J., & Noe, R. (2000). Toward an Integrative Theory of Training Motivation: A Meta-Analytic Path Analysis of 20 Years of Research. *The Journal of Applied Psychology*, *85*(5), 678–707. doi:10.1037/0021-9010.85.5.678 PMID:11055143

Cortellazzo, L., Bruni, E., & Zampieri, R. (2019). The role of leadership in a digitalized world: A review. *Frontiers in Psychology*, *10*, 1938. Advance online publication. doi:10.3389/fpsyg.2019.01938 PMID:31507494

Dang, A., Khanra, S., & Kagzi, M. (2022). Barriers towards the continued usage of massive open online courses: A case study in India. *International Journal of Management Education*, *20*(1), 100562. doi:10.1016/j.ijme.2021.100562

Deci, E. L., & Ryan, R. M. (2000). The "what" and "why" of goal pursuits: Human needs and the self-determination of behavior. *Psychological Inquiry*, *11*(4), 227–268. doi:10.1207/S15327965PLI1104_01

Dennen, V. P. (2005). From message posting to learning dialogues: Factors affecting learner participation in asynchronous discussion. *Distance Education*, *26*(1), 127–148. doi:10.1080/01587910500081376

Dweck, C. (2007). *Mindset: The new psychology of success*. Ballantine Books.

Eisenbeiss, S. A. (2012). Re-thinking ethical leadership: An interdisciplinary integrative approach. *The Leadership Quarterly*, *23*(5), 791–808. doi:10.1016/j.leaqua.2012.03.001

Gegenfurtner, A., Ebner, M., & Harper, B. (2017). Taking a closer look at motivational aspects of gamified online courses: A case study. *Interactive Learning Environments*, *25*(4), 479–491.

Gokak, A. J. H., Mehendale, S., & Bhāle, S. M. (2022). Modelling and analysis for higher education shadow institutions in Indian context: An ISM approach. *Quality & Quantity*, *57*(4), 3425–3451. doi:10.1007/s11135-022-01514-6 PMID:36091487

GouvenelleC.FloraM.FlorenceT. (2023). Digital tools in occupational health, brakes or levers for building multidisciplinary dynamics, https://arxiv.org/abs/2307.05998

Hicks, W. D., & Klimoski, R. J. (1987). Entry into Training Programs and Its Effects on Training Outcomes: A Field Experiment. *Academy of Management Journal*, *30*(3), 542–552. doi:10.2307/256013

Jaiswal, A., & Arun, C. J. (2022). Working from home during COVID-19 and its impact on Indian employees' stress and creativity. *Asian Business & Management*, 1–25. doi:10.1057/s41291-022-00202-5

Khan, A. N., & Khan, N. A. (2022). The nexuses between transformational leadership and employee green organisational citizenship behaviour: Role of environmental attitude and green dedication. *Business Strategy and the Environment, 31*(3), 921–933. doi:10.1002/bse.2926

Kim, C., & Keller, J. M. (2010). Motivation, volition and belief change strategies to improve mathematics learning. *Journal of Computer Assisted Learning, 26*(5), 407–420. doi:10.1111/j.1365-2729.2010.00356.x

Kluger, A. N., & DeNisi, A. (1996). The effects of feedback interventions on performance: A historical review, a meta-analysis, and a preliminary feedback intervention theory. *Psychological Bulletin, 119*(2), 254–284. doi:10.1037/0033-2909.119.2.254

Knowles, M. S. (1950). *Informal Adult Education*. Association Press.

Knowles, M. S., Holton, E. F., III, & Swanson, R. A. (2020). The Adult Learner. Taylor and Francis.

Kolb, D. A. (1984). *Experiential Learning: Experience as the Source of Learning and Development*. Prentice Hall.

Kraiger, K., Fisher, S., Grossman, R., Mills, M. J., & Sitzmann, T. (2022). Online IO graduate education: Where are we and where should we go? *Industrial and Organizational Psychology: Perspectives on Science and Practice, 15*(2), 151–171. doi:10.1017/iop.2021.144

Lapitan, L. D. Jr, Tiangco, C. E., Sumalinog, D. A. G., Sabarillo, N. S., & Diaz, J. M. (2021). An effective blended online teaching and learning strategy during the COVID-19 pandemic. *Education for Chemical Engineers, 35*, 116–131. doi:10.1016/j.ece.2021.01.012

Lazazzara, A., & Bombelli, C. M. (2011). HRM practices for an ageing Italian workforce: The role of training. *Journal of European Industrial Training, 35*(8), 808–825. doi:10.1108/03090591111168339

Lewin, K. (1951). *Field Theory in Social Science*. Harper.

Lindeman, E. C. (1926a). Andragogik: The Method of Teaching Adults. *Worker Education, 4*, 38.

Lindeman, E. C. (1926b). *The Meaning of Adult Education*. New Republic.

Malik, A., Budhwar, P., Mohan, H., & Srikanth, N. R. (2023). Employee experience—the missing link for engaging employees: Insights from an MNE's AI-based HR ecosystem. *Human Resource Management*, *62*(1), 97–115. doi:10.1002/hrm.22133

Mandi, J., Kotary, J., Berden, S., Mulamba, M., Bucarey, V., Guns, T., & Fioretto, F. (2023). *Decision-Focused Learning: Foundations, State of the Art, Benchmark and Future Opportunities*. Working Paper Series, Cornell University; doi:10.48550/arXiv.2307.13565

Manyika, J., Lund, S., Chui, M., Bughin, J., Woetzel, J., Batra, P., Ko, R., & Sanghvi, S. (2017). *Jobs lost, jobs gained: Workforce transitions in a time of automation*. McKinsey Global Institute. Retrieved May 22, 2023, from https://www.mckinsey.com/global-themes/future-of-organizations-and-work/what-the-future-of-work-willmean-for-jobs-skills-and-wages

Meister, J. C., & Willyerd, K. (2010). Mentoring millennials. *Harvard Business Review*, *88*(5), 68–72. PMID:20429252

Miao, J., Chang, J., & Ma, L. (2022). Teacher–student interaction, student–student interaction and social presence: Their impacts on learning engagement in online learning environments. *The Journal of Genetic Psychology*, *183*(6), 514–526. doi:10.1080/00221325.2022.2094211 PMID:35815529

Mitchell, C., Cours Anderson, K., Laverie, D., & Hass, A. (2021). Distance be damned: The importance of social presence in a pandemic constrained environment. *Marketing Education Review*, *31*(4), 294–310. doi:10.1080/10528008.2021.1936561

Mushtaque, I., Waqas, H., & Awais-E-Yazdan, M. (2022). The effect of technostress on the teachers' willingness to use online teaching modes and the moderating role of job insecurity during COVID-19 pandemic in Pakistan. *International Journal of Educational Management*, *36*(1), 63–80. doi:10.1108/IJEM-07-2021-0291

Neeley, T., & Leonardi, P. (2022). Developing a digital mindset. *Harvard Business Review*, *100*(5–6), 50–55.

Noe, R., & Colquitt, J. (2002). Planning for Training Impact. In Creating, Implementing, and Managing Effective Training and Development. Jossey-Bass.

Noe, R. A. (1986). Trainee Attributes and Attitudes: Neglected Influences on Training Effectiveness. *Academy of Management Review*, *11*(4), 736–749. doi:10.2307/258393

Noe, R. A. (2023). *Employee Training and Development*. McGraw Hill.

Pasupathi, M. (2013). *How we learn. The Great Courses*. The Teaching Company.

Pham, N. T., Jabbour, C. J. C., Usman, M., Ali, M., & Phan, H. L. (2022). How does training boost employees' intention to implement environmental activities? An empirical study in Vietnam. *International Journal of Manpower, 43*(8), 1761–1782. doi:10.1108/IJM-04-2021-0238

Pink, D. H. (2008). *Drive: The surprising truth about what motivates us*. Riverhead Books.

Pintrich, P. R., & De Groot, E. V. (1990). Motivational and self-regulated learning components of classroom academic performance. *Journal of Educational Psychology, 82*(1), 33–40. doi:10.1037/0022-0663.82.1.33

Pollock, R. V. H., Jefferson, A. M., & Wick, C. W. (2015). *The Six Disciplines of Breakthrough Learning: How to Turn Training and Development into Business Results*. Wiley. doi:10.1002/9781119153832

Praveen M. Kulkarni, PM, Lakshminarayana K, Gokhale,P, Tigadi, BS, Veshne,N & Kulkarni, AV(2023). Employee Motivation and Its Relationship with Online Training. Jindal Journal of Business Research. 1-17.

Quinones, M. A. (1995). Pretraining Context Effects: Training Assignments as Feedback. *The Journal of Applied Psychology, 80*(2), 226–238. doi:10.1037/0021-9010.80.2.226

Rahman, M. F. W., Kistyanto, A., & Surjanti, J. (2022). Does cyberloafing and person organization fit affect employee performance? The mediating role of innovative work behavior. *Global Business and Organizational Excellence, 41*(5), 44–64. doi:10.1002/joe.22159

Ranjit, G. (2022). Explicating intrinsic motivation's impact on job performance: Employee creativity as a mediator. *Journal of Strategy and Management, 15*(4), 647–664.

Reeve, J., Jang, H. R., & Jang, H. (2018). Personality-based antecedents of teachers' autonomy-supportive and controlling motivating styles. *Learning and Individual Differences, 62*, 12–22. https://doi.org/. lindif.2018.01.001 doi:10.1016/j

Rothwell, W. J., Imroz, S. M., & Bakhshandeh, B. (Eds.). (2021). *Organization Development Interventions*. Routledge. doi:10.4324/9781003019800

Rouiller, J., & Goldstein, I. (1993). The Relationship Between Organizational Transfer Climate and Positive Transfer of training. *Human Resource Development Quarterly, 4*(4), 377–390. doi:10.1002/hrdq.3920040408

Salas, E., Tannenbaum, S. I., Kraiger, K., & Smith-Jentsch, K. A. (2012). The science of training and development in organizations: What matters in practice. *Psychological Science in the Public Interest*, *13*(2), 74–101. doi:10.1177/1529100612436661 PMID:26173283

Schmude, T., Koesten, L., Möller, T., & Tschiatschek, S. (2023). Applying Interdisciplinary Frameworks to Understand Algorithmic Decision-Making, https://doi.org//arXiv.2305.16700 doi:10.48550

Schon, D. A. (1987). *Educating the Reflective Behaviour*. Jossey-Bass.

Singh, A., Sharma, S., & Paliwal, M. (2021). Adoption intention and effectiveness of digital collaboration platforms for online learning: The Indian students' perspective. *Interactive Technology and Smart Education*, *18*(4), 493–514. doi:10.1108/ITSE-05-2020-0070

Singh, C., Maries, A., Heller, K., & Heller, P. (2023). Instructional Strategies that Foster Effective Problem-Solving, /arXiv.2304.05585 doi:10.1063/9780735425477_017

Singh, J., Evans, E., Reed, A., Karch, L., Qualey, K., Singh, L., & Wiersma, H. (2022). Online, hybrid, and face-toface learning through the eyes of faculty, students, administrators, and instructional designers: Lessons learned and directions for the post-vaccine and post-pandemic/COVID-19 world. *Journal of Educational Technology Systems*, *50*(3), 301–326. doi:10.1177/00472395211063754

Song, L., Singleton, E. S., Hill, J. R., & Koh, M. H. (2016). Improving online learning: Student perceptions of useful and challenging characteristics. *The Internet and Higher Education*, *7*(1), 59–70. doi:10.1016/j.iheduc.2003.11.003

Tannenbaum, S. I., Mathieu, J. E., Salas, E., & Cannon-Bowers, J. A. (1991). Meeting Trainees' Expectations: The Influence of Training Fulfillment on the Development of Commitment, Self-Efficacy, and Motivation. *The Journal of Applied Psychology*, *76*(6), 759–769. doi:10.1037/0021-9010.76.6.759

Turban, E., Outland, J., King, D., Lee, J. K., Liang, T., & Turban, D. C. (2017). Innovative EC systems: From e-government to E-learning, e-Health, sharing economy, and P2P commerce. Springer texts in business and economics (pp. 167–201). Springer. doi:10.1007/978-3-319-58715-8_5

Vallerand, R. J. (1997). Toward a hierarchical model of intrinsic and extrinsic motivation. In M. P. Zanna (Ed.), Advances in experimental social psychology. Academic Press. doi:10.1016/S0065-2601(08)60019-2

Vikas, S., & Mathur, A. (2022). An empirical study of student perception towards pedagogy, teaching style and effectiveness of online classes. *Education and Information Technologies*, *27*(1), 589–610. doi:10.1007/s10639-021-10793-9 PMID:34720659

Vroom, V. H. (1994). *Work and motivation*. Jossey-Bass.

Yang, J. (2023). The impact of Industry 4.0 on the world of work and the call for educational reform. In D. Guo (Ed.), *The frontier of education reform and development in China: Articles from educational research* (pp. 285–298). Springer Nature. doi:10.1007/978-981-19-6355-1_15

Yang, S., Nachum, O., Du, Y., Wei, J., Abbeel, P., & Schuurmans, D. (2023). *Foundation Models for Decision Making: Problems, Methods, and Opportunities*. Working Paper Series, Cornell University. doi:10.48550/arXiv.2303.04129

ZhouB.WangP.WanJ.LiangY.WangF. (2022). Effective Vision Transformer Training: A Data-Centric Perspective. https://arxiv.org/abs/2209.15006

Chapter 8
Examining the Relationship Between Learning Design and Organizational Citizenship Behavior

Jennifer A. Bockelman
https://orcid.org/0009-0001-5671-5684
Adler University, USA

ABSTRACT

This chapter will explore how training and development programs contribute to increased motivation to engage in prosocial organizational behaviors or organizational citizenship behaviors (OCBs). OCB refers to behaviors outside of an employee's core role that he or she performs for the benefit of an organization or other organizational members. While organizations have a considerable interest in increasing the motivation of employees to exhibit OCB, OCB may not be recognized by an organization's performance measurement system. Research has attempted to define predictors of OCB, such as personality traits, employee attitudes, and leadership behaviors. Potential motivations behind OCB will be explored, as well as adult learning theories that are most likely to promote OCB. In addition, this chapter will provide recommendations for the design of training and development with the goal of encouraging OCB and reducing counterproductive work behaviors (CWB).

DOI: 10.4018/979-8-3693-1674-0.ch008

INTRODUCTION

Motivation, or its absence, can be considered a pivotal factor when evaluating an organization's ability to attain competitive advantage. Most people can separate the colleagues who constantly go above and beyond from those who appear to be counting down the minutes until they can sign off for the day. These perceptions do not inform the observer of what those employees may be experiencing cognitively. This describes the major problem of assessing motivation – it is a hypothetical construct that cannot be observed (Luthans, 2011). The best we can do is identify behaviors that likely speak to the presence or absence of motivation. Yet organizations have a vested interest in understanding what motivates an employee to perform desired behaviors. That motivation may stem from various incentives, such as pay, promotional opportunities, or job security. Nevertheless, these incentives alone cannot tell the full story when it comes to prosocial organizational behavior (POB). POBs are particularly desirable for employers as employees often engage in these behaviors without an explicit promise of monetary or other compensation.

Training and development programs can contribute to an increase in prosocial behaviors and a decrease in antisocial behaviors. This chapter will examine how training and development can provide employees with the skill set to increase their prosocial behaviors (i.e., organizational citizenship behaviors) while decreasing the prevalence of antisocial behaviors (i.e., counterproductive work behaviors). We will begin with a summary of the research around POB and organizational citizenship behavior (OCB). We will then review existing theories that provide frameworks for understanding the motivation behind employees' willingness to engage in these behaviors and the benefits of OCB on organizational performance. Finally, we will focus on specific training and development models that can be incorporated into learning programs designed to inspire OCB and other prosocial behaviors.

Prosocial Behaviors

Prosocial behaviors have been referenced within academic literature in various forms for several decades. However, Ervin Staub was one of the first scholars to define and conceptualize the term as we understand it today. As the name implies, prosocial behaviors benefit others (Staub, 1978). The definition sounds relatively straightforward until one considers that contrasting perspectives may create conflict as to whether a behavior is prosocial. For example, take a manager who steps in to handle work for an overwhelmed subordinate. The immediate action may be beneficial (i.e., lessening that employee's workload). However, if the manager repeatedly takes over work for his or her direct report, this can hamper the employee's development and create an unhealthy dependency on the manager. In addition, the manager may indirectly harm him or herself by taking on an individual contributor's role in addition to their own role, which has the potential to lead to burnout. At that point, one can argue that the actions are no longer beneficial and, therefore, no longer prosocial. Does the intent behind the behavior carry more weight or the outcome?

Brief and Motowidlo (1986) argued that prosocial organizational behavior must involve an intent to benefit the company or other people, even if those actions ultimately harm the intended beneficiaries. They categorized prosocial behavior into two categories: functional or dysfunctional. Consider a tenured employee who has found multiple ways to circumvent established processes to get their job done faster. This employee may take a new hire under their wing and, to help that employee learn the ropes more quickly, teach the new hire those shortcuts. In the short term, the new employee reaches optimal productivity levels in a shorter period. However, the circumvented processes likely exist for a reason, and both the tenured and new employees could be putting the company in danger of regulation violations, litigation, or safety concerns. In addition, the new hire, who likely is under heightened scrutiny during the onboarding period, may be more susceptible to disciplinary action for not following the established processes.

Interest in prosocial organizational behaviors has increased exponentially in the past several years (Podsakoff et al., 2000). The desire to understand what motivates someone to engage in prosocial behaviors is understandable when considering the long-term positive impact on society. Prosocial behavior has been found to alleviate physiological symptoms of stress, increase feelings of self-worth and happiness, and improve social connection (Aknin et al., 2010; Aknin et al., 2015; Lazar & Eisenberger, 2021; Klein, 2016). Moreover, some theorize that prosocial behavior evolved as a condition necessary for the survival of humans (Simpson & Beckes, 2010). The same could be said for the survival of organizations. Behaviors that go beyond role requirements, such as mentoring a colleague, surfacing organizational challenges, or complimenting the organization publicly, are considered necessary for effective organizational functioning (Brief & Motowidlo, 1986). Brief and Motowidlo categorized these actions as POB if they meet the following four criteria: 1) an organizational member performs these actions, 2) these actions occur while the organizational member is operating within his or her organizational role, 3) the actions are directed towards other organizational members or the organization itself, and 4) the actions are intended to benefit the organization or other organizational members.

The above paragraphs highlight the broad definition of POB. Some have argued that the phrase should be retired due to the breadth of that definition (Organ, 2014; Van Dyne et al., 1995). Recently, concepts such as OCB, initially considered a subset of POB, have emerged as a more defined way to conceptualize positive activities within a company that organizations would be incentivized to promote.

Organizational Citizenship Behavior (OCB)

Organizational Citizenship Behavior entered the organizational psychology lexicon in the 1980s. Bateman and Organ (1983) first conceptualized "citizenship behaviors" as social behaviors that support the functioning of a group but are not prescribed for an actor's role or performance. Organ later expanded upon this concept with the term "organizational citizenship behaviors," which was defined as helpful, constructive behaviors that provide benefit to organizational members or an organization but are not directly related to an individual's role within the organization or formally recognized within the company's performance measurement system (1988). OCB can be considered a subset of POB as the broader category may include behaviors codified into an employee's role or directly impact that employee's performance. For example, a manager is often expected to coach, mentor, and support their direct reports as part of the formal job description. These actions meet all four criteria of Brief and Motowidlo's definition of POB. However, because managers are often measured by the ability to coach their team as part of that manager's performance, those coaching behaviors would not fall within the definition of OCB. A more appropriate OCB example would be an individual contributor who takes it upon himself or herself to coach and mentor a colleague. This voluntary behavior is unlikely to be required as part of the respective contributor's formal job role yet may still have both short and long-term benefits for the company.

The proliferation of attention on OCB has led to a wide array of behaviors that could fall within this construct. To organize these behaviors, some have proposed dimensions predicated upon those actions that directly benefit the organization, OCB-O, and actions that directly benefit individual organizational members, or OCB-I (Williams & Anderson, 1991). Organ (1988) further deconstructed his OCB model into five dimensions, which can also be seen in Figure 1:

1. **Altruism.** These behaviors comprise of discretionary actions to help others with workplace-related problems. Others have referred to this dimension as "helping behavior" (Podsakoff et al., 2000).
2. **Sportsmanship.** These themes relate to one's attitude in processing negative experiences at work. These employees refrain from complaining when things don't go their way. They may also put the companies' best interests above their own.
3. **Conscientiousness.** This dimension looks at how a person complies with company rules and procedures. Another way to think of this category is an organizational member's obedience to the company, even if no one may be monitoring that obedience. The rigor with which these employees adhere to the organization's rules and procedures sets them apart from the general compliance

that all employees are expected to have, which is why these behaviors can fall under OCB. Others have called this dimension "organizational compliance" (Podsakoff et al., 2000).
4. **Civic Virtue.** As citizens might display their civic virtue by voting or running for town council, employees can display organizational civic virtue by engaging in company governance activities.
5. **Courtesy.** Employees who display behaviors within this category take the initiative to prevent workplace problems from occurring.

Figure 1. Organ's Five Dimensions of Organizational Citizenship Behaviors

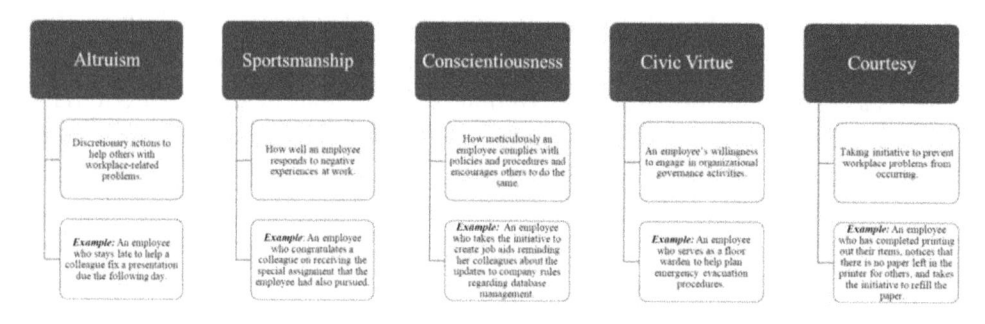

Altruism	Sportsmanship	Conscientiousness	Civic Virtue	Courtesy
Discretionary actions to help others with workplace-related problems.	How well an employee responds to negative experiences at work.	How meticulously an employee complies with policies and procedures and encourages others to do the same.	An employee's willingness to engage in organizational governance activities.	Taking initiative to prevent workplace problems from occurring.
Example: An employee who stays late to help a colleague fix a presentation due the following day.	*Example:* An employee who congratulates a colleague on receiving the special assignment that the employee had also pursued.	*Example:* An employee who takes the initiative to create job aids reminding her colleagues about the updates to company rules regarding database management.	*Example:* An employee who serves as a floor warden to help plan emergency evacuation procedures.	*Example:* An employee who has completed printing out their items, notices that there is no paper left in the printer for others, and takes the initiative to refill the paper.

Podsakoff et al. also expanded and organized the various OCB actions presented within the literature into several dimensions (2000). Most of his dimensions are similar to Organ's, with the exception of courtesy, which does not seem to align with any of Podsakoff's dimensions. Podsakoff et al. added three dimensions which are not found in Organ's original conceptualization:

1. **Individual Initiative.** These behaviors revolve around voluntary seeking out additional work beyond what is required of one's role. An example might be an employee who routinely volunteers for stretch assignments.
2. **Organizational Loyalty.** Employees within this category promote and defend the company from internal and external attacks. They remain committed to the organization through the highs and the lows. This may look like an employee who responds to a colleague's complaints about their organization's benefits by promoting the company's generous parental leave policies.
3. **Self-Development.** Unlike the other six themes, this last one emphasizes how the employee helps himself or herself instead of how he or she directly helps the larger organization or other members. Employees who engage in self-development seek to improve their knowledge, skills, or abilities through

training, education, mentorship, etc. This would still fall under OCB as there may be an indirect benefit to the organization through stronger talent.

Related Prosocial Organizational Behavior Constructs

Throughout the literature, one might see references to other constructs that are conceptually very similar to OCB, such as Extra Role Behaviors (ERB), contextual performance, and organizational spontaneity. ERB as a construct separate from organizational citizenship behaviors has been challenged. Van Dyne et al. (1995) defined ERB as all voluntary, deliberate behaviors that benefit or are intended to benefit an organization and do not fall within one's job role. This definition seems familiar because it shares multiple common elements with Organ's definition of OCB. However, Van Dyne et al. specify that ERB should not be construed merely as prosocial behavior that occurs within a work environment; there must be an intended benefit at the organizational level. This is dissimilar to POB and OCB, where the intended benefit can be for either the organization or other organizational members.

Analyzing behaviors that benefit organizational members but not the organization, and vice versa, can become quite complex. In addition, defining what behaviors do and do not fall within the construct of a job function is also a challenge. Let's return to the hypothetical situation of a manager coaching his employees. Earlier, it was noted that this would not fall within OCB as a manager is expected to coach employees as part of his or her role. However, let's say that the manager sets additional time outside his working hours to provide extra coaching to his employee, late into the night or on the weekends. Are these actions still a part of the manager's position? From the manager's perspective, he is going above and beyond his role to develop his employee. On the other hand, from the senior leader's perspective, the job is salaried, and managers may often be expected to stay late or work outside normal hours if their teams need them. In addition, even if the manager's decision to stay late and provide extra coaching is technically not a part of his role, his leader will likely appreciate that behavior, and he could see a direct benefit in the form of recognition on an annual performance rating, which goes against Organ's initial OCB definition. Organ (1997) recognized that the landscape around job roles and task performance had changed and modified his definition of OCB to include all "performance that supports the social and psychological environment in which task performance takes place" (p.95). This revised definition makes it easier to differentiate task performance, which is specific to a role, from citizenship performance, which may look similar across multiple roles (Borman et al., 2001).

The nuances that differentiate POB, OCB, and ERB are subtle, complex, and divisive. Some argue that these constructs are so similar that they should be considered the same construct, and any differences should be highlighted as part of the conversation around behaviors (Organ, 2014). Others caution against incorporating different constructs into one overarching construct (Van Dyne et al., 2014). An examination of these arguments is outside of the scope of this chapter. The more important question is why some employees exhibit more motivation to support the organization in ways that go beyond their prescribed job duties. As OCB is the most well-known and well-researched of the prosocial organizational behavior constructs, we will use that term as we explore the research behind employees' motivations to exhibit these desired behaviors.

The Benefits of Organizational Citizenship Behavior

It's unlikely to surprise anyone that employers receive a significant benefit from a work culture that promotes and encourages OCB. As engaging in these behaviors may not translate directly into monetary or other performance rewards, one could argue that employers can reap the benefits from their workforce without being forced to pay the costs through raises, promotions, or bonuses. While that cynical view may be true of some organizations, having an organizational culture that encourages and promotes OCB provides value for both the employer and the employee. A team with high levels of OCB may be rewarded with more autonomy after proving that they can help one another, display loyalty to the company, or commit to following departmental policies. These behaviors build camaraderie among team members and trust levels among peers, superiors, the team, which can result in increased OCB levels (Da Silva et al., 2019; Konovsky & Pugh, 1994). One study found that OCB actions falling within the Altruism, Sportsmanship, and Civic Virtue dimensions increased productivity, promoted effective sales tactics, decreased customer complaints, and enhanced operational efficiency (Podsakoff & MacKenzie, 2014).

We have already briefly touched on the benefits for the individual who engages in OCB, but there is much more to explore with this topic. Many of us may relate to the experience of working for an organization where our colleagues step in to help out a peer who is overwhelmed, or there is an interest in bringing a spirit of levity to the workplace through games and social functions. Over the course of our adult lives, we will spend tens of thousands of hours at work; most of us would prefer to spend that time in a helping environment where people seem to genuinely want to be there. The camaraderie that develops among team members through displays of OCB can evolve into genuine friendship, which has been found to enhance happiness, promote career development, and decrease stress (Berman et al., 2002; Wang et al., 2023).

Moreover, contrary to the stereotype of the employee doing the bare minimum to scrape by, employees often express the desire to prove themselves by taking on more than their role requires (Low et al., 2016). Not only do these employees expect this of themselves, but they also feel that their managers should expect them to want to go above and beyond their roles. The value that meaningful work can bring to our lives cannot be overstated. While there may be times that a job is just a job performed to meet the economic requirements of living, OCB can provide meaning to employees by allowing them to engage in genuinely fulfilling work, even if it is not directly related to the work that they were hired to do. For example, over the past several decades, Employee Resource Groups (ERGs) have emerged as networks for professionals based on a common shared identity, such as ethnicity, gender, or sexual orientation. These groups are often led by employees who have voluntarily chosen to do so with no promise of monetary compensation. Nevertheless, the bonds forged through these shared identities help foster a cohesive and meaningful work environment beyond monetary compensation.

The above benefits may provide insight into an individual's motivation to engage in OCB. The motivation that prompts specific behavior can be complex, and, as previously noted, the motivation itself cannot be directly observed. However, we can explore characteristics, attitudes, contexts, or tactics that may prompt someone to exhibit OCB.

Motivation and Organizational Citizenship Behavior

Researchers often study behaviors that prompt motivation through two dimensions: extrinsically motivated behaviors and intrinsically motivated behaviors. Individuals are extrinsically motivated to pursue certain behaviors through the implied or explicit promise of material gain, such as monetary rewards, public recognition, and promotional opportunities (Cerasoli et al., 2014). Intrinsically motivated individuals are instead driven by their desires (e.g., task enjoyment, the desire to stay busy, or the feeling of accomplishment from exceeding expectations). One of the key components of OCB is that there is no explicit promise of an extrinsic incentive. Historically, employers and researchers assumed that it was solely extrinsic motivation that stimulated desired performance. With that assumption, it can be difficult to understand an employee's motivation to help a coworker with a project, join a party planning committee, or take on stretch assignments for an understaffed department, especially if they know they will not receive any immediate reward for these actions. Consequentially, researchers have focused their efforts on understanding the intrinsic motivation that compels OCB actions, generating research around three different predictors: personality, employee attitudes, and leadership.

Personality

Organizational psychologists and scholars have had a strong interest in understanding how personality influences general performance. Understandably, if organizations could point to certain traits or characteristics that lead to higher sales, more productivity, or excellent customer service, those companies would benefit from hiring individuals with the identified attributes. Intelligence initially emerged as the dominant trait that could predict task performance (Organ & McFall, 2004). However, as theories around citizenship behavior and contextual performance began to take root, researchers turned to other non-cognitive personality traits to attempt to explain variance in these types of behaviors. The results have been mixed.

While there are several models for understanding personality, the Five-Factor Model of Personality remains one of the most popular frameworks for examining the relationship between personality and OCB. Building off the work of prior researchers who studied personality traits, Costa and McCrae determined that the five following groupings accounted for all personality descriptors: Openness, Conscientiousness, Extraversion, Agreeableness, and Neuroticism (1999). Some studies have found support for the theory that these personality groupings can serve as a predictor for the display of OCB. Mahajan (2017) found that Conscientiousness, Agreeableness, Openness, and Extraversion all correlated positively with OCB. However, other meta-analyses have found inconsistent and weak correlations between personality attributes and OCB (Organ, 1994). One exception is the factor of Conscientiousness, which has surfaced repeatedly as a direct predictor for OCB as well as a moderator for the relationship between job satisfaction and OCB (Borman et al., 2001; Bowling, 2010).

Finally, some studies have found a strong correlation between various measures of personality variables and counterproductive work behaviors (CWB) such as non-approved absences, company rule violations, and theft (Organ & McFall, 2004). Although CWBs are often tied to OCBs and other extra-role behavior, the two are distinct constructs and do not influence the other (Bowling, 2010). In other words, an employee who does not engage in OCB is not significantly more likely to display CWB. We will explore counterproductive work behaviors in more detail later in this chapter.

Many of us might feel that there must be some aspect of the personality that drives employees to perform discretionary behaviors that that may not be recognized, rewarded, or compensated by their employer. One proposed explanation is that personality traits may relate more to the manner in which OCB is performed, not necessarily the frequency (Organ & McFall, 2004). For example, individuals who fall on the higher side of the Agreeableness dimension may exhibit more empathy and care when helping a frustrated colleague with a technology issue than another employee who falls on the lower end of the Agreeableness dimension. Yet the second employee may also volunteer his or her time to help with the technology issue, perhaps because he or she has a strong background in technology and knows that they can resolve the problem quickly as long as they focus on the task and not the person.

Furthermore, Organ and McFall (2004) posited that the workplace may actually suppress or enhance certain parts of one's personality depending on how that individual perceives the culture and expectations for their behavior. In other words, an employee who is skilled at monitoring his or her environment for behavior cues may be more adept at "reading the room" and understanding that participating in workplace committees as a form of civic virtue is more likely to get them noticed by upper management. They may choose to engage in this behavior, despite having no innate desire to do so. Organ and McFall suggested that future research into this area should make modifications to research design to account for the complex way that personality may show itself in the workplace and perhaps yield more fruitful results.

While direct links between personality and OCB frequency are not strongly supported by research, there has been more favorable research linking personality to job satisfaction and job satisfaction to OCB levels.

Employee Attitudes

While personality has often taken center stage in the search for consistent predictors of OCB, the study of OCB emerged based on the desire to link some element of performance to job satisfaction (Organ & McFall, 2004). In contrast to task performance, which can be more readily associated with technical skills and training, OCB and other manifestations of extra-role behaviors were hypothesized to be more closely tied to an employee's cognitive and affective states. In other words, an employee who hates their job, whether that's due to poor person-organization fit or a micromanaging, unsupportive boss, may still meet expectations when it comes to task performance if they have the technical skill to do the job. However, it is unlikely that they will engage in discretionary behaviors that go above and beyond the role that pays them.

Moreover, one's personality may predispose an employee to have higher or lower levels of job satisfaction. For instance, studies have found that those who tend to be higher in Neuroticism are more likely to express dissatisfaction with their jobs (Judge et al., 2002). Other Big Five dimensions such as Extraversion and Conscientiousness have also been found to show a correlation with job satisfaction, but whether the correlation was positive or negative changed depending on the type of job (Harari et al., 2018; Sterns et al., 1983).

The interest in understanding predictors of job satisfaction stems from the belief that an employee's orientation towards their employer affects multiple facets of their performance. For example, Bateman and Organ (1983) found that job satisfaction could be positively linked to stronger levels of OCB. This indicates that organizational members, consciously or unconsciously, choose to engage in behavior that supports the social and psychological work environment when they feel socially and psychologically supported. This type of "quid pro quo" forms the basis for social exchange theory, which states that humans engage in social currency transactions, similar to economic transactions. The difference is that with social exchange, the transactions become obligations based on an informal contract that may or may not be fulfilled (Blau, 1964; Konovsky & Pugh, 1994).

Employees who feel valued and supported by their organization may feel obligated to exhibit positive behavior that goes beyond their prescribed job duties. Conversely, that employee may also expect that displays of OCB create an obligation for additional compensation based on the organizational informal contract. At the heart of social exchange theory lies organizational justice and fairness. Research supports that employees will respond to feelings of fairness (or lack thereof) by increasing or decreasing OCB levels (Moorman, 1991). These responses are magnified when the feelings of fairness are related to interactions with one's supervisor or manager.

Leadership Behaviors

Leadership behaviors may play an outsized role when examining the motivation behind OCB. Supervisors and managers serve as a physical representation of the company. While employees can differentiate between exchanges with their leader and exchanges with their company, the quality of their exchange with their leader significantly impacts the employee's perception of organizational support (Wayne et al., 1997). Therefore, one's interactions and relationships with their supervisor often inform how one views their employer and, consequentially, how one responds to perceived favorable or unfavorable treatment. Effective leadership, characterized by the leader's ability to develop their team, communicate goals and standards, inspire innovation, and recognize top performance, was associated with leaders reporting higher levels of organizational citizenship behavior on their teams (Dubey et al., 2023). Favorable interactions with one's leader have also been linked to higher levels of OCB, leading researchers to explore whether specific leadership styles are more likely to elicit stronger displays of OCB actions.

Pillai et al. (1999) looked at two specific leadership constructs to study this question: transformational and transactional leadership. Transformational leaders refer to those who serve as an ideal influence for those they lead, who motivate and generate enthusiasm to get the work done, who inspire innovation and creativity, and who can personalize their interactions to accommodate individual differences (Bass & Riggio, 2006). Transformational leadership has been linked to procedural justice, which refers to how employees perceive the fairness of the processes used to determine performance and other organizational outcomes (Pillai et al., 1999). On the other hand, transactional leaders focus on processes and procedures while employing corrective action to correct deviations from standards; involve themselves more in the day-to-day operational tasks rather than long-term strategic change; and motivate by providing rewards contingent on carrying out the desired task (Bass & Riggio, 2006; Burke, 2017). Transactional leadership has been linked with distributive justice, which refers to an employee's perception of the fairness of organizational outcomes, instead of the processes used to achieve those outcomes (Pillai et al., 1999). Transformational leadership is often held up as the leadership model to which one should aspire. Interestingly, Pillai and the team of researchers found that favorable perceptions of distributive justice were more likely to predict higher OCB levels, an association that they did not find with procedural justice. While transformational leadership was also found to have an indirect influence on OCB, this finding indicates that there are components of both types of leadership that may positively influence employees to engage in OCB activities.

In summary, there are many sources of motivation for the display of OCB. These motivations may change depending on the context or the person. Theoretical frameworks within the training and development fields are relevant to understanding how a learning program can be designed to encourage a culture of citizenship behavior. While there is limited evidence on the ability of training programs to impact one's personality, the research is more promising when looking at the impact of training on job satisfaction, employee attitudes, and effective leadership.

Adult Learning Theory and Citizenship Behavior

George and Jones (1997) argued that our understanding of why OCB occurs was limited by the lack of research into the specific context in which the OCB actions occur. Adult learning theories serve as one way to understand the learning context in which OCB may occur. Adult learning theories have become critical to developing training strategies. While these theories tend to advocate for a particular learning methodology that best complements an adult's learning style, empirical evidence supporting one methodology over another has been mixed. Regardless, there are components of several adult learning theories that provide promising clues to their impact on encouraging organizational citizenship behavior. We will examine four of them in This chapter: andragogy, transformative learning theory, experiential learning theory, and social learning theory.

Andragogy

Andragogy has existed for centuries but did not enter the mainstream lexicon until the 1970s. Around that time, Malcolm Knowles developed a theoretical framework for adult learning that centered on the adult directing and actively participating in his or her learning, as opposed to pedagogy, which emphasizes the teacher's role in directing the student (Knowles, 1989/2003). In Knowles's conceptualization of andragogy, the teacher's role is to help facilitate the student's desire to learn. He believes that adults not only have the capacity to direct their own learning but also crave that autonomy. As such, the students should be involved in the process of planning their own learning (Knowles, 1968/2003). His experience influenced him to believe that adults were much more likely to be engaged in learning developed and presented by their peers. With the classes he taught at Boston University, he would have his students split into teams to learn about a topic and then instruct the rest of the class on that topic. Knowles also proposed representative planning councils where students would serve on that committee as representatives of the learning population and work with facilitators to plan the curriculum. An employee who is high on the OCB dimensions of individual initiative, civic virtue, and self-development would likely be one of the first to volunteer on such a committee and have significant influence over their fellow learners.

Helping and supporting one's peers is considered one of the key features of an andragogical teaching methodology (Sinelnikova et al., 2022). This type of prosocial behavior has been supported in empirical studies looking at educators who trend towards an andragogical approach. One study found that andragogical educators were more likely express affection and inclusion by initiating and actively maintaining close, intimate relationships with other (Holmes, 1980). This was in opposition to educators who leaned towards a pedagogical approach. These educators seemed to align more with a need to maintain their relationships with others by controlling their behavior. This approach may end up backfiring; studies have found that higher managerial control levels can dampen the exhibition of OCB (Allen et al., 2015). We can conclude that interpersonal behaviors which support an organizational environment where employees feel valued and respected is one way to encourage desired performance through OCB.

A learning environment based on andragogical principles not only encourages relationship building, it requires a high level of personal involvement of employees (Kessels & Poell, 2004). This level of involvement leads to a knowledge network where employees are encouraged to challenge groupthink, share knowledge, innovate, and pursue career development, all of which generate social capital. Kessels and Poell concetpualized social capital as similar to economic capital. However, social capital relies on the resources within an organization's social networks to create value for the organization. The learning generated within these knowledge and social networks eventually becomes spontaneous and cannot be explicitly controlled formally by management. In other words, these behaviors form the context for organizational spontaneity to occur.

This chapter has not explored the literature pertaining to organizational spontaneity in detail, as the conceptualization of this term is extraordinarily similar to OCB. George and Brief (1992) defined organizational spontaneity as "extra-role behaviors that are performed voluntarily and that contribute to organizational effectiveness" (p. 311). These behaviors include helping colleagues, protecting the company, making constructive suggestions, developing individually, and sharing goodwill. One may wonder how this definition differs from OCB at all. George and Brief differentiate organizational spontaneity by the fact that the company's formal performance system can award these behaviors. While Organ's original definition of OCB specifically excluded behaviors directly recognized by the company, as previously noted, Organ revised his definition in 1997 to remove the requirement that these behaviors are excluded from an organization's performance measurement system. In short, at this time, there is virtually no difference between organizational spontaneity and OCB.

Transformative Learning Theory

Transformative learning and andragogy both share the same philosophical reliance on the emancipation of the learner, meaning that the learner is encouraged to engage in dialogue to establish meaning in their own education and their self-direction (Wals et al., 2008). Transformative learning emphasizes the reassessment of prior beliefs to derive insight and education from that reassessment (Mezirow, 1990). Mezirow based this theory on the assumption that, throughout their lives, adults have developed belief systems that influence how, what, and why they learn. These belief systems may work against individuals and become constraining rather than helpful, as the learner is unable to integrate data that does not match preconceived notions. Transformative learning resolves that conflict by encouraging continuous reflection on prior beliefs. The goal of this learning methodology is to encourage inclusive, self-directed, and socially responsible ways of thinking (Mezirow, 1997).

The critical thinking referenced above is crucial to transformative learning (Hart et al., 2016). Moreover, the critical thinking required to closely examine one's preconceived notions is similar to the critical thinking required to process negative experiences in a positive manner (sportsmanship) or proactively work to prevent workplace problems from occurring (courtesy). As such, an environment where transformative learning occurs can also align quite nicely with OCB. Hart et al. (2016) argued that the presence of OCB influences transformative learning, instead of the other way around. For example, employees willing to challenge and be challenged in the effort to improve the organization are more likely to generate an environment where transformative learning occurs. In addition, those who display altruism or helping behavior towards their colleagues can reduce conflict within the company. This environment would create psychological safety where one can feel free to engage in thinking that challenges the preconceived notions of themselves or other organizational members.

Transformative learning requires that an individual not only take responsibility for their own learning but also hold their organization accountable for creating and sharing knowledge (Rieckmann, 2021). Through this multi-level emphasis on learning, organizational members can be motivated to surface organizational issues that require change and design and implement solutions for those issues. For instance, this chapter previously referenced ERGs as networks that employees generally run on a volunteer basis. After a series of 2020 racially motivated killings within the United States (e.g., George Floyd, Ahmaud Arbery, Breonna Taylor), ERGs that served Black Americans as their affinity members advocated for increased awareness of the history of racial violence within the U.S. as well as policy changes that ensured equitable career opportunities for a diverse workforce. This is one example of how transformative learning has been used to empower a workforce to autonomously engage in actions that create a more just society.

Experiential Learning Theory

Kolb's experiential learning theory was influenced by leading figures in the fields of organizational development, learning, and social psychology (Kolb, 1984). He viewed experience as central to the learning process, differentiating it from other models that emphasize the behavioral and cognitive processes in learning. Because humans continuously have new experiences, Kolb posited that learning continuously occurs. Similarly to transformative learning, experiential learning involves ridding the mind of outdated ideas. The difference is with the process. In transformative learning, the learner begins an active process of reflection and re-examination to remove ideas which are no longer relevant. In experiential learning, the learner learns from his or her interactions with others and how those interactions meet or defy expectations.

For example, suppose an individual has previously interacted with a authoritative and overly prescriptive manager. In that case, that individual may have learned through their interactions with that manager that an employee performs best if they accept direction without question and focus on fulfilling their prescribed job's requirements. If that individual moves to a new team and interacts with a manager who encourages challenge and innovation, that employee may feel that it is expected of him or her to now look for extra-role tasks to do. There may be a cognitive element at play here that the individual may not be aware of. Therefore, while experiential learning emphasizes the role of experience, Kolb still views it as a holistic theory that combines experience with behavior and cognition.

Experiential learning also emphasizes the role that one's environment plays in this process. Outdoor experiential training combines the basic tenets of experiential training while moving the experiences outside (Kim et al., 2019). This type of training usually occurs in the wilderness (although it can occur in any outdoor setting, such as a park or a campsite) and includes a series of training exercises designed to evoke positive behavioral changes. These training exercises should be completely unrelated to the participants' roles, ensuring the experience is truly novel (Williams et al., 2003). Those who advocate for outdoor experiential training contend that it improves individual self-confidence and self-efficacy, accelerates team bonding, and reduces stress. All these factors likely lead to enhanced levels of job satisfaction, one theorized precursor to increased levels of OCB. Research has suggested that outdoor experiential training can increase altruism within employees and make them more likely to display individual initiative, courtesy, or organizational loyalty by increasing their willingness to surface change-oriented ideas (Kim et al., 2019).

Social Learning Theory

Like experiential learning theory, social learning theory leans into how people learn through their experiences. However, instead of people learning only through their direct experiences, they are also capable of learning through observing the experiences of others (Bandura, 1977). Albert Bandura, who is credited with developing this theory, argued that all knowledge that can be gained through direct experiences can also be gained through observing the experiences of others and the outcomes of those experiences. For example, an employee who observes a colleague's promotion following their work on a voluntary, special assignment may attribute that promotion to the work on the special project. That employee may then "learn" that if she also completes special projects, she will be in line for a promotion, even though this reward has not been explicitly promised or communicated to her. Her learning comes simply from her observation of her colleagues.

Figure 2 depicts the four processes that must be present for social learning to occur.

1. **Attentional processes.** This refers to the person's ability to recognize the components of another person's behavior. For someone unable to attend to the behavior around them, all the role modeling in the world will not influence that individual. Some individuals may display a star quality that invites more attention. Organizations have an interest in ensuring that these influential employees are modeling desired behaviors.

2. **Retention processes.** There is no value in observing behavior if a person cannot retain the features of what they saw. Observers can assist with their retention processes through rehearsal. Unfortunately, not all behaviors can be rehearsed, which may provide an unfair advantage for those with more advanced retention processes.
3. **Motoric reproduction processes.** The observer must have the skill to reproduce the behavior physically. They may be inhibited by being unable to directly observe all components of behavior or by their physical limitations in reproduction.
4. **Reinforcement and motivational processes.** If there is no reward for the observed behavior (or the reward is not visible), it is unlikely to be reproduced. Conversely, the same outcome will occur if the behavior is disciplined.

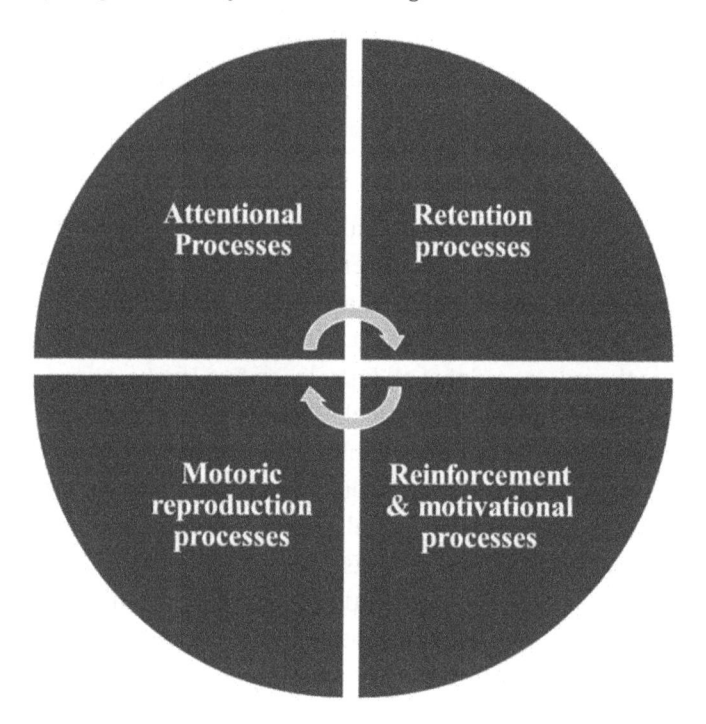

Figure 2. The four processes of social learning

One common element among the above learning theories is that they all emphasize a learner's self-efficacy, which is perceived as critical to developing prosocial organizational behaviors such as OCB and organizational spontaneity (George & Jones, 1997). This focus on self-efficacy should form a critical component of the design for a training program, especially if a desired outcome of the program is to positively impact OCB.

Training Programs' Impact on OCB

Examining dominant adult learning theories provides us with a context to view how learning can impact OCB and vice-versa. The primary purpose of training and development programs is to provide employees with the skill set needed to be successful in their jobs and provide the organization with a competitive advantage. Adding to and enhancing an employee's skillset allows them to engage in all manners of prosocial organizational behavior, regardless of the specific learning theory applied (George & Jones, 1997). That's because an individual with a low skill level will likely be constrained in their ability to:

1. Help others as they do not have the skill set to be helpful, even if they do have the desire.
2. Show conscientiousness through complying with organizational processes, as they may not have knowledge of those processes or the skill level to execute them.
3. Be involved in the company's governance as they are more focused on learning the core aspects of their job. Understandably, they lack the time, energy, or capacity to perform extra-role behaviors that are not guaranteed to come with any form of recognition or reward.
4. Publicly share their company's values as they may not be aware of the company's beneficial practices and products.

Training Programs' Impact on Job Satisfaction and Motivation

Training programs go beyond simply upskilling employees to create a culture that encourages OCB. Training and development programs can influence employee satisfaction, a predictor of OCB and motivation in general. Job satisfaction and motivation are often linked with one another – as well as confused with one another. Both constructs are subjective, cognitive, and emotional states that are difficult objectively measure and may exhibit day-to-day variability. Nonetheless, job satisfaction is often theorized to be a predictor of motivation, which serves as the eventual outcome (Kian et al., 2014). This is supported by research which has consistently found positive correlation between job satisfaction and motivation (Ayub & Rafif, 2011; Ismail & Abd Razak, 2016; Lut, 2012).

Many would consider it common sense to assume that employees with higher levels of job satisfaction will also be more likely to go above and beyond their company. Yet what makes an employee more likely to be happy with their job? Is it the pay, the organizational values, the emotional intelligence of the manager, or access to on-site amenities? There's also personality which, as noted earlier in the chapter, has some ties to job satisfaction while studies have also shown strong support for the theory that personality impacts an employee's motivation to learn (Major et al., 2006; Roberts et al., 2018; Rowold, 2007). Nevertheless, one factor that shows a consistent correlation with satisfaction is the employee's level of engagement. Research indicates that an employee's engagement at work is a more significant predictor of job satisfaction when compared to other factors (Swancott & Davis, 2023). When employees perceive that they have received high-quality training, they are more likely to exhibit high levels of work engagement and organizational loyalty (Humeera et al., 2023; Karatepe, 2013). This may be because employees interpret the opportunity to receive such training as a signal that they are valued and integral to the organization's success. This increased level of engagement also leads to more frequent displays of extra-role behavior during customer interactions.

Training Programs' Impact on Counterproductive Work Behaviors (CWB)

A quality training and development program can not only increase motivation and job satisfaction – it can also decrease the frequency of counterproductive work behaviors (CWB). CWB are inappropriate, harmful, or unlawful behaviors that threaten the health of an organization (Martinko et al., 2002). A wide spectrum encompasses these behaviors, from routinely showing up late to work to workplace acts of violence. The motivations behind these behaviors are complex. Employees may perceive the organization as unfair and retaliate through the display of OCB (e.g., an employee who feels that they were unfairly denied a promotion and, consequentially, begins to call out of work frequently without explanation as they seek other employment). Employees may also assess the potential disciplinary actions that are levied against those who engage in these types of behaviors and determine that it is unlikely that those actions will apply to themselves (e.g., a senior executive who witnesses other executives engage in fraudulent behaviors with no repercussions may begin to exhibit those same behaviors). It seems likely that an employee's attitude or job satisfaction are likely predictors of a willingness to display deviant work-related behaviors.

It is rational to want to root out those who are more likely to engage in CWB before they ever officially join an organization. Consequentially, one area of focus has been to develop tests (e.g., alcohol tests, stress tolerance tests, integrity tests) that can be used during employee selection to eliminate applicants who exhibit deviant tendencies (MacLane & Walmsley, 2010). As noted previously, research linking personality to CWB has been more promising than the links we have seen between personality and OCB (Ferreira & Nascimento, 2016; MacLane & Walmsley, 2010; Spector, 2010). One possible explanation for this discrepancy is that deviant behavior that can be identified through a test is more likely to clearly show up in a person's behavior as well.

If certain personality traits can serve as a predictor of CWB, then one may have the question as to whether training and development programs can have any impact on an individual's personality. While research supports that personality changes are possible even into one's elder years, studies have struggled to find consistent evidence of training having any long-term impact on personality traits (Sander et al., 2017). On the other hand, there is evidence of direct links between training programs and CWB. One study found a negative correlation between opportunities for professional development and CWB, indicating that as those development opportunities increased, CWB actions decreased (Guo et al., 2019). The authors theorized that employees who positively perceive the available opportunities to grow at work exhibit decreased negative job attitudes and increased organizational loyalty. In addition, employees who experience higher levels of well-being at work (measured by self-descriptions that used adjectives such as interested, excited, and enthusiastic) were less likely to exhibit destructive behaviors. A learning and development program that excites the learner and generates enthusiasm while providing them with the skills for career advancement can promote affective well-being and workplace engagement.

Learning Organizations and OCB

High levels of engagement can also be tied to the company's attitude towards learning. Organizations adept at obtaining, developing, and sharing knowledge while incorporating those learnings into all areas of their business (otherwise known as learning organizations) create sustained competitive advantage through employee investment (Islam et al., 2012). Organizations that rank strongly on their learning culture may drive OCB through an environment that encourages its workforce to show initiative in sharing knowledge with others. Because organizational members are immersed in a culture of continuous, systemic learning processes, they may engage in more systemic behavior by going outside of their core job functions to benefit the organization (Basim et al., 2009). Continuous learning through dialogue and inquiry has been implicated as important factors in predicting OCB.

Learning organizations are skilled at encouraging demonstrations of extra-role behavior (Yin Yin Lau et al., 2020). These organizations generally exhibit four characteristics: 1) an opportunity for individual learning and the sharing of that learning, 2) knowledge that can be created through reflection on new experiences, 3) employees who are encouraged to participate in decision-making processes through shorter chains-of-command, and 4) leaders who create the psychological and environmental safety to allow for experimentation with new ideas. When examining the relationship between a learning organization and higher levels of OCB, researchers have examined whether the employee perceives that the organization rewards learning, shares knowledge across all employees, provides mentorship and coaching, and recognizes innovation and risk-taking. Organizations that exhibit these factors also have higher levels of self-reported OCB. This effect was positively compounded by employees who also perceived favorable team relationships.

Leadership and OCB

Interactions with the leader of the team often drive those team relationships. While multiple leadership styles may produce desired performance depending on the situation, the quality of one's leadership skills can have beneficial or detrimental effects on their employee. Organizations expend significant money on leadership development programs without much evidence that they work (Druckman et al., 1997). Moreover, 54% of employees do not trust their manager to do the right thing (DDI, 2023). As previously discussed, trust levels have been indicated to show positive correlations with OCB. Additionally, within that same survey, top leaders within the company expressed concerns about the skills of their managers and supervisors. Research indicates that organizations with a strong leader talent pipeline are not only significantly more likely to engage top talent, but they are also much more likely to be in the top tier of industry performance.

Leaders identified the following skills as critical to their roles: identifying top talent, strategic thinking, change management, decision-making, and influencing others (DDI, 2023). Unfortunately, most leaders state that they do not receive much training in any of these areas. Leaders are eager for learning opportunities and signified that they prefer learning experiences such as instructor-led training and professional coaching much more than other experiences such as internal coaching or digital learning. The internal coaching category includes coaching from their manager, which was surprisingly ranked very low on preferred learning experiences. However, leaders who perceived the coaching from their managers to be effective were much more likely to value it. Therefore, the low preference for manager coaching may be more reflective of the quality of the coaching rather than the actual desire for it. These findings are critical to developing high-quality training programs to build upon the leadership skills necessary to drive engagement, enhance job satisfaction, and increase OCB levels. The literature supports that training in emotional intelligence behaviors (such as increased manager support) and technical training that increases manager self-efficacy can lead to higher levels of employee engagement (Jungert et al., 2022; Luthans & Peterson, 2002).

Even beyond increasing the engagement of direct reports, leaders' engagement and job satisfaction can also be positively impacted by high-quality training programs, which can lead to higher levels of OCB on the leaders' part. Research on group-level OCB has begun to emerge, focusing on the manager or supervisor's part in role modeling POB for their team. Studies have observed that displays of leader OCB were likely to positively impact team OCB levels, especially when the team views the leader as a role model worth emulating (Yaffe & Kark, 2011). This aligns with the research on social learning theory previously enumerated within this chapter. Several recommendations for developing leaders' skills through training are presented below:

1. Organizations should provide training that increases leaders' ability to operate within a virtual and hybrid environment, especially when identifying and developing other talent.
2. Talent departments should identify the key leadership skills general to all company leaders and specific to certain roles and partner with training departments to design training to accommodate those general and role-specific profiles.
3. Senior leaders should combine training and development with career conversations to provide managers and supervisors with purpose and support as they navigate their advancement through the pipeline.

CONCLUSION

Organizational citizenship behaviors and other prosocial organizational behaviors are key to driving a high-performance, engaged work culture. OCB includes a variety of discretionary behaviors that may or may not be rewarded by the organization. Motivation to engage in these behaviors also varies but likely is based on a combination of personality, employee attitudes, and leadership role modeling. While displays of OCB may be more innate within specific personality traits, training programs significantly enhance employee job satisfaction and effective leadership skills to drive these prosocial behaviors. When designing training programs to increase OCB levels, the following characteristics should be considered for inclusion in the design:

1. Training should include components of self-direction and active participation of the learner.
2. Interpersonal interactions should be emphasized to build relationships and increase the direct and indirect experiences that lead to knowledge gain and sharing.

3. High-quality technical training is as critical as social or behavioral training, providing employees with the skills to feel comfortable in their roles. That comfort level is a precursor to having the capacity and desire to engage in OCB.
4. A specific training program should be an integrated part of the learning organization framework.
5. Leaders should have training specific to their roles to increase OCB at their level and inspire them to role model those behaviors for their teams.

Individuals and organizations both stand to reap significant benefits from a culture that values and promotes prosocial behavior. Training and development programs should be ready to partner with change agents and organizational leaders in driving their companies into the top performance tier.

REFERENCES

Aknin, L. B., Barrington-Leigh, C. P., Dunn, E. W., Helliwell, J. F., Biswas-Diener, R., Kemeza, I., Nyende, P., Ashton-James, C. E., & Norton, M. I. (2010). Prosocial spending and well-being: Cross-cultural evidence for a psychological universal. *Journal of Personality and Social Psychology, 104*(4), 635–652. doi:10.1037/a0031578 PMID:23421360

Aknin, L. B., Broesch, T., Hamlin, J. K., & Van de Vondervoort, J. W. (2015). Prosocial behavior leads to happiness in a small-scale rural society. *Journal of Experimental Psychology. General, 144*(4), 788–795. doi:10.1037/xge0000082 PMID:26030168

Allen, M. R., Adomdza, G. K., & Meyer, M. H. (2015). Managing for innovation: Managerial control and employee level outcomes. *Journal of Business Research, 68*(2), 371–379. doi:10.1016/j.jbusres.2014.06.021

Ayub, N., & Rafif, S. (2011). The relationship between work motivation and job satisfaction. *Pakistan Business Review, 13*(2), 332-347. https://www.researchgate.net/publication/342864521_The_Relationship_between_Work_Motivation_and_Job_Satisfaction

Bandura, A. (1977). *Social learning theory*. Prentice-Hall.

Basim, H. N., Şeşen, H., Sözen, C., & Hazir, K. (2009). The effect of employees' learning organization perceptions on organizational citizenship behaviors. *Selcuk University Social Sciences Institute Journal, 22*, 55–66. https://www.academia.edu/en/1082627/The_Effect_of_Employees_Learning_Organization_Perceptions_on_Organizational_Citizenship_Behaviors

Bass, B. M., & Riggio, R. E. (2006). *Transformational Leadership*. Lawrence Erlbaum Associates, Inc. doi:10.4324/9781410617095

Bateman, T. S., & Organ, D. W. (1983). Job satisfaction and the good soldier: The relationship between affect and employee "citizenship." *Academy of Management Journal, 26*(4), 587–595. doi:10.2307/255908

Berman, E. M., West, J. P., & Richter, M. N. Jr. (2002). Workplace relations: Friendship patterns and consequences (according to managers). *Public Administration Review, 62*(2), 217–230. doi:10.1111/0033-3352.00172

Blau, P. (1964). *Exchange and power in social life*. John Wiley & Sons, Inc.

Borman, W. C., Penner, L. A., Allen, T. D., & Motowidlo, S. J. (2001). Personality predictors of citizenship performance. *International Journal of Selection and Assessment, 9*(1-2), 52–69. doi:10.1111/1468-2389.00163

Bowling, N. A. (2010). Effects of Job Satisfaction and Conscientiousness on Extra-Role Behaviors. *Journal of Business and Psychology, 25*(1), 119–130. doi:10.1007/s10869-009-9134-0

Brief, A. P., & Motowidlo, S. J. (1986). Prosocial organizational behaviors. *Academy of Management Review, 11*(4), 710–725. doi:10.2307/258391

Burke, W. W. (2017). *Organization Change: Theory and Practice* (5th ed.). SAGE Publications, Inc.

Cerasoli, C. P., Nicklin, J. M., & Ford, M. T. (2014). Intrinsic motivation and extrinsic incentives jointly predict performance: A 40-year meta-analysis. *Psychological Bulletin, 140*(4), 980–1008. doi:10.1037/a0035661 PMID:24491020

Conte, J. M., & Landy, F. J. (2019). *Work in the 21st Century: An Introduction to Industrial and Organizational Psychology* (6th ed.). Wiley.

Costa, P. T., & McCrae, R. R. (1999). A five-factor theory of personality. *The five-factor model of personality: Theoretical perspectives, 2*, 51-87.

Da Silva, W. F. C., Da Consolação Paiva, W., & Da Silva, H. A. (2019). Correlations between trust and the organizational citizenship behaviors: Reflections and considerations for public managers from a municipality in Minas Gerais. *British Journal of Management, 12*(2), 317–335. doi:10.5902/19834659

DDI. (2023). *Global Leadership Forecast 2023.* https://media.ddiworld.com/research/glf2023.pdf

Druckman, D., Singer, J. E., & Van Cott, H. (1997). *Enhancing Organizational Performance.* National Academy Press. doi:10.17226/5128

Dubey, P., Pathak, A. K., & Sahu, K. K. (2023). Assessing the influence of effective leadership on job satisfaction and organisational citizenship behaviour. *Rajagiri Management Journal, 17*(3), 221–237. doi:10.1108/RAMJ-07-2022-0108

Ferreira, M. F., & Nascimento, E. D. (2016). Relationship between personality traits and counterproductive work behaviors. *Psico-USF, 21*(3), 677–685. doi:10.1590/1413-82712016210319

George, J. M., & Brief, A. P. (1992). Feeling good-doing good: A conceptual analysis of the mood at work-organizational spontaneity relationship. *Psychological Bulletin, 112*(2), 310–322. doi:10.1037/0033-2909.112.2.310 PMID:1454897

George, J. M., & Jones, G. R. (1997). Organizational spontaneity in context. *Human Performance, 10*(2), 153–170. doi:10.1207/s15327043hup1002_6

Guo, Z., Xie, B., Chen, J., & Wang, F. (2019). The relationship between opportunities for professional development and counterproductive work behaviors: The mediating role of affective well–being and moderating role of task-contingent conscientiousness. *International Journal of Mental Health Promotion, 21*(3), 111–122. doi:10.32604/IJMHP.2019.011040

Harari, M. B., Thompson, A. H., & Viswesvaran, C. (2018). Extraversion and job satisfaction: The role of trait bandwidth and the moderating effect of status goal attainment. *Personality and Individual Differences, 123,* 14–16. doi:10.1016/j.paid.2017.10.041

Hart, T. A., Gilstrap, J. B., & Bolino, M. C. (2016). Organizational citizenship behavior and the enhancement of absorptive capacity. *Journal of Business Research, 69*(10), 3981–3988. doi:10.1016/j.jbusres.2016.06.001

Holmes, M. R. (1980). Interpersonal behaviors and their relationship to the andragogical and pedagogical orientations of adult educators. *Adult Education, 31*(1), 18–29. doi:10.1177/074171368003100102

Humeera, N., & Mufeed, S. A. (2023). Role of HRM practices in enhancing employee engagement: A literature review. *IUP Journal of Management Research, 22*(3), 40–64.

Islam, T., Anwar, F., Khan, S. U. R., Rasli, A., Ahmad, U. N. B. U., & Ahmed, I. (2012). Investigating the mediating role of organizational citizenship behavior between organizational learning culture and knowledge sharing. *World Applied Sciences Journal, 19*(6), 795–799.

Ismail, A., & Abd Razak, M. R. (2016). A study on job satisfaction as a determinant of job motivation. *Acta Universitatis Danubius, 12*(3), 30–44.

Judge, T. A., Heller, D., & Mount, M. K. (2002). Five-factor model of personality and job satisfaction: A meta-analysis. *The Journal of Applied Psychology, 87*(3), 530–541. doi:10.1037/0021-9010.87.3.530 PMID:12090610

Jungert, T., Gradito Dubord, M. A., Högberg, M., & Forest, J. (2022). Can managers be trained to further support their employees' basic needs and work engagement: A manager training program study. *International Journal of Training and Development, 26*(3), 472–494. doi:10.1111/ijtd.12267

Karatepe, O. M. (2013). High-performance work practices and hotel employee performance: The mediation of work engagement. *International Journal of Hospitality Management, 32*, 132–140. doi:10.1016/j.ijhm.2012.05.003

Kessels, J. W., & Poell, R. F. (2004). Andragogy and social capital theory: The implications for human resource development. *Advances in Developing Human Resources, 6*(2), 146–157. doi:10.1177/1523422304263326

Kian, T. S., Yusoff, W. F. W., & Rajah, S. (2014). Job satisfaction and motivation: What are the difference among these two. *European Journal of Business and Social Sciences, 3*(2), 94–102.

Kim, S. H., Childs, M., & Williams, J. (2019). The effects of outdoor experiential training on part-time student employees' organizational citizenship behavior. *Journal of Hospitality and Tourism Management, 41*, 90–100. doi:10.1016/j.jhtm.2019.10.009

Klein, N. (2016). Prosocial behavior increases perceptions of meaning in life. *The Journal of Positive Psychology, 12*(4), 354–361. doi:10.1080/17439760.2016.1209541

Knowles, M. S. (2003). Androgogy – Not pedagogy. In P. Jarvis & C. Griffin (Eds.), *Adult and Continuing Education – Major Themes in Education* (pp. 226–233). Routledge Taylor & Francis Group. (Original work published 1968)

Knowles, M. S. (2003). Excerpt from 'How my ideas evolved and changed. In P. Jarvis & C. Griffin (Eds.), *Adult and Continuing Education – Major Themes in Education* (pp. 234–239). Routledge Taylor & Francis Group. (Original work published 1989)

Kolb, D. A. (1984). *Experiential Learning: Experience as the Source of Learning and Development*. Prentice-Hall, Inc.

Konovsky, M. A., & Pugh, S. D. (1994). Citizenship behavior and social exchange. *Academy of Management Journal, 37*(3), 656–669. doi:10.2307/256704 PMID:10134637

Lazar, L., & Eisenberger, N. I. (2022). The benefits of giving: Effects of prosocial behavior on recovery from stress. *Psychophysiology, 59*(2), 1–16. doi:10.1111/psyp.13954 PMID:34676898

Low, C. H., Bordia, P., & Bordia, S. (2016). What do employees want and why? An exploration of employees' preferred psychological contract elements across career stages. *Human Relations, 69*(7), 1457–1481. doi:10.1177/0018726715616468

Lut, D. M. (2012). Connection between job motivation, job satisfaction and work performance in Romanian trade enterprises. *Economics and Applied Informatics, 18*(3), 45–50.

Luthans, F. (2011). *Organizational Behavior: An Evidence-Based Approach* (12th ed.). The McGraw-Hill Companies, Inc.

Luthans, F., & Peterson, S. J. (2002). Employee engagement and manager self-efficacy: Implications for managerial effectiveness and development. *Journal of Management Development, 21*(5), 376–387. doi:10.1108/02621710210426864

MacLane, C. N., & Walmsley, P. T. (2010). Reducing counterproductive work behavior through employee selection. *Human Resource Management Review, 20*(1), 62–72. doi:10.1016/j.hrmr.2009.05.001

Mahajan, R. (2017). Impact of big five personality traits on OCB and satisfaction. *International Journal of Business Insights & Transformation, 11*(1), 46–51.

Major, D. A., Turner, J. E., & Fletcher, T. D. (2006). Linking proactive personality and the Big Five to motivation to learn and development activity. *The Journal of Applied Psychology, 91*(4), 927–935. https://psycnet.apa.org/doi/10.1037/0021-9010.91.4.927. doi:10.1037/0021-9010.91.4.927 PMID:16834515

Martinko, M. J., Gundlach, M. J., & Douglas, S. C. (2002). Toward an integrative theory of counterproductive workplace behavior: A causal reasoning perspective. *International Journal of Selection and Assessment, 10*(1-2), 36–50. doi:10.1111/1468-2389.00192

Mezirow, J. (1990). A transformation theory of adult learning. In *Adult Education Research Annual Conference Proceedings* (Vol. 31, pp. 141-146). Academic Press.

Mezirow, J. (1997). Transformative learning: Theory to practice. *New Directions for Adult and Continuing Education, 1997*(74), 5–12. doi:10.1002/ace.7401

Moorman, R. H. (1991). Relationship between organizational justice and organizational citizenship behaviors: Do fairness perceptions influence employee citizenship? *The Journal of Applied Psychology, 76*(6), 845–855. doi:10.1037/0021-9010.76.6.845

Organ, D. W. (1988). *Organizational citizenship behavior: The good soldier syndrome*. Lexington Books.

Organ, D. W. (1994). Personality and organizational citizenship behavior. *Journal of Management, 20*(2), 465–478. doi:10.1177/014920639402000208

Organ, D. W. (2014). Organizational citizenship behavior: It's construct clean-up time. *Human Performance, 10*(2), 85–97. doi:10.1207/s15327043hup1002_2

Organ, D. W., & McFall, J. B. (2004). Personality and citizenship behavior in organizations. In B. Schneider & D. B. Smith (Eds.), *Personality and Organizations* (pp. 291–314). Lawrence Erlbaum Associates, Inc., doi:10.4324/9781410610034-22

Pillai, R., Schriesheim, C. A., & Williams, E. S. (1999). Fairness perceptions and trust as mediators for transformational and transactional leadership: A two-sample study. *Journal of Management, 25*(6), 897–933. doi:10.1177/014920639902500606

Podsakoff, P. M., & MacKenzie, S. B. (2014). Impact of organizational citizenship behavior on organizational performance: A review and suggestions for future research. *Human Performance, 10*(2), 133–151. doi:10.1207/s15327043hup1002_5

Podsakoff, P. M., MacKenzie, S. B., Paine, J. B., & Bachrach, D. G. (2000). Organizational citizenship behaviors: A critical review of the theoretical and empirical literature and suggestions for future research. *Journal of Management, 26*(3), 513–563. doi:10.1177/014920630002600307

Rieckmann, M. (2021). Emancipatory and transformative Global Citizenship Education in formal and informal settings: Empowering learners to change structures. *Tertium Comparationis, 26*(2), 174-186. https://elibrary.utb.de/doi/abs/10.31244/tc.2020.02.10

Roberts, Z., Rogers, A., Thomas, C. L., & Spitzmueller, C. (2018). Effects of proactive personality and conscientiousness on training motivation. *International Journal of Training and Development, 22*(2), 126–143. doi:10.1111/ijtd.12122

Rowold, J. (2007). The impact of personality on training-related aspects of motivation: Test of a longitudinal model. *Human Resource Development Quarterly, 18*(1), 9–31. doi:10.1002/hrdq.1190

Sander, J., Schmiedek, F., Brose, A., Wagner, G. G., & Specht, J. (2017). Long-term effects of an extensive cognitive training on personality development. *Journal of Personality, 85*(4), 454–463. doi:10.1111/jopy.12252 PMID:26998917

Simpson, J. A., & Beckes, L. (2010). Evolutionary perspectives on prosocial behavior. In M. Mikulincer & P. R. Shaver (Eds.), *Prosocial motives, emotions, and behavior: The better angels of our nature* (pp. 35–53). American Psychological Association. doi:10.1037/12061-002

Sinelnikova, V., Ivchenko, T., Pistunova, T., Regesha, N., & Skazhenyk, M. (2022). Enhancing the performance of andragogic education. *Journal of Curriculum and Teaching, 11*(1), 245–254. doi:10.5430/jct.v11n1p245

Spector, P. E. (2010). The relationship of personality to counterproductive work behavior (CWB): An integration of perspectives. *Human Resource Management Review, 21*(4). Advance online publication. doi:10.1016/j.hrmr.2010.10.002

Staub, E. (1978). *Positive social behavior and morality: Social and personal influences* (Vol. 1). Academic Press Inc.

Sterns, L., Alexander, R. A., Barrett, G. V., & Dambrot, F. H. (1983). The relationship of extraversion and neuroticism with job preferences and job satisfaction for clerical employees. *Journal of Occupational Psychology, 56*(2), 145–153. doi:10.1111/j.2044-8325.1983.tb00122.x

Swancott, L. J., & Davis, S. K. (2023). Service with a smile? Engagement is a better predictor of job satisfaction than emotional intelligence. *Current Psychology (New Brunswick, N.J.), 42*(17), 14647–14651. doi:10.1007/s12144-022-02818-4

Van Dyne, L., Cummings, L. L., & Parks, J. M. (1995). Extra role behaviors: In pursuit of construct and definitional clarity. *Research in Organizational Behavior, 17*, 215–285. https://www.researchgate.net/publication/309563728_Extra-role_behaviors_In_pursuit_of_construct_and_definitional_clarity

Wals, A. E., Geerling-Eijff, F., Hubeek, F., Van der Kroon, S., & Vader, J. (2008). All mixed up? Instrumental and emancipatory learning toward a more sustainable world: Considerations for EE policymakers. *Applied Environmental Education and Communication, 7*(3), 55–65. doi:10.1080/15330150802473027

Wang, S., Liu, Y., Zhang, J., & Li, S. (2023). Why, how and when the double-edged sword of workplace friendship impacts differentiated organizational citizenship behavior: A relationship motivation theory approach. *Current Psychology (New Brunswick, N.J.), 42*(16), 13838–13855. doi:10.1007/s12144-022-03818-0

Wayne, S. J., Shore, L. M., & Liden, R. C. (1997). Perceived organizational support and leader-member exchange: A social exchange perspective. *Academy of Management Journal, 40*(1), 82–111. doi:10.2307/257021

Williams, L. J., & Anderson, S. E. (1991). Job satisfaction and organizational commitment as predictors of organizational citizenship and in-role behaviors. *Journal of Management, 17*(3), 601–617. doi:10.1177/014920639101700305

Williams, S. D., Graham, T. S., & Baker, B. (2003). Evaluating outdoor experiential training for leadership and team building. *Journal of Management Development, 22*(1), 45–59. doi:10.1108/02621710310454851

Yaffe, T., & Kark, R. (2011). Leading by example: The case of leader OCB. *The Journal of Applied Psychology, 96*(4), 806–826. doi:10.1037/a0022464 PMID:21443315

Yin Yin Lau, P., Park, S., & McLean, G. (2020). Learning organization and organizational citizenship behaviour in West Malaysia: Moderating role of team-oriented culture. *European Journal of Training and Development, 44*(8/9), 847–864. doi:10.1108/EJTD-01-2020-0007

KEY TERMS AND DEFINITIONS

Andragogy: An adult learning theory that emphasizes the role an adult plays in directing his or her own learning.

Counterproductive Work Behavior: Detrimental actions performed by an organizational member that can harm the organization or other organizational members.

Experiential Learning Theory: An adult learning theory that emphasizes the role of new events and situations in learning.

Five-Factor Model of Personality: A framework for conceptualizing an individual's characteristics or traits and divides those traits into five dimensions: Openness, Conscientiousness, Extraversion, Agreeableness, and Neuroticism.

Organizational Citizenship Behavior: Actions performed by an organizational member that go beyond task performance, the requirements of the job role, and provide value to the organization or other members.

Prosocial Organizational Behavior: Actions performed by an organizational member that benefit the organization or other organizational members.

Social Learning Theory: An adult learning theory that emphasizes the ability to learn through observing the experiences of others.

Transformative Learning Theory: An adult learning theory that emphasizes the role of reflection and reassessment of prior beliefs in driving learning.

Chapter 9
Motivating Workplace Learners From a Place of Psychological Safety

Rachel Frost
https://orcid.org/0009-0006-8627-3588
Adler University, USA

ABSTRACT

This chapter delves into motivating workplace learners through the lens of psychological safety and adult learning theories. Grounded in self-determination theory, the exploration of felt support underscores the impact of intrinsic motivation on continuous learning and development. Multigenerational knowledge sharing is examined, revealing the interplay between psychological safety and generational cohort dynamics. The measurable impact of people-first training strategies and transformational leadership principles are emphasized for their positive effects on workplace thriving. A trauma-informed approach is integrated, advocating for inclusive and supportive organizational cultures. Lastly, insights from academic studies are woven throughout to contribute to a comprehensive understanding of effective strategies for fostering psychological safety, motivation, and holistic thriving in workforce development programs.

"*A psychologically safe work environment is one in which employees feel safe to voice ideas, willingly seek feedback, provide honest feedback, collaborate, take risks and experiment.*" (Newman et al., 2017, p. 521)

DOI: 10.4018/979-8-3693-1674-0.ch009

Copyright © 2024, IGI Global. Copying or distributing in print or electronic forms without written permission of IGI Global is prohibited.

INTRODUCTION

While the term "Psychological safety" remains linked to qualitative, subjective interpretation, a growing body of quantifiable evidence underscores its profound impact on workplace learning and employee motivation. In the realm of workplace dynamics, Kark and Carmeli's (2009) seminal study illustrates the essential factor of psychological safety for enhancing employees' vitality while mitigating defensiveness and anxiety linked to the learning process. Additionally, the study by Lui and Keller (2021) underscores psychologically safe environments as fertile grounds for learning and engagement. A comprehensive meta-analysis conducted by Newman et al. (2017), spanning eighty-three studies, reinforces a consistent theme: A psychologically safe work environment transcends subjective good vibes; it emerges as an ecosystem wherein employees feel secure to voice ideas, seek and provide feedback, collaborate, take risks, and experiment. The analysis further establishes a predictive relationship between psychological safety and consequential learning and performance outcomes across all organizational levels (Newman et al., 2017).

Psychological safety also extends beyond a learner's capacity to speak, question, and risk freely; it embodies a holistic sense of safety and belonging. In the wake of collective and individual traumas permeating the professional sphere, as highlighted by Manning (2022), organizations are grappling with the ongoing issues and repercussions of COVID-19. These include heightened levels of burnout and stress among employees due to prolonged remote work arrangements, increased workload demands, and uncertainty surrounding job security and future organizational changes. Alongside a global pandemic, persistent challenges posed by racial violence, political upheaval, and environmental disasters have intensified workplace stressors. The surge in anxiety and depression statistics in the U.S. (American Institute of Stress, 2023) underscores the imperative for organizations to adapt and proactively support their employees' wellbeing through unforeseen challenges (Manning, 2022). Age diversity in the workplace and the issue of generational cohort perception also bring the challenge of psychological safety to the forefront with its effect on knowledge sharing, mentoring, and training initiatives.

This chapter aims to unravel the underlying theories that scaffold psychological safety, drawing from Social Learning Theory, Self-Determination Theory, Social Exchange Theory, Organizational Support Theory, and Social Identity Theory. Through the lens of a "people first" strategy, we will explore practical applications in training and development. Ultimately, we will illuminate the enduring value of cultivating psychologically safe learning atmospheres, where employee motivation not only takes root but thrives sustainably.

The History of the Psychological Safety Concept

The humanistic approach of psychologist Carl Rogers (1902-1987) was a forerunner of the principles of psychological safety. Rogers' theory was that people needed "unconditional positive regard, genuineness, and empathy" to be empowered to meet their full capabilities and potential for good (Rogers, 1957). This person-centered approach was echoed by Abraham Maslow (1908-1970), whose 1943 Theory of Motivation posited that humans are motivated by basic physiological and safety needs before they can focus on higher-level needs of "belongingness" and self-actualization (Maslow, 1943). Researchers and MIT professors, Edgar Stein and Warren Bennis, were the first to suggest that perceptions of psychological safety in the workplace reduce threat and encourage unconstrained collaboration (1965).

William Kahn (1990) resurrected and expounded on the concept with his influential grounded theory paper which revealed a significant relationship between employee engagement and psychological safety at work. He described psychological safety as a condition in which one can freely share knowledge, thoughts, or ideas "without fear of negative consequences to self-image, status or career" (Kahn, 1990:708). Amy Edmondson later expanded on this idea with her quantifiable research conclusions that psychological safety is an "enabler of learning" (Edmondson, 1999). Furthermore, her studies suggested that a psychologically safe workplace provides opportunities for people to speak up about ideas, questions, fears, or disagreements without fear of being shut down or punished in some way (Edmondson, 1999; Edmondson & Lei, 2014, Edmondson, 2018). More recently, Timothy Clark's research suggests that there are 4 Stages of psychological safety: Inclusion safety, Learner Safety, Contributor Safety, and Challenger Safety (Clark, 2020). Clark proposes that each stage is vital if an organization wants to motivate a diverse workforce with an open flow of ideas, collaboration, and innovation.

Relevance to Workplace Motivation and Learning

Learning is the ability to acquire new skills or knowledge and apply it directly to one's work (Edmondson, 1999). Psychological safety reduces anxiety associated with workplace learning, suggesting that a psychologically safe organizational climate facilitates an agile learning environment. This is where open communication and collaboration are promoted, enabling individuals to quickly adapt to changing circumstances, acquire new skills, and respond effectively to emerging challenges.

Edmondson (2020) underscores that although psychological safety is crucial, it is not the ultimate goal. The goal is excellence and establishing psychological safety is the means to the goal (The Kings Fund video, 2020). This insight positions psychological safety as a pivotal conduit leading to more impactful workplace training initiatives. Given that training and development serve as the primary drivers of organizational growth, the cultivation of psychological safety becomes instrumental in fostering an environment conducive to learning and knowledge sharing. As highlighted by Korte (2007), these processes are intricately woven into the fabric of group dynamics and social interactions (p. 172).

Recognizing that individuals dedicate a significant portion of their lives to work, the significance of interpersonal communication and the perception of psychological safety within the workplace cannot be overstated. Edmondson's assertion thus resonates deeply with the understanding that a psychologically safe environment is a means to achieve organizational excellence and a foundation for the vitality of workplace learning and growth initiatives. Organizations with learning agility not only think holistically and systematically about the training needs of their human capital but can adapt to unpredictable market climates more quickly than competitors (Garvin et al., 2008). Psychological safety tops the list as a distinguishing characteristic of a supportive learning environment (Garvin et al., 2008), signaling that it is acceptable to ask questions, take risks, own mistakes, learn from mistakes, or offer minority viewpoints (Newman et al., 2017).

Aligned with the emphasis on psychological safety as a catalyst for workplace excellence and learning, the concept of workforce learning engagement comes to the forefront. Defined as an affective-cognitive state where employees actively create, acquire, and transfer knowledge (Garvin et al., 2008), training and development become a vital component in the organizational growth narrative. The positive association between employee perceptions of psychological safety and learning behavior is not only an individual phenomenon but extends to team dynamics as well (Newman et al., 2017). Lui and Keller's (2021) study further fortifies this connection by revealing that psychologically safe environments contribute to team member motivation and engagement (p. 44). This interplay between psychological safety, workforce learning engagement, and team dynamics underscores the relationship between a supportive training environment and the cultivation of a motivated and knowledgeable workforce.

Malcolm Knowles' andragogical theory (1980) further reinforces this connection by emphasizing the importance of tailoring learning experiences to meet the unique needs and characteristics of adult learners. When applied in the workplace context, this theory suggests that training programs should provide opportunities for employees to take ownership of their learning, apply new knowledge and skills to real-world challenges, and engage in collaborative problem-solving with their peers.

Theoretical Support

Malcolm Knowles' andragogical theory provides a framework for understanding how adults learn best and emphasizes the importance of learners' autonomy, self-direction, and readiness to learn. According to Knowles (1980), adult learners are motivated by internal factors such as relevance to their lives and previous experiences. They prefer learning that is problem-centered, task-oriented, and immediately applicable to their work or personal goals. Additionally, Knowles highlights the significance of adult learners' active involvement in the learning process, emphasizing the role of collaboration, reflection, and self-assessment (Frazier & Tupper, 2018).

The integration of psychological safety principles with Knowles' andragogical theory aligns with the idea of creating a supportive and empowering learning environment for adult learners. When adult learners feel psychologically safe, they are more likely to take ownership of their learning, engage in meaningful discussions, share their perspectives, and explore new ideas without fear of judgment or failure. This sense of safety and autonomy fosters a deeper level of engagement and motivation, leading to enhanced learning outcomes and personal growth.

Furthermore, by honoring adult learners' autonomy and life experiences, educators can tailor their instructional strategies to meet the diverse needs and preferences of learners. This may involve offering opportunities for self-directed learning, incorporating real-life examples and case studies, providing choices in learning activities, and encouraging reflection on how new knowledge or skills can be applied in different contexts. When adults have autonomy in their learning process and can see the direct application of new knowledge or skills to their lives or work, they are more likely to be intrinsically motivated to engage in learning activities and pursue continuous growth and development.

Intrinsic Motivation

Within the complex nuances of adult motivation, the internal forces propelling individuals often eclipse external incentives (Frazier & Tupper, 2018). Grounded in this understanding, the Self-Determination Theory posits that intrinsic motivation, stemming from autonomy, competence, and relatedness, serves as the bedrock for human motivation and self-regulation (Ryan & Desi, 2017). Translating this theory into the workplace context, employees exhibit heightened motivation for learning and development when their fundamental psychological needs are met (Frazier & Tupper, 2018) and there is immediate and meaningful application for the learning (Bouchrika, 2023). In this symbiotic relationship, psychological safety emerges as the catalyst, amplifying intrinsic motivation and setting in motion a feedback cycle that fuels personal transformation and cultivates collaborative learning environments (Dewey et al., 2020, p. 78).

The adage "What gets rewarded gets repeated," often attributed to B.F. Skinner, encapsulates the motivational power of rewarding behavior. Acknowledging individual strengths and providing positive reinforcement enhances participants' internal drive for learning. The trifecta of intrinsic motivation, Self-Determination Theory, and psychological safety shape a workplace environment to be conducive to continuous learning, growth, and collaborative success.

Collaborative Learning

The dynamics of workplace groups and learning cohorts also find resonance in Social Identity Theory, where individuals consistently define their identity within the prevailing social context to maintain a positive self-image (Tajfel & Turner, 2004). Organizational culture acts as a strong socialization agent (Joy & Kolb, 2009) and the commonality of purpose becomes the cohesive agent. Psychological safety, a cornerstone in this context, places a premium on social connection and a sense of belonging (Clark, 2020). In workplace environments where individuals feel group pride and support from their colleagues, they are more inclined to share ideas, engage in collaborative endeavors, and express themselves without the looming fear of social repercussions (Edmondson, 1999). Psychological safety is realized within a group setting and shared behaviors (Lynn & Sarro, 2022). In a nurturing and collaborative atmosphere, individual contributions and successes are appreciated and become a potent incentive for ongoing growth and shared achievements within the cohort (Dewey et al., 2020, p. 78). A learning environment that fosters interdependence not only contributes to intrinsic motivation for group members but also fortifies psychological safety by acknowledging and supporting individual contributions to the collective learning journey.

Experiential Learning

David Kolb believed that learning styles are shaped by genetics, life experiences, and environmental demands placed upon individuals (Joy & Kolb, 2009). Experiential learning theory suggests that growth is interactive and cyclical in nature through cognitive (thinking), affective (emotions and feelings), and psychomotor (kinesthetic) learning domains (Joy & Kolb, 2009). Both Kolb and Knowles (1980) place the individual at the active center of the learning process and emphasize the influential role of past experiences and reflection in shaping learning trajectories. In such an environment, the diverse experiences of group members are not merely acknowledged but valued, fostering inclusivity (Clark, 2020). The integration of experiential learning theory with psychological safety principles provides a comprehensive framework for creating an inclusive and growth-oriented learning environment across cognitive, affective, and psychomotor domains.

Workforce Development practitioners play a crucial role in removing obstacles (Clark, 2020) and determining the right resources to enhance the learning conditions and accessibility for all individuals (Praslova, 2021). Implementing the experiential learning cycle for adults, "touches all the bases" (Joy & Kolb, 2009) as individuals are encouraged to experiment, reflect, think, and act in ways that best align with their learning styles. Offering this choice in self-directed and relevant learning content not only underscores the components of Self-Determination Theory as individuals take ownership of their deficiencies (Ryan & Desi, 2000), but enables a transformative learning experience (Bouchrika, 2023; Joy & Kolb, 2009). In inclusive, psychologically safe environments, employees feel liberated to engage in learning styles that best suit them without fear of failure (Edmondson, 1999). Experiential learning theory, underscores the dynamic nature of learning (Joy & Kolb, 2009) and gives adult learners a "theory of action" to influence and solidify new behaviors (Gavin & McBrearty, 2019, p. 20).

When a training program aligns with employees' natural and motivating learning styles, there is improved "alignment with organizational culture, values or strategic intent" (Andrews and Liang, 2018, p. 2) Gratton & Erickson (2013) point to the deep psychological and motivating power of meaningful work for individuals and teams. A well-designed training initiative prepares employees for meaningful work and engages the feedback loop for overall employee satisfaction. Organizations that build intentionally strong teams consistently invest in their employees' well-being, motivation, and creative input, which is likely to increase organizational trust (Gratton & Erickson, 2013, p. 76).

Organizational Trust

Organizational Support Theory delves into the dynamics between employers and employees, hinging on the crucial notion of perceived organizational support—the extent to which employees believe their contributions are valued and their well-being is prioritized within the workplace (Baran et al., 2012, para. 1). Training is multifaceted with both relational and transactional dimensions (Arnold, 1996) and a comprehensive examination illuminates the interconnected nature of psychological contracts and psychological safety. Rooted in the Social Exchange Theory (Arnold, 1996), the psychological contract finds its foundation in a cultural norm of reciprocity. Instances of perceived breaches in the psychological contract prompt employees to adjust their motivation and contributions accordingly (Lub et al., 2016, p. 655). Organizations oblivious to the significance of trust and the social contract face the risks of increased turnover and diminished productivity, necessitating critical interventions (Choitz & Wagner, 2021, p. 13).

Drawing parallel trajectories, organizations embracing an empowering approach to workforce development and training may be perceived as upholding and honoring the psychological contract (Bouchrika, 2023). As a result, a positive social exchange is established, fostering a psychologically safe environment conducive to the growth of adult learners within the realm of training and development.

Feedback and Growth

Aligned with the foundational assumptions of Self-Determination Theory (Ryan & Desi, 2000), adults are viewed as perpetual seekers, continuously striving "to understand themselves through the integration of new experiences and connections with others" (Nwoko & Yazdani, 2023, p. 131). In a training and development landscape fortified by psychological safety, a robust feedback culture emerges as a natural byproduct, enhancing learning agility as a deliberate practice of improvement (Aguinis, 2019). In this nurturing environment, adult learners find their intrinsic need met to comprehend the value and purpose behind their learning, increasing their buy-in. In organizations where employees perceive a climate of "feedback receptivity" (Chawla et al., 2016) and psychological safety, intrinsic motivation flourishes, propelling individuals not only to contribute actively but also to challenge ideas—a fertile ground for innovation (Clark, 2020). Constructive feedback can be viewed not merely as an evaluative tool but as a dynamic, two-way interaction in the developmental journey of adult learners (Nwoko & Yazdani, 2023).

The infusion of psychological safety principles into workplace training and development aligns with the motivational framework articulated by self-determination theory and the fundamental principles underpinning adult learning theories (Ryan & Desi, 2017; Knowles, 1980). This harmonious integration fosters an environment wherein employees experience a profound sense of empowerment, competence, connection, and motivation, propelling them toward active and sustained engagement in continuous learning and development (Kark & Carmeli, 2009). Beyond nurturing individual growth, this synthesis contributes to a positive and flourishing organizational culture.

Psychological Safety's Effect on Age Diversity in Training

The interplay between psychological safety and training is discernible in the multifaceted landscape of generational cohorts within the workforce. With four major generations currently contributing to the organizational milieu—Baby Boomers (1946-1964), Generation X (1965-1980) Generation Y or Millennials (1981-1995), and Generation Z (1997-2012)—each cohort brings distinct worldviews, ideals, and conflict management styles shaped by their formative experiences (Olckers & Booysen, 2021). The research study by Lub et al. (2016) posits that each generational cohort builds mental schemas regarding psychological contracts and related work outcomes, underlining the influence of generational perspectives on workplace dynamics.

Social identity theory provides a lens to understand how generational identity manifests in the workplace. According to Lyons et al. (2019), generational identity is strongest in individuals with a high need for positive self-esteem and subjective uncertainty avoidance. The meta-analysis study done by Burton et al. (2019) reviewed 121 peer-reviewed articles and identified five core themes of generational cohort differences in the workplace: team dynamics, conflict, leadership, wages/work environment, and commitment. Interestingly, they found that most research studies focused on Millennial characteristics and dynamics. The fact that millennials make up an estimated 50% of the current workforce may explain this phenomenon. Otherwise, it may signify the seismic cultural shift ushered in by this cohort and those succeeding them with the advent of advanced technology.

In addition to the noticeable shift towards tech fluency in recent generations, Gerhardt et al. (2022) highlight a significant change in attitudes toward mental health. According to their findings, Millennial and Gen Z employees demonstrate more openness in expressing their concerns about mental health in the workplace, a subject that their older counterparts often prefer to keep more private. Younger generations may feel more confident to challenge the status quo and "the way things have always been done" in the workplace.

Andree's (2018) hypothetical case study explored the generational perspectives of training and conflict management in the world of healthcare and nursing, especially among female Baby Boomers and Millennials. Burton et al. (2019) explained that women are most often represented in the nursing and teaching professions because these were the most culturally acceptable career paths for women of the Boomer generation (Burton et al., 2019). Given how gender identity is shaped by the cultural and historical norms in each generational cohort, a suggestion for future research would be how different genders of various generations may perceive psychological safety in the workplace.

Actual vs. Perceived Differences

Individual perception is not only a core part of psychological safety but also a principal component of social identity. There have been numerous studies evaluating how generational cohorts diverge in behavioral and workplace attachment; However, Olckers & Booysen, (2021) point out that academic literature thus far has not accounted for generational cohort perception of psychological ownership (Olckers & Booysen, 2021, p. 2). Lester et al.'s (2012) study raised the important question of actual versus perceived generational differences at work. They recognize the tendency for perceived differences to influence actual differences because each generational cohort interprets the other's actions filtered through their own set of values and perceptions. By asking the question of actual versus perceived differences, the Lester et al. (2012) study was able to quantify "I value" statements by each generational cohort. Armed with this empirical knowledge that perceived generational cohort differences are often greater than actual generational cohort differences can make a huge difference in how companies navigate conflict resolution and managerial training (Lester et al., 2012).

For example, Baby Boomers often value extreme optimism, loyalty, strong work ethic, and respect for authority (Burton et al., 2019). Gen X often have a high self-concept and are more committed to their careers than the organization (Olckers & Booysen, 2021). Millennials, who make up an estimated 50% of the current workforce, (Field, 2019) often value constant stimulation, independence, and instant feedback and challenges (Olckers & Booysen, 2021). Emerging research on Generation Z, though limited, suggests a unique technological skill set and perspectives that differentiate them from previous generations (Leslie et al., 2021).

In the face of these differences, the imperative is not to view generational disparities as conflicting but rather as opportunities for enrichment, empowerment, and mentorship. Andree (2018) advocates for recognizing the strengths, resources, and abilities of individuals from different generations as assets for positive change.

Of course, not all challenges encountered in workplace relations can be solely attributed to a generational gap in understanding. Within generational cohorts, substantial variations exist in personalities, socioeconomics, gender perspectives, ethnic and cultural backgrounds, and familial influences. Empowering individuals to take ownership of resolving conflicts and embracing intergenerational diversity through mentorship are key strategies for promoting a holistic perspective of generational diversity and knowledge sharing within teams (Edmondson, 2018).

Generational Knowledge Sharing

Knowledge sharing is a vital component of the learning process by which we actively acquire and assimilate new information (Gerpott et al., 2021). Individuals dedicate approximately one-third of their lifespan to their professional endeavors, and as longevity increases, so does the wealth of experience that individuals accumulate, presenting ample opportunities for knowledge-sharing within the professional domain.

Lyons et al. (2019) emphasize the organizational setting as a "central theater" for the manifestation of generational identity (p. 11). However, Gerpott et al.

(2021) bring attention to the potential challenges in open knowledge sharing within multigenerational groups, citing diversity research which suggests a diminished likelihood of engagement in such sharing (p. 3778). Tajfel & Turner (2004) suggests that in the workplace age is a salient individual characteristic that is "automatically assessed and triggers social categorization processes" (Gerpott et al., 2021) The presence or absence of psychological safety in age-diverse training groups emerges as a critical factor influencing active and open knowledge sharing, potentially mitigating inhibitions and exclusionary behaviors rooted in the apprehension of critique. Recognizing these insights holds relevance for training and development leaders, given the inherent difficulty in controlling age diversity composition and participants' social perceptions within training groups.

As Gerpott et al. (2021) shed light on the complexities associated with multigenerational groups, the importance of encouraging active knowledge-sharing becomes pronounced. In this context, Clark (2020) asserts that learner safety operates as a reciprocal relationship, involving encouragement in exchange for engagement and the recognition of the individual's permission to make mistakes during the learning process (Edmondson, 2018). Recognizing the pivotal role of psychological safety in training settings, Clark (2020) offers proactive measures to enhance its presence. These steps encompass fostering relational curiosity, reinforcing the learning potential of all employees, and eliciting the wisdom of older cohorts to share lessons learned through lived experiences (LeaderFactor, 2023). Implementing these strategies increases the likelihood of motivating engagement and shaping a new social identity within the training group (Korte, 2007).

Balancing Perspective

While the generational cohort theory holds merit, a mediating study conducted in Nigeria by Nwoko and Yazdani (2023) challenges the prevailing notion that generational distinctions, particularly in the context of extrinsic and intrinsic motivation, are notably pronounced. In contrast to the widespread perception of distinct generational preferences, the research suggests that the influence of intrinsic motivation on employee engagement maintains a positive trajectory across generations. The scholars underscore the existence of shared values among employees, contending that work engagement correlates more strongly with organizational culture than with inherent generational categorization (Nwoko & Yazdani, 2023, p. 139). Nevertheless, despite these findings, it is imperative to acknowledge the perceived or actual generational identity when formulating training programs. This acknowledgment becomes essential not due to inherent generational disparities but to address the fundamental psychological needs of autonomy, competence, and relatedness (Ryan & Desi, 2000). Recognizing and catering to these core needs can exert a substantial influence on motivation across all generational cohorts, underscoring the imperative of fostering a psychologically safe environment for knowledge sharing in the development of effective training initiatives.

PSYCHOLOGICAL SAFETY'S ROLE IN CULTIVATING A "PEOPLE-FIRST" TRAINING STRATEGY

Setting the Stage With Inclusion

In the realm of organizational initiatives aimed at Diversity, Equity, and Inclusion (DEI), Dalavai (2020) advocates for a comprehensive strategy integrating corporate training, transparent dialogues, and prescriptive positive language to articulate the desired organizational culture. Further, the establishment of employee resource groups is proposed to facilitate constructive discussions and perpetuate meaningful change (Dalavai, 2020, p. 25). This multifaceted approach propels training and development initiatives towards embracing an "inclusion mindset" (Connors, 2019), providing learners with the necessary psychological safety to transcend their comfort zones (Clark, 2020).

However, the creation of psychological safety requires addressing unconscious bias, inherent in every individual and workplace (Dalavai, 2020). Awareness is pivotal for recognizing and extending connection. Although still under research, major companies like Google have initiated unconscious bias training for workforce development. Porath (2016) notes that after such training at Google, participants were more likely to perceive the company's culture as fair, objective, and attuned to diversity than those in the control group (p. 13). Dr. Timothy Clark's research introduces a four-stage model of psychological safety, with "inclusion safety" identified as the foundational stage. According to Clark (2020), this initial stage is imperative for constructing psychological safety, and its absence jeopardizes the realization of subsequent stages, including learning safety, contributing safety, and challenging safety. The establishment of inclusion safety is thus positioned as a cornerstone in the architecture of psychological safety within the training and development landscape.

Leadership Style Matters

Considerable empirical evidence underscores the significant impact of transformational leadership in fostering a conducive environment for learning and knowledge sharing within the workplace (Garvin et al., 2008; Arnold & Walsh, 2013; Shafaei & Nejati, 2023). The four dimensions of transformational leadership—

intellectual stimulation, individualized consideration, inspirational motivation, and idealized influence—have been identified as key drivers (Yin et al., 2020) that positively influence these aspects. Transformational leadership emerges as a buffer against negative experiences, such as customer incivility, and mitigates work demands, including perceptions of stress (Arnold et al., 2015, p. 368).

Yin et al. (2020) suggest that psychological safety operates as a full mediator, linking the intricate relationship between transformational leadership dimensions and their effects, even across international contexts. The research by Frazier and Tupper (2018) reinforces this finding, contending that a supervisor's prosocial motivation and adeptness in cultivating a safe work environment contribute to heightened perceptions of psychological safety among employees, ultimately fostering a sense of thriving (Frazier & Tupper, 2018, p. 584). This phenomenon is described as a "trickle-down effect" (Frazier & Tupper, 2018) where perceived psychological safety from leaders has a cascading impact, not only amplifying employee motivation for learning but potentially influencing customer perceptions of service quality as well (Dang et al., 2022).

The language of leaders is often the first indication to others of the safety and inclusion of a space. Of course, *felt* inclusion is more impactful than *stated* inclusion, but language opens the door to feelings (Brown, 2013). Gerbrandt et al. (2021) recommend that leaders must establish trust before employees will believe that the organization has their well-being in mind (Gerbrandt et al., 2021, p. 33). Brené Brown, social researcher and data scientist, has written extensively about vulnerability as the key component for effective leadership. When leaders are authentic and honest about what they don't know (Brown, 2013), share past mistakes or lessons learned (Edmondson, 2018), are receptive to feedback, and share power (Clark, 2020), they give their constituents unconscious permission to do the same.

Shafaei & Nejati (2023) accentuate the human need for meaningful work and posit that inclusive leadership, intertwined with psychological safety, not only enhances the meaningfulness of work but also unlocks employees' full learning potential (Shafaei & Nejati, 2023, p. 3). The synergy of psychological safety and inclusive leadership across generations creates an environment where learners are more inclined to view failure as an opportunity for learning, thereby reducing negative emotions and decreasing turnover intentions (Lui & Keller, 2021, p. 40). Leaders who establish an atmosphere where employees feel supported, valued, and free to express themselves significantly contribute to the psychological safety of learners (Clark, 2020). Furthermore, aligning with andragogy principles (Knowles, 1980), learning facilitators who emphasize a person-centered approach over an authoritative "guru factor" aid in a transformative learning experience for adults (Bouchrika, 2023). This multifaceted leadership approach lays the groundwork for a robust and effective learning environment.

Understanding Trauma and Its Impact on Learning and Motivation

There is a growing awareness and call for resources related to trauma awareness in the workplace, exemplified by Choitz & Wagner's (2021) research for the *National Fund for Workforce Solutions*. Their examination highlights an existing abundance of research studies and tools concerning trauma-informed care in healthcare and social sciences; however, they identify a notable gap in analogous resources within the organizational and workforce development realms (Choitz & Wagner, 2021, p. 4). Praslova (2021) echoes these concerns in her contribution to the Society for Human Resource Management (SHRM) blog, asserting that organizations are poised for greater success in the post-pandemic era if they draw insights from the trauma-informed models and leadership employed in the first-responder and helping professions.

Becoming "trauma-informed" does not require a degree in psychology; rather, it requires a practitioner or trainer to realize the widespread impact and experiences of trauma on adult learners and how that affects them in the workplace (Champine et al., 2022). In this context, the intersection of psychological safety and a trauma-informed approach becomes essential, with Manning (2022) emphasizing the unique and enduring impact of organizational support on human capital.

Psychological safety and trauma-informed care in training and development share a significant relationship, particularly in fostering supportive and empowering learning environments. Praslova (2021) advocates for the widespread integration of a trauma-informed mindset and corresponding behaviors for workforce development and organizational resilience (Praslova, 2021, para. 6). Trauma-informed workplaces "create a sense of belonging, connection, and safety through their attitudes, policies and practices" (Gerbrandt et al., 2021, p. 6) which removes psychological barriers to learning.

What Is Trauma?

According to The Substance Abuse and Mental Health Services Administration in the U.S. Department of Health and Human Services (SAMHSA), "Individual trauma results from an event, series of events, or set of circumstances that is experienced by an individual as physically or emotionally harmful or life-threatening and that has lasting adverse effects on the individual's functioning and mental, physical, social, emotional, or spiritual well-being." (SAMSHA, 2014). Traumatic experiences may be a one-time event or ongoing and multifaceted. Stress responses from trauma can alter cognitions by changing neural pathways in the brain (SAMSHA, 2014). These rewired pathways can have a lasting effect on physical and mental health, profoundly influencing individuals' perceptions of the world, and heightening hypervigilance while diminishing a sense of safety (Choitz & Wagner, 2021). Psychological safety is much more than feeling safe to speak. It is a general feeling of safety and belonging, despite the various individual and collective traumas humans bring with them to the workplace.

A broad spectrum of causes, such as adverse childhood experiences, domestic violence, racism, sexual assault, bias, and harassment, can lead to trauma and distress (SAMSHA, 2014). Approximately 50% of the population experiences at least one traumatic event during their lifetime (Manning, 2022). Manning (2022) highlights the recent tumultuous years marked by a global pandemic, economic uncertainty, political upheaval, and environmental disasters, resulting in a surge in anxiety and depression (U.S. Census Bureau, 2022). The Cognitive Triad of Traumatic Stress, based on Beck et al. (1979), elucidates how trauma influences cognitive patterns about self, the world, and the future. Living in a VUCA (volatile, uncertain, complex, ambiguous) world, characterized by failures and setbacks (Lawrence, 2013, p. 3), impacts learners' belief in their ability to navigate challenges (SAMSHA, 2014). Trauma, often seen as an "invisible wound" (Gerbrandt et al., 2021, p. 13), elicits unique and subjective emotional responses with diverse impacts. Praslova (2021) underscores the role of diversity awareness in recognizing heightened stress responses due to historical injustices, discrimination, and various mental or physical health conditions.

Despite the unexpected challenges organizations face, it is crucial to remember that trauma is not a new phenomenon. Manning (2022) emphasizes that the strategies employed by organizations to support people during periods of trauma can yield meaningful and long-lasting impact (Manning, 2022). The establishment of a psychological contract between employers and employees hinges on mutual trust, and trust is enhanced by awareness and action (Lub et al., 2016). In this regard, the cultivation of an empathetic environment, the suspension of assumptions, and the scrutiny of cultural biases become indispensable.

The study by McCluney (2017) delves into the racial-identity trauma experienced by many black and brown individuals, framing it as a "psychological injury" resulting from racially motivated incidents that overwhelm an individual's coping capacity, cause bodily harm, or threaten life integrity (McCluney, 2017). Bryant-Davis (2019) cites Crenshaw's seminal study on intersectionality and the way marginalized people experience cultural identity and oppression which is qualitatively distinct from the trauma experiences of a dominant culture group (Bryant-Davis, 2019, para. 1). McCluney (2017) advocates for a strength-based perspective that focuses on empowering organizations and employees to implement educational and prosocial behaviors, moving beyond the debilitating outcomes of racial trauma. Gerbrandt et al. (2021), researchers associated with the Crisis & Trauma Resource Institute, contribute to the discourse by examining the far-reaching impact of traumatic experiences, emphasizing their effects across relationships, communities, and workplaces.

Trauma-Informed Approach to Training and Development

Perceived psychological safety among learners not only enhances motivation for learning but also plays a crucial role in enhancing overall performance and nurturing prosocial behaviors, thereby emphasizing its extensive implications (Frazier & Tupper, 2018, p. 584). Choitz & Wagner (2021) suggest that although no one chooses to go through trauma or stressful situations, everyone has a choice in how they respond to toxic stress and trauma (Choitz & Wagner, 2021, p. 3). This underscores the necessity of understanding the neurobiological and physiological underpinnings of trauma and adopting healthier response mechanisms. Given the reliance of workplaces on healthy, optimized brain function, employers and workforce development organizations emerge as logical conduits for disseminating such knowledge and information (Gerbrandt et al., 2021).

Choitz & Wagner (2021) draw attention to SAMHSA's (2014) four Rs rubric to describe a "trauma-informed" organization, program, or system: Realizing the widespread impact of trauma and exploring potential recovery paths; Recognizing signs and symptoms of trauma; Responding by fully integrating trauma knowledge into policies and practices; Actively resisting re-traumatization through care and intentionality. These overlap and support the five key principles for a "trauma-informed" organization, according to Gerbrandt et al. (2021), which are promoting awareness, shifting attitudes, fostering safety, providing choice, and highlighting strengths (Gerbrandt et al. (2021, p. 11) to create a more resilient and engaged workforce.

The establishment of a healthy corporate culture is posited as instrumental in fostering employee engagement and connection, integral components contributing to the overarching concept of psychological safety. This resonates with the perspective of trauma expert Dr. Gabor Mate (n.d.), who posits that "safety is not the absence of threat. It is the presence of connection," reinforcing the profound interconnectedness between fostering a trauma-informed workplace culture and ensuring the well-being of its members.

Measurable impact

The impact of psychological safety in the workplace is underscored by compelling research data, illuminating the profound consequences of neglecting this crucial aspect. Workplaces devoid of psychological safety witness a decline in employee well-being, engagement, and overall thriving, compounding the impact of existing life stressors carried by individuals (Manning, 2020). This lack of thriving among employees has significant repercussions for both businesses and the economy. The American Psychological Association estimates that workplace stress incurs a staggering cost of $500 billion annually to the U.S. economy (APA, 2015). This financial burden is manifested through the loss of billions of workdays each year due to job-related stress (American Institute of Stress). Gallup (2023) cited that workers' self-reported daily stress reached a record high, increasing from 38% in 2019 to 43% in 2020. Furthermore, workplace stress contributes to nearly a 50 percent increase in voluntary turnover (American Institute of Stress, n.d.), exacerbating organizational challenges.

Beyond the direct impacts of workplace stress, a deficiency in employee engagement exacts its toll on organizations and the broader economy. Thriving employees contribute essential benefits to the organization, such as vitality, continuous learning, good health, effective leadership, and the establishment of a positive work/life balance (Porath, 2016, p. 10). Gallup (2023) finds that managers play an outsized role in the stress workers feel on the job, which influences their daily stress overall. Addressing psychological safety not only mitigates these adverse effects but also provides an avenue for organizations to analyze and calculate the return on investment (ROI) associated with their activities. By incorporating psychological safety metrics into HR assessments of workforce development programs, organizations gain valuable insights into how their initiatives contribute to overall growth.

Initiating the cultivation of psychological safety involves a comprehensive approach that begins with recruitment and selection, proceeds through respectful onboarding techniques, and extends into organizational training and coaching strategies. According to Porath (2016), this approach has been shown to increase civility, job satisfaction, and organizational commitment while concurrently reducing turnover. To assess the effectiveness of these strategies, organizations can employ surveys and data analytics to gauge employee engagement, satisfaction, and attrition rates. However, a results-oriented measurement only tells part of the story regarding the psychological safety of a workplace.

The intangible value of psychological safety in training and learning goals extends beyond traditional performance metrics, incorporating a holistic perspective that encompasses employee well-being, engagement, and overall organizational effectiveness. Embedding psychological safety outcomes into the balanced scorecard for training and learning goals necessitates a thorough evaluation of individual, departmental, and organizational training needs. This strategic alignment ensures that training initiatives not only target specific skill development but also contribute to broader organizational objectives.

Limitations of Psychological Safety

A plethora of research studies have found a positive correlation between psychological safety and learning behavior, information sharing, creativity, innovation, voice, and proactive activity (Frazier et al., 2017, Newman et al., 2017). However, several studies have found limiting factors to the beneficial components of psychological safety. Deng et al.'s (2019) study in China yields insights into the cultural distinctions between individualistic and collectivist societies concerning the moderating role of psychological safety in group average work motivation. The authors posit that collectivistic societies inherently possess accountability driven by social pressure to avoid failing the group. In contrast, individualistic societies lack such moderating elements. Consequently, in the absence of intentional accountability, a high psychological safety climate serves as a "social shield," potentially fostering a sense of complacency among group members and hindering individual work motivation within groups (Deng et al., 2019, p. 1119).

Eldor et al., (2023) also assert that high levels of psychological safety may be counterproductive and yield unfavorable performance outcomes, particularly in roles involving standardized (routine) tasks. This finding holds significance as previous research has predominantly explored psychological safety in the context of creativity, innovation, and risk-taking behaviors. Eldor et al.'s (2023) study underscores the relevance of considering how heightened psychological safety could potentially distract and perplex individuals engaged in tasks that necessitate the avoidance of creativity, innovation, and risk-taking behaviors. Furthermore, both Eldor et al. (2023) and Deng et al. (2019) contend that the moderating influence of "collective accountability" mitigates the adverse impact of elevated psychological safety levels in specific contexts.

Edmondson (2018) and Clark (2020) agree that psychological safety should never be a cover to slack off, avoid difficult conversations, or eschew accountability for actions. Rather, the act of assessing the nuanced context of the workplace learning situations, giving learners the support they need according to their role, and seeking collective accountability creates a psychologically safe place for all learners.

Recommendations

As highlighted earlier, numerous recent studies have demonstrated the positive implications of a high psychological safety climate within the workplace. However, a noteworthy gap exists in the literature concerning factors contributing to the establishment of psychological safety in organizational settings (Lui & Keller, 2021). Drawing a parallel connection, the presence of psychological safety intersects with trauma-informed care in the workplace (Manning, 2022). Adopting a "trauma-informed" approach involves practitioners and trainers recognizing the pervasive impact and diverse experiences of trauma, including generational and racial trauma, and the heightened stress that individuals carry into their relationships, communities, and workplaces (Gerbrandt et al., 2021). The profound influence of organizational support on individuals, both psychologically and emotionally, is emphasized by Porath (2016) and Choitz & Wagner (2021). Consequently, there is a compelling need for more comprehensive research on factors that support workplace psychological safety, particularly within the domain of training and development.

Additionally, most studies cited were conducted in the United States within an individualistic culture and specific historical events that shaped various generational cohorts. The generational identity theories and social frameworks are often developed from a Western mindset (Parry & Urwin, 2011). Future studies regarding workplace trauma-informed approaches and comparing cultural differences with multigenerational perspectives of psychological safety would be of considerable value.

CONCLUSION

Emphasizing the need for a more nuanced understanding of a healthy and psychologically safe workplace, Porath (2016), Gerbrandt et al. (2021) and Praslova (2021) point to the combined effort of CDC and SAMHSA to provide *Six Principles for a Trauma-Informed Approach* with safety, trustworthiness & transparency, collaboration & mutuality, empowerment, voice & choice and cultural, historical and gender inclusion (SAMHSA, 2014).

In the context of training and development, the integration of a trauma-informed approach contributes to the creation of a holistic, and supportive learning environment. Each principle reinforces the others, emphasizing the importance of psychological safety, trust, collaboration, empowerment, and inclusivity in training programs.

Safety: Workplace trainers provide unwavering support for learners to take risks and grow beyond their comfort zones. They play a pivotal role in creating a safe learning environment that supports intrinsic motivation.

Trustworthiness & Transparency: A clear description of the purpose, structure, and learning outcomes of the training is communicated and aligned with organizational goals and immediate learner benefits. Training leaders model authenticity and vulnerability, increasing trust and establishing a strong foundation for group connection and cohesion.

Peer Support: Social exchanges and support are woven into the training design to establish the shared experiences of human experiences, fostering a sense of community and comradery. It also encourages knowledge sharing, mentoring, and problem-solving in age-diverse groups.

Collaboration & Mutuality: A "people first" training program has an intentional, collaborative, and power-sharing dynamic where diverse perspectives and experiences are respected in the social learning process, and collective accountability exists for learning and achievement.

Empowerment, Voice & Choice: Training options and individualized learning paths empower an adult learner's drive for autonomy and make the learning content relevant and applicable. Transformational leaders reinforce learning potential by providing a foundation of feedback receptivity and enabling learners to voice their needs, questions, and concerns without fear of reprisal.

Cultural, Historical, and Gender Inclusion: Training programs are accessible to all, countering hidden and overt bias, and ensuring that the learning space is inclusive and welcoming to individuals from diverse backgrounds and abilities.

The integration of these principles into training and development initiatives represents a strategy that transcends the mere acquisition of skills and knowledge. By emphasizing psychological safety, trust, and the overall well-being of all participants, these initiatives become a holistic endeavor that not only empowers individuals but also nurtures a collaborative and inclusive organizational culture.

As encapsulated in the often-attributed quote to Maya Angelou, "People will forget what you said; people will forget what you did. But people will never forget how you made them feel." This sentiment resonates with the fundamental tenet of a "people-first" ethos, where organizational intentionality in enhancing employee motivation, psychological safety, and learning agility becomes the cornerstone of a thriving and cohesive workplace. The enduring legacy of such an approach lies not only in the tangible outcomes of training but in the indelible impact it leaves on the individuals within the organization.

REFERENCES

Aguinis, H. (2019). *Performance Management* (4th ed.). Chicago Business Press.

American Institute of Stress. (2023). *Workplace stress.* http://www.stress.org/workplace-stress/

American Psychological Association. (2015). *Paying with our health: Stress in America.* https://www.apa.org/news/press/releases/stress/2014/stress-report.pdf

Andree, S. (2018). Embracing generational diversity: Reducing and managing workplace conflict/Accepter la diversity generationnelle: Reduire et gerer les conflits en milieu de travail. *ORNAC Journal, 36*(4), 13.

Andrews, P., & Laing, G. (2018). Evaluating the outcomes of a training program through an ROI evaluation: A case study. *e-Journal of Social & Behavioural Research in Business, 9*(3), 1–9.

Arnold, J. (1996). The psychological contract: A concept in need of closer scrutiny? *European Journal of Work and Organizational Psychology, 5*(4), 511–520. doi:10.1080/13594329608414876

Arnold, K. A., & Walsh, M. M. (2015). Customer incivility and employee well-being: Testing the moderating effects of meaning, perspective taking, and transformational leadership. *Work and Stress, 29*(4), 362–378. doi:10.1080/02678373.2015.1075234

Baran, B., Shanock, L. & Miller, L. (2012). Advancing organizational support theory into the twenty-first-century world of work. *Journal of Business and Psychology. 27*(10). 1007/s10869-011-9236-3.

Bouchrika, I. (2023, July 28). *The andragogy approach: Knowles' adult learning theory principles*. Research.com. https://research.com/education/the-andragogy-approach

Brown, B. (2013). Daring greatly: how the courage to be vulnerable transforms the way we live, love, parent, and lead (Center Point large print ed.). Thorndike, ME: Center Point Large Print.

Bryant-Davis, T. (2019). The cultural context of trauma recovery: Considering the posttraumatic stress disorder practice guideline and intersectionality. *Psychotherapy (Chicago, Ill.), 56*(3), 400–408. doi:10.1037/pst0000241 PMID:31282715

Burton, C. M., Mayhall, C., Cross, J., & Patterson, P. (2019). Critical elements for multigenerational teams: A systematic review. *Team Performance Management, 25*(7/8), 369–401. doi:10.1108/TPM-12-2018-0075

Carmeli, A., & Gittell, J. H. (2009). High-quality relationships, psychological safety, and learning from failures in work organizations. *Journal of Organizational Behavior, 30*(6), 709–729. doi:10.1002/job.565

Champine, R. B., Hoffman, E. E., Matlin, S. L., Strambler, M. J., & Tebes, J. K. (2022). What does it mean to be trauma-informed?": A mixed-methods study of a trauma-informed community initiative. *Journal of Child and Family Studies, 31*(2), 459–472. doi:10.1007/s10826-021-02195-9 PMID:35018088

Chawla, N., Gabriel, A., Dahling, J., & Patel, K. (2016, July). Feedback dynamics are critical to improving performance management systems. *Industrial and Organizational Psychology: Perspectives on Science and Practice*, *9*(02), 260–266. doi:10.1017/iop.2016.8

Choitz, V., & Wagner, S. (2021). *A Trauma Informed approach to the workforce*. The National Fund for Workforce Solutions. https://nationalfund.org/wp-content/uploads/2021/04/A-Trauma-Informed-Approach-to-Workforce.pdf

Clark, T. R. (2020). *The 4 Stages of Psychological Safety: Defining the Path to Inclusion and Innovation*. Berrett-Koehler.

Columbia Law School. (n.d.). https://www.law.columbia.edu/pt-br/news/2017/06/kimberle-crenshaw-intersectionality

Connors, A. (2019). Adopt an inclusion mindset. *Talent Development*, *73*(12), 18–20.

Crenshaw, K. (2017*). Kimberlé Crenshaw on Intersectionality, More than Two Decades Later*. Academic Press.

Dalavai, E. V. (2020). Building a positive organizational culture through antiracism. *Talent Development*, *74*(12), 24–26.

Dang, V. T., Nguyen, H. N., Hoang, T. H., Nguyen, T. H., Tran, V. T., Nguyen, Q. H., & Nguyen, N. (2022). Gyms' indoor environmental quality and customer emotion: The mediating roles of perceived service quality and perceived psychological safety. *Leisure Studies*, *41*(2), 263–280. doi:10.1080/02614367.2021.1975803

Deng, H., Leung, K., Lam, C. K., & Huang, X. (2019). Slacking Off in Comfort: A dual-pathway model for psychological safety climate. *Journal of Management*, *45*(3), 1114–1144. doi:10.1177/0149206317693083

Dewey, S., Codallos, K., Barry, R., Drenkhahn, K., Glover, M., Muthig, A., Roberts, S. L., & Abbott, B. (2020). Higher education in prison: A pilot study of approaches and modes of delivery in eight prison administrations. *Journal of Correctional Education*, *71*(1), 57–89.

Edmondson, A. (1999). Psychological safety and learning behavior in work teams. *Administrative Science Quarterly*, *44*(2), 350–383. doi:10.2307/2666999

Edmondson, A. C. (2018). *The fearless organization*. John Wiley & Sons.

Edmondson, A. C., & Lei, Z. (2014). Psychological safety: The history, renaissance, and future of an interpersonal construct. *Annual Review of Organizational Psychology and Organizational Behavior, 1*(1), 23–43. doi:10.1146/annurev-orgpsych-031413-091305

Eldor, L., Hodor, M., & Cappelli, P. (2023). The limits of psychological safety: Nonlinear relationships with performance. *Organizational Behavior and Human Decision Processes, 177,* 104255. doi:10.1016/j.obhdp.2023.104255

Field, M. (2019, June 10). *Work evolved: Building a successful multigenerational workforce.* Forbes Magazine. https://www.forbes.com/sites/forbestechcouncil/2019/06/10/work-evolved-building-a-successful-multigenerational-workforce/?sh=1581a96878cb

Forsyth, D. R. (2015). *The Psychology of Groups.* Noba. https://nobaproject.com/modules/the-psychology-of-groups

Frazier, M. L., & Tupper, C. (2018). Supervisor prosocial motivation, employee thriving, and helping behavior: A trickle-down model of psychological safety. *Group & Organization Management, 43*(4), 561–593. doi:10.1177/1059601116653911

Gallup. (2023). *State of the global workforce: 2023 report.* Gallup. https://www.gallup.com/workplace/349484/state-of-the-global-workplace.aspx

Garvin, D. A., Edmondson, A., & Gino, F. (2008, March). *Is yours a learning organization?* Academic Press.

Gavin, J., & McBrearty, M. (2019). *Lifestyle wellness coaching* (3rd ed.). Human Kinetics. doi:10.5040/9781492595595

Gerbrandt, N., Grieser, R., & Enns, V. (2021). *A little book about trauma-informed workplaces.* Crisis & Trauma Resource Institute. ACHIEVE Publishing.

Gerpott, F. H., Lehmann-Willenbrock, N., Wenzel, R., & Voelpel, S. C. (2021). Age diversity and learning outcomes in organizational training groups: The role of knowledge sharing and psychological safety. *International Journal of Human Resource Management, 32*(18), 3777–3804. doi:10.1080/09585192.2019.1640763

Gratton, L., & Erickson, T. J. (2013). Eight ways to build collaborative teams. Academic Press.

Grote, G., & Metzgar, C. (2016). Promoting Safety by Increasing Uncertainty. *Professional Safety, 61*(1), 22–23.

Joy, S., & Kolb, D. A. (2009). Are there cultural differences in learning styles? *International Journal of Intercultural Relations, 33*(1), 69–85. doi:10.1016/j.ijintrel.2008.11.002

Kahn, W. A. (1990). Psychological conditions of personal engagement and disengagement at work. *Academy of Management Journal, 33*(4), 692–724. doi:10.2307/256287

Kark, R., & Carmeli, A. (2009). Alive and creating: The mediating role of vitality and aliveness in the relationship between psychological safety and creative work involvement. *Journal of Organizational Behavior, 30*(6), 785–804. doi:10.1002/job.571

Katzenbach, K. M. E., & Gratton, L. (Eds.), *HBR's 10 must reads on teams.* Harvard Business Review Press.

Knowles, M. S. (1980). The modern practice of adult education: From pedagogy to andragogy: Revised and Updates. New York, NY: Association Press.

Korte, R. (2007). A review of social identity theory with implications for training and development. *Journal of European Industrial Training, 31*(3), 166–180. doi:10.1108/03090590710739250

LeaderFactor. (2023). *The 4 stages.* LeaderFactor. https://www.leaderfactor.com

Leslie, B., Anderson, C., Bickham, C., Horman, J., Overly, A., Gentry, C., Callahan, C., & King, J. (2021). Generation Z perceptions of a positive workplace environment. *Employee Responsibilities and Rights Journal, 33*(3), 171–187. doi:10.1007/s10672-021-09366-2

Liang, J., Farh, C. I. C., & Farh, J.-L. (2012). Psychological antecedents of promotive and prohibitive voice: A two-wave examination. *Academy of Management Journal, 55*(1), 71–92. doi:10.5465/amj.2010.0176

Liu, Y., & Keller, R. T. (2021). How psychological safety impacts R&D project teams' performance. *Research Technology Management, 64*(2), 39–45. doi:10.1080/08956308.2021.1863111

Lopez-Garrido, G. (2023, July 10). *Self-Determination Theory: How it explains motivation.* Simply Psychology. https://www.simplypsychology.org/self-determination-theory.html

Lub, X. D., Bal, P. M., Blomme, R. J., & Schalk, R. (2016). One job, one deal… or not: Do generations respond differently to psychological contract fulfillment? *International Journal of Human Resource Management*, *27*(6), 653–680. doi:10.1080/09585192.2015.1035304

Lynn, B., & Sarro, E. (2022, Oct. 20). *5 things you may not know about psychological safety*. Neuroleadership Institute. https://neuroleadership.com/your-brain-at-work/5-things-psych-safety

Manning, K. (2022, March 31). *We need trauma-informed workplaces*. Harvard Business Review. https://hbr.org/2022/03/we-need-trauma-informed-workplaces

Maslow, A. H. (1943). A theory of human motivation. *Psychological Review*, *50*(4), 370–396. doi:10.1037/h0054346

McCluney, C. L., Bryant, C. M., King, D. D., & Ali, A. A. (2017). Calling in Black: A dynamic model of racially traumatic events, resourcing, and safety. *Equality, Diversity and Inclusion*, *36*(8), 767–786. doi:10.1108/EDI-01-2017-0012

Newman, A., Donohue, R., & Eva, N. (2017). Psychological safety: A systematic review of the literature. *Human Resource Management Review*, *27*(3), 521–535. doi:10.1016/j.hrmr.2017.01.001

Nwoko, C., & Yazdani, K. (2023). Self-Determination Theory: The mediating role of generational differences in employee engagement. *Journal of Business & Management Studies*, *5*(4), 130–142. doi:10.32996/jbms.2023.5.4.14

Olckers, C., & Booysen, C. (2021). Generational differences in psychological ownership. *SA Journal of Industrial Psychology*, *47*, 1–13. doi:10.4102/sajip.v47i0.1844

Pappas, C. (2013). *The adult learning theory - andragogy - of Malcolm Knowles*. eLearning Industry. https://elearningindustry.com/the-adult-learning-theory-andragogy-of-malcolm-knowles

Parry, E., & Urwin, P. (2011). Generational differences in work values: A review of theory and evidence. *International Journal of Management Reviews*, *13*(1), 79–96. doi:10.1111/j.1468-2370.2010.00285.x

Porath, C. (2016). *Creating a more human workplace where employees and business thrive*. SHRM Foundation. https://www.shrm.org/hr-today/trends-and-forecasting/special-reports-and-expert-views/Documents/Human-Workplace.pdf

Praslova, L. (2021, March 23). *Trauma-informed workplace: Kindness works best.* SHRM Blog. https://blog.shrm.org/blog/trauma-informed-organizational-behavior-kindness-works-better

Rogers, C. R. (1957). *The necessary and sufficient conditions of therapeutic personality change.* Academic Press.

Rogers, C. R. (1957). The necessary and sufficient conditions of therapeutic personality change. *Journal of Consulting Psychology, 21*(2), 95–103. doi:10.1037/h0045357

Ryan, R. M., & Deci, E. L. (2000). Self-determination theory and the facilitation of intrinsic motivation, social development, and well-being. *The American Psychologist, 55*(1), 68–78. doi:10.1037/0003-066X.55.1.68 PMID:11392867

Ryan, R. M., & Deci, E. L. (2017). *Self-determination theory: Basic psychological needs in motivation, development, and wellness.* The Guilford Press., doi:10.1521/978.14625/28806

Schein, E. H. (1993). How can organizations learn faster? The challenge of entering the green room. *Sloan Management Review, 34*(2), 85–92.

Shafaei, A., & Nejati, M. (2023). Creating meaningful work for employees: The role of inclusive leadership. *Human Resource Development Quarterly, 1*, hrdq.21512. Advance online publication. doi:10.1002/hrdq.21512

Substance Abuse and Mental Health Services Administration (SAMHSA). (2014). *SAMHSA's concept of trauma and guidance for a trauma-informed approach.* SAMHSA's Trauma and Justice Strategic Initiative. https://ncsacw.samhsa.gov/userfiles/files/SAMHSA_Trauma.pdf

Tajfel, H., & Turner, J. C. (2004). The social identity theory of intergroup behavior. In J. T. Jost & J. Sidanius (Eds.), *Political psychology* (pp. 276–293). Psychology Press. doi:10.4324/9780203505984-16

The Kings Fund. (2020) *The importance of psychological safety* [Video]. The Kings Fund. https://www.youtube.com/watch?v=eP6guvRt0U0

U.S. Census Bureau. (2022). *Household pulse survey.* https://www.census.gov/programs-surveys/household-pulse-survey.html

Yin, J., Ma, Z., Yu, H., Jia, M., & Liao, G. (2020). Transformational leadership and employee knowledge sharing: Explore the mediating roles of psychological safety and team efficacy. *Journal of Knowledge Management, 24*(2), 150–171. doi:10.1108/JKM-12-2018-0776

Chapter 10
Motivating Employees Through Continuous Professional Development and Training in the Retail Sector

Gurmeet Singh
 https://orcid.org/0009-0004-6969-2778
Glasgow Caledonian University, UK

Vipin Nadda
 https://orcid.org/0009-0002-1041-2941
University of Sunderland in London, UK

Sunil Saini
Aksum University, Ethiopia

Waseem Akram
University of West of Scotland, UK

ABSTRACT

Training and development could be a real motivating force for the company if they are provided in a well-organized manner. These activities could be considered as major strengths for HR management and can provide a firm base to the organizational objectives as it increases the individual's capacities. The major aim of this chapter is to get a better understanding of the benefits of training and continuous development in the retail sector. The major objective of this chapter is to contribute to making companies aware of the genuine benefits of training and continuous development. Further, the retail sector organizations can surely improve their training techniques

DOI: 10.4018/979-8-3693-1674-0.ch010

Copyright © 2024, IGI Global. Copying or distributing in print or electronic forms without written permission of IGI Global is prohibited.

and it will help them to adopt accurate teaching techniques. Different factors such as management, working conditions, reward system, teamwork, etc. can directly affect the performance of employees. It is significant for business to adopt various strategies through which they can continuously develop the performance of their employees.

INTRODUCTION

In the recent years many business houses has focused upon two most significant activities under the corporate world. These are training and development activities which are currently playing a very important role. Increasing level of competition is evident in every industry whether it is of manufacturing, services, retail, outsourcing etc (Marchington and Wilkinson, 2008). An employee whether operating at higher level or general level, requires training services at any time. It is a type of investment for the company which can offer them valuable returns and outcomes. It can well develop the employees towards long term career goals & objectives and also results in greater job satisfaction (Huemann, Keegan and Turner, 2007). Indeed, a more satisfied individual will work for longer period of time with the company. Training & development are adopted with the purpose of improving the performance of the employees. Employees are one of the most precious assets of the company. So every firm wants to make sure that their workers have the required talent and skill which can improve the productivity of their business (Kougias, Seremeti and Kalogeras, 2013). Requirement of training and development activities arises when company feels that their overall business performance is decreasing also affecting the profitability. It helps in eliminating the loopholes and gapes in the business. Employees feel motivated and inspired towards their work (Cattermole, Johnson, and Jackson, 2014). Here it is important for the company to handle these conditions carefully. Importance and need of training must be properly conveyed to a worker. He must not feel that these activities are undertaken because he is weak or fragile. This will definitely bring good results for them as well the business (Wilson and Western, 2001). One of the important things is that these two activities are very essential in a firm which is on the path of growth and development. Training is related with grasping the essential skill and abilities for a certain work. There is a objective behind it for instance understanding a process or operating a system (Berge and et. al., 2002).

Training and development are regarded as the vital function of human resource management. They are aimed at improving the performance of the individual and groups in organizational settings (Taylor, Murphy and Price, 2006). In a nutshell human resource training and development should be of nature that it designs all the resources with effective oiling making something that the business can take forward. If these types of activities are not appropriate then bureaucratic set up is the outcome which is a type of constrain to every people in the business (Skaggs and Youndt, 2004). Training is given to them in compliance with the goals and objectives of the business. It brings them on par with those confined targets. It also matches them with trends of the industry. Hence all these things will ensure effective performance from the workers (Boxall, 2003).

All the new employees can reach to the level of motivated & committed employees if they succeed in getting required training & learning (McBain, 2007). Unskilled workers become skilled when their potential and capabilities are enhanced in more effective manner through development approaches. Again, potential managers can become competent managers if they are given right kind of training & learning experiences. So, it can be derived that individuals at all level needs improvement is their working (Cattermole, Johnson and Jackson, 2014).

When discussions are made regarding the competitive industries, retail industry comes out as far-reaching and very influential. Training and development is treated as the difference in success and failures. It is not just because of the complex business processes are involved but also the entire focus is on the customer relation (Millar, 2012). These activities in this industry are also far complex than in other industries. It is because of the amount of direct exposure staff with have with consumers. Apart from teaching to be polite and welcoming while attending the customers, they also guide the employees to behave consistently in the line with the values of the products that they represent (Taylor, Murphy and Price, 2006). Each of the retail sales professional must be trained in a manner that they can deliver their performance with high morale and motivation. Not all retailers are established equal when it comes to retaining talent. Some of the companies will able to attract and inspire certain kind of employees through the potential of specialized products that they sell (Kougias, Seremeti and Kalogeras, 2013). It can also be possible because of the unique and distinctive culture of the enterprise.

Retail is one of the sectors which is majorly dependent on the quality of products and services of employees. Organizations can gain many advantages if workers are highly skilled and efficient (Wilson and Western, 2001). But it is also evident that they need proper training and development activities which can ensure maximum efforts and hard work from them. So this study is conducted with the purpose of identifying the impacts of training and development activities on the employees. It will try to discover what can be major significance of continuous development for the cited company and in the overall retail sector (Taylor, Murphy and Price, 2006).

IMPORTANCE OF TRAINING IN THE RETAIL INDUSTRY

According to Marchington and Wilkinson (2008), a properly trained and learned staff will offer many valuable results for the company. A company will be primarily competing on the price unless their employees are trained better than the competitors. They have to be armed with more product knowledge and strategies in order to solve the problems of the customers. Mostly it can be observed that every retail firm spends a huge expenditure on marketing and advertising of products in order to attract the people towards the stores. But this can be a waste of money if their sales forces are not able to give valuable information about the product to the customers (Niazi, 2011). People will leave the store without buying anything if employees cannot make them confident about their purchasing decision. And this thing is not tolerable for any retailer for too long period. So in this industry there are many areas where training requirement is must and needed for great productivity.

Firstly, product knowledge, salesmen in retail stores must know what they are selling and should have the complete information about the product. Attributes and advantages of all the products must be familiar to them (Kougias, Seremeti and Kalogeras, 2013). Having combination of right knowledge and enthusiasm, employees can raise the standard of sales. Along with that they are also required to grasp all the in-store procedures. These procedures include range of tasks and activities (Hassi, 2012). Every activity taken by them has its own importance. These activities includes receiving & storing merchandise in the stores, pricing them, handling special orders, process for opening & closing store, handling cash & sales receipts, store security, recognizing merchandise for markdowns etc (Wilson and Western, 2001). All these functions have their respective importance, and it cannot be ignored. For their execution employees must be given required training and learning. This will help in eliminating all the complexities associated with the business (Berge and et. al., 2002). Customer service also plays an important role in this context. They expect value for the payment they are giving or they will be out of the door. People want to be treated in vibrant and respected manner and also want their queries to be solved at immediate point of time. Workers who are trained properly helps in converting the shoppers into buyers (Skaggs and Youndt, 2004). They also ensure repetitive business and promote the retail company as best in its niche segment.

According to McBain (2007), Customer perception towards the products and services also plays an important role here. This is one of the most significant reasons for training of staff. Whenever a person walks through a retail store, he carries a certain perception about it. That perception may be predisposed by branding, advertising or on the basis of past experiences. Spending options of the people will be influenced by many factors. One of the biggest of them is primarily the experiences that they have with the staff of the store. People will like to buy the products if they are welcomed with comfortable and warm environment. Purchase will not take place if they feel irritated or uncomfortable (Cattermole, Johnson and Jackson, 2014). So here training is the opportunity of the company to influence the behaviour of the staff. It ensures that every personnel have the potential of executing required tasks at the most basic level. This basic level ranges from opening and closing procedures (Taylor, Murphy and Price, 2006). While on the other hand incompetence of employees can result into undo a sale and other operational problems (Millar, 2012).

IMPACT OF TRAINING ON EMPLOYEE PERFORMANCE

Nowadays the training and development has become essential element for the H R management (Niazi., 2011). Companies are putting extra emphasis on the designing the special and unique training modules which can directly help the employees to improve their performance or to understand their potential as well. Various management experts have observed that the impact of training and development is very high on the different aspects of employees (Kougias, Seremeti and Kalogeras, 2013).

In the real-world growth and development of the organization is affected by a number of factors. In the context of the present research during the development of company employee training plays an important role (Newstrom & Davis, 2002). It helps in improving the performance as well as productivity of the business. Through this company can come in better positions to face the competition and to stay at the top. Hence this suggests that there is a significant difference between the firms that provide training to their workers and firms that do not. Existing literatures renders evidence of certain effects of training and development on their performance (McCourt & Derek, 2003). Some of the studies have been conducted taking account the performance of employees specifically. While on the other side others have provided a general picture of the company's performance. The two are linked with each other in one way or another. This states that employee performance has an influence on company's performance (Torrington, Hall & Taylor, 2005). Related to the above subject Wright & Geroy (2001), experienced that through effectual training & development programs there can be changes in the competencies of the staff. It not only improves their skills and talent required to do the current job but also enhances their knowledge and attitude, essential for the future jobs.

According to Swart and et al (2005), concluded that training is the measure of dealing with the gapes and deficit related to their skills and performance. As per their views filling the gap is concerned with applying a suitable training intervention in order to develop required abilities and skills of the workers. Along with that they also stated that through training companies will be able to recognize at which level their people are working. It can also be identified whether they are performing good or not. This will help in modifying their knowledge and potentials as per the requirements of the business (Wognum, 2001). It is being observed that every individual have certain amount of knowledge related to different jobs. However it is important that this is not sufficient and they need to be modified according to the new requirements of work.

According to, Wright & Geroy (2001), competencies of the individuals changes through effective training procedures. It not only improves their skills and talent required to do the current job but also enhances their knowledge, abilities, and capabilities for the future jobs. All these, result in greater productivity for the company. Competencies of the staff are developed through training and it helps them in executing their job in a competitive manner. Further issues like turnover, complaints of dissatisfaction, absenteeism etc. can be minimized when they are trained in well manner (Swart, Mann, Brown & Price, 2005).

Advantages of Training and Development

The major factor or benefits which a company can enjoy due to training and continuous development are as follows:

Employee motivation: The motivational level of employees could boost by providing them appropriate training. The training which company is providing to their employees must be related to their job profile and it must help them to learn new concepts (Hassi, 2012). In the absence of it they will not render genuine efforts. Financial and non-financial rewards are one of the method of motivation. Better remuneration and salary can attract any of the individual. It also includes other type of benefits such as fringe benefits, etc. Presence of motivation can make working simpler and for company it is easier to cover up the costs linked with training (Cattermole, Johnson and Jackson, 2014).

Employee productivity or performance: It is another factor which has direct relationship with the training and development. It is very natural that if employees are getting complete training about their job profile, then it will automatically improve their working efficiency and enable them to perform better (Adamson and Caple, 1996). Apart from this it is comprehensibly understandable that without such aspects it is impossible to raise the level of company's performance as well. Training and development activities directly affects the productivity & performance of the firm. If workers are trained properly it will reflect in their performance (Taylor, Murphy and Price, 2006).

Employee engagement: As it is mentioned above that employee motivation and performance is the positive result of training and development which further lead towards the employee engagement, another objective of HR management (Berge and et. al., 2002). According to Marchington and Wilkinson (2008) employee engagement is essential with a view of company's continuous growth and development. If employees are feeling inclined towards the company then they can gain the competitive advantage and the company can make the full use of their employee's potential. It is important that workers should feel involved towards goals and objectives of the organization.

Employee retention: it is another factor which can be easily achieved if company is having strong and effective training modules (Trim, 2004). The continuous development opportunities enable the company to win the trust of their employees and can retain them for the longer period of time. It is prevalent that employee remain associated with those companies who provide growth opportunities to their employees and ensure their career development (Skaggs and Youndt, 2004). Hence these are the major elements which have declared that without training it is impossible to win the faith of employees and there are lots of other factors which could be treated as benefits of training (Huemann, Keegan and Turner, 2007). Apart from this it is required to understand that companies must be aware with the nature of their business and accordingly they can select the appropriate training sessions and style (Cattermole, Johnson and Jackson, 2014).

Increase in profitability: Profit is one of the major objectives of every firm. It is important to have greater profitability so that business can be continued for a long period of time. Reinvested profits are the source of finance for them as they make investment in other business operations from this money (Wilson and Western, 2001). Training is a type of investment for the organization as they are spending money on their employees. Every company expects that they get valuable returns on the investment that they make. It is important to recover the costs which they have incurred on training and development of the staff (Newstrom & Davis, 2002). So, it can be said training will help in raising the level of profitability within the business. Innovation is also another major factor behind it. It is essential that business should respond to all changes and innovations in the environment. Training can also enhance the innovation skills of the employees (McCourt & Derek, 2003).

Workforce flexibility - It also increase the skills set of the employees. It enables them to make involvement in wider range of tasks and responsibilities. Greater motivation and confidence in workers is evident which means they become less dependent on the management and supervision (Swart, Mann, Brown & Price, 2005). It also improves their skills related to communication, professionalism, conscientiousness, creativity etc. These skills can emerge and enhanced though effective training and development.

Factors Affecting the Performance of Employees

There can be many factors which affect the performance of the employees in the organization. These factors are as follows:

Management (subordinate leadership) - According to Swart, Mann, Brown & Price (2005), innovative HRM activities improve performance like use of systems related to enhance workers participation and flexibility in the design of work and decentralization of managerial tasks & responsibilities. Planning with the people and not for the people delivers a positive relationship to performance improvements when the company make efforts for speed, flexibility and constant innovation. There can be greater level of mutual trust between management and employees for example when workers are given liberty to make involvement in the decision-making process (Marchington and Wilkinson, 2008).

Working conditions - Although working conditions do not have a direct impact on the working conditions of the production and output but it does matters for the employees. Hazardous and dangerous working conditions put life of the employees in danger. It can result into unexpected accidents which can put life of an individual on stake (Niazi, 2011). So working conditions plays an important role because it is also a source of motivation and inspiration for the employees. They feel encouraged when they are surrounded by good and safe infrastructure. Their encouragement is shown in their working and performance (Evans, Pucik & Barsoux 2002). But if they are faced with bad conditions, it places negative impact on their moral. So it is important that company should establish working conditions that do not affect the workers negatively. There can be measures and approaches which can motivate them to work harder and with complete efforts (Edmond & Noon, 2001).

Reward Systems - Reward systems are established to attract and retain quality human resources. These are most effective sources of improvements and motivation for the staff. Company can implement both financial and non-financial system for them (Debrah & Ofori, 2006). Additionally firm should adopt rewards systems that are similar to the industry in which they operate. They can set performance standards in relation to goals and objectives of the company.

Team work - This is the situation where two or more people make interactions towards a common aim. Working becomes easier when people work together in teams and it facilitates coordination and integration (Afshan, Sobia, Kamran, & Nasir, 2012). It places a positive impact on their performance increasing the morale of the employees. Further it increases the profitability and productivity of the employees. It also encourages open communication between the staff and also help in acquiring skills which enables them to achieve objective is more specified period. This can be very difficult when an individual is working alone and it can create synergy also (Ahuja, 2006).

CONCLUSION

Employees are the key essential of company and they should be properly trained and learned in order to gain more valuable results. Moreover, the proper results can be concluded with respect to the retail industry as it requires huge expenses on marketing and advertising of products in order to attract the people towards their stores. In this respect it have been identified that salesman is an important person who needs to properly communicate with all their clients in order to provide them better information about their products and services. There are various tools are available through which company can continuously develop their workers but with the changes in time they need to give high attention towards gaining benefits of training and development. Moreover, in the present dissertation descriptive analysis has been used with the help of quantitative tools. Results attained form it is that company can gain higher competitive advantage by continuously developing their employees and providing them proper training. It have been identified that using different tools for training and development helps the company in gaining higher market share. The overall findings from the data analysis part present a clear picture of the benefits of training and continuously developing employees. Further, better conclusion can be find out from all the objectives and for this purpose all the theories and concepts that contributes in the given subject matter have been identified. It is being found that retail industry can easily gain high market share with giving appropriate information to all their clients about their products. This industry serves various merchandising goods to customers as per their requirements. It is the main responsibility of all their employees to keep their customer satisfied. For this purpose, first they should know that what they are selling and they should have complete information about the products. With due respect it have been identified that employees can make their clients happy by giving them proper information about their services. It is concluded in respect to sales person as it is the most important person of the company. They can easily sell different products of company with having combination of right knowledge and enthusiasm. For the execution of different functioning such as receiving & storing merchandise in the stores, handling special orders, process for opening & closing store, handling cash & sales receipts it is essential to have trained employees. Further, it is concluded for that in order to gain more productivity companies needs to provide high class training to all their workers. They can plan various training and development activities. The planned activity performed within the business and it is essential to develop the skills and knowledge to sale the items. Right kind of training and education provide great amount of payoffs and incentives. It will boost the performance of employees and they can easily achieve their target. Training of staff members can also be decided as per the customer perception towards their products and services. It helps them in gaining customer loyalty and further they can improve their business operations. Customer perception is related to the different things such as branding, advertising etc. Retail store should maintain the comfortable and warm environment. Training is an opportunity of the company to influence the behaviour of staff. Moreover, training and development is essential in the retail industry as it directly affects the employee turnover as well as behaviour of worker at the workplace.

From this given objective it is being found that company can employees both can get benefits from the training and development. Companies are putting extra efforts in providing high class training to all their employees. With the help of this it is also essential to put extra emphasise on designing part. Companies need to set unique training module for this purpose so that they can achieve higher competitive advantage. It have been concluded that impact of training and development is very high and it is essential for the growth of employees as well as real world. Company can come in better positions to face the competition and to stay at the top. It has its highest impact on the performance of the employees in relation to their job. Companies also need to provide the training according to the employee's strength and weaknesses. It helps them in boosting their performance and further they can easily contribute towards the success of industry. Moreover, with the help of the descriptive analysis it have been identified that training directly affects the performance of workers. If company uses good techniques and modules in order to provide them training than they can easily achieve their target. It makes a huge difference between those companies who does not provide training to their staff members. Training module should be changed or modified according to the according to the new requirements of work. In order to fulfill the performance gap organizations need to develop appropriate training and development plan. With the help of the effective training procedures competencies of individual have been changing. Further, it have been recognized that training and continuously developing employees helps in gaining profitability and productivity of company. If employee perform well than they can serve high quality products to their entire employee. It results in increasing customer loyalty as well as higher market share.

From the above section it has been founded that there are various factors that highly affects the performance of workers. Different factors such as management, working condition, reward system; team work etc can directly affect the performance of employees. It the situation where people work as a team and make interaction with each other produces effective results. It put positive environment in company as all the workers perform collaboratively. It helps in increasing the morale of all the employees. In addition to this, it also have been identified that working condition of company directly impact on the production and production and output of the company. It is the source of employee's motivation and inspiration as positive working culture motivates them in perform effectively. They always feel encouraged when they are surrounded by good and safe infrastructure. It is also identified from the above section that company can monitor the performance of all their employees and give them reward according to their performance. They can implement financial and non financial rewards for their workers and also set performance standards in relation to target and objectives of the company.

Recommendations

As training and development plays vital role in achieving success of company as well as their increasing market share. Hence, it is important for business to adopt various strategies through which they can continuously develop the performance of all their employees. Here are some recommendations through which they can develop effective training plan. One of the most important responsibilities of company is to understand the nature of their business and prepare their training plan according to that. In order to properly implement it they need to understand the skills of employees and provide them training as per their strength and weakness. There should be different training plan for different streams as IT people needs to be trained by highly skilled technical people. On the other hand HR strategies needs to be implemented by giving proper plan. The module of overall training and development plan should be set with the highly skilled management people so that they can give proper suggestions. Further, they can take feedbacks from all their workers that at which stage of their work they are facing difficulties. On the basis of this part they can prepare their module and provide them training so that workers can easily overcome with the problems they are facing. It is the proper solution through which each and every staff member performs effectively and share their strength and weakness. In the behavioral aspect management people should choose various strategies through which they can create a proper working environment. It is essential for all the management people to work as a team so that they can effectively communicate to each other. It always helps in boosting the performance level of employees. They can provide various rewards such as promotion, appraisal etc. in order to improve the performance of all their employees. Working condition and culture of company should motivate so that company can provide high class services to all their customers.

In addition to this, company can adopt various training and development methods such as i.e. on-the-job and off-the-job methods. Iceland is a retail industry that serves their customer at a very small scale and it is essential for them to adopt these methods in order to gain higher competitive advantage. Various on-the-job methods can be adopted by company such as job rotation, special projects, experience etc. With the help of shifting and movement of an employee from one job to another in regular intervals helps them in boosting their productivity. Further, they can adopt

Off-the-job methods such as conferences and seminars, special courses and lectures, programmed learning, case study methods etc. These are the different methods in which employees can increase their capability of public speaking and further they can improve their learning skills. With attending seminar and conferences individual can increase their learning and improve their communication skills. Ice land is a retail industry, and it is essential for all their employees to provide proper specification about all their products so that they can easily attract huge numbers of clients. Thus, it can be said that if Iceland follows the above-mentioned recommendations than its practices can become flawless, and all employees perform effectively. Moreover, companies can improve their productivity and increase their market share.

REFERENCES

Adamson, P., & Caple, J. (1996). The training and development audit evolves: Is your training and development budget wasted? *Journal of European Industrial Training, 20*(5), 3–12. doi:10.1108/03090599610119674

Afshan, S., Sobia, I., Kamran, A., & Nasir, M. (2012). Impact of training on employee performance: A study of telecommunication sector in Pakistan. *Interdisciplinary Journal of Contemporary Research in Business, 4,* 6.

Ahuja, K. 2006. Personnel management. Kalyani Publishers.

Baum, T., & Devine, F. (2007). Skills andtraining in the hotel sector: The Case of front office employment in Northern Ireland. *Tourism and Hospitality Research, 7*(3-4), 269–280. doi:10.1057/palgrave.thr.6050046

Boxall, P. (2003). HR strategy and competitive advantage in the service sector. *Human Resource Management Journal, 13*(3), 5–20. doi:10.1111/j.1748-8583.2003.tb00095.x

Cattermole, G., Johnson, J., & Jackson, D. (2014). Employee engagement creates a brighter economic future at Jupiter Hotels. *Strategic HR Review, 13*(2), 81–85. doi:10.1108/SHR-11-2013-0110

Creswell, W. J. (2003). Research Design: Qualitative, Quantitative, and Mixed Methods Approaches. *Sage (Atlanta, Ga.).*

Debrah, Y. A., & Ofori, G. (2006). Human Resource Development of Professionals in an Emerging Economy: The Case of the Tanzanian Construction Industry. *International Journal of Human Resource Management, 17*(3), 440–463. doi:10.1080/09585190500521425

Edmond, H., & Noon, M. (2001). *A dictionary of human resource management*. Oxford University Press.

Effectiveness of Training in Organizations. A Meta-Analysis of Design and Evaluation Features. (2003). http://www.ispi.org/archives/resources/EffectivenessofTrainingArthur_etal.pdf

Evans, P., Pucik, V., & Barsoux, J.-L. (2002). *The Global Challenge: Framework for International Human Resource Management*. McGraw-Hill.

Grbich, C. (2012). Qualitative Data Analysis: An Introduction. *Sage (Atlanta, Ga.)*.

Hassi, A. (2012). Islamic perspectives on training and professional development. *Journal of Management Development*, *31*(10), 1035–1045. doi:10.1108/02621711211281816

Huemann, M., Keegan, A., & Turner, R. J. (2007). Human resource management in the project-oriented company: A review. *International Journal of Project Management*, *25*(3), 315–323. doi:10.1016/j.ijproman.2006.10.001

Jackson, S. (2010). *Research Methods: A Modular Approach*. Cengage Learning.

Kenney, J., & Reid, M. (2006). *Training Interventions*. Institute of Personnel Management.

Kimmel, A. J. (2009). *Ethical Issues in Behavioral Research: Basic and Applied Perspectives* (2nd ed.). John Wiley & Sons.

Kougias, I., Seremeti, L., & Kalogeras, D. (2013). Mobility of Eastern European citizens: Training and development. *European Journal of Training and Development*, *37*(8), 766–778. doi:10.1108/EJTD-03-2013-0033

Kuada, J. (2012). *Research Methodology: A Project Guide for University Students*. Samfundslitteratur.

Marchington, M., & Wilkinson, A. (2008). *Human Resource Management at Work*. CIPD.

McBain, D. (2007). The practice of engagement: Research into current employee engagement practice. *Strategic HR Review*, *6*(6), 16–19. doi:10.1108/14754390780001011

McCourt, W., & Derek, E. (2003). *Global Human Resource Management: Managing People in Developing and Transitional Countries*. Edward Elgar. doi:10.4337/9781781950104

Merriam, B. S. (2009). *Qualitative Research: A Guide to Design and Implementation* (3rd ed.). John Wiley & Sons.

Millar, G. (2012). Employee engagement – a new paradigm. *Human Resource Management International Digest, 20*(2), 3–5. doi:10.1108/09670731211208085

NaumanB. (2010). http://www.binishnauman.com/index.php?option=com_content&view=article&id=134:what-is-more-important-training-or-development-of-employees--manager-today-article-by-binish-naumanpdf&catid=54:publication

Newstrom, W. J., & Davis, K. (2002). *Organizational Behavior: Human Behavior at Work* (11th ed.). McGraw-Hill/Irwin.

Niazi, A. D. (2011). Training and Development Strategy and Its Role in Organizational Performance. *Journal of Public Administration and Governance., 1*(2), 42. doi:10.5296/jpag.v1i2.862

Rasinger, M. S. (2008). *Quantitative Research in Linguistics: An Introduction.* Continuum International Publishing Group.

Rogers, T. T., Pasztor, M. E., & Kleinpeter, B. C. (2003). The Impact of Training on Worker Performance and Retention: Perceptions of Child Welfare Supervisors. *Professional Development: The International Journal of Continuing Social Work Education, 6*(3), 1–2.

Skaggs, C. B., & Youndt, M. (2004). Strategic Positioning, Human Capital, and Performance in Service Organizations: A Customer Interaction Approach. *Strategic Management Journal, 25*(1), 85–99. doi:10.1002/smj.365

Skaggs, C. B., & Youndt, M. (2004). Strategic Positioning, Human Capital, and Performance in Service Organizations: A Customer Interaction Approach. *Strategic Management Journal, 25*(1), 85–99. doi:10.1002/smj.365

Strategic Training and Development: A Gateway to Organizational Success. (2008). http://missionfacilitators.com/wp-content/uploads/2013/03/Strategic-Training-Development-SHRM-2008.pdf

Stuart, R. (2013). *Essentials of Human Resource Training and Development.* http://www.hrps.org/blogpost/736528/160480/Essentials-of-Human-Resource-Training-and-Development

Sullivan, P. (2011). Qualitative Data Analysis Using a Dialogical Approach. *Sage (Atlanta, Ga.).*

Swart, J., Mann, C., Brown, S., & Price, A. (2005). *Human Resource Development: Strategy and Tactics*. Elsevier Butterworth-Heinemann Publications.

Taylor, L. III, Murphy, B., & Price, W. (2006). Goldratt's thinking process applied to employee retention. *Business Process Management Journal, 12*(5), 646–670. doi:10.1108/14637150610691055

Taylor, R., & Davies, D. (2004). Aspects of training and remuneration in the accommodation industry. *Journal of European Industrial Training, 28*(6), 1–2. doi:10.1108/03090590410542693

Torrington, D., Hall, L., & Taylor, S. (2005). *Human Resource Management* (6th ed.). Prentice Hall.

Trim, J. R. P. (2004). Human resource management development and strategic management enhanced by simulation exercises. *Journal of Management Development, 23*(4), 399–413. doi:10.1108/02621710410529820

Wilson, J., & Western, S. (2001). Performance appraisal: An obstacle to training and development? *Career Development International, 6*(2), 93–100.

Wognum, A. A. M. (2001). Vertical Integration of HRD Policy within Companies. *Human Resource Development International, 4*(3), 407–421. doi:10.1080/13678860010006149

Wright, P., & Geroy, D. G. (2001). Changing the mindset: The training myth and the need for word-class performance. *International Journal of Human Resource Management, 12*(4), 586–600. doi:10.1080/09585190122342

Chapter 11
Role of Training and Development in Employee Motivation:
Tourism and Hospitality Sector

Amrik Singh
 https://orcid.org/0000-0003-3598-8787
Lovely Professional University, India

Amjad Imam Ansari
 https://orcid.org/0000-0002-6899-8562
Lovely Professional University, India

ABSTRACT

The contemporary hotel industry is facing many challenges that are closely connected to the changes that occur both in the field of tourist demand and tourist supply. The changes refer to the quality of services at first place, since the needs of tourists change rapidly towards higher quality and different products. Having in mind the character of the activities in the hospitality industry where direct contact between employees and guests is necessary for providing and realizing the services, the success of service realization and fulfilling guests' satisfaction depends the most on the employees. The present study aims to explore the issue of staff training in the hospitality sector as an important management activity for improved service quality. This study explores the importance of appropriate employee structure within the process of providing services. Staff training in the hospitality sector is very important for the continuous training of currently employed staff and for new employees as well.

DOI: 10.4018/979-8-3693-1674-0.ch011

INTRODUCTION

In today's conditions, long-term success and competitive advantage of enterprises depend on giving importance to humans because many of the resources owned by enterprises can be imitated, except for human resources. Therefore, it is important to ensure that human resources do their activities voluntarily. In other words, the motivation of individuals to work is an important factor in the success of the enterprise. In the dynamic landscape of contemporary workplaces, employee motivation stands as a cornerstone for organizational success. While various factors contribute to motivation, training and development emerge as pivotal strategies to nurture and sustain a motivated workforce. This chapter delves into the multifaceted relationship between employee motivation and training and development initiatives, exploring how organizations can harness these tools to drive engagement, productivity, and growth. There are many factors that affect employees' motivations (Singh and Bathla, 2023; Sharma and Singh, 2024; Singh and Singh, 2024; Singh and Hassan, 2024a; Singh, 2024a; Singh, 2024b; Singh and Kumar, 2022; Singh and Hassan, 2024b, Singh and Kumar, 2021; Sharma and Singh, 2024; Ansari and Singh, 2023; Ambardar and Singh, 2017; Ambardar et al., 2022; Bhalla et al., 2023).. These can be summarized as economic, psycho-social and organizational and managerial tools. In this study, it is aimed to reveal the effects of educational activities on employee motivation which are evaluated within the scope of organizational and managerial motivation tools. Training and development activities with motivation will be evaluated as two main variables. Human resource management is a strategic, comprehensive and internally consistent approach to human management, the most valuable asset of the organization (Singh, 2024; Ambardar and Singh, 2017). It is defined as the management of activities in order to ensure the satisfaction, motivation and high performance of the labor force within the organization. Human resources management aims to ensure the superiority of the enterprise by combining the individual wishes and organizational goals of the employees for the growth and development of the organization. In order for the management to recruit appropriate people, it is necessary to know in detail what these works and the personal and social characteristics required by the job. These determinations are performed through business analysis. Business analysis is the cornerstone of human resources management. Without performing a thorough analysis of all tasks, it is difficult to perform other human resource functions sufficiently. A thorough assessment of the entire office, operational, technical and administrative affairs, business analysis for salary, training, performance evaluation and publicity decisions provides a solid foundation. One of the authorities on motivation is Higgins. Higgins (2005) developed a motivational theory called regulatory focus that discusses how two factors play into each decision: prevention and promotion. Prevention refers to the concept of an individual acting in a way required for safety or security. Examples included a person performing a required safety training that is not appealing or having to pay a bill. Neither action is what a person wants to do, but the person understands that the action must be done. Promotion focuses on how a person acts when the activity has some meaning to the person. This focus includes enrolling in a university program because of an enjoyment in the topic or thoughts on how a degree will benefit the person long term (Singh, 2024; Ambardar and Singh, 2017; Singh and Bathla, 2023; Sharma and Singh, 2024; Singh and Singh, 2024; Singh and Hassan, 2024a; Singh, 2024a; Singh, 2024b; Singh and Kumar, 2022; Singh and Hassan, 2024b, Singh and Kumar, 2021; Sharma and Singh, 2024; Ansari and Singh, 2023; Ambardar and Singh, 2017; Ambardar et al., 2022; Bhall et al., 2023). Higgins et al. (2010) discussed how this theory of regulatory fit also influences the interest in activities for individuals. The concept that the person may be motivated differently because of promotion versus preservation showed that the activity must be conveyed to match this regulatory focus. Motivation ties directly into the perception of an employee. By using surveys or questionnaires, organizations can try to gauge the perception of an employee. Beausaert, Segers, and Gijselaers (2011) used data from this type of questionnaire to determine the development and validation of programs. By using a development plan such as this for an employee, organization leaders can see changes in the performance of an employee. Hameed and Waheed (2011) reviewed how organizations use the results of these types of perception surveys to develop strategic plans in programs within the organization. The connection of the two means that an organization can track the development of an employee and the motivation along with it. Overall, training programs are effective when the employee is involved, but the lack of written research on the correct way to implement training prevents organizations from standardizing programs. Common research themes are that employee motivation and involvement are key elements in training program success. Hardman and Robertson (2012) concluded from a literature review that successful training programs within an organization are private because of the desire for organizations to keep a competitive advantage. Freeman (2009) argued that training program success is dependent on the self-efficacy of a person to complete the training. Mayfield and Mayfield (2012) found leadership influence and self-efficacy both increase training program effectiveness more than the training program itself. All three studies showed that while organizational training plans are key components of the program's success, two of the vital factors to training success are the self-efficacy of the trainee and communication from the trainer and organizational leaders. Government training had the most different answers of the three areas of training. Ten participants felt that government training was inadequate or did not do a good job in providing learners with information with quality education. Major factors that people cited for this lack of quality included reliance on CBTs for delivery, outdated materials and information, multiple trainings due almost simultaneously, and lack of integration with corporate or academic programs (Singh, 2024; Ambardar and Singh, 2017; Singh and Bathla, 2023; Sharma and Singh, 2024; Singh and Singh, 2024; Singh and Hassan, 2024a; Singh, 2024a; Singh, 2024b; Singh and Kumar, 2022; Singh and Hassan, 2024b, Singh and Kumar, 2021; Sharma and Singh, 2024; Ansari and Singh, 2023; Ambardar and singh, 2017; Ambardar et al., 2022; Bhalla et al., 2023). Participants that felt government training had good quality responded that the programs used contracted organizations to help develop the material, applied directly to their primary job responsibilities, had relevance to outside credentialing, and involved an interactive delivery model to include hands-on training and classroom instruction. One constant response for government training was that participants felt government training was good at focusing on regulations, requirements, and standards for learners that were more broad-based. Higher education responses were reliant on the participant's degree program, level of education, and delivery method. Individuals involved with technical programs such as information technology or a focused business program felt more engaged, while participants with generalized degrees did not feel their higher education was relevant to the position as a project manager or consultant. Participants with undergraduate education only felt that the higher education was not as beneficial; however, individuals with any graduate education experience typically responded positively on how the education helped them prepare for leading teams and projects. Those that had some classroom experience, residencies, or team assignments to interact with others felt interaction with others prepared them for project management more than those that solely relied on distance learning programs. Individuals of all experience levels, industries, and positions stated that effects on workplace productivity are substantial when poor quality training is in place (Singh and Bathla, 2023; Sharma and Singh, 2024; Singh and Singh, 2024; Singh and Hassan, 2024a; Singh, 2024a; Singh, 2024b; Singh and Kumar, 2022; Singh and Hassan, 2024b, Singh and Kumar, 2021; Sharma and Singh, 2024; Ansari and Singh, 2023; Ambardar and singh, 2017; Ambardar et al., 2022; Bhall et al., 2023). While factors of poor quality varied as shown in the third theme, all participants agreed on the potential effects on workplace productivity from poor training. Individuals responded that poor training often leads to the following issues. We are living in a global village.

LITERATURE REVIEW

Theoretical Background

The world is becoming smaller and our business is becoming larger as the result of globalization. In this regard the companies must be competitive to face the challenges of the globalization. The competitive advantages of the firm depend on the knowledge and skills possessed by the employees (Drucker, 1999; Singh, 2024; Ambardar and Singh, 2017; Singh, 2024a; Singh, 2024b; Singh and Kumar, 2022; Singh and Hassan, 2024b, Singh and Kumar, 2021; Sharma and Singh, 2024; Ansari and Singh, 2023; Ambardar et al., 2022). Training and development have become one of the necessary functions in most organizations, because they lead to high performance in the same field and are important part of human resource department, it has a significant effect on the success of an organization through improving employee performance (Mozael, 2015; Singh, 2024; Ambardar and Singh, 2017).There is significant positive relationship exists between employee training and development and the employee performance (Naveed, 2014; Singh, 2024a; Singh, 2024b; Singh and Kumar, 2022; Singh and Hassan, 2024b, Singh and Kumar, 2021; Sharma and Singh, 2024; Ansari and Singh, 2023; Ambardar and singh, 2017; Ambardar et al., 2022).Currently hotels are facing extensive competition, continuously changing technological and business environment. Globalization and ever-changing customer needs have added up more challenges on business organizations. In order to meet these challenges, the industries are seeking to reach its targeted profit level by ensuring proper training and development of employees. Employees are most precious asset for any company as they can build up or destroy reputation of company and they can affect profitability (Elnaga and Imran, 2013; Singh, 2024; Ambardar and Singh, 2017). Training and development have become one of the necessary functions in most organizations, because they lead to high performance in the same field and are important part of human resource department, it has a significant effect on the success of an organization through improving employee performance (Mozael, 2015). The existing organizations should deal with training necessitates linked up with altering and growing internationalization of industry, diverse national point of view and a varied workforce (Abdus, 2011; Singh, 2024a; Singh, 2024b; Singh and Kumar, 2022; Singh and Hassan, 2024b, Singh and Kumar, 2021; Sharma and Singh, 2024; Ansari and Singh, 2023; Ambardar and singh, 2017; Ambardar et al., 2022). Training is of much significance in achieving the objectives of the organization by keeping in view the interest of employees and organization (Stone, 2002). Training includes but not limited to software training, management training whereas development focuses primarily on the activities that improve employee skills for future endeavors. Firms are now facing new changes due to the rapid pace of technological and global development. Technological advancements have brought about the need of competencies and capabilities needed to perform a specific task. In order to manage these challenges, more enhanced and efficient training programs are needed by all corporations (Figure 1).

Figure 1. Conceptual model of the study

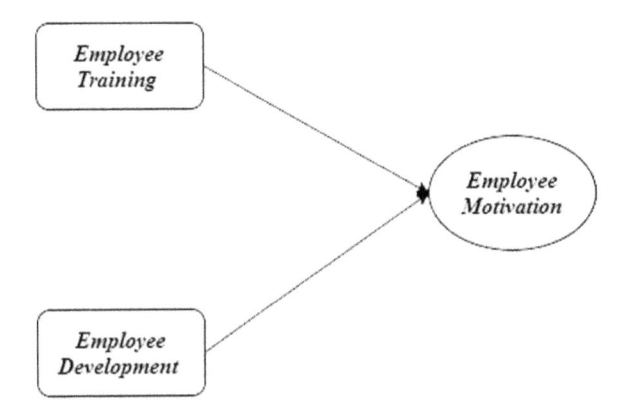

```
   Employee
   Training  ─────────┐
                      ▼
                  Employee
                  Motivation
                      ▲
   Employee  ─────────┘
   Development
```

Employee Training

Training is the learning process that is the indispensable part of human resource development. According to Abbas Z. (2014) training as an essential element to an employee for the development of the companies because some of the employees have lack of knowledge skills and competencies and failed to accomplish task on timely basis. Besides, Training is a learning activity directed towards the acquisition of specific knowledge and skills for the purpose of an occupation or task. The focus of training is the job or task for example, the need to have efficiency and safety in the operation of particular machines or equipment, or the need for an effective sales force to mention but a few (Cole, 2002). According to Saleem et al. (2011) training is an organized increase from the know-how skills and sensations needed for staff members to execute efficiently in the offered process, as well as, to operate in underling situation. Furthermore, training also increases the abilities of employee"s very effective way by motivating them and converting them in to well organize and well-mannered, that ultimately affects the performance of organization. However, Laing (2009) training is defined as an indicator to enhance superior skills, knowledge, capabilities and outlook of the employees that results in effective performance of the workers. Moreover, he adds one more thing, that is, training extends the production of the organization. In line with this is the believe that training is important mean to improve the employees" productivity which ultimately affects the organization performance and effectiveness (Singh and Mohanty, 2012; Singh, 2024a; Singh, 2024b; Singh and Kumar, 2022; Singh and Hassan, 2024b, Singh and Kumar, 2021; Sharma and Singh, 2024; Ansari and Singh, 2023; Ambardar and singh, 2017; Ambardar et al., 2022). Further researchers added that technological developments, atomization, mechanization, changing environment and organizational change have gradually led some employers to the realization that success relies on the skills and abilities of their employees, and this means considerable and continuous investment in training and development Khan et al. (2011).Training the act of increasing the knowledge, skills, abilities of an employee for doing a specific job .It an is an organized increase from the know-how skills and sensations needed for staff members to execute efficiently in the offered process, as well as, to operate in underling situation Saleem et al. (2011). Moreover, Laing (2009) assumed that training as an indicator to enhance superior skills, knowledge, capabilities and outlook of the employees results in effective performance of the workers. However, Singh and Mohanty (2012) believe that training is important mean to improve the employee's productivity which ultimately affects the organization performance and effectiveness. On the other hand, Training must be talked in such a way that it covers the employee's performance-development needs and is in accordance with their job descriptions. In addition to the previous arguments, McConnell (2004) supports a partnership approach between the employees and their companies in determining training needs, as well as the involvement of the employees in setting up training goals. Besides Mehrdad et al. (2009) also said that training techniques are classified into behavioral or On-the-job (orientations, job instruction training, apprenticeships, internships and assistantships, job rotation and coaching) and cognitive or off-the-job (Lectures, computer-based training, games and simulations etc.

The Role of Training in Context With Employee Motivation

Training and development initiatives encompass a broad spectrum of activities designed to enhance employees' knowledge, skills, and competencies. From onboarding programs to leadership development workshops, these interventions cater to diverse learning needs and career aspirations across all levels of the organization:

Skill Enhancement: Training programs offer employees the opportunity to acquire new skills or refine existing ones, equipping them with the capabilities required to perform their roles effectively. Whether it's technical skills in IT, soft skills in communication, or leadership skills, targeted training interventions contribute to competency development and job satisfaction (Singh, 2024a; Singh, 2024b; Singh and Kumar, 2022; Singh and Hassan, 2024b, Singh and Kumar, 2021; Sharma and

Singh, 2024; Ansari and Singh, 2023; Ambardar and singh, 2017; Ambardar et al., 2022).

Career Progression: Development opportunities signal to employees that their growth and advancement are valued within the organization. Through mentorship programs, cross-functional projects, and tuition assistance, employees are empowered to chart their career trajectories and pursue their professional aspirations with confidence.

Adaptability and Innovation: In today's fast-paced business environment, adaptability and innovation are critical for organizational success. Training and development initiatives that foster creativity, critical thinking, and problem-solving skills enable employees to navigate ambiguity, embrace change, and contribute to continuous improvement initiatives.

Employee Development

Employees are always regarded with development in career-enhancing skills which leads to employee motivation and retention. There is no doubt that a well-trained and developed staff will be a valuable asset to the company and thereby will increase the chances of their efficiency and effectiveness in discharging their duties. On the other hand, development means those learning opportunities designed to help employees to grow. Development is not primarily skills oriented. Instead, it provides the general knowledge and attitudes, which will be helpful to employers in higher positions (Sekhar et al., 2013; Singh and Bathla, 2023; Sharma and Singh, 2024). Development programs are regarded as specific framework for helping employees to develop their personal and professional skills, knowledge, attitudes, behavior and consequently improve their abilities to perform specific task in the organization. It provides knowledge about business environment, management principles and techniques, human relations, specific industry analysis and the like is useful for better management of company (Nohria et al., 2008; Singh and Singh, 2024; Singh and Hassan, 2024a; Singh, 2024a; Singh, 2024b; Singh and Kumar, 2022; Singh and Hassan, 2024b, Singh and Kumar, 2021; Sharma and Singh, 2024; Ansari and Singh, 2023; Ambardar and Singh, 2017; Ambardar et al., 2022; Bhalla et al., 2023). Manpower development focused on turning out human resource that is needed for effective.

Best Practices in Context With Employee Development

While the benefits of training and development are evident, realizing its full potential requires a strategic and holistic approach. Here are some best practices to consider:

Needs Assessment: The conduct thorough needs assessments to identify skill gaps, learning objectives, and training priorities aligned with organizational goals and employee development needs.

Customization and Flexibility: Design training programs that are tailored to diverse learning styles, preferences, and job roles. Offer a mix of traditional classroom training, online courses, workshops, and experiential learning opportunities to accommodate different learning preferences and schedules.

Continuous Feedback and Evaluation: Gather feedback from participants throughout the training process to assess effectiveness, relevance, and engagement levels. Use this feedback to refine and improve training programs iteratively.

Integration with Performance Management: Integrate training and development initiatives with performance management processes to ensure alignment with organizational goals and individual development plans. Provide opportunities for employees to apply newly acquired skills and receive recognition for their contributions.

Leadership Support and Role Modeling: Cultivate a culture of learning and development from the top down by encouraging leaders to actively participate in training programs and champion lifelong learning initiatives within their teams.

Employee Motivation

Motivation is the driving force that compels individuals to act and persevere towards the achievement of organizational goals. At its core, motivation is intended to support changes in behavior (Naile & Selesho, 2014; Singh and Bathla, 2023; Sharma and Singh, 2024). It is a force that empowers a person to take action toward a specific goal. Since effective leadership is all about doing things the right way, it is also possible to motivate employees. The leader must win the trust of the team members and inspire them to follow him in order to accomplish these objectives. However, the staff needs to be motivated in order to gain their trust and enable them to perform their duties for the company effectively. It encompasses a complex interplay of intrinsic and extrinsic factors that influence employees' attitudes, behaviors, and performance within the workplace (Rajhans, 2012; Ambardar and singh, 2017; Ambardar et al., 2022; Bhalla et al., 2023; Singh and Singh, 2024; Singh and Hassan, 2024a; Singh, 2024a; Singh, 2024b; Singh and Kumar, 2022; Singh and Hassan, 2024b, Singh and Kumar, 2021; Sharma and Singh, 2024; Ansari and Singh, 2023). Key theories such as Maslow's Hierarchy of Needs, Herzberg's Two-Factor Theory, and Locke and Latham's Goal-Setting Theory provide valuable insights into the psychological mechanisms underlying motivation. In the context of employee motivation, training and development serve as catalysts that unlock potential, enhance skills, and cultivate a sense of purpose and fulfillment among employees (Shahzadi et al., 2014). By investing in continuous learning opportunities, organizations can empower their workforce, foster a culture of innovation, and adapt to evolving market dynamics effectively (William,2010).Effective training and development initiatives have a profound impact on employee motivation, yielding several tangible benefits for both individuals and organizations.

Increased Engagement: Employees who participate in meaningful learning experiences are more engaged and committed to their work. By aligning training programs with employees' interests and career goals, organizations can ignite a sense of purpose and enthusiasm that transcends daily tasks.

Enhanced Job Satisfaction: Investing in employees' professional growth demonstrates a commitment to their well-being and success. As employees acquire new skills and make tangible progress in their careers, they experience greater job satisfaction and are more likely to remain loyal to the organization.

Improved Performance: Training and development interventions directly contribute to enhanced job performance and productivity. Employees who receive regular feedback, coaching, and opportunities for skill development are better equipped to meet and exceed performance expectations, driving overall organizational success.

Retention and Talent Development: In a competitive labor market, organizations that prioritize employee development differentiate themselves as employers of choice. By fostering a culture of continuous learning and investing in talent development, organizations can attract, retain, and nurture top talent, ensuring long-term sustainability and growth.

METHODOLOGY

The current study's foundation is a thorough examination of the literature on role of training and development in employee motivation: tourism and hospitality sector. The study determines the total number of included papers using the extensive literature review approach. Extensive literature review is a methodical approach to collecting data, primarily secondary data. At this stage, data must be critically assessed, and findings must be synthesized using either a qualitative or quantitative approach.

CONCLUSION

Employee motivation is a dynamic force that drives organizational success, and training and development play a central role in nurturing and sustaining that motivation. Due to high competition, they need to upgrade their skills, according to the job positions. A scope of training courses includes different programs with a wide range of issues that meet industry standards and can lead to employee' professional development and improved service quality delivery. By investing in employees' professional growth, organizations can empower their workforce, enhance performance, and foster a culture of innovation and excellence. Through strategic planning, customization, and ongoing evaluation, organizations can maximize the impact of training and development initiatives, creating a motivated and engaged workforce poised for success in today's competitive landscape. Many organizations have come to the realization of the importance of the role of training and development programs as it increases the organization's staff efficiency, skills and productivity. Through training employees' need for supervision gets decreased and they can make better decisions on their own and involved in effective problem solving. Training gives basis to personal development by helping employees to develop leadership talent and communication skills, it decreases their fear in attempting new tasks and enables them to handle stress, frustration and conflicts. These factors give them a chance to perform better which result in developing feelings of satisfaction towards their job (Singh and Bathla, 2023; Sharma and Singh, 2024; Singh and Singh, 2024; Singh and Hassan, 2024a; Singh, 2024a; Singh, 2024b; Singh and Kumar, 2022; Singh and Hassan, 2024b, Singh and Kumar, 2021; Sharma and Singh, 2024; Ansari and Singh, 2023; Ambardar and singh, 2017; Ambardar et al., 2022; Bhalla et al., 2023). Training develops required talents and capabilities in employees which ensure that each and every employee can give contribution towards organization's strategic objectives. To enhance both customer satisfaction and efficiency, a company must have qualified and driven personnel. In this sense, motivation refers to a person's readiness to put forth effort and take initiative in support of corporate objectives. Creating and maintaining employee motivation is a problem for any manager. Managers should employ motivating aspects including performance, recognition, responsibility, and the work itself in addition to concentrating on minimizing job unhappiness such as working conditions, salary, supervision, and relationships with coworkers.

REFERENCES

Ambardar, A., & Singh, A. (2017). Quality of work life practices in Indian hotel industry. *International Journal of Hospitality and Tourism Systems*, *10*(1), 22–33.

Ambardar, A., Singh, A., & Singh, V. (2023). Barriers in Implementing Ergonomic Practices in Hotels- A Study on five star hotels in NCR region. *International Journal of Hospitality and Tourism Systems*, *16*(2), 11–17.

Ansari, A. I., Singh, A., & Singh, V. (2023). The impact of differential pricing on perceived service quality and guest satisfaction: An empirical study of mid-scale hotels in India. *Turyzm/Tourism*, 121–132. doi:10.18778/0867-5856.33.2.10

Beausaert, S., Segers, M., & Gijselaers, W. (2011). The Personal Development Plan Practice Questionnaire: The development and validation of an instrument to assess the employee's perception of personal development plan practice. *International Journal of Training and Development, 15*(4), 249–270. doi:10.1111/j.1468-2419.2011.00375.x

Bhalla, A., Singh, P., & Singh, A. (2023). Technological Advancement and Mechanization of the Hotel Industry. In R. Tailor (Ed.), *Application and Adoption of Robotic Process Automation for Smart Cities* (pp. 57–76). IGI Global. doi:10.4018/978-1-6684-7193-7.ch004

Carter, C. A. (2011, April 26). *The influence of business ownership and selected demographic characteristics on the perceived effectiveness of an entrepreneurship training program among female participants.* Louisiana State University and Agricultural and Mechanical College. Retrieved from http://etd.lsu.edu/docs/available/etd-04212011-091948/

Cilesiz, S. (2011). A phenomenological approach to experiences with technology: Current state, promise, and future directions for research. *Educational Technology Research and Development, 59*(4), 487–510. doi:10.1007/s11423-010-9173-2

Farooq, M., & Khan, M. A. (2011). Impact of training and feedback on employee performance. *Far East Journal of Psychology & Business, 5*(1), 23–33. Retrieved from http://www.fareastjournals.com/

Freeman, E. W. (2009). *Training effectiveness: The influence of personal achievement goals on posttraining self-efficacy* (Doctoral dissertation). Available from ProQuest Dissertations and ThesesDatabase. (UMI No. 3395162)

Gaither, K. A. (2009). *Comparing perceived effectiveness of e-learning and traditional training in the business environment* (Doctoral dissertation). Available from ProQuest Dissertations and Theses Database. (UMI No. 3362657)

Halvorson, H. G., & Higgins, E. T. (2013). Know what really motivates you. *Harvard Business Review, 91*(3), 117–120. https://hbr.org/magazine PMID:23451530

Hardman, W., & Robertson, L. (2012). What motivates employees to persist with online training? One Canadian workplace study. *International Journal of Business, Humanities & Technology, 2*(5), 66–78. Retrieved from http://www.ijbhtnet.com/

Higgins, E. (2005). Value from regulatory fit. *Current Directions in Psychological Science, 14*(4), 209–213. doi:10.1111/j.0963-7214.2005.00366.x

Higgins, E. T., Cesario, J., Hagiwara, N., Spiegel, S., & Pittman, T. (2010). Increasing or decreasing interest in activities: The role of regulatory fit. *Journal of Personality and Social Psychology, 98*(4), 559–572. doi:10.1037/a0018833 PMID:20307129

Hutchins, H. M., Burke, L. A., & Berthelsen, A. M. (2010). A missing link in the transfer problem? Examining how trainers learn about training transfer. *Human Resource Management, 49*(4), 599–618. doi:10.1002/hrm.20371

Kohn, S. L. (2009). *The effects of choice and training reputation on training effectiveness* (Doctoral dissertation). Available from ProQuest Dissertations and Theses Database. (UMI No. 3367278)

Maddox, W. T., & Markman, A. B. (2012). The motivation-cognition interface in learning and decision making. *Current Directions in Psychological Science, 19*(2), 106–110. doi:10.1177/0963721410364008 PMID:20556228

Naile, I., & Selesho, J. M. (2014). The role of leadership in employee motivation. *Mediterranean Journal of Social Sciences, 5*(3), 175–182. doi:10.5901/mjss.2014.v5n3p175

Nohria, N., Groysberg, B., & Lee, L. E. (2008). Employee Motivation. *Harvard Business Review*, 1.

Rajhans, K. (2012). Effective organizational communication: A key to employee motivation and performance. *Interscience Management Review, 2*(2), 81–85.

Sekhar, C., Patwardhan, M., & Singh, R. K. (2013). A literature review on motivation. *Global Business Perspectives, 1*, 471-487.

Shahzadi, I., Javed, A., Pirzada, S. S., Nasreen, S., & Khanam, F. (2014). Impact of employee motivation on employee performance. *European Journal of Business and Management, 6*(23), 159–166.

Sharma, M., & Singh, A. (2024). Enhancing Competitive Advantages Through Virtual Reality Technology in the Hotels of India. In S. Kumar, M. Talukder, & A. Pego (Eds.), *Utilizing Smart Technology and AI in Hybrid Tourism and Hospitality* (pp. 243–256). IGI Global. doi:10.4018/979-8-3693-1978-9.ch011

Sharma, R., & Singh, A. (2024). Use of Digital Technology in Improving Quality Education: A Global Perspectives and Trends. In V. Nadda, P. Tyagi, R. Moniz Vieira, & P. Tyagi (Eds.), *Implementing Sustainable Development Goals in the Service Sector* (pp. 14–26). IGI Global. doi:10.4018/979-8-3693-2065-5.ch002

Singh, A. (2024a). Quality of Work-Life Practices in the Indian Hospitality Sector: Future Challenges and Prospects. In M. Valeri & B. Sousa (Eds.), *Human Relations Management in Tourism* (pp. 208–224). IGI Global. doi:10.4018/979-8-3693-1322-0.ch010

Singh, A. (2024b). Virtual Research Collaboration and Technology Application: Drivers, Motivations, and Constraints. In S. Chakraborty (Ed.), *Challenges of Globalization and Inclusivity in Academic Research* (pp. 250–258). IGI Global. doi:10.4018/979-8-3693-1371-8.ch016

Singh, A., & Bathla, G. (2023). Fostering Creativity and Innovation: Tourism and Hospitality Perspective. In P. Tyagi, V. Nadda, V. Bharti, & E. Kemer (Eds.), *Embracing Business Sustainability through Innovation and Creativity in the Service Sector* (pp. 70-83). IGI Global.

Singh, A., & Hassan, S. C. (2024). Service Innovation Through Blockchain Technology in the Tourism and Hospitality Industry: Applications, Trends, and Benefits. In S. Singh (Ed.), *Service Innovations in Tourism: Metaverse, Immersive Technologies, and Digital Twin* (pp. 205–214). IGI Global. doi:10.4018/979-8-3693-1103-5.ch010

Singh, A., & Hassan, S. C. (2024a). Identifying the Skill Gap in the Workplace and Their Challenges in Hospitality and Tourism Organisations. In Contemporary Challenges in Social Science Management: Skills Gaps and Shortages in the Labour Market (Contemporary Studies in Economic and Financial Analysis, Vol. 112B). Emerald Publishing Limited. doi:10.1108/S1569-37592024000112B006

Singh, A., & Kumar, S. (2021). Identifying Innovations in Human Resources: Academia and Industry Perspectives. In A. Pathak & S. Rana (Eds.), *Transforming Human Resource Functions With Automation* (pp. 104–120). IGI Global. doi:10.4018/978-1-7998-4180-7.ch006

Singh, V., & Singh, A. (2024b). Digital Health Revolution: Enhancing Well-Being Through Technology. In V. Nadda, P. Tyagi, R. Moniz Vieira, & P. Tyagi (Eds.), *Implementing Sustainable Development Goals in the Service Sector* (pp. 213–219). IGI Global. doi:10.4018/979-8-3693-2065-5.ch016

William, A. N. (2010). Employee motivation and performance. *Business Management*, *8*, 5–11.

Compilation of References

Adams, K. M., Hester, P. T., Bradley, J. M., Meyers, T. J., & Keating, C. B. (2014). Systems theory as the foundation for understanding systems. *Systems Engineering*, *17*(1), 112–123. doi:10.1002/sys.21255

Adamson, P., & Caple, J. (1996). The training and development audit evolves: Is your training and development budget wasted? *Journal of European Industrial Training*, *20*(5), 3–12. doi:10.1108/03090599610119674

Adeyemo, D. A., & Aremu, A. O. (1999). Career commitment among secondary school teachers in Oyo state, Nigeria: The Role of biographical mediators. *Nigerian Journal of Applied Psychology*, *5*(2), 184–194.

Afshan, S., Sobia, I., Kamran, A., & Nasir, M. (2012). Impact of training on employee performance: A study of telecommunication sector in Pakistan. *Interdisciplinary Journal of Contemporary Research in Business*, *4*, 6.

Aguinis, H. (2019). *Performance Management* (4th ed.). Chicago Business Press.

Ahuja, K. 2006. Personnel management. Kalyani Publishers.

Ajila, C., & Abiola, A. (2004). Influence of Rewards on Workers Performance in an Organization. *Journal of Social Sciences*, *8*(1), 7–12. doi:10.1080/09718923.2004.11892397

Aknin, L. B., Barrington-Leigh, C. P., Dunn, E. W., Helliwell, J. F., Biswas-Diener, R., Kemeza, I., Nyende, P., Ashton-James, C. E., & Norton, M. I. (2010). Prosocial spending and well-being: Cross-cultural evidence for a psychological universal. *Journal of Personality and Social Psychology*, *104*(4), 635–652. doi:10.1037/a0031578 PMID:23421360

Aknin, L. B., Broesch, T., Hamlin, J. K., & Van de Vondervoort, J. W. (2015). Prosocial behavior leads to happiness in a small-scale rural society. *Journal of Experimental Psychology. General*, *144*(4), 788–795. doi:10.1037/xge0000082 PMID:26030168

Albulescu, M., & Bibu, N. (2020). Change management strategy and ITIL implementation process in an IT company—Study case. In G. Prostean, J. Lavios Villahoz, L. Brancu, & G. Bakacsi (Eds.), *Innovation in Sustainable Management and Entrepreneurship. SIM 2019. Springer Proceedings in Business and Economics*. Springer. doi:10.1007/978-3-030-44711-3_46

Compilation of References

Allen, M. R., Adomdza, G. K., & Meyer, M. H. (2015). Managing for innovation: Managerial control and employee level outcomes. *Journal of Business Research, 68*(2), 371–379. doi:10.1016/j.jbusres.2014.06.021

Allen, S. J., Rosch, D. M., & Riggio, R. E. (2022). Advancing leadership education and development: Integrating adult learning theory. *Journal of Management Education, 46*(2), 252–283. doi:10.1177/10525629211008645

Alshaikh, M. (2020). Developing cybersecurity culture to influence employee behavior: A practice perspective. *Computers & Security, 98*, 102003. doi:10.1016/j.cose.2020.102003

Al-Yaaribi, A., & Kavussanu, M. (2018). Consequences of prosocial and antisocial behaviors in adolescent male soccer players: The moderating role of motivational climate. *Psychology of Sport and Exercise, 37*, 91–99. doi:10.1016/j.psychsport.2018.04.005

Ambardar, A., & Singh, A. (2017). Quality of work life practices in Indian hotel industry. *International Journal of Hospitality and Tourism Systems, 10*(1), 22–33.

Ambardar, A., Singh, A., & Singh, V. (2023). Barriers in Implementing Ergonomic Practices in Hotels- A Study on five star hotels in NCR region. *International Journal of Hospitality and Tourism Systems, 16*(2), 11–17.

American Institute of Stress. (2023). *Workplace stress*. http://www.stress.org/workplace-stress/

American Psychological Association. (2015). *Paying with our health: Stress in America*. https://www.apa.org/news/press/releases/stress/2014/stress-report.pdf

Andersen, N. A. (2020). The constitutive effects of evaluation systems: Lessons from the policymaking process of Danish active labour market policies. *Evaluation, 26*(3), 257–274. doi:10.1177/1356389019876661

Anderson, D. (2016). *Organization Development: The Process of Leading Organizational Change* (6th ed.). Sage Publications, Inc.

Andree, S. (2018). Embracing generational diversity: Reducing and managing workplace conflict/ Accepter la diversity generationnelle: Reduire et gerer les conflits en milieu de travail. *ORNAC Journal, 36*(4), 13.

Andrews, P., & Laing, G. (2018). Evaluating the outcomes of a training program through an ROI evaluation: A case study. *e-Journal of Social & Behavioural Research in Business, 9*(3), 1–9.

Ansari, A. I., Singh, A., & Singh, V. (2023). The impact of differential pricing on perceived service quality and guest satisfaction: An empirical study of mid-scale hotels in India. *Turyzm/Tourism*, 121–132. doi:10.18778/0867-5856.33.2.10

Antony, J., Sony, M., McDermott, O., Jayaraman, R., & Flynn, D. (2023). An exploration of organizational readiness factors for Quality 4.0: An intercontinental study and future research directions. *International Journal of Quality & Reliability Management, 40*(2), 582–606. doi:10.1108/IJQRM-10-2021-0357

Anuradha. (2021, September 2). *What is the difference between subculture and counterculture*. PEDIAA. https://pediaa.com/what-is-the-difference-between-subculture-and-counterculture/

Argyris, C. (1982). *Reasoning, Learning and Action*. Jossey-Bass.

Ariely, D. (2011). *The upside of irrationality: The unexpected benefits of defying logic*. Harper Perennial. doi:10.1109/AERO.2011.5747214

Arnold, J. (1996). The psychological contract: A concept in need of closer scrutiny? *European Journal of Work and Organizational Psychology*, *5*(4), 511–520. doi:10.1080/13594329608414876

Arnold, K. A., & Walsh, M. M. (2015). Customer incivility and employee well-being: Testing the moderating effects of meaning, perspective taking, and transformational leadership. *Work and Stress*, *29*(4), 362–378. doi:10.1080/02678373.2015.1075234

Arnott, D., & Gao, S. (2022). Behavioral economics in information systems research: Critical analysis and research strategies. *Journal of Information Technology*, *37*(1), 80–117. doi:10.1177/02683962211016000

Assens-Serra, J., Boada-Cuerva, M., Serrano-Fernández, M., & Agulló-Tomás, E. (2021). Gaining a better understanding of the types of organizational culture to manage suffering at work. *Frontiers in Psychology*, *12*, 782488. Advance online publication. doi:10.3389/fpsyg.2021.782488 PMID:34880819

Awais Bhatti, M., & Kaur, S. (2010). The role of individual and training design factors on training transfer. *Journal of European Industrial Training*, *34*(7), 656–672. doi:10.1108/03090591011070770

Ayub, N., & Rafif, S. (2011). The relationship between work motivation and job satisfaction. *Pakistan Business Review*, *13*(2), 332-347. https://www.researchgate.net/publication/342864521_The_Relationship_between_Work_Motivation_and_Job_Satisfaction

Balakrishnan, S. R., Soundararajan, V., & Parayitam, S. (2022). Recognition and rewards as moderators in the relationships between antecedents and performance of women teachers: Evidence from India. *International Journal of Educational Management*, *36*(6), 1002–1026. doi:10.1108/IJEM-12-2021-0473

Baldwin, T. T., Magjuka, R. J., & Loher, B. (1991). The perils of participation: Effects of the choice of training on trainee motivation and learning. *Personnel Psychology*, *44*(1), 51–65. doi:10.1111/j.1744-6570.1991.tb00690.x

Baluch, A. M., & Ridder, H.-G. (2020). Mapping the research landscape of strategic human resource management in nonprofit organizations: A systematic review. *Nonprofit and Voluntary Sector Quarterly*, *50*(3), 591–614.

Bandura, A. (1977a). *Social learning theory*. Prentice-Hall.

Bandura, A. (1977b). Self-efficacy: Toward a unifying theory of behavioral change. *Psychological Review*, *84*(2), 191–215. doi:10.1037/0033-295X.84.2.191 PMID:847061

Bandura, A. (2019). Applying theory for human betterment. *Perspectives on Psychological Science*, *14*(1), 12–15. doi:10.1177/1745691618815165 PMID:30799756

Baporikar, N. (2015). Understanding professional development for educators. [IJSEM]. *International Journal of Sustainable Economies Management*, *4*(4), 18–30. doi:10.4018/IJSEM.2015100102

Baporikar, N. (2016b). Lifelong learning in knowledge society. In *Impact of Economic Crisis on Education and the Next-Generation Workforce* (pp. 263–284). IGI Global. doi:10.4018/978-1-4666-9455-2.ch012

Baporikar, N. (2017). Knowledge transfer issues in teaching: Learning management. In *Innovation and Shifting Perspectives in Management Education* (pp. 58–78). IGI Global. doi:10.4018/978-1-5225-1019-2.ch003

Baporikar, N. (2020). Learning link in organizational tacit knowledge creation and dissemination. *International Journal of Sociotechnology and Knowledge Development*, *12*(4), 70–88. doi:10.4018/IJSKD.2020100105

Baporikar, N. (2021). Effect of Reward on Motivation and Job Satisfaction. *International Journal of Applied Management Sciences and Engineering*, *8*(1), 12–51. doi:10.4018/IJAMSE.2021010102

Baporikar, N. (Ed.). (2016a). *Management education for global leadership*. IGI Global.

Baran, B., Shanock, L. & Miller, L. (2012). Advancing organizational support theory into the twenty-first-century world of work. *Journal of Business and Psychology.* 27(10). 1007/s10869-011-9236-3.

Baron, R. A. (1983). *Behavior in organizations*. Allyn & Bacon, Inc.

Basim, H. N., Şeşen, H., Sözen, C., & Hazir, K. (2009). The effect of employees' learning organization perceptions on organizational citizenship behaviors. *Selcuk University Social Sciences Institute Journal*, *22*, 55–66. https://www.academia.edu/en/1082627/The_Effect_of_Employees_Learning_Organization_Perceptions_on_Organizational_Citizenship_Behaviors

Bass, B. M., & Riggio, R. E. (2006). *Transformational Leadership*. Lawrence Erlbaum Associates, Inc. doi:10.4324/9781410617095

Basset-Jones, N., & Lloyd, G. F. (2005). Does Herzberg"s motivation theory have staying power? *Journal of Management Development*, *24*(10), 929–943. doi:10.1108/02621710510627064

Bateman, T. S., & Organ, D. W. (1983). Job satisfaction and the good soldier: The relationship between affect and employee "citizenship." *Academy of Management Journal*, *26*(4), 587–595. doi:10.2307/255908

Bauer, K., Orvis, K., Ely, K., & Surface, E. (2016). Re-examination of Motivation in Learning Contexts:Meta-analytically Investigating the Role Type of Motivation Plays in the Prediction of Key TrainingOutcomes. *Journal of Business and Psychology*, *31*(1), 33–50. doi:10.1007/s10869-015-9401-1

Baum, T., & Devine, F. (2007). Skills andtraining in the hotel sector: The Case of front office employment in Northern Ireland. *Tourism and Hospitality Research*, 7(3-4), 269–280. doi:10.1057/palgrave.thr.6050046

BDC. (n.d.). *Organizational culture*. Entrepreneur's Toolkit. https://www.bdc.ca/en/articles-tools/entrepreneur-toolkit/templates-business-guides/glossary/organizational-culture

Beausaert, S., Segers, M., & Gijselaers, W. (2011). The Personal Development Plan Practice Questionnaire: The development and validation of an instrument to assess the employee's perception of personal development plan practice. *International Journal of Training and Development*, 15(4), 249–270. doi:10.1111/j.1468-2419.2011.00375.x

Becerra, M., & Mshigeni, S. (2022). A quasi-experimental evaluation of a flipped class in a public health course. *Journal of Applied Learning and Teaching*, 5(1), 178–182.

Beckhard, R., & Wendy, P. (1992). *Changing the essence: The art of creating and leading fundamental change in organizations* (Vol. 10). Jossey-Bass.

Bednarek, R. (2023). Using interpretive methods to unleash the potential of human resource development. *Human Resource Development Review*, 22(1), 169–186.

Bell, B. S., Tannenbaum, S. I., Ford, J. K., Noe, R. A., & Kraiger, K. (2017). 100 years of training and development research: What we know and where we should go. *The Journal of Applied Psychology*, 102(3), 305–323. doi:10.1037/apl0000142 PMID:28125262

Bellou, V. (2010). Organizational culture as a predictor of job satisfaction: The role of gender and age. *Career Development International*, 15(1), 4–19. doi:10.1108/13620431011020862

Belte, A. (2021). New avenues for HRM roles: A systematic literature review on HRM in hybrid organizations. *German Journal of Human Resource Management*, 36(2), 157–176.

Bereiter, C. (1990). Aspects of an Educational Learning Theory. *Review of Educational Research*, 60(4), 603–624. doi:10.3102/00346543060004603

Berman, E. M., West, J. P., & Richter, M. N. Jr. (2002). Workplace relations: Friendship patterns and consequences (according to managers). *Public Administration Review*, 62(2), 217–230. doi:10.1111/0033-3352.00172

Besley, T., & Persson, T. (2022). Organizational dynamics: Culture, design, and performance. *Journal of Law Economics and Organization*, ewac020. Advance online publication. doi:10.1093/jleo/ewac020

Bhalla, A., Singh, P., & Singh, A. (2023). Technological Advancement and Mechanization of the Hotel Industry. In R. Tailor (Ed.), *Application and Adoption of Robotic Process Automation for Smart Cities* (pp. 57–76). IGI Global. doi:10.4018/978-1-6684-7193-7.ch004

Bhatti, M. K., Soomro, B. A., & Shah, N. (2022). Predictive power of training design on employee performance: An empirical approach in Pakistan's health sector. *International Journal of Productivity and Performance Management*, 71(8), 3792–3808. doi:10.1108/IJPPM-09-2020-0489

Bijaniaram, R., Tehrani, M., Noori, R., & Pak, J. (2023). What does it take for organizations to adopt massive open online courses (MOOCs)? A fuzzy DANP analysis. *Journal of the Knowledge Economy*, 1–36. doi:10.1007/s13132-023-01178-z

Bishop, J. (1987). The recognition & Reward of Employee Performance. *Journal of Labor Economics*, 5(4), S36–S56. doi:10.1086/298164

Blau, P. (1964). *Exchange and power in social life*. John Wiley & Sons, Inc.

Bond, M. A., & Blevins, S. J. (2020, March). Using faculty professional development to foster organizational change: A social learning framework. *TechTrends*, 64(2), 229–237. doi:10.1007/s11528-019-00459-2

Booysen, L. (2013). The development of inclusive leadership practice and processes. In B. M. Ferdman & B. R. Deane (Eds.), *Diversity at Work: The Practice of Inclusion.*, doi:10.1002/9781118764282.ch10

Borman, W. C., Penner, L. A., Allen, T. D., & Motowidlo, S. J. (2001). Personality predictors of citizenship performance. *International Journal of Selection and Assessment*, 9(1-2), 52–69. doi:10.1111/1468-2389.00163

Bouchrika, I. (2023, July 28). *The andragogy approach: Knowles' adult learning theory principles*. Research.com. https://research.com/education/the-andragogy-approach

Bowling, N. A. (2010). Effects of Job Satisfaction and Conscientiousness on Extra-Role Behaviors. *Journal of Business and Psychology*, 25(1), 119–130. doi:10.1007/s10869-009-9134-0

Boxall, P. (2003). HR strategy and competitive advantage in the service sector. *Human Resource Management Journal*, 13(3), 5–20. doi:10.1111/j.1748-8583.2003.tb00095.x

Bragas, C. M., Bragas, L. F., & Soliman, C. (2022). The Changing Workforce And Its Implications To Productivity: A Literature Review. Sachetas An International, Peer Reviewed. *Open Access & Multidisciplinary Journal.*, 1(2), 55–69.

Bridges, W. (1986). Managing organizational transitions. *Organizational Dynamics*, 15(1), 24–33. doi:10.1016/0090-2616(86)90023-9

Brief, A. P., & Motowidlo, S. J. (1986). Prosocial organizational behaviors. *Academy of Management Review*, 11(4), 710–725. doi:10.2307/258391

Brown, B. (2013). Daring greatly: how the courage to be vulnerable transforms the way we live, love, parent, and lead (Center Point large print ed.). Thorndike, ME: Center Point Large Print.

Bryant-Davis, T. (2019). The cultural context of trauma recovery: Considering the posttraumatic stress disorder practice guideline and intersectionality. *Psychotherapy (Chicago, Ill.)*, 56(3), 400–408. doi:10.1037/pst0000241 PMID:31282715

Bunch, K. (2009). The influence of organizational culture on training effectiveness. In C. D. Hansen & Y. T. Lee (Eds.), *The Cultural Context of Human Resource Development*. Palgrave Macmillan. doi:10.1057/9780230236660_12

Burke, L. A., & Hutchins, H. M. (2007). Training Transfer: An Integrative Literature Review. *Human Resource Development Review*, *6*(3), 263–296. Advance online publication. doi:10.1177/1534484307303035

Burke-Smalley, L. A., & Mendenhall, M. E. (2020). Facilitating Transfer of Learning in Professional Development Programs: A Cognitive-Behavioral Tool. *Management Teaching Review*, *7*(2), 155–163. doi:10.1177/2379298120953532

Burke, W. W. (2002). *Organizational Change: Theory and Practice*. Sage.

Burke, W. W. (2017). *Organization Change: Theory and Practice* (5th ed.). SAGE Publications, Inc.

Burton, C. M., Mayhall, C., Cross, J., & Patterson, P. (2019). Critical elements for multigenerational teams: A systematic review. *Team Performance Management*, *25*(7/8), 369–401. doi:10.1108/TPM-12-2018-0075

By, R. T. (2005). Organisational change management: A critical review. *Journal of Change Management*, *5*(4), 369–380. doi:10.1080/14697010500359250

Cabral, A. M., & Marques, J. P. C. (2022). How innovation can influence customer satisfaction – A case study of the Saccharum Hotel in Madeira. *International Journal of Innovation Science*, *15*(1), 80–93. doi:10.1108/IJIS-03-2021-0061

Caffarella, R. S., & Daffron, S. (2013). *Planning programs for adult learners: A practical guide* (3rd ed.). Jossey-Bass.

Campbell, J. P., & Pritchard, R. D. (1976). Motivation theory in industrial and organizational psychology. In M. D. Dunnette & L. M. Hough (Eds.), *Handbook of Industrial and Organizational Psychology* (pp. 63–130). Wiley.

Carmeli, A., & Gittell, J. H. (2009). High-quality relationships, psychological safety, and learning from failures in work organizations. *Journal of Organizational Behavior*, *30*(6), 709–729. doi:10.1002/job.565

Carraher, R., Gibson, A., & Buckley, R. (2006). Compensation in the Baltic and the USA. *Baltic Journal of Management*, *1*(1), 7–23. doi:10.1108/17465260610640840

Carter, C. A. (2011, April 26). *The influence of business ownership and selected demographic characteristics on the perceived effectiveness of an entrepreneurship training program among female participants*. Louisiana State University and Agricultural and Mechanical College. Retrieved from http://etd.lsu.edu/docs/available/etd-04212011-091948/

Cattermole, G., Johnson, J., & Jackson, D. (2014). Employee engagement creates a brighter economic future at Jupiter Hotels. *Strategic HR Review*, *13*(2), 81–85. doi:10.1108/SHR-11-2013-0110

Cawsey, Deszca, & Ingols. (2012). *Organisational Change: An Action-Oriented Toolkit* (2nd ed.). Academic Press.

Cerasoli, C. P., Nicklin, J. M., & Ford, M. T. (2014). Intrinsic motivation and extrinsic incentives jointly predict performance: A 40-year meta-analysis. *Psychological Bulletin*, *140*(4), 980–1008. doi:10.1037/a0035661 PMID:24491020

Cervone, D. (2023). Theory and Application in Personality Science: The Case of Social-Cognitive Theory. *Psychology and Developing Societies*, *35*(2), 231–250. doi:10.1177/09713336231178366

Champine, R. B., Hoffman, E. E., Matlin, S. L., Strambler, M. J., & Tebes, J. K. (2022). What does it mean to be trauma-informed?": A mixed-methods study of a trauma-informed community initiative. *Journal of Child and Family Studies*, *31*(2), 459–472. doi:10.1007/s10826-021-02195-9 PMID:35018088

Chang, S., & Lee, M. (2007). A study on the relationship among leadership, organizational culture, the operation of learning organization and employees' job satisfaction. *The Learning Organization*, *14*(2), 155–185. doi:10.1108/09696470710727014

Chao, G. T. (2012). Organizational socialization: Background, basics, and a blueprint for adjustment at work. In Oxford University Press eBooks (pp. 579–614). doi:10.1093/oxfordhb/9780199928309.013.0018

Chatterjee, S., & Kar, A. K. (2020). Why do small and medium enterprises use social media marketing and what is the impact: Empirical insights from India. *International Journal of Information Management*, *53*, 102103. doi:10.1016/j.ijinfomgt.2020.102103

Chawla, N., Gabriel, A., Dahling, J., & Patel, K. (2016, July). Feedback dynamics are critical to improving performance management systems. *Industrial and Organizational Psychology: Perspectives on Science and Practice*, *9*(02), 260–266. doi:10.1017/iop.2016.8

Chawla, P. (2020). Impact of employer branding on employee engagement in business process outsourcing (BPO) sector in India: Mediating effect of person–organization fit. *Industrial and Commercial Training*, *52*(1), 35–34. doi:10.1108/ICT-06-2019-0063

Chawla, S., Sareen, P., & Gupta, S. (2022). Wellness programs an employee engagement technique pre and during pandemic: A systematic literature review. *ECS Transactions*, *107*(1), 3505–3521. doi:10.1149/10701.3505ecst

Checkland, P. (1999). Systems thinking. In W. Currie & B. Galliers (Eds.), *Rethinking Management Information Systems: An Interdisciplinary Perspective* (pp. 45–56). Oxford University Press. doi:10.1093/oso/9780198775331.003.0004

Chenglieh, P. (1985). In Search of the Chinese style of management. *Malaysian Management Review*, *20*(3).

Chen, L., Jiang, W.-J., & Zhao, R.-P. (2022). Application effect of Kolb's experiential learning theory in clinical nursing teaching of traditional Chinese medicine. *Digital Health*, *4*, 1–5. doi:10.1177/20552076221138313 PMID:36406155

Chen, T. Y., Chang, P. L., & Yen, C. W. (2004). A study of career needs, career development programs, job satisfaction and the turnover intensity of R & D personnel. *Career Development International*, *9*(4), 424–437. doi:10.1108/13620430410544364

Chen, Y., & Lou, H. (2002). Toward an understanding of the behavioral intention to use a groupware application. *Journal of Organizational and End User Computing*, *14*(4), 1–16. doi:10.4018/joeuc.2002100101

Chiaburu, D. S., & Tekleab, A. G. (2005). Individual and contextual influences on multiple dimensions of training effectiveness. *Journal of European Industrial Training*, *29*(8), 604–626. doi:10.1108/03090590510627085

Choitz, V., & Wagner, S. (2021). *A Trauma Informed approach to the workforce*. The National Fund for Workforce Solutions. https://nationalfund.org/wp-content/uploads/2021/04/A-Trauma-Informed-Approach-to-Workforce.pdf

Chowkase, A. A., Datar, K., Deshpande, A., Khasnis, S., Keskar, A., & Godbole, S. (2022). Online learning, classroom quality, and student motivation: Perspectives from students, teachers, parents, and program staff. *Gifted Education International*, *38*(1), 74–94. doi:10.1177/02614294211060401

Cho, Y. (2023). Special issue on qualitative methods for theory building in HRD: Why now? *Human Resource Development Review*, *22*(1), 3–6. doi:10.1177/15344843221146358

Chuang, S. (2021). The applications of constructivist learning theory and social learning theory on adult continuous development. *Performance Improvement*, *60*(3), 6–14. doi:10.1002/pfi.21963

Cilesiz, S. (2011). A phenomenological approach to experiences with technology: Current state, promise, and future directions for research. *Educational Technology Research and Development*, *59*(4), 487–510. doi:10.1007/s11423-010-9173-2

Clardy, A. (2018). 70-20-10 and the dominance of informal learning: A fact in search of evidence. *Human Resource Development Review*, *17*(2), 153–178. doi:10.1177/1534484318759399

Clark, C. S., Dobbins, G. H., & Ladd, R. T. (1993). Exploratory Field Study of Training Motivation. *Group & Organization Management*, *18*(3), 292–307. doi:10.1177/1059601193183003

Clark, T. R. (2020). *The 4 Stages of Psychological Safety: Defining the Path to Inclusion and Innovation*. Berrett-Koehler.

Colquitt, J., LePine, J., & Noe, R. (2000). Toward an Integrative Theory of Training Motivation: A Meta-Analytic Path Analysis of 20 Years of Research. *The Journal of Applied Psychology*, *85*(5), 678–707. doi:10.1037/0021-9010.85.5.678 PMID:11055143

Columbia Law School. (n.d.). https://www.law.columbia.edu/pt-br/news/2017/06/kimberle-crenshaw-intersectionality

Combe, M. (2014). *Change readiness: Focusing change management where it counts*. Project Management Institute.

Conmy, S. (n.d.). *What are the four types of corporate culture?* The Corporate Governance Institute. https://www.thecorporategovernanceinstitute.com/insights/lexicon/what-are-the-four-types-of-corporate-culture/

Connors, A. (2019). Adopt an inclusion mindset. *Talent Development*, *73*(12), 18–20.

Conte, J. M., & Landy, F. J. (2019). *Work in the 21st Century: An Introduction to Industrial and Organizational Psychology* (6th ed.). Wiley.

Cortellazzo, L., Bruni, E., & Zampieri, R. (2019). The role of leadership in a digitalized world: A review. *Frontiers in Psychology*, *10*, 1938. Advance online publication. doi:10.3389/fpsyg.2019.01938 PMID:31507494

Costa, P. T., & McCrae, R. R. (1999). A five-factor theory of personality. *The five-factor model of personality: Theoretical perspectives, 2,* 51-87.

Crenshaw, K. (2017*). Kimberlé Crenshaw on Intersectionality, More than Two Decades Later.* Academic Press.

Creswell, W. J. (2003). Research Design: Qualitative, Quantitative, and Mixed Methods Approaches. *Sage (Atlanta, Ga.).*

Cummings, T. G., & Worley, C. G. (2009). *Organization Development & Change* (9th ed.).

Da Silva, W. F. C., Da Consolação Paiva, W., & Da Silva, H. A. (2019). Correlations between trust and the organizational citizenship behaviors: Reflections and considerations for public managers from a municipality in Minas Gerais. *British Journal of Management*, *12*(2), 317–335. doi:10.5902/19834659

Dalain, A. F. (2023). Nurturing employee engagement at workplace and organizational innovation in time of crisis with moderating effect of servant leadership. *SAGE Open*, *13*(2). doi:10.1177/21582440231175150

Dalavai, E. V. (2020). Building a positive organizational culture through antiracism. *Talent Development*, *74*(12), 24–26.

Dang, A., Khanra, S., & Kagzi, M. (2022). Barriers towards the continued usage of massive open online courses: A case study in India. *International Journal of Management Education*, *20*(1), 100562. doi:10.1016/j.ijme.2021.100562

Dang, V. T., Nguyen, H. N., Hoang, T. H., Nguyen, T. H., Tran, V. T., Nguyen, Q. H., & Nguyen, N. (2022). Gyms' indoor environmental quality and customer emotion: The mediating roles of perceived service quality and perceived psychological safety. *Leisure Studies*, *41*(2), 263–280. doi:10.1080/02614367.2021.1975803

Day, D. V., Griffin, M., & Louw, K. R. (2014). The climate and culture of leadership in organizations. In Oxford University Press eBooks. doi:10.1093/oxfordhb/9780199860715.013.0006

Day, D. V., Bastardoz, N., Bisbey, T. M., Reyes, D. L., & Salas, E. (2021). Unlocking Human Potential through Leadership Training & Development Initiatives. *Behavioral Science & Policy*, *7*(1), 41–54. doi:10.1177/237946152100700105

DDI. (2023). *Global Leadership Forecast 2023*. https://media.ddiworld.com/research/glf2023.pdf

Debrah, Y. A., & Ofori, G. (2006). Human Resource Development of Professionals in an Emerging Economy: The Case of the Tanzanian Construction Industry. *International Journal of Human Resource Management*, *17*(3), 440–463. doi:10.1080/09585190500521425

Deci, E. L., & Ryan, R. M. (2000). The "what" and "why" of goal pursuits: Human needs and the self-determination of behavior. *Psychological Inquiry*, *11*(4), 227–268. doi:10.1207/S15327965PLI1104_01

Deeprose, D. (1994). *How to recognize and reward employees*. AMACOM.

Deng, H., Leung, K., Lam, C. K., & Huang, X. (2019). Slacking Off in Comfort: A dual-pathway model for psychological safety climate. *Journal of Management*, *45*(3), 1114–1144. doi:10.1177/0149206317693083

Dennen, V. P. (2005). From message posting to learning dialogues: Factors affecting learner participation in asynchronous discussion. *Distance Education*, *26*(1), 127–148. doi:10.1080/01587910500081376

Dewey, S., Codallos, K., Barry, R., Drenkhahn, K., Glover, M., Muthig, A., Roberts, S. L., & Abbott, B. (2020). Higher education in prison: A pilot study of approaches and modes of delivery in eight prison administrations. *Journal of Correctional Education*, *71*(1), 57–89.

Dodoo, J. E., & Al-Samarraie, H. (2021). A systematic review of factors leading to occupational injuries and fatalities. *Journal of Public Health (Berlin)*, *31*(1), 99–113. doi:10.1007/s10389-020-01427-4

Druckman, D., Singer, J. E., & Van Cott, H. (1997). *Enhancing Organizational Performance*. National Academy Press. doi:10.17226/5128

Dubey, P., Pathak, A. K., & Sahu, K. K. (2023). Assessing the influence of effective leadership on job satisfaction and organisational citizenship behaviour. *Rajagiri Management Journal*, *17*(3), 221–237. doi:10.1108/RAMJ-07-2022-0108

Dweck, C. (2007). *Mindset: The new psychology of success*. Ballantine Books.

Dwyer, R. J. (2004). Employee development using adult education principles. *Industrial and Commercial Training*, *36*(2), 79–85. doi:10.1108/00197850410524851

Eby, L. T., Freeman, D. M., Rush, M. C., & Lance, C. E. (1999). Motivational bases of affective organizational commitment: A partial test of an integrative theoretical model. *Journal of Occupational and Organizational Psychology*, *72*(4), 463–483. doi:10.1348/096317999166798

Edmond, H., & Noon, M. (2001). *A dictionary of human resource management*. Oxford University Press.

Edmondson, A. (1999). Psychological safety and learning behavior in work teams. *Administrative Science Quarterly, 44*(2), 350–383. doi:10.2307/2666999

Edmondson, A. C. (2018). *The fearless organization*. John Wiley & Sons.

Edmondson, A. C., & Lei, Z. (2014). Psychological safety: The history, renaissance, and future of an interpersonal construct. *Annual Review of Organizational Psychology and Organizational Behavior, 1*(1), 23–43. doi:10.1146/annurev-orgpsych-031413-091305

Effectiveness of Training in Organizations. A Meta-Analysis of Design and Evaluation Features. (2003). http://www.ispi.org/archives/resources/EffectivenessofTrainingArthur_etal.pdf

Eisenbeiss, S. A. (2012). Re-thinking ethical leadership: An interdisciplinary integrative approach. *The Leadership Quarterly, 23*(5), 791–808. doi:10.1016/j.leaqua.2012.03.001

Eldor, L., Hodor, M., & Cappelli, P. (2023). The limits of psychological safety: Nonlinear relationships with performance. *Organizational Behavior and Human Decision Processes, 177*, 104255. doi:10.1016/j.obhdp.2023.104255

Errida, A., & Lotfi, B. (2020). Measuring change readiness for implementing a project management methodology: An action research study. *Academy of Strategic Management Journal, 19*(1), 1–17.

Errida, A., & Lotfi, B. (2021). The determinants of organizational change management success: Literature review and case study. *International Journal of Engineering Business Management, 13*. Advance online publication. doi:10.1177/18479790211016273

Evangelist-Roach, M. (2020). *Workforce Agility Strategies for Improving the Success Rate of Change Initiatives* (Doctoral dissertation, Walden University).

Evans, P., Pucik, V., & Barsoux, J.-L. (2002). *The Global Challenge: Framework for International Human Resource Management*. McGraw-Hill.

Farooq, M., & Khan, M. A. (2011). Impact of training and feedback on employee performance. *Far East Journal of Psychology & Business, 5*(1), 23–33. Retrieved from http://www.fareastjournals.com/

Feinberg, R., Bock, B., Bolton, R., Chambers, K. S., Claus, P. J., Deva, I., Gray, J. P., Güvenç, B., Hudson, C., Keesing, R. M., Lingenfelter, S., Mark, A. K., Montague, S. P., Ravenhill, P. L., Sewell, D., & Watson-Gegeo, K. A. (1979). Schneider's symbolic culture theory: An Appraisal [and Comments and Reply]. *Current Anthropology, 20*(3), 541–560. https://www.jstor.org/stable/2742111. doi:10.1086/202324

Ferreira, M. F., & Nascimento, E. D. (2016). Relationship between personality traits and counterproductive work behaviors. *Psico-USF, 21*(3), 677–685. doi:10.1590/1413-82712016210319

Field, M. (2019, June 10). *Work evolved: Building a successful multigenerational workforce.* Forbes Magazine. https://www.forbes.com/sites/forbestechcouncil/2019/06/10/work-evolved-building-a-successful-multigenerational-workforce/?sh=1581a96878cb

Fischer-Lescano, A. (2011). Critical Systems Theory: A Challenge for Law and Society. *Philosophy and Social Criticism, 38*(1), 3–23. doi:10.1177/0191453711421600

Ford, T. G., Lavigne, A. L., Fiegener, A. M., & Si, S. (2020). Understanding district support for leader development and success in the accountability era: A review of the literature using social-cognitive theories of motivation. *Review of Educational Research, 90*(2), 264–307. doi:10.3102/0034654319899723

Forsyth, D. R. (2015). *The Psychology of Groups.* Noba. https://nobaproject.com/modules/the-psychology-of-groups

Francis, A. (n.d.). *Charles Handy's Model of organizational culture.* MBA Knowledge Base. https://www.mbaknol.com/management-principles/charles-handys-model-of-organizational-culture/

Fraraccio, M. (2023, September 21). *Management theory of Charles Handy.* Business. https://www.business.com/articles/management-theory-of-charles-handy/

Frazier, M. L., & Tupper, C. (2018). Supervisor prosocial motivation, employee thriving, and helping behavior: A trickle-down model of psychological safety. *Group & Organization Management, 43*(4), 561–593. doi:10.1177/1059601116653911

Freeman, E. W. (2009). *Training effectiveness: The influence of personal achievement goals on posttraining self-efficacy* (Doctoral dissertation). Available from ProQuest Dissertations and ThesesDatabase. (UMI No. 3395162)

Freifeld, L. (2023, November 15). *2023 Training Industry Report.* Training. https://trainingmag.com/2023-training-industry-report/#:~:text=final%20purchase%20decision-TRAINING%20EXPENDITURES,the%20payroll%20of%20small%20companies

Frey, B. (1997). On the Relationship between Intrinsic and Extrinsic Work Motivation. *International Journal of Industrial Organization, 15*(4), 427–439. doi:10.1016/S0167-7187(96)01028-4

Gaither, K. A. (2009). *Comparing perceived effectiveness of e-learning and traditional training in the business environment* (Doctoral dissertation). Available from ProQuest Dissertations and Theses Database. (UMI No. 3362657)

Gallemard, J. (2023, August 25). Implicit Knowledge - What is It & How to Transfer in The Workplace. *Smart Tribune.* https://blog.smart-tribune.com/en/implicit-knowledge

Gallup. (2023). *State of the global workforce: 2023 report.* Gallup. https://www.gallup.com/workplace/349484/state-of-the-global-workplace.aspx

Garavan, T. N., O'Brien, F., Duggan, J., Gubbins, C., Lai, Y., Carbery, R., Heneghan, S., Lannon, R., Sheehan, M., & Grant, K. (2020). The current state of research on training effectiveness. In Springer eBooks (pp. 99–152). doi:10.1007/978-3-030-48900-7_5

Compilation of References

Garavan, T. N., O'Donnell, D., McGuire, D., & Watson, S. (2007). Exploring Perspectives on Human Resource Development: An Introduction. *Advances in Developing Human Resources*, *9*(1), 3–10. doi:10.1177/1523422306294342

Garner, J. K., & Shank, M. D. (2023). Using adult learning theory to explore student perceptions of the flipped class method. *Journal of Marketing Education*, 1–16. doi:10.1177/02734753231196501

Garrow, V. (2009). *OD: past, present and future*. Institute for Employment Studies.

Gartner, K. N., & Nollen, S. D. (1989). Career experiences, perceptions of employment practices and psychological commitment to the organization. *Human Relations*, *42*(11), 975–991. doi:10.1177/001872678904201102

Garvin, D. A., Edmondson, A., & Gino, F. (2008, March). *Is yours a learning organization?* Academic Press.

Gavin, J., & McBrearty, M. (2019). *Lifestyle wellness coaching* (3rd ed.). Human Kinetics. doi:10.5040/9781492595595

Gegenfurtner, A., Ebner, M., & Harper, B. (2017). Taking a closer look at motivational aspects of gamified online courses: A case study. *Interactive Learning Environments*, *25*(4), 479–491.

George, J. M., & Brief, A. P. (1992). Feeling good-doing good: A conceptual analysis of the mood at work-organizational spontaneity relationship. *Psychological Bulletin*, *112*(2), 310–322. doi:10.1037/0033-2909.112.2.310 PMID:1454897

George, J. M., & Jones, G. R. (1997). Organizational spontaneity in context. *Human Performance*, *10*(2), 153–170. doi:10.1207/s15327043hup1002_6

Gerbrandt, N., Grieser, R., & Enns, V. (2021). *A little book about trauma-informed workplaces*. Crisis & Trauma Resource Institute. ACHIEVE Publishing.

Gerpott, F. H., Lehmann-Willenbrock, N., Wenzel, R., & Voelpel, S. C. (2021). Age diversity and learning outcomes in organizational training groups: The role of knowledge sharing and psychological safety. *International Journal of Human Resource Management*, *32*(18), 3777–3804. doi:10.1080/09585192.2019.1640763

Gittner, A. B., Dennis, S. A., & Forbis, J. S. Jr. (2023). Diversion: A systems theory perspective. *Journal of Contemporary Criminal Justice*, *39*(4), 485–489. doi:10.1177/10439862231189415

Glaveski, S. (2021, January 20). *Where Companies Go Wrong with Learning and Development*. Harvard Business Review. https://hbr.org/2019/10/where-companies-go-wrong-with-learning-and-development

Gokak, A. J. H., Mehendale, S., & Bhāle, S. M. (2022). Modelling and analysis for higher education shadow institutions in Indian context: An ISM approach. *Quality & Quantity*, *57*(4), 3425–3451. doi:10.1007/s11135-022-01514-6 PMID:36091487

GouvenelleC.FloraM.FlorenceT. (2023). Digital tools in occupational health, brakes or levers for building multidisciplinary dynamics, https://arxiv.org/abs/2307.05998

Graham, J. (2005). Organizational change management and projects. Paper presented at PMI® Global Congress 2005—North America, Toronto, Ontario, Canada. Newtown Square, PA: Project Management Institute.

Gratton, L., & Erickson, T. J. (2013). Eight ways to build collaborative teams. Academic Press.

Grbich, C. (2012). Qualitative Data Analysis: An Introduction. *Sage (Atlanta, Ga.)*.

Grossman, R., & Salas, E. (2011). The transfer of training: What really matters. *International Journal of Training and Development*, *15*(2), 103–120. doi:10.1111/j.1468-2419.2011.00373.x

Grote, G., & Metzgar, C. (2016). Promoting Safety by Increasing Uncertainty. *Professional Safety*, *61*(1), 22–23.

Guo, Z., Xie, B., Chen, J., & Wang, F. (2019). The relationship between opportunities for professional development and counterproductive work behaviors: The mediating role of affective well-being and moderating role of task-contingent conscientiousness. *International Journal of Mental Health Promotion*, *21*(3), 111–122. doi:10.32604/IJMHP.2019.011040

Guzowski, L. (2022, February 2). *Effective conflict resolution in the workplace with Thomas Kilmann model*. Human. https://www.human.pm/post/thomas-kilmann-model-conflict-resolution-workplace

Hajjar, E. L. (2018). Exploring the Factors That Affect Employee Training Effectiveness: A Case Study in Bahrain. *SAGE Open*, *8*(2). doi:10.1177/2158244018783033

Halvorson, H. G., & Higgins, E. T. (2013). Know what really motivates you. *Harvard Business Review*, *91*(3), 117–120. https://hbr.org/magazine PMID:23451530

Hammer, E. (2021). HRD interventions that offer a solution to work-life conflict. *Advances in Developing Human Resources*, *23*(2), 142–152. doi:10.1177/1523422321991192

Harari, M. B., Thompson, A. H., & Viswesvaran, C. (2018). Extraversion and job satisfaction: The role of trait bandwidth and the moderating effect of status goal attainment. *Personality and Individual Differences*, *123*, 14–16. doi:10.1016/j.paid.2017.10.041

Hardman, W., & Robertson, L. (2012). What motivates employees to persist with online training? One Canadian workplace study. *International Journal of Business, Humanities & Technology*, *2*(5), 66–78. Retrieved from http://www.ijbhtnet.com/

Harrison, R. (2000). Employee Development. Beekman Publishing.

Hart, T. A., Gilstrap, J. B., & Bolino, M. C. (2016). Organizational citizenship behavior and the enhancement of absorptive capacity. *Journal of Business Research*, *69*(10), 3981–3988. doi:10.1016/j.jbusres.2016.06.001

Hassi, A. (2012). Islamic perspectives on training and professional development. *Journal of Management Development*, *31*(10), 1035–1045. doi:10.1108/02621711211281816

Haun, C. N. (2022). Diversity management and cultural competence in the healthcare field. In Springer eBooks (pp. 3378–3381). doi:10.1007/978-3-030-66252-3_3472

Hayes, J. (2018). *The theory and practise of change management*. Red Globe Press.

Hebets, E. A. (2018). A Scientist's Guide to Impactful Science Communication: A Priori Goals, Collaborative Assessment, and Engagement with Youth. *BioEssays*, *40*(8), 1800084. Advance online publication. doi:10.1002/bies.201800084 PMID:29882972

Hedin, N. S. (2010). Experiential Learning: Theory and Challenges. *Christian Education Journal*, *7*(1), 109–117. doi:10.1177/073989131000700108

Heinz, K. (2023, October 20). *The 4 types of organizational culture and their benefits*. Built In. https://builtin.com/company-culture/types-of-organizational-culture

Herzberg, F. (2003). *One more time: how do you motivate employees? Harvard Business Review on Motivating People*. Harvard Business School Press.

Hetler, A. (2023, September 13). *11 signs of toxic workplace culture*. WhatIs. https://www.techtarget.com/whatis/feature/Signs-of-toxic-workplace-culture

Heydari, M. R., Taghva, F., Amini, M., & Delavari, S. (2019). Using Kirkpatrick's model to measure the effect of a new teaching and learning methods workshop for health care staff. *BMC Research Notes*, *12*(1), 388. Advance online publication. doi:10.1186/s13104-019-4421-y PMID:31292006

Hicks, W. D., & Klimoski, R. J. (1987). Entry into Training Programs and Its Effects on Training Outcomes: A Field Experiment. *Academy of Management Journal*, *30*(3), 542–552. doi:10.2307/256013

Higgins, E. (2005). Value from regulatory fit. *Current Directions in Psychological Science*, *14*(4), 209–213. doi:10.1111/j.0963-7214.2005.00366.x

Higgins, E. T., Cesario, J., Hagiwara, N., Spiegel, S., & Pittman, T. (2010). Increasing or decreasing interest in activities: The role of regulatory fit. *Journal of Personality and Social Psychology*, *98*(4), 559–572. doi:10.1037/a0018833 PMID:20307129

Holmes, M. R. (1980). Interpersonal behaviors and their relationship to the andragogical and pedagogical orientations of adult educators. *Adult Education*, *31*(1), 18–29. doi:10.1177/074171368003100102

Holst, J. D., & Kuk, L. (2018). A dissection of experiential learning theory: Alternative approaches to reflection. *Adult Learning*, *29*(4), 151–157.

Huemann, M., Keegan, A., & Turner, R. J. (2007). Human resource management in the project-oriented company: A review. *International Journal of Project Management*, *25*(3), 315–323. doi:10.1016/j.ijproman.2006.10.001

Humeera, N., & Mufeed, S. A. (2023). Role of HRM practices in enhancing employee engagement: A literature review. *IUP Journal of Management Research, 22*(3), 40–64.

Hutchins, H. M., Burke, L. A., & Berthelsen, A. M. (2010). A missing link in the transfer problem? Examining how trainers learn about training transfer. *Human Resource Management, 49*(4), 599–618. doi:10.1002/hrm.20371

Huysman, M., & de Wit, D. (2004). Practices of managing knowledge sharing: Towards a second wave of knowledge management. *Knowledge and Process Management, 2*(1), 81–92. doi:10.1002/kpm.192

Islam, T., Anwar, F., Khan, S. U. R., Rasli, A., Ahmad, U. N. B. U., & Ahmed, I. (2012). Investigating the mediating role of organizational citizenship behavior between organizational learning culture and knowledge sharing. *World Applied Sciences Journal, 19*(6), 795–799.

Ismail, A., & Abd Razak, M. R. (2016). A study on job satisfaction as a determinant of job motivation. *Acta Universitatis Danubius, 12*(3), 30–44.

Israilidis, J., Siachou, E., & Kelly, S. (2021) Why organizations fail to share knowledge: an empirical investigation and opportunities for improvement. *Information Technology & People, 34*(5), 1513-1539.

Jackson, L. D. (2009). *Revisiting Adult Learning Theory through the Lens of an Adult Learner. Journal Name, Volume(Issue)*. Page Range.

Jackson, M. K. (2022). Working remotely: How organizational leaders and HRD practitioners used the experiential learning theory. *New Horizons in Adult Education and Human Resource Development, 46*, 1–5.

Jackson, S. (2010). *Research Methods: A Modular Approach*. Cengage Learning.

Jaiswal, A., & Arun, C. J. (2022). Working from home during COVID-19 and its impact on Indian employees' stress and creativity. *Asian Business & Management*, 1–25. doi:10.1057/s41291-022-00202-5

Jick, T. D. (1990). Note: the recipients of change. In *Harvard Business School 9-491-039*. Harvard Business School Press.

Joy, S., & Kolb, D. A. (2009). Are there cultural differences in learning styles? *International Journal of Intercultural Relations, 33*(1), 69–85. doi:10.1016/j.ijintrel.2008.11.002

Judge, T. A., Heller, D., & Mount, M. K. (2002). Five-factor model of personality and job satisfaction: A meta-analysis. *The Journal of Applied Psychology, 87*(3), 530–541. doi:10.1037/0021-9010.87.3.530 PMID:12090610

Juneja, P. (n.d.). *Edgar Schein's model of organization culture*. Management Study Guide. https://www.managementstudyguide.com/edgar-schein-model.htm

Jungert, T., Gradito Dubord, M. A., Högberg, M., & Forest, J. (2022). Can managers be trained to further support their employees' basic needs and work engagement: A manager training program study. *International Journal of Training and Development*, *26*(3), 472–494. doi:10.1111/ijtd.12267

Kabiri, S., Akbari, H., & Hosseini, S. A. (2020). Performance-enhancing drug use among professional athletes: A longitudinal test of social learning. *Crime and Delinquency*, *68*(5), 869–893.

Kabiri, S., Smith, H., & Akers, R. L. (2020). A Social Learning Model of Antisocial Coaching Behavior. *International Journal of Offender Therapy and Comparative Criminology*, *64*(8), 874–889. doi:10.1177/0306624X19899608 PMID:31928277

Kahn, W. A. (1990). Psychological conditions of personal engagement and disengagement at work. *Academy of Management Journal*, *33*(4), 692–724. doi:10.2307/256287

Karatepe, O. M. (2013). High-performance work practices and hotel employee performance: The mediation of work engagement. *International Journal of Hospitality Management*, *32*, 132–140. doi:10.1016/j.ijhm.2012.05.003

Kark, R., & Carmeli, A. (2009). Alive and creating: The mediating role of vitality and aliveness in the relationship between psychological safety and creative work involvement. *Journal of Organizational Behavior*, *30*(6), 785–804. doi:10.1002/job.571

Katzenbach, K. M. E., & Gratton, L. (Eds.), *HBR's 10 must reads on teams*. Harvard Business Review Press.

Katz, R., & Van Maanan, J. (1977). The loci of work satisfaction: Job interaction and policy. *Human Relations*, *30*(5), 469–486. doi:10.1177/001872677703000505

Kaur, G. (2022, February 9). *What is knowledge management? definition, process, examples, strategy, best practices, and Trends*. Spiceworks. https://www.spiceworks.com/collaboration/content-collaboration/articles/what-is-knowledge-management/

Kenney, J., & Reid, M. (2006). *Training Interventions*. Institute of Personnel Management.

Kern, M., & Zapf, D. (2021). Ready for change? A longitudinal examination of challenge stressors in the context of organizational change. *Journal of Occupational Health Psychology*, *26*(3), 204–223. doi:10.1037/ocp0000214 PMID:33705194

Kessels, J. W., & Poell, R. F. (2004). Andragogy and social capital theory: The implications for human resource development. *Advances in Developing Human Resources*, *6*(2), 146–157. doi:10.1177/1523422304263326

Keswani, D. (2020, April 27). *Understanding organizational subcultures and countercultures*. Amity. https://www.ekoapp.com/blog/understanding-organizational-subcultures-and-countercultures

Khalid, M. S., Zhan-Yong, Q., & Bibi, J. (2021). The impact of learning in a diversified environment: Social and cognitive development of international students for global mindset. *European Journal of Training and Development*, *46*(5/6), 373–389. doi:10.1108/EJTD-12-2020-0175

Khan, A. N., & Khan, N. A. (2022). The nexuses between transformational leadership and employee green organisational citizenship behaviour: Role of environmental attitude and green dedication. *Business Strategy and the Environment, 31*(3), 921–933. doi:10.1002/bse.2926

KhankhojeM. (2016). Change management in healthcare organizations. *Social Science Research Network*. doi:10.2139/ssrn.3232774

Kian, T. S., Yusoff, W. F. W., & Rajah, S. (2014). Job satisfaction and motivation: What are the difference among these two. *European Journal of Business and Social Sciences, 3*(2), 94–102.

Kim, C., & Keller, J. M. (2010). Motivation, volition and belief change strategies to improve mathematics learning. *Journal of Computer Assisted Learning, 26*(5), 407–420. doi:10.1111/j.1365-2729.2010.00356.x

Kimmel, A. J. (2009). *Ethical Issues in Behavioral Research: Basic and Applied Perspectives* (2nd ed.). John Wiley & Sons.

Kim, S. H., Childs, M., & Williams, J. (2019). The effects of outdoor experiential training on part-time student employees' organizational citizenship behavior. *Journal of Hospitality and Tourism Management, 41*, 90–100. doi:10.1016/j.jhtm.2019.10.009

Klein, N. (2016). Prosocial behavior increases perceptions of meaning in life. *The Journal of Positive Psychology, 12*(4), 354–361. doi:10.1080/17439760.2016.1209541

Klier, J. D., Bamberger, M., & Raimondo, E. (2022). Grounding Evaluation Capacity Development in Systems Theory. *Evaluation, 28*(2), 231–250. doi:10.1177/13563890221088871

Klonoff, D. C. (2019). Behavioral Theory: The Missing Ingredient for Digital Health Tools to Change Behavior and Increase Adherence. *Journal of Diabetes Science and Technology, 13*(2), 276–281. doi:10.1177/1932296818820303 PMID:30678472

Kluger, A. N., & DeNisi, A. (1996). The effects of feedback interventions on performance: A historical review, a meta-analysis, and a preliminary feedback intervention theory. *Psychological Bulletin, 119*(2), 254–284. doi:10.1037/0033-2909.119.2.254

Knowles, M. S. (1980). The modern practice of adult education: From pedagogy to andragogy: Revised and Updates. New York, NY: Association Press.

Knowles, M. S., Holton, E. F., III, & Swanson, R. A. (2020). The Adult Learner. Taylor and Francis.

Knowles, M. S. (1950). *Informal Adult Education*. Association Press.

Knowles, M. S. (2003). Androgogy – Not pedagogy. In P. Jarvis & C. Griffin (Eds.), *Adult and Continuing Education – Major Themes in Education* (pp. 226–233). Routledge Taylor & Francis Group. (Original work published 1968)

Knowles, M. S. (2003). Excerpt from 'How my ideas evolved and changed. In P. Jarvis & C. Griffin (Eds.), *Adult and Continuing Education – Major Themes in Education* (pp. 234–239). Routledge Taylor & Francis Group. (Original work published 1989)

Compilation of References

Knowles, S. (2021). Coaching for transformational, cultural change. In *Positive Psychology Coaching*. Springer. doi:10.1007/978-3-030-88995-1_20

Kobiruzzaman, M. M. (2022). Netflix Organizational Change & Structure Case Study 2022. Newsmoor- Best Online Learning Platform. https://newsmoor.com/netflixorganizational-change-organizational-managementchange-examples

Kohn, S. L. (2009). *The effects of choice and training reputation on training effectiveness* (Doctoral dissertation). Available from ProQuest Dissertations and Theses Database. (UMI No. 3367278)

Kolb, A., & Kolb, D. (2005). Learning styles and learning spaces: Enhancing experiential learning in higher education. *Academy of Management Journal*, *4*(2), 193–212.

Kolb, D. (1984). *Experiential learning: Experience as the source of learning and development*. Prentice Hall.

Kolb, D. A. (1984). *Experiential Learning: Experience as the Source of Learning and Development*. Prentice Hall.

Kolb, D. A. (2015). *Experiential learning: experience as the source of learning and development* (2nd ed.). Pearson Education.

Konovsky, M. A., & Pugh, S. D. (1994). Citizenship behavior and social exchange. *Academy of Management Journal*, *37*(3), 656–669. doi:10.2307/256704 PMID:10134637

Korte, R. (2007). A review of social identity theory with implications for training and development. *Journal of European Industrial Training*, *31*(3), 166–180. doi:10.1108/03090590710739250

Kougias, I., Seremeti, L., & Kalogeras, D. (2013). Mobility of Eastern European citizens: Training and development. *European Journal of Training and Development*, *37*(8), 766–778. doi:10.1108/EJTD-03-2013-0033

Kraiger, K., Fisher, S., Grossman, R., Mills, M. J., & Sitzmann, T. (2022). Online IO graduate education: Where are we and where should we go? *Industrial and Organizational Psychology: Perspectives on Science and Practice*, *15*(2), 151–171. doi:10.1017/iop.2021.144

Kreutzer, R. T., & Land, K. (2014). The Necessity of Change Management: Why our traditional communication and organizational structures are becoming obsolete. In Springer eBooks (pp. 209–248). doi:10.1007/978-3-642-54401-9_9

Kuada, J. (2012). *Research Methodology: A Project Guide for University Students*. Samfundslitteratur.

Kumar, P. (2023, October 26). *The importance of aligning the company culture with employee training*. eLearning Industry. https://elearningindustry.com/importance-of-aligning-company-culture-with-employeetraining#:~:text=It%20fosters%20a%20sense%20of, into%20their%20roles%20and%20responsibilities.&text=When%20employees%20feel%20that%20the,out%20of%20their%20comfort%20zones.

Kwon, H. R., & Silva, E. A. (2019). Mapping the landscape of behavioral theories: Systematic literature review. *Journal of Planning Literature*, *35*(2), 161–179. doi:10.1177/0885412219881135

Kwon, H. R., & Silva, E. A. (2023). Matching Behavioral Theories and Rules with Research Methods in Spatial Planning-Related Fields. *Journal of Planning Literature*, *38*(2), 245–259. doi:10.1177/08854122231157708

Landy, F. J., & Becker, W. S. (1990). Motivation theory reconsidered. In B. M. Staw & L. L. Cummings (Eds.), *Work in Organizations* (pp. 1–38). Jai Press.

Lang, D. L. (1992). Organizational culture and commitment. *Human Resource Development Quarterly*, *2*(3), 191–196. doi:10.1002/hrdq.3920030211

Lapitan, L. D. Jr, Tiangco, C. E., Sumalinog, D. A. G., Sabarillo, N. S., & Diaz, J. M. (2021). An effective blended online teaching and learning strategy during the COVID-19 pandemic. *Education for Chemical Engineers*, *35*, 116–131. doi:10.1016/j.ece.2021.01.012

Larentis, F., Antonello, C. S., & Slongo, L. A. (2018). Development of inter-organizational culture: the elements. In Springer eBooks (pp. 27–46). doi:10.1007/978-3-030-00392-0_3

Lawler, E. E. (2003). *Treat people right*. Jossey-Bass Inc. McGraw-Hill Irwin.

Lazar, L., & Eisenberger, N. I. (2022). The benefits of giving: Effects of prosocial behavior on recovery from stress. *Psychophysiology*, *59*(2), 1–16. doi:10.1111/psyp.13954 PMID:34676898

Lazazzara, A., & Bombelli, C. M. (2011). HRM practices for an ageing Italian workforce: The role of training. *Journal of European Industrial Training*, *35*(8), 808–825. doi:10.1108/03090591111168339

LeaderFactor. (2023). *The 4 stages*. LeaderFactor. https://www.leaderfactor.com

Leonard, H. S., & Lang, F. (2010). Leadership development via action learning. *Advances in Developing Human Resources*, *12*(2), 225–240. doi:10.1177/1523422310367800

Leslie, B., Anderson, C., Bickham, C., Horman, J., Overly, A., Gentry, C., Callahan, C., & King, J. (2021). Generation Z perceptions of a positive workplace environment. *Employee Responsibilities and Rights Journal*, *33*(3), 171–187. doi:10.1007/s10672-021-09366-2

Leslie, H. J. (2021). Facilitation fundamentals: Redesigning an online course using adult learning principles and trifecta of student engagement framework. *Journal of Research in Innovative Teaching & Learning*, *14*(2), 271–287. doi:10.1108/JRIT-09-2019-0068

Lester, J. N. (2022). Introduction to special issue: Qualitative research methodologies and methods for theory building in human resource development. *Human Resource Development Review*, *22*(1), 1–8.

Lewin, K. (1951). *Field Theory in Social Science*. Harper.

Liang, J., Farh, C. I. C., & Farh, J.-L. (2012). Psychological antecedents of promotive and prohibitive voice: A two-wave examination. *Academy of Management Journal*, *55*(1), 71–92. doi:10.5465/amj.2010.0176

Li, B. (2023). Thinking diffractively with data in human resource development. *Human Resource Development Review*, *22*(1), 15–35. doi:10.1177/15344843221135670

Li, C. K. W. (2022). The applicability of social structure and social learning theory to explain intimate partner violence. *Journal of Interpersonal Violence*, *37*(23-24), 1–26. doi:10.1177/08862605211072166 PMID:35200042

Lim, D. H. (2000). Training design factors influencing transfer of training to the workplace within an international context. *Journal of Vocational Education and Training*, *52*(2), 243–258. doi:10.1080/13636820000200118

Lindeman, E. C. (1926a). Andragogik: The Method of Teaching Adults. *Worker Education*, *4*, 38.

Lindeman, E. C. (1926b). *The Meaning of Adult Education*. New Republic.

Lindgreen, A., Di Benedetto, C. A., Brodie, R. J., & Zenker, S. (2022). Teaching: How to ensure quality teaching, and how to recognize teaching qualifications. *Industrial Marketing Management*, *100*, A1–A5. doi:10.1016/j.indmarman.2021.11.008

Liu, Y., & Keller, R. T. (2021). How psychological safety impacts R&D project teams' performance. *Research Technology Management*, *64*(2), 39–45. doi:10.1080/08956308.2021.1863111

Locke, E. A. (1976). The nature and causes of job satisfaction. In M. D. Dunnette (Ed.), *Handbook of industrial and organizational psychology* (pp. 1297–1349). Rand McNally.

Lopez-Garrido, G. (2023, July 10). *Self-Determination Theory: How it explains motivation*. Simply Psychology. https://www.simplypsychology.org/self-determination-theory.html

Low, C. H., Bordia, P., & Bordia, S. (2016). What do employees want and why? An exploration of employees' preferred psychological contract elements across career stages. *Human Relations*, *69*(7), 1457–1481. doi:10.1177/0018726715616468

Lub, X. D., Bal, P. M., Blomme, R. J., & Schalk, R. (2016). One job, one deal…or not: Do generations respond differently to psychological contract fulfillment? *International Journal of Human Resource Management*, *27*(6), 653–680. doi:10.1080/09585192.2015.1035304

Lucas, L. M., & Ogilvie, D. (2006). Things are not always what they seem. How reputations, culture and incentives influence knowledge transfer. *The Learning Organization*, *13*(1), 7–24. doi:10.1108/09696470610639103

Lumen Learning. (n.d.). *Key dimensions of organizational culture*. Principles of Management. https://courses.lumenlearning.com/wm-principlesofmanagement/chapter/reading-key-dimensions-of-organizational-culture/

Lut, D. M. (2012). Connection between job motivation, job satisfaction and work performance in Romanian trade enterprises. *Economics and Applied Informatics*, *18*(3), 45–50.

Luthans, F. (1998). Organizational Behavior. Boston: Irwin McGraw-Hill. Luthans, Fred, Harriette S. McCaul, Nancy G. Dodd (1985). Organizational Commitment: A Comparison of American, Japanese, and Korean Employees. *Academy of Management Journal*, *28*(1), 213–219. doi:10.2307/256069

Luthans, F. (2011). *Organizational Behavior: An Evidence-Based Approach* (12th ed.). The McGraw-Hill Companies, Inc.

Luthans, F., & Peterson, S. J. (2002). Employee engagement and manager self-efficacy: Implications for managerial effectiveness and development. *Journal of Management Development*, *21*(5), 376–387. doi:10.1108/02621710210426864

Lynn, B., & Sarro, E. (2022, Oct. 20). *5 things you may not know about psychological safety*. Neuroleadership Institute. https://neuroleadership.com/your-brain-at-work/5-things-psych-safety

MacIntosh, E., & Doherty, A. (2010). The influence of organizational culture on job satisfaction and intention to leave. *Sport Management Review*, *13*(2), 106–117. doi:10.1016/j.smr.2009.04.006

MacLane, C. N., & Walmsley, P. T. (2010). Reducing counterproductive work behavior through employee selection. *Human Resource Management Review*, *20*(1), 62–72. doi:10.1016/j.hrmr.2009.05.001

Maddox, W. T., & Markman, A. B. (2012). The motivation-cognition interface in learning and decision making. *Current Directions in Psychological Science*, *19*(2), 106–110. doi:10.1177/0963721410364008 PMID:20556228

Mahajan, R. (2017). Impact of big five personality traits on OCB and satisfaction. *International Journal of Business Insights & Transformation*, *11*(1), 46–51.

Major, D. A., Turner, J. E., & Fletcher, T. D. (2006). Linking proactive personality and the Big Five to motivation to learn and development activity. *The Journal of Applied Psychology*, *91*(4), 927–935. https://psycnet.apa.org/doi/10.1037/0021-9010.91.4.927. doi:10.1037/0021-9010.91.4.927 PMID:16834515

Malik, A., Budhwar, P., Mohan, H., & Srikanth, N. R. (2023). Employee experience—the missing link for engaging employees: Insights from an MNE's AI-based HR ecosystem. *Human Resource Management*, *62*(1), 97–115. doi:10.1002/hrm.22133

Malik, M. I., & Ahsan, R. (2019). Towards innovation, co-creation and customers' satisfaction: A banking sector perspective. *Asia Pacific Journal of Innovation and Entrepreneurship*, *13*(3), 311–325. doi:10.1108/APJIE-01-2019-0001

Mambo, S., & Smuts, H. (2022). The impact of organisational culture on knowledge management: The case of an international multilateral organisation. *EPiC Series in Computing*, 184–171. doi:10.29007/bkxv

Mandi, J., Kotary, J., Berden, S., Mulamba, M., Bucarey, V., Guns, T., & Fioretto, F. (2023). *Decision-Focused Learning: Foundations, State of the Art, Benchmark and Future Opportunities.* Working Paper Series, Cornell University; doi:10.48550/arXiv.2307.13565

Manning, K. (2022, March 31). *We need trauma-informed workplaces.* Harvard Business Review. https://hbr.org/2022/03/we-need-trauma-informed-workplaces

Manyika, J., Lund, S., Chui, M., Bughin, J., Woetzel, J., Batra, P., Ko, R., & Sanghvi, S. (2017). *Jobs lost, jobs gained: Workforce transitions in a time of automation.* McKinsey Global Institute. Retrieved May 22, 2023, from https://www.mckinsey.com/global-themes/future-of-organizations-and-work/what-the-future-of-work-willmean-for-jobs-skills-and-wages

Marchington, M., & Wilkinson, A. (2008). *Human Resource Management at Work.* CIPD.

Mariati, & Mauludin, H. (2018). The influence of organizational culture and work motivation on employee performance, job satisfaction as intervening variable (Study on Secretariat Staff of Pasuruan Regency). *IOSR Journal of Business and Management (IOSR-JBM), 20*(8). Available at SSRN: https://ssrn.com/abstract=3228300

Martinelli, M., Silverman, J., & Helou, J. E. (2023, September 1). *Design tactics for training transfer.* ATD. https://www.td.org/magazines/td-magazine/design-tactics-for-training-transfer

Martinko, M. J., Gundlach, M. J., & Douglas, S. C. (2002). Toward an integrative theory of counterproductive workplace behavior: A causal reasoning perspective. *International Journal of Selection and Assessment, 10*(1-2), 36–50. doi:10.1111/1468-2389.00192

Maslow, A. H. (1943). A theory of human motivation. *Psychological Review, 50*(4), 370–396. doi:10.1037/h0054346

Matthews, P. (2023, September 22). *The Case for Learning Transfer.* People Alchemy. https://peoplealchemy.com/blog/the-case-for-learning-transfer/

McBain, D. (2007). The practice of engagement: Research into current employee engagement practice. *Strategic HR Review, 6*(6), 16–19. doi:10.1108/14754390780001011

McCluney, C. L., Bryant, C. M., King, D. D., & Ali, A. A. (2017). Calling in Black: A dynamic model of racially traumatic events, resourcing, and safety. *Equality, Diversity and Inclusion, 36*(8), 767–786. doi:10.1108/EDI-01-2017-0012

McConnell, T. R. (1942). Introduction. In N. B. Henry (Ed.), Theories of learning (41st Yearbook, National Society for the Study of Education, Part 2 (pp. 3-13). Chicago: University of Chicago Press.

McCourt, W., & Derek, E. (2003). *Global Human Resource Management: Managing People in Developing and Transitional Countries.* Edward Elgar. doi:10.4337/9781781950104

McMahon, M., & Patton, W. (2022). The Systems Theory Framework of career development: News of difference and a journey towards acceptance. *Australian Journal of Career Development, 31*(3), 195–200. doi:10.1177/10384162221120464

Meek, V. L. (1988). Organizational culture: Origins and weaknesses. *Organization Studies*, *9*(4), 453–473. doi:10.1177/017084068800900401

Meister, J. C., & Willyerd, K. (2010). Mentoring millennials. *Harvard Business Review*, *88*(5), 68–72. PMID:20429252

Merriam, B. S. (2009). *Qualitative Research: A Guide to Design and Implementation* (3rd ed.). John Wiley & Sons.

Mezirow, J. (1990). A transformation theory of adult learning. In *Adult Education Research Annual Conference Proceedings* (Vol. 31, pp. 141-146). Academic Press.

Mezirow, J. (1997). Transformative learning: Theory to practice. *New Directions for Adult and Continuing Education*, *1997*(74), 5–12. doi:10.1002/ace.7401

Miao, J., Chang, J., & Ma, L. (2022). Teacher–student interaction, student–student interaction and social presence: Their impacts on learning engagement in online learning environments. *The Journal of Genetic Psychology*, *183*(6), 514–526. doi:10.1080/00221325.2022.2094211 PMID:35815529

Millar, G. (2012). Employee engagement – a new paradigm. *Human Resource Management International Digest*, *20*(2), 3–5. doi:10.1108/09670731211208085

Miller, D. (2002). Successful Change Leaders: What makes them? What do they do that is different? *Journal of Change Management*, *2*(4), 359–368. doi:10.1080/714042515

Mind Tools Content Team. (n.d.). *Hofstede's cultural dimensions*. Mind Tools. https://www.mindtools.com/a1ecvyx/hofstedes-cultural-dimensions

Mirzoyan, S., & Tovmasyan, G. (2022). The role and necessity of change management in organizations. Investing CRM as an effective system to manage customer relations. *Business Ethics and Leadership*, *6*(1), 6–13. doi:10.21272/bel.6(1).6-13.2022

Mishra, A. (2021, May 14). *Thomas Kilmann conflict model*. Management Weekly. https://managementweekly.org/thomas-kilmann-conflict-resolution-model/

Mitchell, C., Cours Anderson, K., Laverie, D., & Hass, A. (2021). Distance be damned: The importance of social presence in a pandemic constrained environment. *Marketing Education Review*, *31*(4), 294–310. doi:10.1080/10528008.2021.1936561

Moorman, R. H. (1991). Relationship between organizational justice and organizational citizenship behaviors: Do fairness perceptions influence employee citizenship? *The Journal of Applied Psychology*, *76*(6), 845–855. doi:10.1037/0021-9010.76.6.845

Morris, T. H. (2020). Experiential learning: A systematic review and revision of Kolb's model. *Interactive Learning Environments*, *28*(8), 1064–1077. doi:10.1080/10494820.2019.1570279

Mukhalalati, B. A., & Taylor, A. (2019). Adult learning theories in context: A quick guide for healthcare professional educators. *Journal of Medical Education and Curricular Development*, 6, 6. doi:10.1177/2382120519840332 PMID:31008257

Mukherjee, K. (2015). *Organizational Development and Change*. Pearson.

Mushtaque, I., Waqas, H., & Awais-E-Yazdan, M. (2022). The effect of technostress on the teachers' willingness to use online teaching modes and the moderating role of job insecurity during COVID-19 pandemic in Pakistan. *International Journal of Educational Management*, 36(1), 63–80. doi:10.1108/IJEM-07-2021-0291

Naile, I., & Selesho, J. M. (2014). The role of leadership in employee motivation. *Mediterranean Journal of Social Sciences*, 5(3), 175–182. doi:10.5901/mjss.2014.v5n3p175

Nauman B. (2010). http://www.binishnauman.com/index.php?option=com_content&view=article&id=134:what-is-more-important-training-or-development-of-employees--manager-today-article-by-binish-naumanpdf&catid=54:publication

Neeley, T., & Leonardi, P. (2022). Developing a digital mindset. *Harvard Business Review*, 100(5–6), 50–55.

Newman, A., Donohue, R., & Eva, N. (2017). Psychological safety: A systematic review of the literature. *Human Resource Management Review*, 27(3), 521–535. doi:10.1016/j.hrmr.2017.01.001

Newstrom, W. J., & Davis, K. (2002). *Organizational Behavior: Human Behavior at Work* (11th ed.). McGraw-Hill/Irwin.

Ng, K. H., & Ahmad, R. (2018). Personality traits, social support, and training transfer: The mediating mechanism of motivation to improve work through learning. *Personnel Review*, 47(1), 39–59. doi:10.1108/PR-08-2016-0210

Niazi, A. D. (2011). Training and Development Strategy and Its Role in Organizational Performance. *Journal of Public Administration and Governance.*, 1(2), 42. doi:10.5296/jpag.v1i2.862

Nickerson, C. (2023, October 24). *Hofstede's cultural dimensions theory & examples*. Simply Psychology. https://www.simplypsychology.org/hofstedes-cultural-dimensions-theory.html

Nimon, K. (2015). Secondary Data Analyses from Published Descriptive Statistics: Implications for Human Resource Development Theory, Research, and Practice. *Advances in Developing Human Resources*, 17(1), 26–39. doi:10.1177/1523422314559805

Noe, R., & Colquitt, J. (2002). Planning for Training Impact. In Creating, Implementing, and Managing Effective Training and Development. Jossey-Bass.

Noe, R. A. (1986). Trainee Attributes and Attitudes: Neglected Influences on Training Effectiveness. *Academy of Management Review*, 11(4), 736–749. doi:10.2307/258393

Noe, R. A. (2023). *Employee Training and Development*. McGraw Hill.

Nohria, N., Groysberg, B., & Lee, L. E. (2008). Employee Motivation. *Harvard Business Review*, 1.

Normore, A. H., Javidi, M., & Long, L. W. (2019). Handbook of Research on Strategic Communication, Leadership, and Conflict Management in Modern Organizations. In Advances in human resources management and organizational development book series. doi:10.4018/978-1-5225-8516-9

Nwoko, C., & Yazdani, K. (2023). Self-Determination Theory: The mediating role of generational differences in employee engagement. *Journal of Business & Management Studies, 5*(4), 130–142. doi:10.32996/jbms.2023.5.4.14

Odigie, H. A., & Li-Hua, R. (2008). Unlocking the channel of tacit knowledge transfer. *The Learning Organization, 32*(4), 124–141.

Okoye, K. R., & Edokpolor, J. E. (2021). Effect of industrial work experience in developing technical and vocational education undergraduates' employability skills. *Asian Journal of Assessment in Teaching and Learning, 11*(1), 1–12. doi:10.37134/ajatel.vol11.1.1.2021

Olckers, C., & Booysen, C. (2021). Generational differences in psychological ownership. *SA Journal of Industrial Psychology, 47*, 1–13. doi:10.4102/sajip.v47i0.1844

Organ, D. W. (1988). *Organizational citizenship behavior: The good soldier syndrome*. Lexington Books.

Organ, D. W. (1994). Personality and organizational citizenship behavior. *Journal of Management, 20*(2), 465–478. doi:10.1177/014920639402000208

Organ, D. W. (2014). Organizational citizenship behavior: It's construct clean-up time. *Human Performance, 10*(2), 85–97. doi:10.1207/s15327043hup1002_2

Organ, D. W., & McFall, J. B. (2004). Personality and citizenship behavior in organizations. In B. Schneider & D. B. Smith (Eds.), *Personality and Organizations* (pp. 291–314). Lawrence Erlbaum Associates, Inc., doi:10.4324/9781410610034-22

Ottawa University. (2021, January 12). *5 benefits of training and development*. Why Is Training and Development Important? https://www.ottawa.edu/online-and-evening/blog/january-2021/5-benefits-of-training-and-development

Pappas, C. (2013). *The adult learning theory - andragogy - of Malcolm Knowle*s. eLearning Industry. https://elearningindustry.com/the-adult-learning-theory-andragogy-of-malcolm-knowles

Pappas, S., & McKelvie, C. (2022, October 17). *What is culture?* Live Science. https://www.livescience.com/21478-what-is-culture-definition-of-culture.html

Parent, J. D., & Lovelace, K. J. (2018). Employee engagement, positive organizational culture and individual adaptability. *On the Horizon, 26*(3), 206–214. doi:10.1108/OTH-01-2018-0003

Parry, E., & Urwin, P. (2011). Generational differences in work values: A review of theory and evidence. *International Journal of Management Reviews, 13*(1), 79–96. doi:10.1111/j.1468-2370.2010.00285.x

Pasupathi, M. (2013). *How we learn. The Great Courses*. The Teaching Company.

Pathiranage, Y., Jayatilake, L., & Abeysekera, R. (2020). A literature review on organizational culture towards corporate performance. *International Journal of Management, Accounting and Economics, 7*(9), 522-544. https://www.ijmae.com/article_117964.html

Patterson, J. (2023, June 13). *Creating a culture of training and development in the workplace*. Forbes. https://www.forbes.com/sites/forbeshumanresourcescouncil/2023/06/13/creating-a-culture-of-training-and-development-in-the-workplace/?sh=447be1eb1038

Perriton, L. (2022). Guest editorial: Historical perspectives. *Human Resource Development Review, 21*(2), 152–159. doi:10.1177/15344843221088145

Perry, S. A. B., Barefield, T., & Cox, A. B. (2023). Review of the book Generative Knowing: Principles, Methods, and Dispositions of an Emerging Adult Learning Theory, by A. Nicolaides. *New Horizons in Adult Education and Human Resource Development, 35*(3), 176–177. doi:10.1177/19394225231200262

Pham, N. T., Jabbour, C. J. C., Usman, M., Ali, M., & Phan, H. L. (2022). How does training boost employees' intention to implement environmental activities? An empirical study in Vietnam. *International Journal of Manpower, 43*(8), 1761–1782. doi:10.1108/IJM-04-2021-0238

Philip, J., Jiang, Y., & Akdere, M. (2023). Virtual reality technology for workplace training: The case for developing cultural intelligence. *International Journal of Cross Cultural Management, 23*(3), 557–583. doi:10.1177/14705958231208297

Phillips, J., & Klein, J. D. (2022b). Change Management: From theory to practice. *TechTrends, 67*(1), 189–197. doi:10.1007/s11528-022-00775-0 PMID:36105238

Pillai, R., Schriesheim, C. A., & Williams, E. S. (1999). Fairness perceptions and trust as mediators for transformational and transactional leadership: A two-sample study. *Journal of Management, 25*(6), 897–933. doi:10.1177/014920639902500606

Pink, D. H. (2008). *Drive: The surprising truth about what motivates us*. Riverhead Books.

Pintrich, P. R., & De Groot, E. V. (1990). Motivational and self-regulated learning components of classroom academic performance. *Journal of Educational Psychology, 82*(1), 33–40. doi:10.1037/0022-0663.82.1.33

Podsakoff, P. M., & MacKenzie, S. B. (2014). Impact of organizational citizenship behavior on organizational performance: A review and suggestions for future research. *Human Performance, 10*(2), 133–151. doi:10.1207/s15327043hup1002_5

Podsakoff, P. M., MacKenzie, S. B., Paine, J. B., & Bachrach, D. G. (2000). Organizational citizenship behaviors: A critical review of the theoretical and empirical literature and suggestions for future research. *Journal of Management, 26*(3), 513–563. doi:10.1177/014920630002600307

Pollock, R. V. H., Jefferson, A. M., & Wick, C. W. (2015). *The Six Disciplines of Breakthrough Learning: How to Turn Training and Development into Business Results.* Wiley. doi:10.1002/9781119153832

Polo, F., Cervai, S., & Kantola, J. (2018). Training culture. *Journal of Workplace Learning, 30*(3), 162–173. doi:10.1108/JWL-01-2018-0024

Porath, C. (2016). *Creating a more human workplace where employees and business thrive.* SHRM Foundation. https://www.shrm.org/hr-today/trends-and-forecasting/special-reports-and-expert-views/Documents/Human-Workplace.pdf

Praslova, L. (2021, March 23). *Trauma-informed workplace: Kindness works best.* SHRM Blog. https://blog.shrm.org/blog/trauma-informed-organizational-behavior-kindness-works-better

Praveen M. Kulkarni, PM, Lakshminarayana K, Gokhale,P, Tigadi, BS, Veshne,N & Kulkarni, AV(2023). Employee Motivation and Its Relationship with Online Training. Jindal Journal of Business Research. 1-17.

Pusch, N. (2022). A meta-analytic review of social learning theory and teen dating violence perpetration. *Journal of Research in Crime and Delinquency, 61*(2), 171–223. doi:10.1177/00224278221130004

Qi, Y., Wang, B., & Liu, J. (2023). Behavioural economics theories in information-seeking behaviour research: A systematic review. *Journal of Librarianship and Information Science,* 1–13. doi:10.1177/09610006231219246

Quinones, M. A. (1995). Pretraining Context Effects: Training Assignments as Feedback. *The Journal of Applied Psychology, 80*(2), 226–238. doi:10.1037/0021-9010.80.2.226

Radević, I., Dimovski, V., Lojpur, A., & Colnar, S. (2023). Quality of healthcare services in focus: The role of knowledge transfer, hierarchical organizational structure and trust. *Knowledge Management Research and Practice, 21*(3), 525–536. doi:10.1080/14778238.2021.1932623

Rahi, S., Alghizzawi, M., Ahmad, S., Munawar Khan, M., & Ngah, A. H. (2022). Does employee readiness to change impact organization change implementation? Empirical evidence from emerging economy. *International Journal of Ethics and Systems, 38*(2), 235–253. doi:10.1108/IJOES-06-2021-0137

Rahman, M. F. W., Kistyanto, A., & Surjanti, J. (2022). Does cyberloafing and person organization fit affect employee performance? The mediating role of innovative work behavior. *Global Business and Organizational Excellence, 41*(5), 44–64. doi:10.1002/joe.22159

Rajhans, K. (2012). Effective organizational communication: A key to employee motivation and performance. *Interscience Management Review, 2*(2), 81–85.

Ranjit, G. (2022). Explicating intrinsic motivation's impact on job performance: Employee creativity as a mediator. *Journal of Strategy and Management, 15*(4), 647–664.

Rasinger, M. S. (2008). *Quantitative Research in Linguistics: An Introduction.* Continuum International Publishing Group.

Ratiu, L., David, O. A., & Baban, A. (2016). Developing managerial skills through coaching: Efficacy of a cognitive-behavioral coaching program. *Journal of Rational-Emotive & Cognitive-Behavior Therapy, 34*(4), 244–266. doi:10.1007/s10942-016-0256-9

Reed, M. S., Collins, D., & Cronin, A. (2023). Assessing the efficacy of online learning in disparate business subjects: Lessons from distributed practice theory. *Journal of Management Education, 47*(5), 512–541. doi:10.1177/10525629231178916

Reeve, J., Jang, H. R., & Jang, H. (2018). Personality-based antecedents of teachers' autonomy-supportive and controlling motivating styles. *Learning and Individual Differences, 62,* 12–22. https://doi.org/. lindif.2018.01.001 doi:10.1016/j

Reidhead, C. (2020). Impact of organizational culture on employee satisfaction: A case of Hilton Hotel, United Kingdom. *Journal of Economics and Business, 3*(1). Advance online publication. doi:10.31014/aior.1992.03.01.209

Reis, G. G., Trullén, J., & Story, J. (2016). Perceived organizational culture and engagement: The mediating role of authenticity. *Journal of Managerial Psychology, 31*(6), 1091–1105. doi:10.1108/JMP-05-2015-0178

Rhodes, J., Lok, P., Yu-Yuan Hung, R., & Fang, S. C. (2008). An integrative model of organizational learning and social capital on effective knowledge transfer and perceived organizational performance. *Journal of Workplace Learning, 20*(4), 245–258. doi:10.1108/13665620810871105

Rieckmann, M. (2021). Emancipatory and transformative Global Citizenship Education in formal and informal settings: Empowering learners to change structures. *Tertium Comparationis, 26*(2), 174-186. https://elibrary.utb.de/doi/abs/10.31244/tc.2020.02.10

Ritchie, L. (2021). *Yes I can: Learn to use the power of self-efficacy.* Effic Research Ltd.

Roberts, Z., Rogers, A., Thomas, C. L., & Spitzmueller, C. (2018). Effects of proactive personality and conscientiousness on training motivation. *International Journal of Training and Development, 22*(2), 126–143. doi:10.1111/ijtd.12122

Robledo, M. A. (2023). Organizational culture. In Springer eBooks (pp. 1–3). doi:10.1007/978-3-319-01669-6_553-2

Rogers, C. R. (1957). *The necessary and sufficient conditions of therapeutic personality change.* Academic Press.

Rogers, C. R. (1957). The necessary and sufficient conditions of therapeutic personality change. *Journal of Consulting Psychology, 21*(2), 95–103. doi:10.1037/h0045357

Rogers, T. T., Pasztor, M. E., & Kleinpeter, B. C. (2003). The Impact of Training on Worker Performance and Retention: Perceptions of Child Welfare Supervisors. *Professional Development: The International Journal of Continuing Social Work Education, 6*(3), 1–2.

Rosellini, A., & Hawamdeh, S. (2020). Tacit knowledge transfer in training and the inherent limitations of using only quantitative measures. *Proceedings of the Association for Information Science and Technology, 57*(1). 10.1002/pra2.272

Rothermel, R., & LaMarsh J. (2011). Managing change through employee empowerment. *Global Business and Organizational Excellence: A Review of Research and Best Practices, 31*(2), 17-23.

Rothwell, W. J., Imroz, S. M., & Bakhshandeh, B. (Eds.). (2021). *Organization Development Interventions*. Routledge. doi:10.4324/9781003019800

Rouiller, J., & Goldstein, I. (1993). The Relationship Between Organizational Transfer Climate and Positive Transfer of training. *Human Resource Development Quarterly, 4*(4), 377–390. doi:10.1002/hrdq.3920040408

Rowold, J. (2007). The impact of personality on training-related aspects of motivation: Test of a longitudinal model. *Human Resource Development Quarterly, 18*(1), 9–31. doi:10.1002/hrdq.1190

Rumjaun, A. B., & Narod, F. (2020). Social learning theory—Albert Bandura. In Springer Texts in Education (pp. 85–99). doi:10.1007/978-3-030-43620-9_7

Ryan, R. M., & Deci, E. L. (2000). Self-determination theory and the facilitation of intrinsic motivation, social development, and well-being. *The American Psychologist, 55*(1), 68–78. doi:10.1037/0003-066X.55.1.68 PMID:11392867

Ryan, R. M., & Deci, E. L. (2017). *Self-determination theory: Basic psychological needs in motivation, development, and wellness*. The Guilford Press., doi:10.1521/978.14625/28806

Sahu, A. K., Padhy, R. K., & Dhir, A. (2020). Envisioning the future of behavioral decision-making: A systematic literature review of behavioral reasoning theory. *Australasian Marketing Journal, 28*(4), 145–159. doi:10.1016/j.ausmj.2020.05.001

Salas, E., Tannenbaum, S. I., Kraiger, K., & Smith-Jentsch, K. A. (2012). The science of training and development in organizations: What matters in practice. *Psychological Science in the Public Interest, 13*(2), 74–101. doi:10.1177/1529100612436661 PMID:26173283

Sancho-Thomas, P., Fuentes-Fernández, R., & Fernández-Manjón, B. (2009). Learning teamwork skills in university programming courses. *Computers & Education, 53*(2), 517–531. doi:10.1016/j.compedu.2009.03.010

Sander, J., Schmiedek, F., Brose, A., Wagner, G. G., & Specht, J. (2017). Long-term effects of an extensive cognitive training on personality development. *Journal of Personality, 85*(4), 454–463. doi:10.1111/jopy.12252 PMID:26998917

Sanjaghi, M., Akhavan, P., & Najafi, S. (2013). Fostering knowledge sharing behavior: The role of organizational culture and trust. *International Journal of the Academy of Organizational Behavior Management, 2*(5), 9-33.

Compilation of References

Satyam, B., & Aithal, P. S. (2022). Reimagining an Experiential Learning Exercise in Times of Crisis: Lessons Learned and a Proposed Framework. *Journal of Marketing Education*, *44*(2), 191–202. doi:10.1177/02734753221084128

Schein, E. H. (1993). How can organizations learn faster? The challenge of entering the green room. *Sloan Management Review*, *34*(2), 85–92.

Scherrens, A.-L., Pype, P., Van den Eynden, B., Mertens, F., Stichele, R. V., & Deveugele, M. (2018). The use of behavioural theories in end-of-life care research: A systematic review. *Palliative Medicine*, *32*(1), 1065–1079. doi:10.1177/0269216318758212 PMID:29569998

Schmude, T., Koesten, L., Möller, T., & Tschiatschek, S. (2023). Applying Interdisciplinary Frameworks to Understand Algorithmic Decision-Making, https://doi.org//arXiv.2305.16700 doi:10.48550

Schon, D. A. (1987). *Educating the Reflective Behaviour*. Jossey-Bass.

Sekhar, C., Patwardhan, M., & Singh, R. K. (2013). A literature review on motivation. *Global Business Perspectives*, *1*, 471-487.

Shadmanfaat, S. M., Howell, C. J., Muniz, C. N., Cochran, J. K., Kabiri, S., & Fontaine, E. M. (2020). Cyberbullying perpetration: An empirical test of social learning theory in Iran. *Deviant Behavior*, *41*(3), 278–293. doi:10.1080/01639625.2019.1565513

Shafaei, A., & Nejati, M. (2023). Creating meaningful work for employees: The role of inclusive leadership. *Human Resource Development Quarterly*, *1*, hrdq.21512. Advance online publication. doi:10.1002/hrdq.21512

Shahzadi, I., Javed, A., Pirzada, S. S., Nasreen, S., & Khanam, F. (2014). Impact of employee motivation on employee performance. *European Journal of Business and Management*, *6*(23), 159–166.

Shapira-Lishchinsky, O. (2014). Simulation-based constructivist approach for education leaders. *Educational Management Administration & Leadership*, *43*(6), 972–988. doi:10.1177/1741143214543203

Sharma, M., & Singh, A. (2024). Enhancing Competitive Advantages Through Virtual Reality Technology in the Hotels of India. In S. Kumar, M. Talukder, & A. Pego (Eds.), *Utilizing Smart Technology and AI in Hybrid Tourism and Hospitality* (pp. 243–256). IGI Global. doi:10.4018/979-8-3693-1978-9.ch011

Sharma, R., & Singh, A. (2024). Use of Digital Technology in Improving Quality Education: A Global Perspectives and Trends. In V. Nadda, P. Tyagi, R. Moniz Vieira, & P. Tyagi (Eds.), *Implementing Sustainable Development Goals in the Service Sector* (pp. 14–26). IGI Global. doi:10.4018/979-8-3693-2065-5.ch002

Shuell, T. J. (1986). Cognitive conceptions of learning. *Review of Educational Research*, *56*(4), 411–436. doi:10.3102/00346543056004411

Simpson, J. A., & Beckes, L. (2010). Evolutionary perspectives on prosocial behavior. In M. Mikulincer & P. R. Shaver (Eds.), *Prosocial motives, emotions, and behavior: The better angels of our nature* (pp. 35–53). American Psychological Association. doi:10.1037/12061-002

Sinelnikova, V., Ivchenko, T., Pistunova, T., Regesha, N., & Skazhenyk, M. (2022). Enhancing the performance of andragogic education. *Journal of Curriculum and Teaching, 11*(1), 245–254. doi:10.5430/jct.v11n1p245

Singh, A., & Bathla, G. (2023). Fostering Creativity and Innovation: Tourism and Hospitality Perspective. In P. Tyagi, V. Nadda, V. Bharti, & E. Kemer (Eds.), Embracing Business Sustainability through Innovation and Creativity in the Service Sector (pp. 70-83). IGI Global.

Singh, A., & Hassan, S. C. (2024a). Identifying the Skill Gap in the Workplace and Their Challenges in Hospitality and Tourism Organisations. In Contemporary Challenges in Social Science Management: Skills Gaps and Shortages in the Labour Market (Contemporary Studies in Economic and Financial Analysis, Vol. 112B). Emerald Publishing Limited. doi:10.1108/S1569-37592024000112B006

Singh, C., Maries, A., Heller, K., & Heller, P. (2023). Instructional Strategies that Foster Effective Problem-Solving, /arXiv.2304.05585 doi:10.1063/9780735425477_017

Singh, A. (2024a). Quality of Work-Life Practices in the Indian Hospitality Sector: Future Challenges and Prospects. In M. Valeri & B. Sousa (Eds.), *Human Relations Management in Tourism* (pp. 208–224). IGI Global. doi:10.4018/979-8-3693-1322-0.ch010

Singh, A. (2024b). Virtual Research Collaboration and Technology Application: Drivers, Motivations, and Constraints. In S. Chakraborty (Ed.), *Challenges of Globalization and Inclusivity in Academic Research* (pp. 250–258). IGI Global. doi:10.4018/979-8-3693-1371-8.ch016

Singh, A., & Hassan, S. C. (2024). Service Innovation Through Blockchain Technology in the Tourism and Hospitality Industry: Applications, Trends, and Benefits. In S. Singh (Ed.), *Service Innovations in Tourism: Metaverse, Immersive Technologies, and Digital Twin* (pp. 205–214). IGI Global. doi:10.4018/979-8-3693-1103-5.ch010

Singh, A., & Kumar, S. (2021). Identifying Innovations in Human Resources: Academia and Industry Perspectives. In A. Pathak & S. Rana (Eds.), *Transforming Human Resource Functions With Automation* (pp. 104–120). IGI Global. doi:10.4018/978-1-7998-4180-7.ch006

Singh, A., Sharma, S., & Paliwal, M. (2021). Adoption intention and effectiveness of digital collaboration platforms for online learning: The Indian students' perspective. *Interactive Technology and Smart Education, 18*(4), 493–514. doi:10.1108/ITSE-05-2020-0070

Singh, J., Evans, E., Reed, A., Karch, L., Qualey, K., Singh, L., & Wiersma, H. (2022). Online, hybrid, and face-toface learning through the eyes of faculty, students, administrators, and instructional designers: Lessons learned and directions for the post-vaccine and post-pandemic/COVID-19 world. *Journal of Educational Technology Systems, 50*(3), 301–326. doi:10.1177/00472395211063754

Singh, V., & Singh, A. (2024b). Digital Health Revolution: Enhancing Well-Being Through Technology. In V. Nadda, P. Tyagi, R. Moniz Vieira, & P. Tyagi (Eds.), *Implementing Sustainable Development Goals in the Service Sector* (pp. 213–219). IGI Global. doi:10.4018/979-8-3693-2065-5.ch016

Sithambaram, J., Nasir, M. H. N. B. M., & Ahmad, R. (2021). Issues and challenges impacting the successful management of agile-hybrid projects: A grounded theory approach. *International Journal of Project Management*, *39*(5), 474–495. doi:10.1016/j.ijproman.2021.03.002

Skaggs, C. B., & Youndt, M. (2004). Strategic Positioning, Human Capital, and Performance in Service Organizations: A Customer Interaction Approach. *Strategic Management Journal*, *25*(1), 85–99. doi:10.1002/smj.365

Skinner, B. F. (1988). *About Behaviorism*. Random House.

Smith, R., King, D., Sidhu, R., & Skelsey, D. (Eds.). (2014). *The effective change manager's handbook: Essential guidance to the change management body of knowledge*. Kogan Page Publishers.

Smokowski, P. R., Bacallao, M., & Evans, C. B. R. (2017). Acculturation. In R. Levesque (Ed.), *Encyclopedia of Adolescence*. Springer. doi:10.1007/978-3-319-32132-5_300-2

Song, L., Singleton, E. S., Hill, J. R., & Koh, M. H. (2016). Improving online learning: Student perceptions of useful and challenging characteristics. *The Internet and Higher Education*, *7*(1), 59–70. doi:10.1016/j.iheduc.2003.11.003

Sony, M., Antony, J., & Douglas, A. (2020). Essential ingredients for the implementation of Quality 4.0. *The TQM Journal*, *32*(4), 779–793. doi:10.1108/TQM-12-2019-0275

Spector, P. E. (2010). The relationship of personality to counterproductive work behavior (CWB): An integration of perspectives. *Human Resource Management Review*, *21*(4). Advance online publication. doi:10.1016/j.hrmr.2010.10.002

Srimulyani, V. A., & Hermanto, Y. B. (2022). Organizational culture as a mediator of credible leadership influence on work engagement: Empirical studies in private hospitals in East Java, Indonesia. *Humanities & Social Sciences Communications*, *9*(1), 1–11. doi:10.1057/s41599-022-01289-z PMID:35990765

Staub, E. (1978). *Positive social behavior and morality: Social and personal influences* (Vol. 1). Academic Press Inc.

Stavrinoudis, T., & Kakarougkas, C. (2019). The synthesis of the variables formulates rewards system culture (ReSCulture). In Springer proceedings in business and economics (pp. 577–602). doi:10.1007/978-3-030-03910-3_39

Sterns, L., Alexander, R. A., Barrett, G. V., & Dambrot, F. H. (1983). The relationship of extraversion and neuroticism with job preferences and job satisfaction for clerical employees. *Journal of Occupational Psychology*, *56*(2), 145–153. doi:10.1111/j.2044-8325.1983.tb00122.x

Strategic Training and Development: A Gateway to Organizational Success . (2008). http://missionfacilitators.com/wp-content/uploads/2013/03/Strategic-Training-Development-SHRM-2008.pdf

Stuart, R. (2013). *Essentials of Human Resource Training and Development.* http://www.hrps.org/blogpost/736528/160480/Essentials-of-Human-Resource-Training-and-Development

Substance Abuse and Mental Health Services Administration (SAMHSA). (2014). *SAMHSA's concept of trauma and guidance for a trauma-informed approach.* SAMHSA's Trauma and Justice Strategic Initiative. https://ncsacw.samhsa.gov/userfiles/files/SAMHSA_Trauma.pdf

Sugiyama, K., Cavanagh, K. V., Van Esch, C., Bilimoria, D., & Brown, C. (2016). Inclusive leadership development. *Journal of Management Education, 40*(3), 253–292. doi:10.1177/1052562916632553

Sullivan, P. (2011). Qualitative Data Analysis Using a Dialogical Approach. *Sage (Atlanta, Ga.).*

Sutler-Cohen, S. (2019, March 6). *Core values: What they are, why they matter, and how to define yours.* Medium. https://medium.com/@scoutcoaching/core-values-what-they-are-why-they-matter-and-how-to-define-yours-93164383eada

Swancott, L. J., & Davis, S. K. (2023). Service with a smile? Engagement is a better predictor of job satisfaction than emotional intelligence. *Current Psychology (New Brunswick, N.J.), 42*(17), 14647–14651. doi:10.1007/s12144-022-02818-4

Swart, J., Mann, C., Brown, S., & Price, A. (2005). *Human Resource Development: Strategy and Tactics.* Elsevier Butterworth-Heinemann Publications.

Sweller, J., Ayres, P., & Kalyuga, S. (2011). *Cognitive load theory.* Springer. doi:10.1007/978-1-4419-8126-4

Tajfel, H., & Turner, J. C. (2004). The social identity theory of intergroup behavior. In J. T. Jost & J. Sidanius (Eds.), *Political psychology* (pp. 276–293). Psychology Press. doi:10.4324/9780203505984-16

Tannenbaum, S. I., Mathieu, J. E., Salas, E., & Cannon-Bowers, J. A. (1991). Meeting Trainees' Expectations: The Influence of Training Fulfillment on the Development of Commitment, Self-Efficacy, and Motivation. *The Journal of Applied Psychology, 76*(6), 759–769. doi:10.1037/0021-9010.76.6.759

Taormina, R. J. (2008). Interrelating leadership behaviors, organizational socialization, and organizational culture. *Leadership and Organization Development Journal, 29*(1), 85–102. doi:10.1108/01437730810845315

Taylor, L. III, Murphy, B., & Price, W. (2006). Goldratt's thinking process applied to employee retention. *Business Process Management Journal, 12*(5), 646–670. doi:10.1108/14637150610691055

Taylor, R., & Davies, D. (2004). Aspects of training and remuneration in the accommodation industry. *Journal of European Industrial Training, 28*(6), 1–2. doi:10.1108/03090590410542693

Compilation of References

Tharenou, P. (2010). Training and development in organizations. In A. Wilkinson, N. Bacon, T. Redman, & S. Snell (Eds.), *The Sage handbook of human resource management* (pp. 155–172). Sage. doi:10.4135/9780857021496.n10

The Kings Fund. (2020) *The importance of psychological safety* [Video]. The Kings Fund. https://www.youtube.com/watch?v=eP6guvRt0U0

The World of Work Project. (2022). *Edgar Schein's organizational culture triangle: A simple summary.* https://worldofwork.io/2019/10/edgar-scheins-culture-triangle/

Torrington, D., Hall, L., & Taylor, S. (2005). *Human Resource Management* (6th ed.). Prentice Hall.

Trim, J. R. P. (2004). Human resource management development and strategic management enhanced by simulation exercises. *Journal of Management Development*, *23*(4), 399–413. doi:10.1108/02621710410529820

Tsai, Y. (2011). Relationship between organizational culture, leadership behavior and job satisfaction. *BMC Health Services Research*, *11*(1), 98. doi:10.1186/1472-6963-11-98 PMID:21569537

Turban, E., Outland, J., King, D., Lee, J. K., Liang, T., & Turban, D. C. (2017). Innovative EC systems: From e-government to E-learning, e-Health, sharing economy, and P2P commerce. Springer texts in business and economics (pp. 167–201). Springer. doi:10.1007/978-3-319-58715-8_5

U.S. Census Bureau. (2022). *Household pulse survey.* https://www.census.gov/programs-surveys/household-pulse-survey.html

Uzialko, A. (2023, October 23). *How to develop a New Hire Training Plan.* Business News Daily. https://www.businessnewsdaily.com/15839-new-hire-training.html

Vallerand, R. J. (1997). Toward a hierarchical model of intrinsic and extrinsic motivation. In M. P. Zanna (Ed.), Advances in experimental social psychology. Academic Press. doi:10.1016/S0065-2601(08)60019-2

Van Dyne, L., Cummings, L. L., & Parks, J. M. (1995). Extra role behaviors: In pursuit of construct and definitional clarity. *Research in Organizational Behavior*, *17*, 215–285. https://www.researchgate.net/publication/309563728_Extra-role_behaviors_In_pursuit_of_construct_and_definitional_clarity

Viđak, M., Barać, L., Tokalić, R., Buljan, I., & Marušić, A. (2021). Interventions for Organizational Climate and Culture in Academia: A scoping review. *Science and Engineering Ethics*, *27*(2), 24. Advance online publication. doi:10.1007/s11948-021-00298-6 PMID:33783667

Vikas, S., & Mathur, A. (2022). An empirical study of student perception towards pedagogy, teaching style and effectiveness of online classes. *Education and Information Technologies*, *27*(1), 589–610. doi:10.1007/s10639-021-10793-9 PMID:34720659

Von Bertalanffy, L. (1968). *General System Theory: Foundations, Development.* George Braziller.

Vroom, V. H. (1994). *Work and motivation*. Jossey-Bass.

Wals, A. E., Geerling-Eijff, F., Hubeek, F., Van der Kroon, S., & Vader, J. (2008). All mixed up? Instrumental and emancipatory learning toward a more sustainable world: Considerations for EE policymakers. *Applied Environmental Education and Communication*, *7*(3), 55–65. doi:10.1080/15330150802473027

Wanberg, C. R. (2012). The Oxford handbook of organizational socialization. In Oxford University Press eBooks. doi:10.1093/oxfordhb/9780199763672.001.0001

Wang, S., & Huang, L. (2022). A Study of the Relationship between Corporate Culture and Corporate Sustainable Performance: Evidence from Chinese SMEs. *Sustainability (Basel)*, *14*(13), 7527. doi:10.3390/su14137527

Wang, S., Liu, Y., Zhang, J., & Li, S. (2023). Why, how and when the double-edged sword of workplace friendship impacts differentiated organizational citizenship behavior: A relationship motivation theory approach. *Current Psychology (New Brunswick, N.J.)*, *42*(16), 13838–13855. doi:10.1007/s12144-022-03818-0

Wayne, S. J., Shore, L. M., & Liden, R. C. (1997). Perceived organizational support and leader-member exchange: A social exchange perspective. *Academy of Management Journal*, *40*(1), 82–111. doi:10.2307/257021

Weiner, B. J. (2020). A theory of organizational readiness for change. In *Handbook on implementation science* (pp. 215–232). Edward Elgar Publishing. doi:10.4337/9781788975995.00015

Weinstein, C. E., & Mayer, R. E. (1986). The teaching of learning strategies. In M. C. Wittrock (Ed.), *Handbook of research on teaching* (3rd ed., pp. 315–327). Macmillan.

Westaby, J. D. (2005). Behavioral reasoning theory: Identifying new linkages underlying intentions and behavior. *Organizational Behavior and Human Decision Processes*, *98*(2), 97–120. doi:10.1016/j.obhdp.2005.07.003

Whelan-Berry, K. S., & Somerville, K. A. (2010). Linking change drivers and the organizational change process: A review and synthesis. *Journal of Change Management*, *10*(2), 175–193. doi:10.1080/14697011003795651

Widdifield, J., Bernatsky, S., Pope, J. E., Kuriya, B., Barber, C. E., Eder, L., & Thorne, C. (2021). Evaluation of rheumatology workforce supply changes in Ontario, Canada, from 2000 to 2030. *Healthcare Policy*, *16*(3), 119–135. doi:10.12927/hcpol.2021.26428 PMID:33720829

Widodo, H. P., Perfecto, M. R., Van Canh, L., & Buripakdi, A. (2018). Incorporating cultural and moral values into ELT materials in the context of Southeast Asia (SEA). In H. Widodo, M. Perfecto, L. Van Canh, & A. Buripakdi (Eds.), *Situating Moral and Cultural Values in ELT Materials. English Language Education* (Vol. 9). Springer. doi:10.1007/978-3-319-63677-1_1

William, A. N. (2010). Employee motivation and performance. *Business Management*, *8*, 5–11.

Williams, L. J., & Anderson, S. E. (1991). Job satisfaction and organizational commitment as predictors of organizational citizenship and in-role behaviors. *Journal of Management, 17*(3), 601–617. doi:10.1177/014920639101700305

Williams, S. D., Graham, T. S., & Baker, B. (2003). Evaluating outdoor experiential training for leadership and team building. *Journal of Management Development, 22*(1), 45–59. doi:10.1108/02621710310454851

Wilson, T., & Kelly, S. (2022, November 30). *Barriers to effective training and development.* https://strategichrinc.com/barriers-to-effective-training/

Wilson, J., & Western, S. (2001). Performance appraisal: An obstacle to training and development? *Career Development International, 6*(2), 93–100.

Wognum, A. A. M. (2001). Vertical Integration of HRD Policy within Companies. *Human Resource Development International, 4*(3), 407–421. doi:10.1080/13678860010006149

Wojciechowski, T. W. (2021). The relevance of the dual systems model for social learning theory: Testing for moderation effects. *Criminal Justice and Behavior, 48*(12), 1791–1807. doi:10.1177/00938548211017927

Wright, P., & Geroy, D. G. (2001). Changing the mindset: The training myth and the need for word-class performance. *International Journal of Human Resource Management, 12*(4), 586–600. doi:10.1080/09585190122342

Xie, L. (2018). Leadership and organizational learning culture: A systematic literature review. *European Journal of Training and Development, 43*(1/2), 76–104. doi:10.1108/EJTD-06-2018-0056

Yaffe, T., & Kark, R. (2011). Leading by example: The case of leader OCB. *The Journal of Applied Psychology, 96*(4), 806–826. doi:10.1037/a0022464 PMID:21443315

Yang, S., Nachum, O., Du, Y., Wei, J., Abbeel, P., & Schuurmans, D. (2023). *Foundation Models for Decision Making: Problems, Methods, and Opportunities.* Working Paper Series, Cornell University. doi:10.48550/arXiv.2303.04129

Yang, J. (2023). The impact of Industry 4.0 on the world of work and the call for educational reform. In D. Guo (Ed.), *The frontier of education reform and development in China: Articles from educational research* (pp. 285–298). Springer Nature. doi:10.1007/978-981-19-6355-1_15

Yawson, R. M. (2012). Systems theory and thinking as a foundational theory in human resource development: A myth or reality? *Human Resource Development Review, 12*(1), 53–85. doi:10.1177/1534484312461634

Yergler, J. D. (2012). Organizational culture and leadership. *Leadership and Organization Development Journal, 33*(4), 421–423. doi:10.1108/01437731211229331

Yin Yin Lau, P., Park, S., & McLean, G. (2020). Learning organization and organizational citizenship behaviour in West Malaysia: Moderating role of team-oriented culture. *European Journal of Training and Development*, *44*(8/9), 847–864. doi:10.1108/EJTD-01-2020-0007

Yin, J., Ma, Z., Yu, H., Jia, M., & Liao, G. (2020). Transformational leadership and employee knowledge sharing: Explore the mediating roles of psychological safety and team efficacy. *Journal of Knowledge Management*, *24*(2), 150–171. doi:10.1108/JKM-12-2018-0776

ZhouB.WangP.WanJ.LiangY.WangF. (2022). Effective Vision Transformer Training: A Data-Centric Perspective. https://arxiv.org/abs/2209.15006

Zollers, N. J., Ramanathan, A. K., & Yu, M. (1999). The relationship between school culture and inclusion: How an inclusive culture supports inclusive education. *International Journal of Qualitative Studies in Education : QSE*, *12*(2), 157–174. doi:10.1080/095183999236231

Zulkarnain, Z., Hadiyani, S., Ginting, E. D., & Fahmi. (2024). Commitment, employee engagement and readiness to change among oil palm plantation officers. *SA Journal of Human Resource Management*, *22*, 2471. doi:10.4102/sajhrm.v22i0.2471

About the Contributors

Amjad Imam Ansari, Ph.D. Research Scholar, is an Assistant Professor in the School of Hotel Management and Tourism at Lovely Professional University, Jalandhar, India. His research interest focuses on Hotel Revenue Management, Hospitality Products and Services, Hotel Management, Hotel Sales and Marketing, Tourism Management. He has over 8 years of experiences in academic and industry.

Neeta Baporikar is currently a Professor/Director (Business Management) at Harold Pupkewitz Graduate School of Business, Namibia University of Science and Technology, Namibia. Before this, she was Head-Scientific Research, with the Ministry of Higher Education CAS-Salalah, Sultanate of Oman, Professor (Strategy and Entrepreneurship) at IIIT Pune and BITS India. With a decade-plus of experience in the industry, consultancy, and training, she made a lateral switch to research and academics in 2000. Prof Baporikar holds D.Sc. (Management Studies) USA, Ph.D. (Management), SP Pune University, INDIA with MBA (Distinction) and Law (Hons.) degrees. Apart from this, she is an external reviewer, Oman Academic Accreditation Authority, an Accredited Management Teacher, a Qualified Trainer, an FDP from EDII, a Doctoral Guide, and a Board Member of Academic Advisory Committee in accredited B-Schools. She has to her credit many conferred doctorates, 350+ scientific publications, and authored 30+ books in the areas of Strategy, Entrepreneurship, Management, and Higher Education. She is also a member of the international and editorial advisory board, and reviewer for Emerald, IGI, Inderscience, Wiley, etc.

Jennifer Bockelman is a Global Learning and Development Project Manager for Liberty Mutual Insurance. She manages the development and execution of leadership development and culture change strategies in North America, Europe, and Asia. She earned her Master's in Organizational Conflict Management from Southern Methodist University and is currently enrolled in the Industrial/Organizational Psychology doctoral program at Adler University. Her primary research interest concerns the recruitment and retention of women, minorities, and other historically underrepresented groups in leadership. She is also interested in topics such as learning and development and employee motivation strategies. She is married to her wonderful partner, Josh, and they are the parents to two children.

João Farinha is a Ph.D. in Management from Universidade Europeia, with a Master's degree in Marketing and a Brand Management thesis. He also has an Executive Master's Degree in Marketing Management from the same institution. He also holds a Certificate in Business and Management (Leadership and Emotional Intelligence) from Case Western Reserve University, a Certificate in Business and Management (Entrepreneurship) from the University of Maryland, College Park, and a Certificate in Business and Management (Leadership and Emotional Intelligence) from the Wharton School, University of Pennsylvania (Leadership). He is presently a member of the Governance, Competitiveness, and Public Policy (GOVCOPP) research unit at the University of Aveiro, as well as the Research Centre in Tourism, Sustainability, and Well-Being (CinTurs) research unit at the University of Algarve. Associate professor at ISLA Santarem Lecturing in Management, Human Resources, Operations, and Marketing. Course director for the MBA in Commercial Management and Marketing, as well as the degree in Business Processes and Operations Management and the higher professional technical course in Organization and Industrial Management.

Rachel Frost, SHRM-CP, a senior talent development specialist at a global company. She lives in the Twin Cities of Minnesota with her husband and 5 children. Rachel has a Master's Degree in Industrial-Organizational Psychology from Adler University with a specialty in training and development. Rachel has a passion for incorporating more holistic wellness, trauma-informed leadership and psychological safety knowledge and practice in the workplace. Professional affiliations include SIOP, SEBOC, SHRM, TCSHRM, ATD-GTC.

Mahima Guwalani is a final year student specializing in the area of Human Resources at Narsee Monjee Institute of Management Studies, Bengaluru Campus. She comes from a technical background and having a heart for people she is deeply passionate about HR, Change management and People Analytics, gaining valuable insights into the art of optimising human potential through OD interventions, data-driven decision-making and strives to create exceptional work environments where people can thrive.

Alphonsa Haokip is currently the Headmistress of Christ King High School, Chingjaroi Khullen. She has completed her doctorate entitled, "Attitude, Problem Solving Ability, and Achievement in Mathematics Learning among the Secondary

About the Contributors

School Students of Thadou Kuki Tribe in Manipur". Her areas of interest are Mathematics Learning of Secondary School Students, their problem-solving ability, their academic achievement, mathematics teachers and their concerns, paradigm shift in higher education, and gender issues.

Peace Kumah holds a doctorate degree in Business Administration and MBA (Human Resource Management) degree from Wisconsin International University College, Accra, Ghana. She has several years of teaching experience and occupies leadership positions in various educational institutions. Her research interest includes organizational leadership and motivation, change management, and employment relations.

Rui Martins is a professor in ISLA-Santarém, Department of Management and Economics, Portugal and Student of a PhD in Management from the University of Beira Interior, Portugal and NECE-UBI, Research Centre for Business Sciences. His research focuses on the strategies of Internationalization of SMEs, entrepreneurship, business networks and business creation.

Elizabeth Mize achieved her Master's degrees in English and Education from Rajiv Gandhi University, Rono Hills, Doimukh, Itanagar. She successfully cleared both the NET and SLET examinations in English and Education. Her doctoral degree was conferred upon her by the Department of Education at Rajiv Gandhi University, Doimukh, Itanagar. Dr. Mize has actively participated in numerous national and international seminars and conferences, making valuable contributions through research articles published in journals and chapters in edited books.

Melita Stephen Natal is an Assistant Professor at Amity Business School, Amity University, Greater Noida, UP, India.

Amalia Nedelcut is a lecturer at Babeş-Bolyai University, teaching Management in English, Romanian and German, and other subjects like Project Management, Business Ethics and Organizational Human Behavior. With a Ph.D. in Cultural Management and a master's in Business Engineering, she brings a rich interdisciplinary perspective to her work. Amalia is also a community leader involved in international projects focused on personal development, fostering a global collaboration and empowering individuals to reach their full potential.

Nicholas Patrick holds a Ph.D.in Industrial and Organizational Psychology from Adler University. He has held various teaching or academic positions at many educational institutions, including Lakehead University, Nipissing University, and Northern Lights College. His research and expertise lie in business, English, leadership methodology, industrial and organizational psychology, philosophy, and mathematics. He is passionate about advancing social justice and focuses on improving the student learning experience.

Maria de Fátima Pina holds a PhD in Mathematics from the University of Coimbra and the University of Porto. She is an Adjunct Professor at ISLA Santarém and an Invited Auxiliary Professor at ISCTE - University Institute of Lisbon. She is Member of the Portuguese Mathematics Society, Member of the Portuguese Automatic Control Association, Member of the Information and Technology Research Centre of the ISLA Santarém Research & Development Unit, and affiliate of IFAC - International Federation of Automatic Control. As a researcher at ISR - UC, Institute of Systems and Robotics of the University of Coimbra she worked in different projects, and her current research interests include interdisciplinary areas, such as, Control Theory, Data Science, Dynamical Systems, Computer Vision, Robotics, Social Sciences and Medical Engineering.

V. Muthu Ruben is a distinguished Associate Professor at the School of Law, Christ University, situated in Bengaluru, Karnataka, India. Driven by an extensive scholarly foundation and a steadfast dedication to legal education, Dr. Ruben makes substantial contributions to both the academic community and the domain of law. His proficiency transcends numerous spheres within the realm of law, and he significantly influences the educational journeys of students enrolled at Christ University. Motivated by an ardent interest in legal research, he actively participates in scholarly endeavors, thereby making significant contributions to the ongoing legal dialogue. In addition to his scholarly responsibilities, Dr. V. Muthu Ruben is renowned for his commitment to cultivating an atmosphere that encourages intellectual engagement. His mentorship and counsel motivate pupils to explore into the complexities of the law, fostering the development of critical thinking skills and a profound comprehension of legal principles. In his role as an Associate Professor, Dr. Ruben provides the School of Law with an abundance of expertise, experience, and a forward-thinking perspective, thereby enhancing the institution's dedication to providing superior legal education.

Deepak Sharma has been working as Associate Professor in the area of Human Resources at Narsee Monjee Institute of Management Studies, Bengaluru Campus and has 24 years of experience (with industry & academia combined). He has been Corporate Trainer/HR & Legal Consultant for industry houses as well as Faculty member of leading B-Schools of India namely, International Management Institute popularly known as IMI and Lal Bahadur Shastri Institute of Management, New

About the Contributors

Delhi. He has authored books, research papers/case studies and multiple articles in Economic Times HR World in the area of Human Resources. He imparts Management Development Programmes on Leadership development, Change Management, Team Building and Personal Effectiveness, Negotiation Skills, Industrial Relations, Labour Laws for HR Managers to name a few. His areas of interest include HR systems (namely, Learning & Development, Performance Management & Coaching, Cultural system, Renewal system & Organization Development), Labour Laws, ROI, Leadership Development, Employee experience, Employee engagement, Talent Management, Gender Sensitisation & Sexual Harassment at workplace.

Amrik Singh is working as Professor in the School of Hotel Management and Tourism at Lovely Professional University, Punjab, India. He obtained his Ph.D. degree in Hotel Management from Kurukshetra University, Kurukshetra. He started his academic career at Lovely Professional University, Punjab, India in the year 2007. He has published more than 40 research papers in UGC and peer-reviewed and Scopus/Web of Science) journals. He has published 12 patents and 01 patent has been granted in the inter-disciplinary domain. Dr. Amrik Singh participated and acted as a resource person in various national and international conferences, seminars, research workshops, and industry talks. His area of research interest is accommodation management, ergonomics, green practices, human resource management in hospitality, waste management, AR VR in hospitality, etc. He is currently guiding 8Ph.D. scholars and 2 Ph.D. scholars have been awarded Ph.D.

Ranjit Singha is a Doctorate Research Fellow at Christ (Deemed to be University) and holds the prestigious American Psychological Association (APA) membership. With a strong background in Research and Development, he has significantly contributed to various fields such as Mindfulness, Addiction Psychology, Women Empowerment, UN Sustainable Development Goals, and Data Science. With over 15 years of experience in Administration, Teaching, and Research, both in Industry and Higher Education Institutions (HEI), Mr Ranjit has established himself as a seasoned professional. Mr Ranjit is dedicatedly involved in research and teaching endeavours, primarily focusing on mindfulness and compassion-based interventions. His work in these areas aims to promote well-being and foster positive change in individuals and communities.

Surjit Singha is an academician with a broad spectrum of interests, including UN Sustainable Development Goals, Organizational Climate, Workforce Diversity, Organizational Culture, HRM, Marketing, Finance, IB, Global Business, Business, AI, K12 and Higher Education, Gender and Cultural Studies. Currently a faculty member at Kristu Jayanti College, Dr Surjit also serves as an Editor, reviewer, and author for prominent global publications and journals, including being on the Editorial review board of Information Resources Management Journal and contributor to various publications. With over 13 years of experience in Administration, Teaching, and Research, Dr. Surjit is dedicated to imparting knowledge and guiding students in their research pursuits. As a research mentor, Dr. Surjit has nurtured young minds and fostered academic growth. Dr. Surjit has an impressive track record of over 75 publications, including articles, book chapters, and textbooks, holds two US Copyrights, and has completed and published two fully funded minor research projects from Kristu Jayanti College.

Index

A

Adhocracy Culture 17-18, 31
Adult Learning 2, 79, 83-88, 110, 138, 144, 146-147, 156, 161, 163, 166-167, 176, 187-188, 193, 205-207, 214
Adult Learning Theory 83-88, 187, 205-206

B

Behavioral Theories 82, 88-91, 110

C

Change Management 40-42, 58-65, 68-76, 91, 98, 106, 196
Change Process 62-67, 72, 75
Clan Culture 17-18, 31
Cognitive Theories 82, 91-93, 95, 110
Collective Accountability 224, 226
competitive advantage 8, 177, 193, 195, 239, 241-243, 249-250
contextual factors 90, 164-167
Core Competences 136
Core Values 1, 3-5, 21-22, 26-28, 31, 37
Countercultures 1, 20-21, 26-27, 31
Counterproductive Work Behavior 205
Cultural Alignment 35, 40, 48, 51, 56
Cultural Transformation 35-36, 39-40, 46-49, 51, 56, 73-74
Cultural Values 33-35, 37-40, 43-46, 48-49, 51, 56

E

Employee Attitudes 38, 61, 176, 183, 185, 187, 197
Employee Motivation 1-2, 4, 10, 12, 19-26, 33-38, 44-45, 48, 57, 79, 91, 106, 110, 126, 128-129, 146, 156, 159-161, 164-166, 208, 219, 226, 238, 248-250, 254-258
Employee Satisfaction 33-34, 36, 57, 99, 193, 213
Experiential Learning Theory 83, 100-102, 187, 190-191, 205, 212-213
Extra-Role Behavior 184, 194-195
Extrinsic Motivation 164, 167, 183

F

Factors in Change Management 72
Five-Factor Model of Personality 184, 206

G

Generational Cohort Theory 217
global pandemic 208, 221

H

Hierarchical Culture 17-19, 26, 31
Holistic Thriving 207
human resource 79-80, 82-83, 105-108, 117-119, 129, 144, 152, 220, 234,

249, 252-253, 255
Human Resource Development (HRD) Theory 83, 105-108

I

Intrinsic Motivation 86-87, 144, 157-158, 183, 207, 211-212, 214, 217, 225

J

Job Satisfaction 25, 33, 38, 48, 51, 90, 110, 127, 164, 184-185, 187, 191, 193-194, 196-197, 223, 234, 254, 257

K

Knowledge Exchange 137
Knowledge Transfer 80, 88, 101, 104, 107, 117-118, 129-133, 138-148, 150, 152-153
Knowledge-Sharing 107, 140, 148, 216-217

L

long-term success 46, 249

M

Market Culture 17, 19, 31
Motivating Force 233

O

organizational behavior 57, 81, 97, 110, 177-178, 181-182, 193, 206
Organizational Citizenship Behavior 176-177, 179, 182-183, 186-187, 206
Organizational Culture 1-2, 4-13, 15-28, 31-39, 43-46, 48-51, 57, 79, 88-89, 91, 106, 139, 143, 147-149, 157, 165, 182, 212-214, 217-218, 226
organizational functioning 65, 138, 178
Organizational Objectives 33-34, 45, 68, 99, 105-106, 166, 223, 233

P

Person Culture 17, 31
Power Culture 16, 23, 31
professionals/LnD experts 166, 168
Prosocial Organizational Behavior 177-178, 181-182, 193, 206
psychological safety 190, 207-215, 217-226

R

reflective observation 83, 100
Reward System 9, 127, 149, 234, 242
Role Culture 17, 31

S

Self-Determination Theory 207-208, 211-214
Self-Directed Learning 80, 83-87, 100, 166, 211
Skill Development 41, 83, 91, 102, 104, 139-140, 223, 257
social interaction 86-87, 160, 164-165, 167
Social Learning Theory 35, 39-40, 44, 49-50, 83, 102-105, 187, 191, 197, 206, 208
Systems Theory 79, 83, 96-99, 110

T

Task Culture 16, 31
Tourism and Hospitality 248, 257
Training and Development 1-2, 4, 6, 9, 12-13, 20-28, 32, 34-36, 39, 41-51, 57-58, 63, 79, 83, 90, 105-106, 117-119, 123, 125, 133, 138-140, 156-157, 159, 166, 168, 176-177, 187, 193-195, 198, 208, 210, 214, 217-218, 220, 222, 225-226, 233-235, 237-239, 241-243, 248-249, 252, 254-258
Training Interventions 88, 156-157, 161, 164-166, 254
Training Program 1, 139-140, 143-144, 146-153, 160, 193, 213, 226, 250

Index

Training Strategies 23, 33, 57, 166, 187, 207
Training Transfer 139
Transformational Leadership 186-187, 207, 218-219
Transformative Learning Theory 187, 189, 206
Trauma-Informed Approach 207, 220, 222, 225

W

Working Conditions 234, 240, 258

Publishing Tomorrow's Research Today

Uncover Current Insights and Future Trends in
Business & Management
with IGI Global's Cutting-Edge Recommended Books

Print Only, E-Book Only, or Print + E-Book.
Order direct through IGI Global's Online Bookstore at www.igi-global.com or through your preferred provider.

Developmental Language Disorders in Childhood and Adolescence
ISBN: 9798369306444
© 2023; 436 pp.
List Price: US$ 230

The Sustainable Fintech Revolution: Building a Greener Future for Finance
ISBN: 9798369300084
© 2023; 358 pp.
List Price: US$ 250

Cases on Enhancing Business Sustainability Through Knowledge Management Systems
ISBN: 9781668458594
© 2023; 366 pp.
List Price: US$ 240

5G, Artificial Intelligence, and Next Generation Internet of Things: Digital Innovation For Green and Sustainable Economies
ISBN: 9781668486344
© 2023; 256 pp.
List Price: US$ 280

The Use of Artificial Intelligence in Digital Marketing: Competitive Strategies and Tactics
ISBN: 9781668493243
© 2024; 318 pp.
List Price: US$ 250

AI and Emotional Intelligence for Modern Business Management: Bridging the Gap and Nurturing Success
ISBN: 9798369304181
© 2023; 415 pp.
List Price: US$ 250

Do you want to stay current on the latest research trends, product announcements, news, and special offers? Join IGI Global's mailing list to receive customized recommendations, exclusive discounts, and more.
Sign up at: www.igi-global.com/newsletters.

Scan the QR Code here to view more related titles in Business & Management.

www.igi-global.com | Sign up at www.igi-global.com/newsletters | facebook.com/igiglobal | twitter.com/igiglobal | linkedin.com/igiglobal

Ensure Quality Research is Introduced to the Academic Community

Become a Reviewer for IGI Global Authored Book Projects

The overall success of an authored book project is dependent on quality and timely manuscript evaluations.

Applications and Inquiries may be sent to:
development@igi-global.com

Applicants must have a doctorate (or equivalent degree) as well as publishing, research, and reviewing experience. Authored Book Evaluators are appointed for one-year terms and are expected to complete at least three evaluations per term. Upon successful completion of this term, evaluators can be considered for an additional term.

If you have a colleague that may be interested in this opportunity, we encourage you to share this information with them.

IGI Global's Open Access Journal Program

Publishing Tomorrow's Research Today

Including Nearly 200 Peer-Reviewed, Gold (Full) Open Access Journals across IGI Global's Three Academic Subject Areas: Business & Management; Scientific, Technical, and Medical (STM); and Education

Consider Submitting Your Manuscript to One of These Nearly 200 Open Access Journals for to Increase Their Discoverability & Citation Impact

Web of Science Impact Factor	Journal
6.5	Journal of Organizational and End User Computing
4.7	Journal of Global Information Management
3.2	International Journal on Semantic Web and Information Systems
2.6	Journal of Database Management

Choosing IGI Global's Open Access Journal Program Can Greatly Increase the Reach of Your Research

Higher Usage
Open access papers are 2-3 times more likely to be read than non-open access papers.

Higher Download Rates
Open access papers benefit from 89% higher download rates than non-open access papers.

Higher Citation Rates
Open access papers are 47% more likely to be cited than non-open access papers.

Submitting an article to a journal offers an invaluable opportunity for you to share your work with the broader academic community, fostering knowledge dissemination and constructive feedback.

Submit an Article and Browse the IGI Global Call for Papers Pages

We can work with you to find the journal most well-suited for your next research manuscript. For open access publishing support, contact: journaleditor@igi-global.com

Publishing Tomorrow's Research Today
IGI Global
e-Book Collection

Including Essential Reference Books Within Three Fundamental Academic Areas

Business & Management
Scientific, Technical, & Medical (STM)
Education

- Acquisition options include Perpetual, Subscription, and Read & Publish
- No Additional Charge for Multi-User Licensing
- No Maintenance, Hosting, or Archiving Fees
- Continually Enhanced Accessibility Compliance Features (WCAG)

| Over **150,000+** Chapters | Contributions From **200,000+** Scholars Worldwide | More Than **1,000,000+** Citations | Majority of e-Books Indexed in Web of Science & Scopus | Consists of Tomorrow's Research Available Today! |

Recommended Titles from our e-Book Collection

Innovation Capabilities and Entrepreneurial Opportunities of Smart Working
ISBN: 9781799887973

Advanced Applications of Generative AI and Natural Language Processing Models
ISBN: 9798369305027

Using Influencer Marketing as a Digital Business Strategy
ISBN: 9798369305515

Human-Centered Approaches in Industry 5.0
ISBN: 9798369326473

Modeling and Monitoring Extreme Hydrometeorological Events
ISBN: 9781668487716

Data-Driven Intelligent Business Sustainability
ISBN: 9798369300497

Information Logistics for Organizational Empowerment and Effective Supply Chain Management
ISBN: 9798369301593

Data Envelopment Analysis (DEA) Methods for Maximizing Efficiency
ISBN: 9798369302552

Request More Information, or Recommend the IGI Global e-Book Collection to Your Institution's Librarian

For More Information or to Request a Free Trial, Contact IGI Global's e-Collections Team: eresources@igi-global.com | 1-866-342-6657 ext. 100 | 717-533-8845 ext. 100